Defining the Truth About Contraception

Defining the Truth About Contraception

The Resolution of the Humanae vitae Crisis

Michael C. McGuckian, S.J.

Copyright © 2021 by Michael C. McGuckian, S.J.

ISBN:　　　　Softcover　　　　978-1-6641-6164-1
　　　　　　　eBook　　　　　 978-1-6641-6163-4

All rights reserved. No part of this book may be reproduced or transmitted in any form or by any means, electronic or mechanical, including photocopying, recording, or by any information storage and retrieval system, without permission in writing from the copyright owner.

Any people depicted in stock imagery provided by Getty Images are models, and such images are being used for illustrative purposes only.
Certain stock imagery © Getty Images.

Print information available on the last page.

Rev. date: 03/05/2021

To order additional copies of this book, contact:
Xlibris
844-714-8691
www.Xlibris.com
Orders@Xlibris.com
827490

CONTENTS

Introduction vii

PART 1: THE PROBLEM OF DISSENT

Chapter 1: The Curran Affair 1
Chapter 2: Religious Submission to the Pope: the Problem 12
Chapter 3: The Infallibility of the Church 36
Chapter 4: A Theandric Church and a Human Church 57
Chapter 5: The Incorporation of the Holy Spirit in the Church 66
Chapter 6: From the Theandric Organism to the Human Corporation 111
Chapter 7: Believing In the Church 130
Chapter 8: The Holy Church 'Subsists in' the Catholic Church ... 145
Chapter 9: The Magisterium of the Holy Church 158
Chapter 10: A Secondary Object of Infallibility? 204
Chapter 11: The Moral Teaching of the Church 237
Chapter 12: From the Magisterium of the Church to the Magisterium of the Bishops 264
Chapter 13: The Ordinary Magisterium of the Bishops 285
Chapter 14: Religious Submission to the Pope: the Resolution 298
Chapter 15: Legitimate Dissent from Official Teaching 320
Chapter 16: The Resolution of the *Humanae vitae* Crisis 356

PART 2: DEFINING THE TRUTH ABOUT CONTRACEPTION

Chapter 17: The Procreative Principle 379
Chapter 18: The Failure of the Procreative Principle 406
Chapter 19: The Failure of the Arguments Interpreted 433
Chapter 20: The Genuine Tradition on Contraception 445
Chapter 21: The Inviolability of the Generative Process 466
Chapter 22: Some Objections Answered 482
Chapter 23: A Dogmatic Definition 497

Introduction

This book seeks to propose a resolution of the crisis in the Catholic Church which is focussed on the doctrine of contraception. The doctrine continues to be taught authoritatively and consistently, but it is accepted neither by most Catholics nor, significantly, by most professional moral theologians. After heated debates for many years the topic is no longer discussed very much at all. People have settled into solid convictions on the matter and have no longer any interest in reading what the other side are saying. For those who have come to believe that contraception is a valid option for a Catholic the discussion is over. They are happy to be part of the universal consensus that contraception is a legitimate means of birth control and that, when it used carefully and appropriately, it is a significant force for human liberation, especially for women. On the other hand, there does continue to be discussion and sometimes even heated debate among those who accept the traditional condemnation of contraception. For no generally accepted rationale has yet been found as to why contraception is morally objectionable, and there is even disagreement as to what precisely the act of contraception entails. This discussion, however, goes on in comparatively obscure magazines which are not read by anyone who does not already accept that contraception is wrong. The matter rarely, if ever, arises now in mainstream theological or pastoral journals. So where is the crisis? It is my conviction at least, that when the Pope is insisting on this doctrine and the bishops either support his teaching or remain silent about any reservations they may have, and, at the same time, what seems like a clear majority of Catholic faithful and professional moral theologians continue to ignore it, then, however quiet things may be on the surface, there is a crisis in the Church. The crisis has to be definitively resolved one way or the other, sooner or later, and the longer it continues the higher the price that will eventually have to be paid in the division which must result. Pope John Paul II made strong and sometimes impassioned interventions in support of the teaching, but without any notable impact. The situation is just too complicated for the exercise of pure authority to bring a resolution. A coherent rationale must be found which can meet with acceptance with the broad mass of the faithful before peace can be restored.

There was general recognition of the inadequacy of the rationale for the condemnation of contraception available when the challenge came. Elizabeth Anscombe, in her spirited defence of the doctrine, gave a good assessment of the situation subtending prior to the issuance of *Humanae vitae*. She makes no bones about the fact that the arguments in use at the time were not convincing to many people. She wrote: "The lack of clear accounts of the reason in the teaching was disturbing to many people. Especially, I believe, to many of the clergy whose job it was to give the teaching to the people."[1] She makes an excellent point here about the plight of the clergy. Priests simply cannot preach about a matter of which they are not themselves personally convinced. Preaching is the kind of activity which demands conviction for it to work. And the Working Paper produced by the moral theologians on the Papal Commission on Birth Control recognised the situation when they wrote: 'If we could bring forward arguments which are clear and cogent based on reason alone, it would not be necessary for our commission to exist, nor would the present state of affairs exist in the Church as it is.'[2] Commenting later, John Finnis has spoken of '[t]

---

[1] G. E. M. Anscombe, "Contraception and Chastity," in Janet E. Smith, ed., *Why Humane Vitae was Right: A Reader* (San Francisco: Ignatius Press, 1993), 121-46 at 130.

[2] "The Minority Working Paper, 23 May 1966," in Peter Harris, *et. al.*, *On Human Life: An Examination of Humanae Vitae* (London: Burns & Oates, 1968), 170-202, at 178.

he muddle and forgetfulness ... [which] can be seen throughout the world-wide debate among Catholic theologians and others, the debate that flourished between 1959 and 1967.'[3]

The insecurity of the doctrine appeared also at the highest levels in the Church. Division among the bishops was manifest at the Second Vatican Council.[4] Bishop Reuss, who had written one of the three articles which broke the long consensus, presented a version of his argument at one of the conciliar General Congregations, and his line of thought was supported by other high-ranking and influential bishops. Pope Paul VI had to intervene personally to prevent any further discussion of the matter and had to insist that the traditional teaching was at least mentioned in the chapter on marriage in *Gaudium et spes*. The fact that Pope John XXIII saw the need to appoint a Papal Commission to examine the issue helped to foster the notion that the doctrine was uncertain, and Pope Paul VI's long and anguished deliberations prior to the issuance of *Humanae vitae* strengthened this impression.

In *Humanae vitae* itself, Pope Paul VI recognises that he is facing a new state of affairs giving rise to new questions (HV 3), and he even implicitly admits the weakness of his arguments when he reminds priests that 'the pastors of the Church enjoy a special light of the Holy Spirit in teaching the truth. And this, rather than the arguments they put forward, is why you are bound to such obedience.' (HV 28) And even those most supportive of the traditional teaching admit that the magisterial interventions have failed to resolve the difficulties people are facing. In an intervention twenty years after *Humanae vitae*, a group of four consistent defenders of the encyclical concluded their argument with a clear recognition that confusion still reigned, when they wrote: 'We hope that these clarifications will help to overcome some of the

---

[3] John Finnis, '*Humanae Vitae*: Its Background and Aftermath' *International Review of Natural Family Planning* (1980), 141-53 at 141.

[4] On this see Ambrogio Valsecchi, *Controversy: The birth control debate 1958-1968* (Washington-Cleveland: Corpus Books, 1968), 119-52, Peter Hebblethwaite, *Paul VI: The First Modern Pope* (Paulist Press: New York / Mahwah, 1993), 394, 443-45 and Philip S. Kaufman, O.S.B., *Why You Can Disagree . . . and Remain a Faithful Catholic* (New York: Crossroad, 1991), 4.

confusions occasioned by certain formulations in *Humanae vitae* and *Familiaris consortio* –formulations not of their central teachings, but of their explanations both of why contraception is morally wrong and of why NFP can be morally acceptable.'[5] With such uncertainty and confusion reigning even at the highest levels in the Church, it makes sense that such a difficult teaching should be difficult for many Catholics to accept. What the current consensus among the world-wide episcopate may be is impossible to determine, but the memory of the clear division manifested at the Second Vatican Council surely needs to be healed. The contention here will be that only a full Council of the Church speaking with a manifest moral unanimity can clear the air effectively. A Council will only be able to speak effectively on the basis of a widespread consensus in the Church, which includes bishops, moral theologians, clergy and laity. Complete unanimity would be asking a lot at this stage, but the only hope of any form of consensus is on the basis of a coherent and widely accepted rationale for the teaching to be defined. Such is manifestly not currently available.

The difficulties are located on two closely related levels. A first set of difficulties concern the structure of teaching in the Church. Many Catholics believe that contraception is wrong because that is the official teaching of the Church proclaimed by Pope Pius XI in *Casti connubii* and by Pope Paul VI in *Humanae vitae*. Many others are not convinced. Richard McCormick has written that one 'can say ... that the teaching is clear and certain simply because the papal magisterium has said so. ... In the discussion that has followed *Humanae vitae*, those who have supported the conclusions of the Encyclical have argued in just this way. I believe this is theologically unacceptable.'[6] There is truth in what McCormick says, and it raises the whole problem of dissent, which forms the first part of the book. There are essential points of ecclesiology and fundamental theology which need to be formulated clearly before the matter can be comprehensively resolved. The second set of difficulties

---

[5] Germain Grisez, Joseph Boyle, John Finnis, William E. May, "'Every Marital Act Ought to be Open to New Life,': Toward a Clearer Understanding," The Thomist 52 (1988), 365-426 at 368.

[6] *Theological Studies* 29 (1968), 727-28.

are concerned with the particular point of contraception, and there are unresolved issues here also.

The argument to be presented in this book, then, is that, while *Humanae vitae* is correct in its fundamental teaching that contraception is wrong, there are two major flaws in the encyclical, corresponding to these two levels, which go a long way towards explaining why it has so signally failed to resolve the crisis in the Church's teaching in this matter which arose in the early 1960's. The first flaw concerns the general structure of moral doctrine in the Church. There is a widespread, maybe even universal, understanding in moral theology that when a particular moral norm is a matter of natural law the basis of the teaching must be ultimately grounded on rational argument, and *Humanae vitae* seems to support this view. On this presupposition, however, if the arguments made to support a teaching fail to convince, then the teaching loses its credibility. The second flaw is to be found precisely in this area of the arguments presented by the encyclical in support of the teaching. It will be suggested that the arguments simply do not work, and that it is no surprise that people have not been convinced by them. In the circumstances it makes the teaching of the encyclical difficult, and for most people even impossible, to accept. The failure of these arguments springs from an even more fundamental error, which holds that contraception is a matter of sexual morality.

Contraception, as the name suggests, means interfering in the process of human generation in order to prevent the act of sexual intercourse from resulting in conception. Some forms of contraception impact directly on the act of sexual intercourse, and those that don't can be understood as changing the meaning of the act, even when they do not touch it directly. Contraception, therefore, relates in different ways to two fundamental areas of morality, sex and life. Throughout Christian history, there have been two streams of tradition approaching this matter from one side or the other. Currently, the dominant official position is that contraception is to be understood as a point of sexual morality, falling under the sixth commandment. Pope Paul VI, in *Humanae vitae*, teaches that the traditional condemnation of contraception 'is based on the inseparable connection, established by God, which man on his own initiative may not break, between the unitive significance and the procreative significance which are both inherent to the marriage act.' (HV 12) Pope John Paul II made this principle a key foundation of his teaching on this matter, as for example in *Familiaris consortio* § 32, and he formally taught that contraception is a matter of sexual morality in *Evangelium vitae*, § 13:

> Certainly, from the moral point of view contraception and abortion are *specifically different* evils: the former contradicts the full truth of the sexual act as the proper expression of conjugal love, while the latter destroys the life of a human being; the former is opposed to the virtue of chastity in marriage, the latter is opposed to the virtue of justice and directly violates the divine commandment "You shall not kill".

A fundamental argument of this book is that both Pope Paul VI and Pope John Paul II are wrong in these judgments, and that the genuine Christina tradition in this matter teaches that contraception is not a matter of sexual morality at all, but a life issue, falling under the fifth commandment.

According to Pope John Paul II, in *Familiaris Consortio*, the difference of opinion over contraception 'is a difference which is much wider and deeper than is usually thought, one which involves in the final analysis two irreconcilable concepts of the human person and of human sexuality.' (§ 32) My reading leads me to doubt the Pope's judgment here. I find basically the same sets of ideas at work on both sides of the debate, despite the different conclusions reached. It is not a matter of two sides, with all the light on one side and nothing but darkness on the other. My impression is of muddle and forgetfulness, and a confusion which is widespread, indeed universal, and which includes the Pope himself. This is not at all to suggest that the Pope is wrong on the fundamental substantive issue that contraception is intrinsically evil. But it is to suggest that the Pope is confused, as was Pope Paul VI before him, about what contraception actually is, and why it is wrong, and how we know it is wrong. And this confusion goes a long way towards explaining why so many people have difficulty accepting the teaching.

From the point of view of a Christian teaching, which must of its very nature be based on Tradition, this is a very problematical situation. For it cannot be resolved by somebody discovering a new reason why contraception is wrong. There must be a reason in the Tradition why we know already that it is wrong, if it is wrong. The Church does not teach out of thin air. Everything taught in the Church has to be present in the Tradition in a recognisable form. It cannot be created anew. Development can occur and can be necessary. But there has to be a line of development that can be recognised, and it must be made clear.

It will be argued that there is confusion both on the moral issue of contraception and about the manner of teaching in the Church which makes the problem of dissent almost insoluble, and the confusion in both areas must be dispelled before the crisis we are facing can be resolved. The confusion about teaching is more profound and has to be tackled first. The confusion about magisterium is deepest in regard to moral matters and the determination of one particular moral norm can only be tackled when that more general issue has been sorted out. The book will therefore form two parts. The first will tackle the problem of dissent, and the second will go on to offer a resolution to the crisis over contraception.

Part 1

The Problem of Dissent

The question to be dealt with here first arose for me during a study of the Charles Curran case. Curran was a leading public dissenter from the teaching of *Humanae vitae* in 1968, and he was eventually disciplined for his dissent in 1986. He attempted to enter into a dialogue with the Congregation for the Doctrine of the Faith with the aim of establishing his right to maintain his dissenting views. He made no effort to justify the various positions in dispute, but based his case on a general right of dissent from magisterial teachings which are not defined. He wrote a book, *Faithful Dissent*[1], in which he presented a justification of his position, basing himself on the theology of dissent available in the pre-conciliar manuals of ecclesiology, the theology which was referred to with approval by the Second Vatican Council, and there was undoubtedly logic in his argument. He repeatedly asked the Congregation to point out the error in his logic, but the Congregation did not enter into discussion with him on the matter, though it seems clear, as we shall see from the documents which Curran has published, that the Congregation shared the same basic principles on which Curran based his case for the right to dissent. Eventually, in 1992, in the document Donum veritatis, 'On the role of the theologian in the Church', the Congregation did eventually present its own theology

---

[1] Charles E. Curran, Faithful Dissent (London: Sheed & Ward, 1987).

of dissent. The position presented there, it seems to me, cannot be considered a satisfactory treatment of the issue, as I will hope to show, and hence the present book.

Dissent from a magisterial teaching can be legitimate to the extent that the authority proposing the teaching is fallible. There can be no dissent from an infallible teaching authority. To recognise a teaching authority as infallible is effectively to accept that dissent is out of the question. Correspondingly, to accept that a teaching authority is fallible is effectively to concede that dissent is possible and can be legitimate. Within the Church it is universally accepted that the teachings of the extraordinary Magisterium, the definitions of the Councils and the Popes, are proposed infallibly and that dissent from them is illegitimate. The situation is not so clear in regard to the ordinary Magisterium of the Pope and the bishops. One can only decide on the legitimacy of dissent if one has first discerned whether or not the teaching is proposed infallibly, and so far no clear line of demarcation has been established within the mass of ordinary episcopal teaching between what is proposed infallibly and what is not. This issue emerged clearly after the First Vatican Council and, more than a century later, it remains unresolved.

If dissent from the teaching of the ordinary Magisterium is legitimate in certain circumstances, as the Congregation concedes, on what basis did the Congregation condemn Fr. Curran without offering some further grounds to justify the action? If such dissent is ever legitimate, why is it illegitimate in the instances charged against Curran? That is the question Fr. Curran and the theologians who supported him asked, and the Congregation did not attempt to answer. And the question remains unanswered still. The aim of this book is to answer these questions, and, as will appear, in order to do so it will be necessary to cover the whole issue of Magisterium in the Church and find an alternative approach to that currently in place.

As the subtitle of the book indicates, the long range goal of this work is to contribute to a resolution of the current impasse in the Church on moral issues in general and the issue of contraception in particular. Currently the stand-off is complete. The aim of this book is to seek to find general principles which can be agreed by both sides in the dispute, so that the particular issues might be looked at again together. Every effort is made here to enter sympathetically into the arguments of all the participants in the discussion, and not to allow difference of opinion on the particular issues to get in the way of agreement on the fundamental principles. The focus here is on the general question of public dissent from magisterial teaching, and particular moral questions are being left to one side for appropriate treatment in due course.

Chapter 1

The Curran Affair

The events of the Second Vatican Council caused a shock to the Catholic system. The spectacle of the Bishops from around the world coming to Rome and successfully reversing a number of points of doctrine and discipline which had been insisted upon, with sanctions, over the previous decades brought about a sudden and dramatic change in the attitude to authority among Catholics. The important theological changes took place in the theology of the Church and of Revelation, but, from the point of view of the public at large, the most dramatic change was the reversal of the policy on religious freedom, and the corresponding change in the attitude towards other Christian denominations and non-Christian religions. The significance of what happened did not lie in the particular points of doctrine or discipline which were changed, but simply in the fact of change. As Avery Dulles has remarked: 'By its actual practice of revision, the Council implicitly taught the legitimacy and even the value of dissent. In effect the Council said that the ordinary magisterium of the Roman Pontiff had fallen into error and had unjustly harmed the careers of loyal and able scholars. Some of the thinkers who had resisted official teaching in the pre-conciliar period were among the principal precursors and architects of

Vatican II.'[1] What the Council taught was obviously important. What the Council did, at least in the matter to be discussed here, was more important still.

The crisis of authority in the Catholic Church found a very precise focus with the publication of the encyclical *Humanae vitae* in July 1968. During the troubled period immediately following the Second Vatican Council many people had come to the conclusion that a change was about to be made in the Church's teaching on contraception, and there was widespread consternation and disappointment, as well as, it must also be recognised, profound relief and satisfaction in many other hearts, when Pope Paul VI reaffirmed the traditional doctrine. *Humanae vitae* was released on Monday morning, July 29, 1968. A number of Catholic theologians in the United States, including Charles Curran, were convinced that, in the circumstances, 'it would be important to point out to Roman Catholics that it was not necessary for married couples to choose between using artificial contraception and being Roman Catholic. A loyal Catholic could dissent from such noninfallible teaching.'[2] These men drew up a public statement of their position which contained the following as its central affirmation:

> It is common teaching in the Church that Catholics may dissent from authoritative, noninfallible teachings of the magisterium when sufficient reasons for so doing exist. Therefore, as Roman Catholic theologians, conscious of our duty and our limitations, we conclude that spouses may responsibly decide according to their conscience that artificial contraception in some circumstances is permissible and indeed necessary

---

[1] Avery (later Cardinal) Dulles, 'Doctrinal Authority for a Pilgrim Church,' in Readings in Moral Theology No. 3: The Magisterium and Morality, edd. Charles E. Curran and Richard McCormick, S.J. (New York / Ramsey: Paulist Press, 1982), 247-270. See also Bonaventure Kloppenburg O.F.M., The Ecclesiology of Vatican II (Franciscan Herald Press: Chicago, 1974), 56-57.

[2] Curran, Faithful Dissent, 17.

to preserve and foster the values and sacredness of marriage.³

They defended their publication of this position by stating that 'it is our conviction also that true commitment to the mystery of Christ and the Church requires a candid statement of mind at this time by all Catholic theologians.'⁴ Curran acted as the spokesman for the original group of 87 signers at a press conference on Tuesday morning, July 30. Eventually over 600 persons qualified in the sacred sciences publicly signed this statement. The logic is simple. There is affirmed the right to dissent from 'authoritative, noninfallible teachings of the magisterium.' From that it follows that Catholic spouses may dissent from the teaching of *Humanae vitae*, which was not presented as a definitive judgement by Pope Paul VI. On this basis, the theologians felt bound in conscience to make a public statement to that effect. Years later, Curran would freely concede that this dissent was public and organized, and would still conclude that 'in my judgment the statement was responsible and it has held up very well over the years.'⁵ He still believes that 'it was important for Roman Catholic spouses to know that they did not have to make a choice between using artificial contraception under some conditions and ceasing to be members of the Roman Catholic Church. The Catholic theologian, among others, had an obligation to tell this to Catholic spouses.'⁶

Curran and his colleagues were not alone in taking this line, for the same point was also made by some bishops. On the same July 30, 1968 Cardinal Alfrink, Archbishop of Utrecht in the Netherlands, publicly announced that Catholics do not have to accept *Humanae vitae* without discussion or debate, and subsequently a number of episcopal conferences made statements to the same effect. On August 30, the Belgian Bishops affirmed the right of Catholics to dissent from the

---

3   Charles C. Curran, Robert E. Hunt, Dissent In and For the Church: Theologians and *Humanae vitae* (Sheed & Ward: New York, 1969), 26.
4   Curran, Hunt, Dissent In and For the Church, 26.
5   Curran, Faithful Dissent, 18.
6   Curran, Faithful Dissent, 64.

teaching: 'Someone, however, who is competent in the matter under consideration and capable of forming a personal and well-founded judgment ..., may, after serious examination before God, come to other conclusions on certain points.'[7] On September 21, the Austrian bishops said that the 'since the encyclical does not contain an infallible dogma, it is conceivable that someone feels unable to accept the judgment of the teaching authority of the Church,'[8] and on September 27, the Canadian bishops further developed this point: 'Since they are not denying any point of divine and Catholic faith nor rejecting the teaching authority of the Church, these Catholics should not be considered, or consider themselves, shut off from the body of the faithful.'[9] On October 17, the Scandinavian bishops made a declaration along these same lines.[10] What these Episcopal Conferences are saying is basically the same thing as Curran and his fellow-theologians said in their public statement. They are all presenting the standard theology of dissent, pointing out that it allows a Catholic to have legitimate reservations in regard to a teaching of the ordinary magisterium of the Pope.

Curran did not dissent explicitly from the teaching of *Humanae vitae* in the public statement, but he did so in his subsequent writings. He went on to express his dissent from other moral teachings and built up a considerably bibliography in this sense. It was no surprise, therefore, that his work came to the attention of the Congregation for the Doctrine of the Faith. Even when the Roman disciplinary action got under way against him, Curran retained his certainty as to the validity of his overall position. When he became aware that he was under investigation by the Congregation for the Doctrine of the Faith, he tells us that he 'wanted to make this a teaching moment for the good of theology and the good of the church.' He was convinced that 'the Catholic Church ultimately has to recognize the legitimacy of public

---

[7] *Humanae vitae* and the Bishops: The Encyclical and the Statements of the National Hierarchies, ed. John Horgan (Shannon: Irish University Press, 1972), 65-66.
[8] Curran, Hunt, Dissent In and For the Church, 199.
[9] Horgan, 79.
[10] Horgan, 237.

theological dissent from some noninfallible teaching and the possibility of such dissent in practice by members of the church.' With that in view he 'wanted to make sure that the public understood that I was neither a rebel nor a guerrilla but a loyal Catholic theologian working for what I and many others thought to be the truth and therefore the good of the church.'[11] Curran was, again, very far from alone in adopting this position, for over 750 members of the College Theological Society and the Catholic Theological Society of America signed a statement supporting him.[12]

The first set of 'Observations' sent to Curran by the Congregation for the Doctrine of the Faith in 1979 opens by outlining what the Congregation considered to be the basic issue involved, that of *public* dissent. The document begins by stating: 'The fundamental observation to be made regarding the writings of Father Charles Curran focuses upon his misconceptions of the specific competence of the authentic magisterium of the Church in matters *de fide et moribus*.'[13] The document then outlines the standard doctrine on dissent from ordinary magisterial teaching. 'Insofar as the individual theologian does not have reasons which appear to be clearly valid to him and which derive from his competence in the matter in question to suspend or refuse assent to the teaching of this authentic magisterium, he must heed its teaching, even while recognizing that it might in an exceptional case be mistaken, since it does not enjoy the guarantee of infallibility.'[14] The document then affirms that 'this suspension of assent does not provide grounds for a so-called right to public dissent, for such public dissent would in effect constitute an alternative magisterium contrary to the magisterium of Christ given to the apostles and constantly exercised through the hierarchical magisterium in the Church.'[15] The second set of 'Observations' of 1983 confirms this position: 'The issue of whether

---

[11] Curran, Faithful Dissent, 36.
[12] Curran, Faithful Dissent, 44.
[13] Observations of the Sacred Congregation for the Doctrine of the Faith regarding the Reverend Charles E. Curran (July 1979) in Curran, Faithful Dissent, 118.
[14] Ibid.
[15] Ibid.

a person who privately dissents from the ordinary Magisterium of the Church has the consequent right to dissent publicly is at the basis of the SCDF's difficulties with Father Curran.'[16] This document elaborates a little on the reasons why public dissent is wrong, even when private dissent is justified, for 'to further dissent publicly and to encourage dissent in others runs the risk of causing scandal to the faithful and to assume a certain responsibility for the confusion caused by setting up one's own theological opinion in contradiction to the position taken by the Church.' Curran would seem, therefore, to be correct when he says that 'the central point at issue in the controversy is the possibility of public theological dissent from some non-infallible teaching,'[17] and in taking it that this is also the position, at least as formulated, of the Congregation for the Doctrine of the Faith.[18]

Together with this central point, public dissent, the Congregation also pointed out the dissenting positions adopted by Curran on moral matters, which Curran admitted to at every stage. In his exchange of letters with the Congregation, Curran always focussed on the agreed central issue of public dissent, arguing a case in its favour and seeking reasons for the Congregation's condemnation of it. The Congregation did not enter into discussion of the points Curran raised, and Curran considered himself unjustly treated as a result. In the end he wrote: 'I can only once again plead that reason and justice demand that the Congregation spell out the norms governing dissent especially public dissent, and show how I have violated these norms…'[19] For Curran insisted that his dissent was 'in accord with the norms laid down by the United States bishops in their 1968 pastoral letter "Human Life in Our Day,"'[20] and always insisted that his whole effort was within the communion of the Catholic Church. He wrote: 'The general context

---

[16] Ibid, 201-02.
[17] Charles Curran; 'Public Dissent in the Church', in Readings in Moral Theology No. 6; Dissent in the Church, edd. Charles E. Curran and Richard A. McCormick, S.J., (New York/Mahwah: Paulist Press, 1988), 387-407 at 395 and 401.
[18] Curran, Faithful Dissent, 55.
[19] Curran's Response on August 24, 1984 in Curran, Faithful Dissent, 232.
[20] 'Response of Curran, August 20, 1986' in Readings No. 6, 364-369 at 367.

for this chapter and for the entire case is that of the Roman Catholic Church and Catholic theology. I have made it very clear that I am a believing Catholic and intend to do Catholic theology. Despite my intentions, I still might be wrong; but I maintain that my positions are totally acceptable for a Catholic theologian and a believing Roman Catholic.'[21]

Another significant point of mutual incomprehension between the Congregation and Curran was on the response expected to the teaching of the ordinary magisterium. The current official teaching makes a clear distinction between the assent of faith due to defined doctrine and the religious submission due to ordinary teaching. The doctrine is summarised in Canon 752: 'While the assent of faith is not required, a religious submission of intellect and will is to be given to any doctrine which either the Supreme Pontiff or the College of Bishops ... declare upon a matter of faith or morals, even though they do not intend to proclaim that doctrine by a definitive act.' This distinction is fundamental for Charles Curran's position, and he repeated the point frequently. He wrote: 'From my perspective I have constantly emphasized that my position on dissent in no way involves or contradicts Catholic faith and the assent of faith made by me as a Catholic believer and as a theologian. I do not now and never have challenged what belongs to Catholic faith as such. This point is absolutely crucial for me both as a Catholic believer and a Catholic theologian.'[22] The point is central to Curran's position, for he regards it as the basis of the right to dissent. As he wrote elsewhere: 'The primary theological reason ... for recognizing dissent as a possible legitimate option for Catholics responding to authoritative teaching arises from the fact that the motive is not divine faith.'[23] Throughout the exchange of letters between the Congregation and Curran, the clear focus had been on the principles of dissent from ordinary teaching towards which, according to the standard theory accepted by both parties, religious submission of will

---

[21] Curran, <u>Faithful Dissent</u>, 50.
[22] Letter of Curran to Archbishop Hickey, December 9, 1985 in Curran, <u>Faithful Dissent</u>, 253. See also page 57
[23] 'Dissent, Theology of' in NCE XVI (Supplement 1967-1974), 128.

and intellect is the appropriate response, and not divine faith, as Curran was insisting. Curran was surprised, then, by the opening paragraph of the definitive letter he received from the Congregation in 1985. The letter began by referring 'to some theological and juridical points which give definition to all theological teaching in the Catholic Church. Above all, we must recall the clear doctrine of Vatican Council II regarding the principles for the assent of faith (*Lumen gentium* 25). This doctrine was incorporated in the revised Code of Canon Law which in c. 752 sums up the thought of the Council on this point.'[24] Surely Curran was entitled to be confused by this. The Congregation speaks of a clear doctrine on the assent of faith, and refers to canon 752 which makes an explicit distinction between the assent of faith and religious submission of will and intellect! Curran protested at this and pointed out, correctly, that 'this letter of September 17 marks the first time the Congregation has ever described our differences in terms of the assent of faith.'[25] The Congregation subsequently clarified that it still upheld the distinction between the assent of faith and religious submission. In a letter Archbishop Hickey, of November 11, 1985, it said: 'When canon 752 of the Revised Code was written, to which explicit reference was made in our letter, it rightly distinguished between the assent of faith and religious submission, in accord with the distinction made in *Lumen gentium* 25. The canon noted that even (quidem) when the assent of faith is *not* required, as in the case of some papal positions, the religious submission is still expected.'[26] This confusion is significant from the perspective to be developed in this book, and it will be necessary to return to it later.

The letter of September 17 went on to specify the points of moral doctrine from which Curran was dissenting, contraception and sterilization, abortion and euthanasia, masturbation, pre-marital intercourse and homosexual acts, and the indissolubility of marriage, and to say that 'the Congregation now invites you to reconsider and

---

[24] Curran, Faithful Dissent, 248.
[25] Letter of Curran to Archbishop Hickey, 254.
[26] Quoted in Curran, Faithful Dissent, 251.

to retract those positions which violate the conditions necessary for a professor to be called a Catholic theologian. It must be recognized that the authorities of the Church cannot allow the present situation to continue in which the inherent contradiction is prolonged that one who is to teach in the name of the Church in fact denies her teaching.'[27] Curran responded to this ultimatum indignantly refusing to retract the positions he had been upholding throughout, and this led to a final letter form the Congregation. This letter began:

> The purpose of this letter is to inform you that the Congregation has confirmed its position that one who dissents from the Magisterium as you do is not suitable nor eligible to teach Catholic Theology. ... The several dissenting positions which this Congregation contested, namely, on a right to public dissent from the Ordinary Magisterium, the indissolubility of consummated sacramental marriage, abortion, euthanasia, masturbation, artificial contraception, pre-marital intercourse and homosexual acts, were listed carefully enough in the above-mentioned Observations in July of 1983 and have since been published. There is no point in entering into any detail concerning the fact that you do indeed dissent on these issues.[28]

The Congregation goes on to make one last argument in justification of its procedure, which contains points which will be of concern in the sequel and needs to be placed here for the record.

> There is, however, one concern which must be brought out. Your basic assertion has been that since your positions are convincing to you and diverge only from the 'non-infallible' teaching of the Church, they

---

[27] Curran, Faithful Dissent, 250.
[28] Letter of the Congregation to Curran July 25, 1986 in Curran, Faithful Dissent, 268.

constitute 'responsible' dissent and should therefore be allowed in the Church. In this regard, the following considerations seem to be in order. First of all, one must remember the teaching of the Second Vatican Council which clearly does not confine the infallible Magisterium purely to matters of faith nor to solemn definitions. ... Besides this, the Church does not build its life upon its infallible magisterium alone but on the teaching of its authentic, ordinary magisterium as well.[29]

And it concludes:

> In light of your repeated refusal to accept what the Church teaches and in light of its mandate to promote and safeguard the Church's teaching on faith and morals throughout the Catholic Church, this Congregation, in agreement with the Congregation for Catholic Education, sees no alternative now but to advise the Most Reverend Chancellor that you will no longer be considered suitable nor eligible to exercise the function of a Professor of Catholic Theology.[30]

These final letters of the Congregation caused confusion and dismay among the Catholic academic community in the United States, and a statement of the Catholic Theological Society of America summarized the difficulties. It points out that the Congregation does not make any claim that any of the teachings for which Curran is being disciplined fulfil the conditions necessary for an infallible pronouncement. On this basis it concludes that the 'underlying assumption of the letter, therefore, is that dissent from noninfallible teachings effectively places one outside the body of Catholic theologians,' and wonders 'Which noninfallible teachings are serious enough to provoke such a result,

---

[29] Ibid.
[30] Ibid, 270.

and how are those teachings determined?'[31] The statement goes on to query the precise form of the discipline taken against Curran and ask: 'If one is declared no longer a Catholic theologian, does that modify in any way the theologian's relation to the Catholic Church itself? If so, how? If not, what does such a declaration mean?'[32] These are important questions and need to be answered.

This story of the disciplinary process against Charles Curran undertaken by the Congregation for the Doctrine of the Faith sets the problematic to be dealt with in the first part of this book. It surely represents an unsatisfactory situation where some of the best minds in the Church do not understand the disciplinary measures taken against a respected academic. If a disciplinary measure is not understood, it cannot achieve the goal for which it is designed, to bring order to a situation. The argument to be developed here will hope to show that the confusion and mutual incomprehension are based on the inadequacy of the theological foundation shared by all the parties to the dispute, the Congregation for the Doctrine of the Faith as well as Curran and his supporters and the theological community generally, and that the matter remains unresolved to this day.

---

[31] Statement signed by some past presidents of the Catholic Theological Society of America and the College Theology Society (eventually signed by 750 Catholic theologians in US) in Curran, Faithful Dissent, 282-284 at 283.
[32] Ibid.

Chapter 2

Religious Submission to the Pope: the Problem

Dissent from official teaching has been part of the experience of the Church from the very beginning. In the West, however, during the second millennium official teaching in the Church became more and more the responsibility of the Popes, and so dissent from official teaching was equivalently dissent from the teaching of the Pope. The call for orthodoxy was correspondingly focussed on the exhortation to be submissive to the teaching authority of the Pope. The dominant role of the Pope in the Church is the single most significant characteristic of Western Christendom.[1] This focussing of all teaching and dissenting on the Pope involves a particular difficulty in that the Pope is the supreme authority in the Church and there can, therefore, be no appeal to a higher authority from anything which he enacts. If a problem is discerned with any teaching of the Pope, the difficulty or disagreement immediately becomes dissent and there is no appeal procedure to which one can resort. The situation was quite different during the first millennium in the Church when there was a much more balanced relationship between the Pope and the other Patriarchs and the bishops in general. And, although he had no role in the dominical constitution of the Church, the Emperor had an important role to play. The change

---

[1] On this see John W. O'Malley, 'The Millennium and the Papalization of Catholicism,' America, April 8, 2000, 8-16.

in all this was caused by a remarkable transformation in the role of the Pope in the Church commonly known as the eleventh century reformation or revolution, and the background to this event is relevant to the discussion here.

Throughout the first millennium the unity of the Church and the Empire was so close that the Emperor's role was understood to be practically of divine institution. He was granted the honours due to a bishop, and one of his titles was 'the Equal of the Apostles.' It was the Emperor who called the Ecumenical Councils, and it was he who made law for the Church, as part of the State. This meant that it was the Emperor who was responsible for doctrinal discipline. He was always anxious for the unity of his state, so he ensured that binding doctrinal decisions were only made in cases of necessity. This same concern for unity acted as a support for the collegiality of the bishops and definitive judgments were always made by ecumenical councils. When the Popes seceded from the Empire in the eighth century and cooperated in the establishment of the Western Empire, this traditional system was duplicated, as far as possible, in the West. The significance of all this is that, while this system endured, the Emperor constituted an effective counter-balance to the authority of the Pope in the Church. If a Pope abused his office, he could be brought to account by a recognised procedure controlled by the Emperor, and the procedure was often invoked.

An example of that procedure forms part of the immediate background to the revolution which changed everything. When Charlemagne's empire collapsed, the control of the papacy passed to the great families of the Roman aristocracy. These families used the papacy for their own purposes, and the abuses which flowed from this ensure that the tenth century has to be recognised as the very nadir of the papacy. One only has to read the short summaries of the papacies from Formosus (891-96) to Boniface VII (984-85) to get a grasp of what was happening.[2] This situation was obviously badly in need or reform,

---

[2]   See, for instance, the entries in The Oxford Dictionary of Popes, J.N.D. Kelly, OUP, 1986.

and it was the revival of the Empire under the Ottonian kings which made the reformation possible. King Henry III (1039-56) deposed Pope Benedict IX (1032-45), together with two anti-Popes, Silvester III and Gregory VI in 1046, and proceeded to install Popes of his own choosing. These were the good men who initiated the reformation and proceeded to institute the revolution against the imperial authority which had made their installation possible. These men saw that the fundamental problem was the civil control of the Church, whether imperial or local, and they set about remedying the situation. The College of Cardinals was made the electoral college for new Popes in 1059, excluding both the Empire and the Roman nobility, and thus began the long struggle between Church and State which brought about the freedom of the Church from civil control.

This little bit of history is relevant to the discussion here on two points in particular. The role of the Emperor in the Church, though without apostolic foundation, was nonetheless of great practical value. The Emperor represented an authority of stature which could act as a moderating influence on the exercise of the authority of the Pope, which has no clearly discernible limitations. Now that the Church was free, and the Pope was able to formulate and exercise the fullness of his apostolic authority, there was no longer an effective counter-balance to papal authority, and the situation we face now was brought about. The other point, which will find its relevance in the sequel, is the fact that the situation which lay behind the eleventh-century reformation was a series of bad Popes who themselves needed discipline and were deposed.

The reformation required a whole new development in theology and law for its justification. The Cluniac reformers who originated the development worked out a wide-ranging theory of papal authority, covering the whole range of human affairs, religious and civil. Their policy was summarised in the *Dictatus papae* usually attributed to Pope Gregory VII. Of the principles laid down, those of interest to the issue of teaching authority are these: 'The Pope can be judged by no one; the Roman church has never erred and never will err till the end of time; the Pope alone ... can revise his judgements,' and 'a duly ordained

Pope is undoubtedly made a saint by the merits of St. Peter.'[3] In order to support the Pope's role in teaching throughout the Church a strong papalist theology was developed, which called for obedience to the papal decrees in every area.

These men claimed a wide-ranging authority for the Pope in every area of life, civil and religious, and the judgment of doctrine was a central point. In order to try to maintain discipline throughout the West, this authority was delegated widely, and the result was the medieval Inquisition. In the decretal *Ad abolendum* of 1184, setting up the Inquisition, Pope Lucius III offered a very broad definition of heresy, when he wrote that

> we include, in the same perpetual anathema ... all who presume to think, or to teach, concerning the sacrament of the body and blood of our Lord Jesus Christ, or of baptism, or of the remission of sins, or of matrimony, or of the other sacraments of the Church, otherwise than as the Holy Roman Church teaches and observes; and, generally, all persons whom the said Roman Church, or the individual bishops in their dioceses, with the concurrence of their clergy, or the clergy themselves if the see be vacant, with the consent, if need be, of the neighboring bishops, shall have adjudged to be heretics.[4]

And Pope Gregory IX, in the Decretal *Ille humani generis* of 1231, gave the inquisitors a wide-ranging authority in the judgment of heresy.

---

[3] R. W. Southern, <u>Western Society and the Church in the Middle Ages</u> (Penguin, 1970), 102. (<u>Quod Romanus Pontifex, si canonice fuerit ordinatus, meritis beati Petri indubitanter efficitur sanctus</u> (Dict. 23: <u>Gregorii VII Registrum</u>, ed. E. Caspar, 207).)

[4] <u>Heresy and Authority in Medieval Europe: Documents in Translation,</u> Edited, with an Introduction, by Edward Peters (University of Pennsylvania Press Philadelphia, 1980), 171.

> We seek, urge, and exhort your wisdom, by apostolic letters sent to you under the apostolic seal, that you … seek out diligently those who are heretics or are infamed of heresy. … You may exercise the office thus given to you freely and efficaciously, concerning this and all of the things which we have mentioned above.[5]

There is no wish to rehearse here all the details of the history of the Inquisition, but it is clear that the Popes are claiming for themselves here the authority to judge orthodoxy independently, and to delegate the authority widely. There is no sense here of the caution that marked the first millennium, or the notion that defining doctrine is a comparatively rare event, involving the whole Church and best reserved to the communal wisdom of an ecumenical council. There is an implicit claim here to a wide-ranging infallibility in practice which would gradually become explicit.

Needless to say, the procedure and the claim met with resistance. All the reformers of the second millennium in the West offered resistance to the new pro-active papacy.[6] As Congar tells us: 'The period which preceded the Reformation … was a time of criticism, most particularly on the subject of the Church. … A set of movements of a spiritual tendency succeeded one another for four centuries; a development of theological criticism put forward mainly by Ockham and the Nominalists.'[7] The criticism was to be found among the Apostolicals of different types, the Cathars, the Vaudois, the Poor Men of Lyon, Joachimism, the Spirituals, Wyclif, the Lollards, John Hus and the Bohemians. In the beginning, the critique focused on the temporal power of the Church, and particularly of the papacy. The papacy, it was said, had been corrupted since Pope Sylvester, who accepted the Donation of Constantine. 'The call was for a Church which was only

---

[5] Ibid, 197.
[6] On this see Yves Congar, O., <u>Vraie et fausse réforme dans l'Église</u> (2nd ed.) (Paris : Les Éditions du Cerf, 1968), 336-41.
[7] Ibid, 336-37.

Church, and for pastors who were truly pastors and only pastors.'[8] Eventually the doctrinal authority claimed by the papal theologians became a particular point of grievance. The papal theologians of that period are not much read now, so their teaching has often to be deduced from the complaints of the critics. Consider, for instance, John Wyclif:

> What amazing arrogance therefore is displayed by those who so exaggerate their authority and learning as to consider their traditions, e.g., the decretals, as enjoying an authority equal to or greater than that of the Gospel. They are all liable to err both in faith and morals. It could happen that the Roman Pontiff with his cardinals reach such a pitch of folly as to assert that what they teach as to be done and believed should *ipso facto* be done or believed. ... It is neither an article of faith nor deducible from Scripture or reason that, when the Pope with the consent of the cardinals prescribes something in a bull or letter, he is assisted and kept from error by the Holy Spirit as the authors of Scripture were. No particular Church is to be believed, except insofar as it observes the commandments.[9]

The difficulties which Jan Hus faced from one of the three Popes of his day have relevance here. The conflict which led to his eventual downfall was over the 'crusading bull' of Pope John XXIII, now deemed an anti-pope but no less authoritative for Hus in practice at the time. King Ladislas of Naples was a supporter of Pope Gregory XII, and Pope John XXIII naturally resented the aid given to his deposed and excommunicated Roman rival. On September 9, 1411 he issued a bull declaring a crusade against Ladislas and Gregory, ordering all Church authorities, under pain of excommunication, to declare Ladislas an

---

[8] Ibid, 337.
[9] Michael Hurley, S. J., "Scriptura sola': Wyclif and his Critics,' in <u>Traditio</u> 16 (1960), 275-352 at 289 where Hurley is summarizing some of Wyclif's points in the last chapter of the first book of his <u>De civili dominio</u>.

excommunicate, and calling on all rulers, secular and ecclesiastical, to destroy Ladislas.[10] Hus refused to obey this bull and got into an argument over papal authority in relation to it. Those supporting Pope John XXIII used a strong theology of papal authority and, according to Spinka, it is 'only if we are aware of the extreme and adamant Papalism with which he had to contend can we understand why he [Hus] resorted to such spirited arguments to counter it.'[11] One of Hus' opponents, John of Holesov (Czech mark on the s!), wrote a piece entitled '*An credi possit in papam*', one of the most uninhibited statements of papal theology written in his day. He uses the definition of the Church as the *congregatio fidelium*, and asserts that this congregation is composed 'principally of the ecclesiastics: first the lord pope, then the cardinals, patriarchs, primates, archbishops, bishops, and the lower ecclesiastics, the presbyters and priests; for they comprise the Church principally.'[12] Holesov asked the question if it is appropriate to revere the Pope and all superiors, and replied that we should, obeying, loving, and properly honouring and adoring them![13] Another opponent of Hus, Palec (Czech marks on 'a' and 'c'!), wrote the *Tractatus gloriosus*, on behalf of eight University masters, in which they argue that by refusing to obey the pope's command Hus committed as great a transgression as if he had refused to obey apostolic commands.[14] Hus rejects such an identification. Spinka reports:

> It is false, he declares, to assert that papal bulls are to be believed in the same way as the apostolic letters or the gospels of Christ. Papal bulls are often revoked when it is found that the pope was ill-informed or when he dies. ... Just because the pope claims to speak with

---

[10] Matthew Spinka, John Hus' Concept of the Church (Princeton University Press, 1966), 109-10.
[11] Ibid, 151.
[12] Ibid, 152.
[13] Ibid, 153. He gives the reference to Paul de Vooght, Hussiana (Louvain, Publications universitaires de Louvain, 1960), 116-122, less than half way through.
[14] Ibid, 157.

authority is no proof that his command agrees with the apostolic teaching. To assume that it does would be tantamount to regarding him as incapable of sinning [*impeccabilem*].¹⁵ ... The Apostolic See cannot exceed what is taught in the law of God. ... The faithful have the duty of vigilantly seeking to ascertain 'whether the papal or princely letters contain anything contrary to the law of Chist.' If they find that they do, they should resist them to death and under no circumstances obey them.¹⁶

In response to Hus's criticism, the university doctors call on the king and the royal council to declare as inadmissible any criticism of the bull whatever. For them, it should be accepted unconditionally in accordance with the requirements of the *Decretum*, dist. 94, which says that anyone who impedes a legate of the apostolic see is to be excommunicated.¹⁷

The resistance to an excessive papal authority was also an important part of Luther's difficulty in the beginning of his efforts at reform. He himself was a strong papalist in his early years and recognised the fact himself in later years.¹⁸ At the time, and since, the authority of the Pope has been seen as the central point at issue, in the beginning at least. Joseph Lortz has characterized the attack on the papacy as the quintessence of the Indulgence-theses, and he sees in them an attack on the essential structure of the visible Church, especially on the Pope.¹⁹ Already the report of the University of Mainz of 17 December, 1517 on Luther's Indulgence-theses put forward the diminishing of the papal authority in regard to indulgences as the critical point at issue.²⁰ The

---

15 Ibid, 157-58.
16 Ibid, 161.
17 Ibid, 163.
18 Remigius Bäumer, <u>Martin Luther und der Papst</u> (Münster: Aschendorff, 1970), 7-10.
19 <u>Die Reformation in Deuctschland</u>, Vol. I, (Freiburg im Br.: Herder, 1941), 202.
20 Bäumer, <u>Martin Luther und der Papst</u>, 15.

University of Leipzig declared likewise through its theological faculty on 26 December, 1518, that the matter of indulgences touched upon the authority of the Pope. Indeed, all the first Catholic opponents of Luther, like Prierias, Wimpina, Cajetan and Eck saw in the indulgence-theses an attack on papal authority. In the opinion of Prierias, Luther had rebelled 'against the truth and the Holy See'. He put the theses of the infallibility of the Church and the Pope in the forefront of his arguments against Luther. For him, the Roman Church cannot err, nor can the Pope, when, as Pope, he judges a question of faith and does all in his power to recognise the truth, so that whoever does not hold to the teaching of the Roman Church and the Pope as an infallible rule of faith is to be counted as a heretic.[21] And Johannes Eck also recognized at the beginning of the controversy, that the question of the papal primacy and infallibility was the decisive battlefield for the future, so that in the Leipzig disputation the question of the Pope was one of the central themes of the debate.[22] The first assessment of Luther's Ninety-Five Theses made in Rome was by Prierias, who was the Master of the Sacred Palace, the theologian of the papal court. On the basis of his report Luther was summoned to Rome and, along with the summons, Luther received a copy of Prierias's report. Jared Wicks tells us that in his report, Prierias 'baldly asserted that the authority of the Roman Church and the popes is greater than the authority of Scripture,' and then goes on: 'From the moment Luther read Prierias's concise statements on fundamental doctrinal norms, the question of the criteria of true Christian teaching became a key theme of his reflection and controversy. Luther's eventual contestation of papal authority is to a certain extent a reactive effort to vindicate the rightful authority of Scripture in the face of the one-sided claims made by Prierias for the papal magisterium.'[23]

After he had received the *Dialogus* of Prierias, Luther composed a *Responsio* which reveals important aspects of his thinking at this

---

[21] Ibid, 16.
[22] Ibid, 17.
[23] 'Roman Reactions to Luther: the First Year, 1518,' in Jared Wicks, <u>Luther's Reform: Studies on Conversion and the Church</u> (Mainz: Verlag Philipp von Zabern, 1992), 149-188 at 156.

stage. He saw the opinions he expressed in the Ninety-Five Theses and subsequent works as situated in an area of free opinion not yet settled by authoritative doctrinal decisions, and on occasion he made reference to a coming determination by the Church or by a council. He pointed out that only after such a declaration could there be question of heresy on the part of an obstinate dissenter. The *Responsio* made one clear assertion of the normative character for all Christians of the faith professed by the Roman Church, because Christ miraculously maintains that church in the truth and in continuity with original expressions of Christian belief. Luther was still declaring his openness to accepting an authoritative papal judgment. Wicks goes on: 'Clearly it was a fateful development that Pope Leo's spokesman in the Luther case was eventually a Dominican confrere of Tetzel and Prierias, Tommaso de Vio, Cardinal Cajetan, whose reputation as a Thomist loomed large in early sixteenth-century academic circles. Doctrinal judgments delivered by Cajetan, acting as the Pope's legate, were to put a severe strain on Luther's submissive readiness to accept a Roman determination.'[24] Luther was suspicious of the men being delegated with the judgment of his case, and successfully avoided the demanded appearance in Rome, managing to keep the judgment of the case in Germany. Even so, Cardinal Cajetan was delegated to judge the case, and Luther was convinced that only condemnation and excommunication awaited him. In his judgment, unlike Prierias, Cajetan did not brand Luther's teaching heretical. He had detected errors requiring correction, but not evidence that Luther was diverging from revealed and defined truth. Luther did not accept Cajetan's judgments and made an appeal 'to the Pope better informed.' He protested that the procedures taken against him were improper and unjust. He held that his theses treated a legitimate matter of disputation, since on important aspects of indulgences no definitive, binding doctrine had been laid down by the Church, and since indulgences are not central to the faith, there was no just cause for citing Luther before an ecclesiastical tribunal with reference to his orthodoxy. He maintained that, in such a situation theological disputation is legitimate, especially

---

[24] Ibid, 159.

when done with a readiness to submit to the church's judgment. He also complains about the men delegated to judge his case, since they are all his theological opponents who could have no sympathy with his point of view. On the basis of all this, Luther appeals from the ill-informed Pope Leo, who has allowed the process to unfold in such a manner, to a better informed Pope Leo, from whom Luther awaits a just judgment, as from the spokesman for Christ in his Church. Luther had this appeal formally notarized, but in the event it was never sent.[25] On November 9, 1518, Pope Leo X issued *Cum postquam* setting out the official position on indulgences, but Luther did not accept it.

The question has been raised whether Luther was sincere in these protestations of loyalty to the authority structures of the Church in the early phase of his crisis. Remigius Bäumer asks: 'Was Luther sincere in these declarations, or must they be seen to be tactical?'[26] This issue is of no concern here. Regardless of Luther's state of mind at the time, the points he makes are valid and need to be taken seriously in any effort to resolve the issue of the appropriate response to the doctrinal authority of the Pope. For this point was at stake for all the reformers, as Congar tells us. In one place he writes: 'The intention of the Reformers was quite clear from the beginning. They were part of a whole movement, reacting against a new and excessive development of papal authority, which movement rejected the notion of an absolute power, *unconditional* and discretionary.'[27] And he develops the point:

> The Reforms of the 16th century ... were, at the same time, a refusal of an *unconditional* authority of the Church, and particularly of the Pope. Against a Catholicism where, without considering the nature or the content of what was imposed, one carried to its extreme a purely formal and unlimited authority, people wanted to control the *content* of what was imposed upon them. That was, at least in part, the meaning of

---

[25] Ibid, 178-79.
[26] Bäumer, <u>Martin Luther und der Papst</u>, 25-26.
[27] Congar, <u>Vraie et fausse réforme</u>, 432. (Emphasis in the original.)

> Luther's claim of a criterion of Christian faith based, not on authority alone, but on the internal relationship of doctrines to Jesus Christ crucified, my Saviour. That was also the meaning of the Calvinist critique of implicit faith. It was also the sense of the Anglican appeal to tradition, to history, to reason.[28]

It was not only the dissidents within the Church who wrestled with this issue, for the problem was a commonplace in medieval thought. Congar presents the traditional doctrine that authority of teaching is conditional on purity of doctrine.[29] As St. Augustine put it, when a minister speaks, 'if he speaks the truth, Christ is speaking.'[30] According to Congar, St. Isodore of Seville (c. 560 - 636) sums up the patristic tradition: 'Superiors are to be judged by God, never by their subjects. ... If, however, a superior goes beyond the faith, then he is to be corrected by his subjects.'[31] This condition was completely taken for granted well into the second millennium. For instance, Gratian, after quoting a text of Pope St. Leo the Great condemning those who do not submit to papal authority, commented that this was to be understood of those sanctions or decretals in which nothing was to be found against the decrees of the earlier Fathers or the Gospel precepts.[32] This was a text that Luther could and did use for his purpose.[33] St. Thomas could write that we do not believe the successors of the Apostles unless they announce

---

[28] Congar, Vraie et fausse réforme, 374.
[29] Congar, « Apostolicité de ministère et apostolicité de doctrine, » in Ministères et communion ecclésiale (Paris : Cerf, 1971), 51-94.
[30] 'Tractator loquitur: si vera loquitur, Christus loquitur', Sermo 17, 1 (PL 38, 124).
[31] 'Rectores ergo a Deo judicandi sunt, a suis autem subditis nequaquam judicandi sunt. (...) Quod si a fide exhorbitaverit rector, tunc erit arguendus a subditis' (PL 83, 710).
[32] Hoc autem intelligendum est de illis sanctionibus vel decreatalibus epistolis, in quibus nec precedentium Patrum decretis nec evangelicis praeceptis aliquid contrarium invenitur' (Dictum post c. 7 D. XIX (Friedberg I, 62).)
[33] Congar, Apostolicité, 78.

to us what the Apostles left in the Scriptures,[34] which means that the only mandate the bishops have to be listened to by the faithful is that they preach a doctrine conformed to the Scriptures, and this idea was common at that time. There is the famous text in the *Decretum*: 'The Pope can be judged by no one, unless he is discerned to have deviated from the faith.'[35] The men who commented on this text, the Decretists, were sure that 'the Pope could be judged *a tota ecclesia* … that the whole Church was possessed of an authority superior to the Pope's, and that the mind of the Church was most perfectly expressed by a General Council acting, if necessary, even against the Pope.'[36] The Conciliarist position arose from this, and the tension between Pope and Council lasted for a long time. But the basic respect for the supreme authority of the Pope remained: 'The Pope could not dispense against articles of faith indeed, but in the last resort it was left to the Pope himself to determine whether an article of faith was involved in any particular case. He could not act against the well-being of Church; but it was for the Pope himself to decide how the interests of the Church were best served.'[37] There can be no appeal from the Pope to a higher authority, on the human level, and yet it was seen that the possibility of error in papal teaching has to be dealt with somehow. According to Congar:

> The notion of the possibility of an heretical Pope has a *unanimous* tradition, at least until the Counter-reformation. The formula of St. Isodore we saw above was applied to the Pope, that the faithful have no right to judge their pastor, *except* when he deviates from the true faith. … The idea that a Pope could be heretical appears to us even today to be *methodologically* essential for the

---

[34] St Thomas, De Veritate, q. 14, a. 10, ad 11: 'successoribus autem eorum non credimus nisi in quantum nobis annuntiant ea quae illi in scriptis reliquerunt.' See also IV Sent. D. 19, a. 2, a. 2, q^a 3 ad 1; II-II q. 33 a. 4 ad 2.

[35] '(Papa) a nemine est iudicandus, nisi deprehendatur a fide devius.' Dist. 40, c. 6.

[36] Brian Tierney, Foundations of the Conciliar Theory (Cambridge: University Press, 1955), 67.

[37] Tierney, Foundations, 91.

proper equilibrium of the theology *de sacra hierarchia et speciatim de potestate papae*. We could illustrate it with dozens of texts.[38]

Congar seems to be correct in this. The problem, which Congar never managed to solve, is to find a manner of grounding and handling the possibility of an heretical Pope which does not radically undermine the authority of the papacy which is essential for the unity of the Church.

Despite any and all resistance the strong papal theology grew slowly but surely over the centuries and reached a high point in the nineteenth century. When the Enlightenment thinkers and the political leaders influenced by them tried to destroy the Church, the papacy was seen as the key bastion to be destroyed first. And so it was that, as the Church began to revive during the nineteenth century, orthodox thinkers accepted the same logic and made the papacy the basis of every aspect of the Church's life. At the low point of the depression, the Camaldolese monk, Mauro Cappellari, who became Pope Gregory XVI (1831-46), published, at Rome, *Il Trionfo della S. Sede e della Chiesa* (1799). The Holy See and the Church were very much identified. He argued that the Church is infallible because the Pope, her head and foundation, is infallible. In this way of reasoning he was followed by de Maistre, de Lamennais, and the whole Ultramontane movement of the late nineteenth century.[39] A prime example of this tendency was Cardinal Manning. Manning is quite clear in his mind that the identification of the Church and the Pope represents the traditional belief of the Church. He writes that 'whensoever the perpetuity of the faith and the infallibility of the Church is spoken of, the foremost and governing idea in the mind of the faithful has always been the Divine order and assistance by which S. Peter and his successors have been constituted as the perpetual teachers of the Universal Church, and guides in the way

---

[38] Congar, Apostolicité, 79.
[39] Yves Congar, O., L'Église: De saint Augustin à l'époque moderne (Paris: Les Éditions du Cerf, 1970), 413-414.

of eternal life.'⁴⁰ For him 'it is manifest, that, according to this doctrine, the fountain of infallible teaching is the Divine Head in heaven, through the organ of the visible head of the Church on earth.'⁴¹ He argues from the Pope's position as vicar of Christ to his infallibility. He writes: 'The Vicar of Jesus Christ would bear no proportion to the body if, while it is infallible, he were not. He would bear also no representative character if he were the fallible witness of an infallible Head.'⁴² From this follows a wide-ranging infallibility of the Pope.

> The infallibility of the Head of the Church extends to the whole matter of revelation, that is, to the Divine truth and the Divine law, and to all those facts or truths which are in contact with faith and morals.⁴³ ... In all declarations that such propositions are, as the case may be, heretical or savouring of heresy, or erroneous, or scandalous, or offensive to pious ears, and the like, the assistance of the Holy Spirit certainly preserves the Pontiffs from error; and such judgments are infallible, and demand interior assent from all.⁴⁴ ... In a word, the whole *magisterium* or doctrinal authority of the Pontiff as supreme Doctor of all Christians, is included in this definition of his infallibility. And also all legislative or judicial acts, so far as they are inseparably connected with his doctrinal authority; as, for instance, all judgments, sentences, and decisions, which contain the motives of such acts as derived from faith and morals. Under this will come laws of discipline, canonisation of Saints, approbation of religious Orders, of devotions,

---

[40] The Centenary of Saint Peter and the General Council (London: Longman's, Green, and Co., 1867), 22.
[41] Ibid, 24.
[42] Henry Edward Manning, The Temporal Mission of the Holy Ghost (London: Longmans, Green, and Co., 1866), 82-83.
[43] Ibid, 83.
[44] Ibid, 84.

and the like; all of which intrinsically contain the truths and principles of faith, morals, and piety.[45]

Manning based his theology of authority in the Church on the indwelling of the Holy Spirit. He wrote: 'The voice of the living Church, of this hour, when it declares what God has revealed is no other than the voice of the Holy Spirit, and therefore generates divine faith in those who believe.'[46] He then goes on to present the different ways in which the Holy Spirit speaks in the Church; through the Baptismal Creed, Holy Scripture, Tradition found in all the world, the Decrees of General Councils, and concludes with the teaching of the Pope, of which he writes: 'The Definitions and Decrees of Pontiffs, speaking *ex cathedra*, or as the Head of the Church and to the whole Church, whether by Bull, or Apostolic Letter, or Encyclical, or Brief, to many or to one person, undoubtedly emanate from a divine assistance, and are infallible.'[47] Manning was of the view that all the official teachings of the Pope are infallible, and he was strongly opposed in this, as is well known, by Cardinal Newman. It is also well known that the First Vatican Council did not ratify this theology. It taught that when the Pope makes a definition of the faith, he exercises the infallibility of the Church, but did not affirm or deny Manning's stronger view, which he continued to hold as the teaching of the Council. The status of the rest of Pope's teaching, apart from the *ex cathedra* definitions, became a topic in theology and remains so still.

The strong view of the Pope's authority retains its attraction. Consider the paragraph on the matter in *Donum veritatis*, the document on the role of the theologian from the Congregation for the Doctrine of the Faith. It says:

> Divine assistance is also given to the successors of the apostles teaching in communion with the successor

---

[45] The Vatican Council and its Definitions (London: Longman's, Green, and Co., 1870), 89.
[46] Manning, The Temporal Mission, 81.
[47] Ibid, 81-82.

of Peter, and in a particular way, to the Roman Pontiff as Pastor of the whole Church, when exercising their ordinary Magisterium, even should this not issue in an infallible definition or in a 'definitive' pronouncement but in the proposal of some teaching which leads to a better understanding of Revelation in matters of faith and morals and to moral directives derived from such teaching. One must therefore take into account the proper character of every exercise of the Magisterium, considering the extent to which its authority is engaged. It is also to be borne in mind that all acts of the Magisterium derive from the same source, that is, from Christ who desires that His People walk in the entire truth. For this same reason, magisterial decisions in matters of discipline, even if they are not guaranteed by the charism of infallibility, are not without divine assistance and call for the adherence of the faithful.

Take this in combination with the corresponding clause in the Profession of Faith of 1989, by which a Catholic theologian is to promise to 'adhere with religious submission of will and intellect to the teachings which either the Roman Pontiff or the College of Bishops enunciate when they exercise their authentic Magisterium, even if they do not intend to proclaim these teachings by a definitive act.' We all know, *aliunde*, that these formulations are not based on a claim to infallibility for every official teaching of the Pope or the College of Bishops. The problem is, however, that the room to manoeuvre which we know to exist finds no expression here, and the claim comes perilously close to a claim for an authority which is 'absolute, unconditional, and discretionary.'

Religious Submission at Vatican II[48]

---

[48] On this see Umberto Betti, 'L'Ossequio al magistero pontificio 'non ex cathedra' nel N. 25 della 'Lumen gentium'"<u>Antonianum</u> 62 (1987), 420-461.

This issue arose at the Second Vatican Council, but it was not possible, on the basis of the principles generally agreed at that time, to answer it. The debate had as its point of departure the statement made by Pope Pius XII in *Humani generis*:

> Nor is it to be thought that what is contained in encyclical letters does not of itself demand assent, since the Popes do not exercise in them the supreme power of their Magisterium. Rather, such points are taught by the ordinary magisterium, of which it is true to say: 'He who hears you, hears me'. Often, too, what is expounded and inculcated in encyclical letters already appertains to Catholic doctrine for other reasons. But if the Supreme Pontiffs in their official documents purposely pass judgment on a matter debated until then, it is obvious to all that the matter, according to the mind and will of the same Pontiffs, cannot be considered any longer a question open for discussion among theologians.[49]

In the preparatory phase of the Council, various suggestions were made in regard to this matter. On the one hand there were those who argued that the Pope's judgment should put an end to all opinions to the contrary,[50] and that it should be considered infallible.[51] On the other hand, however, there was an a more general concern that infallibility

---

[49] AAS, 42 (1950), 568.
[50] A. Herrera y Oria, Bishop of Malaga: A. Anoveros Ataun, Titular Bishop of Tabuda, Acta et Documenta II: 2, 225, 468 II.
[51] R. Carboni, Titular Archbishop of Sidon; A. Delahunt, General of the Franciscan Capuchins; S. Congregation for Seminaries and Universities, Acta et Documenta, II: 7, 610; II: 8, 309; III, 321; J. M. Marling, Bishop of Jefferson City, Acta et Documenta II: 6, 345.

should not be attributed to these documents and that the Council should clarify the whole matter.[52]

The first draft of the document on the Church contained the teaching of Pope Pius XII in *Humani generis*.[53] When this document was being examined by the Central Preparatory Commission Cardinal König raised important questions in regard to it. He pointed out that the question arises as to how the obedience we owe to such a declaration is to be distinguished from that offered to a definition, properly so called. The text presupposes that such a declaration is not irreformable and so, although free discussion is no longer possible, the declaration cannot be considered a peremptory definition. He recommended that the exposition should be clarified, so that all papal declarations would not be considered in practice as *ex cathedra* definitions, since they are reformable *de iure*, and sometimes required to be reformed *de facto*.[54] Cardinal Döpfner declared that more needed to be said to satisfy the submissions made under this heading. He mentioned two questions as most important. What is the nature of the internal and religious submission of intellect and will required, when the propositions are not irreformable? What is to be done if doubts arise and new arguments and questions emerge? He referred to the case of the Johannine Comma (DS 3681) and to the Response of the Holy Office of June 2, 1927 (DS 3682), which made clear that the earlier decree did not wish to impede further investigation of the matter, so long as it was conducted properly and with a willingness to accept the judgment of the Church. He suggested that an addition of this kind should be added to the

---

[52] Bishop José Eugenio y Trecu, Bishop of Santander, Antepraep, II: 2, 294; J. McManus, Bishop of Ponce (Puerto Rico), Antepraep, II, 6, 649; Faculty of Theology of the Marianum, Antepraep, IV: 2, 432-33. For more on this see Betti, 'L'Ossequio,' 427ff.

[53] De Ecclesia (Schema propositum a Commissione Theologica), Caput VII: De Ecclesiae magisterio, § 2. Acta et documenta Concilio Oecumenico Vaticano II apparando, Series II (Praeparatoria), Volumen II (Acta pontificiae commissionis centralis praeparatoriae Concilii Oecumenicic Vaticani II), Pars IV (Sessio septima: 12-19 Iunii 1962) (Typis polyglottis Vaticanis, MCMLXVIII). (AP II-II, pars IV.), 623.

[54] Ibid, 643-44.

conciliar decree.[55] Cardinal Frings, commenting on the parallel text in the schema of the preparatory commission on Catholic Education and Seminaries, made the same points.[56]

In reaction to the critical remarks made, two changes were made to the text. The order of the faculties in the phrase was reversed; 'submission of intellect and will' became 'submission of will and intellect'. Introducing this change, Fr Sebastian Tromp, the secretary of the committee, offered an explanation of what was meant by the submission of will and intellect: '… of the will, because we must acknowledge this magisterium as teaching in the name of Christ …; of the intellect, because we must give assent, though not absolute, to the truth proposed, just as in daily human affairs is done and ought to be done, where there is the possibility of error, but no genuine probability.' The text was also changed to affirm that there should be no <u>public</u> discussion of a question decided by the Pope, where before it spoke of <u>free</u> discussion.[57]

His Beatitude Maximos IV Saigh, Melchite Patriarch of Antioch and all the Orient, commenting on a document *De obsequio erga Ecclesiae magisterium in tradendis disciplinis sacris* at the 2nd Congregation of the Central Commission on 13 June 1962, said: 'The "non-infallible" magisterium is, by the very meaning of the term and by definition, fallible, and so susceptible to error. If it is susceptible to error, the intervention of the Pope, like every other human teaching, even of great authority, can give to the doctrine it proposes neither the value of a dogma of faith, nor such a certainty that it removes all foundation of possible discussion. Otherwise, this "fallible" or "non-infallible" teaching would be equivalent, in practice, to an "infallible" definition. The schema must explain clearly what is the <u>interior</u>, essential, difference between the "infallible" teaching of the Roman Pontiffs and their teaching which is theoretically called "fallible", but which is considered practically infallible, since no discussion is admitted. We do not want

---

[55] Ibid, 646-47.
[56] <u>Prae</u> II: 4, 181-182.
[57] Betti, L'Ossequio, 431-32.

to deny the affirmation of the schema, but we ask that an explanation be given, for it would appear that such an affirmation has no other goal than to extend surreptitiously the domain of papal infallibility, and to transform every teaching of the Popes into irreformable certitudes, and so practically into dogmas, and these include, especially in recent years, practically the whole domain of human knowledge.'[58]

At the Council this whole document was rejected and a new one proposed. In the new Schema on the Church, the formula remained that religious submission of will and intellect is due to the ordinary magisterium of the Pope, but the clause prohibiting public discussion after a papal judgment was removed. There were numerous reactions from the Fathers.[59] Some wanted a stronger text, advocating at least a return to the earlier version. A greater number of the Fathers, on the contrary, considered the text still to be too maximalist. It was considered excessive to affirm that the 'non ex cathedra' papal magisterium required a 'religious submission of will and intellect', since this submission is not really different from the assent due to the teaching of the infallible magisterium. It was asked that the expression 'religious submission of will and intellect' be properly grounded[60] and unequivocally explained.[61] There must be removed even the least doubt about the real distinction between the assent due to the non-infallible magisterium and that due to the infallible magisterium.[62] It should be specified that this submission is not to be given without any limitation, but rather 'according to the rules of prudence', which, as in the 1927 decree of the Holy Office, do not exclude further investigations and different conclusions, always adhering to the judgment of the Church.[63] A. Fernández, the general of the Dominicans, pointed out the incompatibility of the duty to accept the ordinary magisterium of the Pope with some points affirmed by

---

[58] Acta Synodalia II (Praeparatoria) 2 Central Commission IV, 199-200.
[59] On these see Betti, L'Ossequio, 437-38.
[60] Cardinal Bea, AS II, 2, 651.
[61] F. Garcia Martínez, tit. Bishop of Sululi: AS, Appendix, 402.
[62] E Conf. of Indonesia: AS II, 1, 785; J. M Reuss, tit. Bishop of Sinope, AS II, 2, 853.
[63] Cleary, Columban, Bishop of Nancheng, AS II 1, 319 n 348, 643f.

the Council itself which contradict points made earlier by Popes.[64] The contradictory nature of the suggestions made meant that the doctrinal commission had no mandate to make any change at all to the text as it stood.[65]

When the text was voted on the result was; 2240 votes, null 2, *placet* 1704, *non placet* 53, *placet iuxta modum* 481. Of the *modi*, a few related to this point, but as before they were in contradictory senses, and the Doctrinal Commission, at its meeting on 27 October, 1964 had no option but to reject them all. It was not that they did not recognise the value of the suggestions made, but if any were accepted it would have meant either altering the substance of the text or raising new problems rather than solving them.[66] The Commission contented itself with recommending the consultation of approved authors on the matter.

The Council may not have been able to teach anything new on this matter, but it spoke volumes by its actions, by the way it treated the teaching of earlier papal encyclicals. The obvious question was raised early on at the Council; to what extent the Council was bound to religious submission to such statements in papal encyclicals. Mgr Michael Schmaus raised the issue at the Preparatory Theological Commission in March 1961, on the question of the identity of the Church of Christ and the Catholic Church: 'A most important question is whether the Council is bound by the encyclicals ... whether it stands under the encyclicals or above them, even if it is clear to all that they possess the highest authority.'[67] No answer was given to this question. However, it is generally agreed that the Council corrected earlier papal teaching on a number of issues, notably ecumenism, religious freedom, and the identity of the Church of Christ and the Catholic Church. One commentator has observed: 'I think it would be true to say that the deepest divisions at Vatican II were between those bishops who saw the council as bound to affirm what had already been taught by the popes,

---

[64] AS III 1, 693 and 697.
[65] Betti, L'Ossequio, 439-40.
[66] Ibid, 443.
[67] Umberto Betti, 'Chiesa di Cristo e Chiesa Cattolica: A proposito di un'espressione della <u>Lumen gentium</u>,' <u>Antonianum</u> 61 (1986), 726-745 at 730 footnote 13.

and those who recognised the need for the Council to improve upon, and in some cases, to correct such teaching.'[68] The significance of this is that we are entitled to presume that the manner of acting of the bishops in Council can be taken as a model of Christian behaviour, and their manner of acceptance of papal encyclicals must be the correct one. The precise point of the obligation of bishops in regard to papal encyclicals was raised at the Council.

Franciscus Franic, Bishop of Spalato or Macarscensis, made a submission on the issue. On the basis of a summary of the reaction of bishops to papal statements throughout the tradition, notably the reaction of the Fathers at Chalcedon to Pope Leo's *Tome*, he suggested that, since Bishops are 'true judges and authoritative teachers in matters of faith and morals,' they should be free to judge papal decisions, to examine them and ask for reasons, suspending their assent for a short time.[69] The matter was not discussed, but it did arise in one of the amendments put forward after the vote on LG 25. The first amendment, from 155 Fathers, the conservative minority leaders, was to the effect that the bishops are obliged to the same religious submission as the rest of the faithful, and this should be formulated in the text.[70] The Doctrinal Commission refused the amendment with the comment that the obligation of the bishops is evident.[71] The obligation of the bishops is the same as that of every other member of the faithful, and their response can be taken as exemplary, and look at what happened. The most dramatic event at the Council was when the Council Fathers comprehensively rejected most of the documents prepared by the pre-conciliar commissions. These documents were carefully prepared by the most trusted advisors of the Holy See, and yet were found to be radically unsatisfactory by the College of Bishops as a whole, acting in Council. The authority of these prepared documents was high, pretty much on a par with the authority of a papal encyclical, though without

---

[68] Francis A. Sullivan S.J., Magisterium: Teaching Authority in the Catholic Church (New York/Ramsey: Paulist Press, 1983), 157.
[69] Acta Conc. V. II – Periodus II, Appendix, 522.
[70] AS III 8, 88.
[71] 'Obligatio Episcoporum de se est evidens.' AS III 8, 88.

the Pope's specific approval. The documents were largely summaries of papal teaching developed in the many encyclicals published during the previous century or so since Pope Gregory XV began the practice. And then there were the particular points in the papal encyclicals themselves which were changed in significant ways. Taking it that these responses of the bishops in Council to these documents were appropriate, surely it is safe to say that the responses cannot reasonably be termed acts of religious submission of will and intellect to the teaching proposed. Can it not therefore be concluded that this event substantiates the claim that it is wrong to expect religious submission to every act of the ordinary papal magisterium? The task ahead is to find a way of grounding a positive answer to this question which leaves the foundations of papal authority intact.

Chapter 3

The Infallibility of the Church

The fundamental premise in this matter is that the theology of dissent can only be based on an accurate concept of the infallibility of the Church as a whole, which doctrine is foundational for the whole edifice of faith. According to Cardinal Newman, 'that the Church is the infallible oracle of truth is the fundamental dogma of the Catholic religion,'[1] and this was a position he maintained constantly throughout his long career.[2] Pope John Paul II spoke of the doctrine in similar terms when speaking to the German bishops in connection with the disciplinary measures taken against Hans Küng who put the doctrine into question. He wrote: 'Although the truth about the infallibility of the Church may indeed seem a less central truth, with a lower position in the hierarchy of truths revealed by God and professed by the Church, it is, however, in a way the key to that certainty with which faith is professed and proclaimed, as well as to the life and behaviour of the faithful. If this essential foundation is shaken or destroyed, even the most elementary truths of our faith begin at once to disintegrate.'[3]

---

[1] An Essay in Aid of a Grammar of Assent, (Notre Dame/London: University of Notre Dame Press, 1979), 231.
[2] Avery Dulles, S.J., 'Newman on Infallibility,' TS 51 (1990) 434-449 at 435.
[3] Letter of Pope John Paul II to the German Episcopal Conference (May 15, 1980); The Pope Speaks, Vol. 25, No. 3 1980, 239-246 at 244.

This infallibility of the Church has never, however, been clearly formulated. At the First Vatican Council, at least one bishop asked that the infallibility of the Church be treated before that of the Pope in order to avoid any confusion in people's minds that there may be somehow two infallibilities.[4] Despite this request, the Fathers made clear that they were not speaking about the infallibility of the Church. They were taking it for granted, and affirming what was being denied at the time, namely, the inerrancy of papal definitions. This is made clear in the *Relatio* of Conrad Martin, bishop of Paderborn, on behalf of the explaining the text of the decree on the inerrancy of papal definitions.[5] At the Second Vatican Council, similar concerns were raised about the different infallibilities, but the matter has never been resolved.[6]

Also, it is not only Catholics who believe in the infallibility of the Church. As Walter (later Cardinal) Kasper affirms: 'It is a universal Christian conviction, to be found in the medieval and the Reformed tradition, that the <u>ecclesia universalis</u> cannot err in faith.'[7] Every Christian in every denomination lays claim to a basic belief in the infallibility of the Church. Take Luther for instance. For him, the true Church is infallible. He wrote: 'The church believes and thinks nothing except what Christ has thought and commanded, much less something contrary to what he thought and commanded.'[8] Althaus tells us that 'Luther is as sure and confident as his opponents are that Christ remains with his church through his Holy Spirit and that he guides and leads it into all truth. He can say, "We, too, confess that the church does everything right." (WA 7, 713.) And although he definitely denies that any one individual in the church after the time of the apostles can claim to be infallible in matters of faith, he is equally certain that the universal church can not err. "Hence, after the Apostles no one should

---

[4] Bishop Louis Regnault, Mansi 52, 407-08.
[5] Mansi 52, 940C-941A.
[6] Archbishop Descuffi of Smyrna, AS II/1, 652-53; Bishop Fidel García Martínez, AS II/2, 105; the Swiss Bishops, AS II/2, 911.
[7] <u>Theologie und Kirche</u> (Mainz: Grünewald, 1987), 56.
[8] Paul Althaus, <u>The Theology of Martin Luther</u> (Philadelphia: Fortress Press, 1966), 338. Althaus refers to WA 38, 203, 216ff; 51, 518.

claim this reputation that he cannot err in the faith, except only the universal church." (WA 39ʳ, 46; LW 34, 113.)'[9] If everyone believes in the infallibility of the Church, the doctrine cannot be of much practical use without a clear concept of what precisely we mean when we make the claim.

The difficulty of achieving clarity on the nature of the infallibility of the Church is rooted in the difficulty of being clear on the nature of the Church herself. This point was clearly noted in a significant effort to handle the problem of dissent made by Joseph Ratzinger at an early stage of his theological career.[10] Writing during the early stages of the Second Vatican Council, Ratzinger wrote that 'we should earnestly inquire as to precisely in what sense debate, criticism, protest, and the right to dissent can be said to arise legitimately from the Church's very nature, and where the line is to be drawn in such matters.'[11] He lays down as the fundamental principle a profound love for the Church and notes that what is needed is 'to investigate the structure of this *sentire Ecclesiam*, this "empathy towards the Church."'[12] In dealing with the question of a proper love for the Church, there are two extremes to be avoided, and Ratzinger adverts to them and makes a plea with which the present writer would wish to be associated.

> The time which sang 'Hymns to the Church' seems to us to lie very far in the past, even though only the span of a generation separates us from it. To speak of the Church other than in criticism, is reckoned today as an *a priori* sign of obscurantism and dangerous reaction. This situation is surely only the obverse of a widespread lack of understanding of the Church authority, which

---

[9] Ibid, 342.
[10] Pope Benedict XVI is an important contributor to the present discussion at every stage, and he will be referred to using the title contemporaneous with the text under consideration.
[11] Joseph Ratzinger, 'Free Expression and Obedience in the Church,' in The Church readings in theology (New York: J. Kenedy & Sons, 1963), 194-217 at 195.
[12] Ibid, 210.

seems to find it difficult to distinguish the essential from the unessential, so that everything which is said or decided by the Church's authority is placed under the same protection of untouchability. Where everything is equally important, nothing is important any more – that seems to be gradually becoming our situation where two one-sided positions mutually destroy each other. Anyone wishing to proceed cautiously in this situation, who would seek to ascertain the right and the limits of criticism, which can be only one part and not the whole, will fall between two stools and will be viewed with mistrust and unease by all sides. Nevertheless, this effort must be made, and the following pages would wish to offer a modest contribution.[13]

He deals with the objection that prophecy has already won its victory in the Church and that there is no room in the present dispensation for protest or criticism. He suggests that to view things in this way 'would be to misconstrue the essence of human history as well as the particular mode by which the New Covenant, indeed the Spirit and the divine, exist in the world.'[14] He appeals here to his understanding of the sinfulness of the Church.

> For … the recall of the Church from Babylon, the transformation from 'whore' to 'bride,' from 'stumbling block' to 'cornerstone' is not a distant event that occurred once and for all at the dawn of her history. There is much more to it than that. She is summoned ever anew. She stands, as it were, ever upon the threshold. And the *pascha*, the 'passing-over' from this world's existence

---

[13] Joseph Ratzinger, 'Freimut und Gehorsam: Das Verhältnis des Christen zu seiner Kirche,' Das neue Volk Gottes: Entwürfe zur Ekklesiologie (Düsseldorf: Patmos-Verlag, 1969), 249-266 at 249.

[14] Joseph Ratzinger, 'Free Expression and Obedience in the Church,' in The Church readings in theology (New York: J. Kenedy & Sons, 1963), 194-217 at 210.

into newness of spirit, remains first and last her vital primary principle. In this sense, the Easter mystery is the abiding form of the Church's existence in this world. ... The Church lives and thrives on the call of the Spirit, in the 'crisis,' that tension aroused by the transition from the old to the new. Was it by chance alone that the great saints had to struggle not only with the world but also within the Church as well; that they wrestled with the temptation of the Church to become 'world' and suffered within the Church and at the hand of the Church? A Francis of Assisi, for example, or an Ignatius of Loyola who, arrested for the third time during [by] the Inquisition, rotted in a Salamanca prison, chained for twenty-two days to his companion Calisto. And yet Ignatius retained enough courage and cheerful faith to say: 'In all of Salamanca there are not so many shackles and chains that I would not put up with more for the love of God.' Thus he renounced no part of his mission and none of his obedience to the Church.[15]

On this basis Ratzinger sets the boundaries within which the appeal from the Church's authorities to the Church herself must be maintained, for there are two extremes to be avoided, rejecting the concrete Church completely or treating her as beyond criticism. He wrote:

> It is doubtless a mistake arbitrarily to reduce the Church to the level of an 'Old Testament' by withdrawing into the 'superiority' of protest, i.e. by attempting to appeal against the Church to an authority which actually cannot and does not exist outside the Church. Yet it is equally wrong to consider the incarnation the whole, the total quintessence, and therefore the end, thus decreeing the Church to be the perfected kingdom

---

[15] Ibid, 210-11.

promised by God, which in effect would be a denial of her great eschatological future, her transformation into judgment and end, as well as an attempt to foist her off as spotless and unimpeachable in this present world. Such action would be false, for her divine mystery is a mystery administered by men and these, men who have not yet attained their goal, *are* the Church.[16]

Ratzinger has clearly laid out the problem we face. How can there be an appeal from within the Church to the Church? We cannot go beyond the Church, as Our Lord went beyond the Old Testament Israel. And yet, according to Ratzinger, the Incarnation has not solved the difficulty, for the Church is not perfect, she is not 'spotless and unimpeachable in this present world.' Surely that only leaves us with paradox! If the Church is not perfect, spotless and unimpeachable, how can she be infallible? I suggest Ratzinger has properly posed the problem, but the solution remains to be found. What is required is a more adequate notion of the Church, on the basis of which the paradoxical mixture of holiness and sin within her can be resolved. For it is necessary to move beyond paradox to clear formulation of the precise locus of infallibility in the Church, and that result must be achieved before the issue of the fallibility in the Church can be successfully dealt with.

The only way out of this situation has been noted by Hans Küng. In his critique of infallibility, Küng noted that non-Christians and Christians outside the Catholic Church have always rejected the claim of infallibility for the Church's magisterium, and that recently, however, 'it has become to a surprising extent at least questionable even within the Catholic Church.'[17] The questioning arises from the general recognition of error in magisterial teaching which, according to Küng 'may not be denied even by the more conservative theologians and Church leaders.'[18] Küng recognises that we are in the presence of a very

---

[16] Ibid, 203.
[17] Hans Küng, <u>Infallible?: An Unresolved Enquiry</u>, (London: SCM Press Ltd, 1994), 27.
[18] Ibid.

serious dilemma. 'On the one hand, it is clear that the promises given to the Church must be acknowledged. No believing Christian who bases himself on the New Testament can dispute this.[19] ... On the other hand, the Church's errors must be acknowledged. No thinking person can fail to recognize this.'[20] To resolve the problem Küng argues for a certain kind of infallibility, or better indefectibility, of the Church, and he refers to the position adopted by the Reformers on the matter.

> For all their rejection of the infallibility of Pope and councils the Reformed Churches accept the infallibility or indefectibility of the Church. ... Luther also believed in the guidance of the Church by the Holy Spirit, which enabled him specifically to ascribe infallibility to it. After the apostles it could be said of no one except the universal Church 'that he cannot err in faith'. (WA, Vol. 39/I, 48.) That Church, however, is not to be simply equated with the official Church, with the Pope and the bishops. It is rather the hidden but very real Church of those who truly believe that it cannot err, because Christ in accordance with his promise remains with it to the end of the world; it is 'the pillar and bulwark of the truth' (1 Tim. 3:15) (WA, Vol. 18, 649f.; Vol. 51, 511.) In this respect the Church had survived even under an erring papacy.[21]

Küng's solution, then, is that, while 'the Church's errors must be acknowledged,' there remains a 'hidden but very real Church,' 'not to be simply equated with the official Church,' which is truly infallible. Küng did not work out his ideas in a satisfactory manner, and his license to teach as a Catholic theologian was withdrawn as a result. If, however, there is to be an acceptable theology of the place of dissent in the Church, there can be no doubt that these issues have to be resolved.

---

[19] Ibid, 142.
[20] Ibid, 143.
[21] Ibid, 160.

It will be argued here that there is much of value in what Küng is proposing, but the distinction he is making needs to be more carefully drawn. There have been suggestions made as to a distinction between a 'hidden' Church of different kinds and the concrete Church of our everyday experience throughout the history of theology, and to date all have been judged to be heterodox. I intend to present yet another, for, as I will argue, a theology of legitimate dissent within the Church demands it.

Dissidence has been part of the experience of the Church from the very beginning. It would hardly be appropriate to call St. Paul's disagreement with St. Peter over the proper Christian attitude to the Law dissidence, but he did oppose the Rock to his face, and the example is one that dissidents have appealed to more than once. It has ever been the practice of the dissidents to appeal to the authority of the universal Church in their difficulties with Church authorities. And that is how it must be, since legitimate dissent can only appeal from the magisterial authorities to God, living and active in his Church. The dissident must appeal to the Church, understood in some way distinct from the concrete institution he deems to be in error. Matthew Spinka, a student and biographer of the great Czech reformer, Jan Hus, has put the point well: 'Like an alluring mirage on the horizon, there shines throughout the history of the Christian Church the image of the ideal Church. St. Paul dreamed of it when he wrote about the glorious Church "without spot or wrinkle or any such thing, that she might be holy and without blemish." (Eph 5:27) Some of the best sons of the Church devoted their lives to the realization of this ideal, ending their lives as martyrs because of their reforming zeal.'[22] The appeal to an ideal Church must relativize the authority of the College of Bishops to some extent, for that is its goal. The problem is to achieve that goal while still upholding with its full force the teaching of our Lord that 'He who hears you hears me,' addressed to the Apostles, and understood within the Catholic faith as applying to the bishops, their successors. Along with belief in the infallibility of the Church, it is necessary to make a place

---

[22] Spinka, <u>John Hus' Concept of the Church</u>, 3.

within a proper understanding of that infallibility for the recognition of the continuing fallibility of the bishops, who remain sinful and fallible men, like all the rest of us.

The difficulty here all along has been that making any distinction between the living authorities in the Church and the Church herself as the ultimate authority has always led to a separation between the two which, instead of putting the authority of the bishops in its proper context, has led to the complete undermining of their authority. It has been part of the faith of the Catholic Church from the beginning that Christ founded his Church on the apostles and that the bishops, as their successors, retain that foundational role. In other words, the institution is an essential part of the mystery of the Church, and the unity of the mystery and the institution cannot be broken within an orthodox theology. As Congar tells us: 'All through the writings of the apostolic age and the earliest period of Christianity, we see treated as identical, without the slightest separation between the two, the community life in Christ and the mystical Body, on the one hand, and the actual community of Christians, on the other.'[23] That unicity of the Church is fundamental to the Catholic vision. However, there remains a tension between the mystery and the institution which is an essential aspect of the issue we are facing.

The ambiguity in the word 'church' shows itself even at the level of grammar and popular usage. The meaning immediately familiar to us now is that of a community, a group of people gathered together in the name of Christ. With this concept in mind, it is appropriate to use the plural of the noun and speak of many 'churches', or Christian communities, of which the Catholic Church is but one among that many. There is, however, another, deeper, meaning of the word, for which the plural is inappropriate. This is the mysterious Church of the New Testament promises; the Body of Christ and the Temple of the Holy Spirit. With this concept in mind, there can only be one Church. It can be called the 'true Church' or the 'holy Church', the 'hidden Church' or the 'universal Church'; the name wouldn't matter

---

[23] Yves Congar, The Mystery of the Church (Baltimore: Helicon Press, 1960), 73.

if the conception was correct. This conviction, that there is only one Church, is shared by all Christians, Protestants as well as Catholics and Orthodox. As the Augsburg Confession formulates it: 'It is also taught that at all times there must be and remain one holy, Christian church.'[24] The goal is to form a proper conception of that one, holy Church.

An Invisible Church and a Visible Church?

A duality in the Church is not only a matter for dissidents, however. It is part of the experience of the Church for us all. One commentator has asked the question in this way: 'Is the Church constituted simply by the ensemble of the members and its reality that of the *whole* which results from the sum of its parts, and no more? Or should one rather conceive it as a reality *sui generis*, transcending the individuals assembled, and thus an original 'subject' which is not to be identified with the human subjects … who constitute it? … We are ever oscillating between these two opposed conceptions.'[25] The challenge is to integrate these two views of the Church.

So far the effort to elaborate a distinction between the concrete Church and the Church-mystery has always led to the separation between an invisible Church and the visible Church. The efforts have arisen in the context of two related issues, the rationalization of dissent and explanation of the place of sin in the Church. An early dissident who separated the mystery from the institution was Tertullian, the first great Latin theologian. A pioneer in many things in theology, Tertullian was a pioneer also in the rationalization of dissent. He disagreed with the official position on the question of the forgiveness of the sin of adultery and the permission of a second marriage, after the death of the first spouse. The details of his dissent are not important here. What is

---

[24] Augsburg Confession on the Church, VII: [German] in The Book of Concord: The Confessions of the Evangelical Lutheran Church, edd. Robert Kolb and Timothy J. Wengert (Minneapolis: Fortress Press, 2000), 42.

[25] Alexandre Durand, S.J., 'Qu'est-ce que l'Église?' Nouvelle Revue Théologique 73 (1951) 912-925, at 912.

important for the future is the distinction which he introduced to justify his dissident position. In the *De pudicitia* he distinguished between the Church of the Spirit and the Church of the Bishops; '*ecclesia spiritus ... non ecclesia numerus episcoporum*'.[26] This distinction is one that would last, a harbinger of the future. Tertullian provided no elaboration of his distinction, so it is impossible to be certain just what he had in mind. However, there can be no doubt that the formula he coined goes right to the heart of the matter, for every heterodox ecclesiology has taken this form, of juxtaposing a spiritual Church of some kind over against the concrete Church led by the bishops.

The issue of sin in the Church was central to St. Augustine's struggles with the Donatists and the Pelagians. In response to these movements St. Augustine formulated distinctions which would dominate Western ecclesiology ever after, and continue to do so still. As Ratzinger has remarked: 'The split between Donatists and Catholics that rent the Church of his African homeland caused the great doctor of the Church to distinguish with a sharpness until then unknown between the theological greatness of the Church as a salvific reality and her empirical existence,'[27] and this is precisely the distinction we wish to gras The Donatists formulated a new concept of the Church as an exclusive caste from which sinners were excluded.[28] They held firmly that the Church is the spotless spouse, the Virgin bride of Christ without spot or wrinkle, as described in Eph 5:27, even on this earth.[29] Against them St. Augustine faced a twofold task. He had to prove the co-existence of good and evil in the visible Church and, at the same time, he had to defend the right of the Catholic Church to the title of Bride without spot or wrinkle.[30] He succeeded completely in the first task. The fact

---

[26] De pudicitia 21, 17; CSEL 20, 271.9-10.
[27] Joseph Ratzinger, Principles of Catholic Theology (San Francisco: Ignatius Press, 1988), 196.
[28] On this see Denis Faul, 'Sinners in the Holy Church: A Problem in the Ecclesiology of St. Augustine,' in Studia Patristica, Vo. IX, Part 3 (Berlin: Akademie-Verlag, 1966), 404-415.
[29] Ibid, 411.
[30] Ibid.

that sinners are members of the Church became established doctrine and has often been reasserted by the Magisterium.

The second task was not so simple, and here St. Augustine initiated a discussion which is yet to be satisfactorily concluded. If there are sinners in the Church, how can she be the spotless Bride? And, although St. Augustine proved conclusively that there are sinners in the Church, he was also sure that in some sense sinners do not belong to the Church. As Faul tells us: 'It is equally clear from other figures that he did not regard sinners as really members of the Church; they do not belong to the pure and spotless Dove, who is the Church. Neither do sinners make up the structure of the Temple of God, nor of the house of God.'[31] To solve this problem, St. Augustine placed the Holy Church in an inner group of 'sinless people who bewail the iniquities taking place in their midst (e.g. Ezekiel 9:4).'[32] The controversy with the Pelagians, however, forced him to change his view. Such a group of sinless people was part of their argument in favour of the possibility of living without sin, and they claimed to be just such a group themselves. In response St. Augustine had to stress the universality of sin, and so '[h]e abandoned his idea of the inner group of *sancti*; he placed all the emphasis now on the innermost circle of the predestined in the mind of God.' Whether or not it represents his own best thought, there is no doubt that the distinction St. Augustine bequeathed to posterity was that of 'a dual conception of the Church in time: that of the authentic, but mysterious, society of the elect, and that of the mixed multitude which, in order to avoid ambiguous adjectives such as phenomenological, empirical, or existential, we will simply call the Church of everyday.'[33]

A turning-point relevant to the development being followed here was the emergence of the proactive papacy in the eleventh century. The great reformers of that age began to use the papacy as key instrument for the reform of the Church, and the new pro-active papacy engendered

---

[31] Ibid, 409. (De baptismo, III, 17, 22; CSEL 51, 213-214; IV, 4, 6; 227; VII, 52, 100; 371-72.)

[32] Ibid, 412.

[33] Pasquale Borgomeo, L'Église de ce temps dans la prédication de saint Augustin (Paris : Études Augustiniennes, 1972), 291.

an adverse reaction which has been part of our experience ever since. It meant that the supreme authority of the Church was now immediately engaged in the day-to-day life of every Christian in the West. The very direct political engagement of the Popes added to the possibilities of irritation among the faithful, so that the complaint was often made that the Church had become the Church of Constantine. It also meant that there was no longer a higher court of appeal in cases of dispute. It had ever been that the Pope was the highest court of appeal against local authorities, and now the Pope was himself acting in the first instance in many important areas. So where was one to turn in case of dispute? The dissidents had no alternative but to appeal to some higher form of the Church and that is where the dispute has centred ever since. The dispute was now over the proper definition of the Church itself, and the role of the Pope within it.[34]

Congar summarizes what happened next in this way: 'Although the successive movements from the end of the eleventh century onwards were very different from one another, they have in common one demand, often sounding like a protest: *less* of the Church, and *more* of Christ! Let religious life be less subject to canon law, to the pope, and more effectively subject to God! The law of Christ, given in the Gospel, is an absolute which must be preferred to laws introduced by ecclesiastical action, for these are human.'[35] It is clear from this that the sense of the mystery of the Church had become severely attenuated. The Church has been separated from Christ and is now seen basically as a human corporation. People don't see beyond the institution, and with the new pro-active papacy which emerged in the eleventh century revolution, the Pope's role as representing the Church is more and more emphasised. Over against this institution, with its many faults and failings, the dissidents find their only higher court of appeal in the Gospel.

At the same time the awareness of the sinfulness of the Church became more pronounced. Han Urs von Balthasar quotes a significant

---

[34] On all this see Yves Congar, O., L'Église: De saint Augustin à l'époque moderne (Paris: Les Éditions du Cerf, 1970), 202ff.
[35] Yves Congar, O., Tradition and Traditions, (London: Burns & Oates, 1966), 138.

text of the Bishop of Paris, William of Auvergne (1190-1249), deemed to be one of the most serious-minded theologians of his time.

> God's beloved is the Church, so long as she walks in the footsteps of the Fathers. But now she has become Babylon through her heinousness and infestation by unclean spirits. For God himself she has become an abomination. ... Heretics call the Church 'whore' and 'Babylon' because of the appalling scandal of the Church being overrun by the degenerate and carnal, a mob so large, riffraff so noisy, that the other members of the Church are hidden and cannot be seen. Although the heretics may have rightly felt and spoken in this way about the degenerate and those who are Christians only in name, they did not extend these terms of abuse to all Christians. We are no longer dealing with a bride but with a monster of terrible deformity and ferocity. It is clear that it cannot be said of her in such a state: 'Thou art all fair, and there is not a spot in thee.'[36]

So the two pressures are in play once again, the need to rationalize dissent and to explain the sin in the Church. And theology begins now to formulate the distinction between the Church of our experience and a higher Church, to which one can appeal from the living authorities. The first to broach the matter in this period was Henry of Ghent (c. 1217- 1293). He suggests that there could be a cleavage between the Church of God and the community of believers 'which is considered as the Church',[37] and this separation was set to become ever more important. The Great Western Schism (1378-1417) exacerbated the situation, and made the need for new ideas more urgent. The pressure

---

[36] Hans Urs von Balthasar, 'Casta Meretrix' in Explorations in Theology: II: Spouse of the Word (San Francisco: Ignatius Press, 1991), 193-288 at 197.
[37] *Prologue to the Sentences*, a. 10, q. 1, n. 4, quoted by George H. Tavard in Holy Writ or Holy Church: The Crisis of the Protestant Reformation (New York: Harper and Brothers, 1959), 23.

was great indeed and has been formulated with surprising frankness by Joseph Ratzinger: 'For nearly half a century, the Church was split into two or three obediences that excommunicated one another, so that every Catholic lived under excommunication by one pope or another, and, in the last analysis, no one could say with certainty which of the contenders had right on his side. The Church no longer offered certainty of salvation; she had become questionable in her whole objective form- -the true Church, the true pledge of salvation, had to be sought outside the institution.'[38]

The first effort to find 'the true Church ... outside the institution' was that of conciliarism. As Congar tells us: 'There was formulated an ecclesiology of the *ecclesia universalis*, alone infallible, under the sign, not of a universal pope-bishop, but of Christ. This was the common basis of all the conciliar theologies which emerged after 1379.'[39] On the theory to be developed here, this conciliarist ecclesiology is fundamentally sound and will be referred to again later. For it is the basic thesis of this book that there does indeed exist an *ecclesia universalis* with Christ as its head to which one can appeal, in a specific sense and manner to be worked out, from the concrete Church with the Pope as its head. The conciliarist mistake was to try and place a council above the Pope, and that did not work, for there is no council above the Pope, since the Pope is the head of the College of Bishops and there cannot be a legitimate council at all without the Pope.

The other ecclesiology which emerged at this time was less acceptable than the conciliarist version. One commentator points out that

> it must be noted that, in view of the poor state of Christianity at the time, a new distinction was made during the Great Western Schism between the earthly Church subject to the miseries of the division and the *Ecclesia spiritualis* made up of the elect and believers - ...

---

[38] Joseph Ratzinger, 'The Ecumenical Situation – Orthodoxy, Catholicism and Protestantism,' in <u>Principles of Catholic Theology</u> (San Francisco: Ignatius Press, 1988), lxx-yy at 196.

[39] Congar, <u>L'Église: De saint Augustin à l'époque moderne</u>, 312.

These formed the true 'universal Church', the other, hierarchical Church on earth, being only a human, changeable, projection, called to model itself, without ever arriving at the goal, on the spiritual archetype which alone possesses the transcendent ecclesial characteristics of which the Scriptures speak ... and which can only be realised fully in the eschatological era.[40]

This was the spiritual ecclesiology of John Wyclif. For him only the saved were of the church, and the damned, whom he called the foreknown (*presciti*), were eternally excluded.[41] The irremediable difficulty with Wyclif's theory was that it 'meant that, in practice, the church as a visible body ceased to exist; for ... he never ceased to emphasize that in this world neither the damned nor the saved could be known.'[42] Jan Hus was heavily influenced by Wyclif. He tried to keep Wyclif's ideas within the bounds of orthodoxy, but that really cannot be done. In common with all the great reformers, there was a genuine love of the Church. In his treatise on the Church he wrote: 'As every earthly pilgrim ought faithfully to believe the holy catholic church just as he ought to love Jesus Christ, the Lord, the bridegroom of that church, and also the church herself his bride ...'[43] But the flaw is in the Wyclifean definition: 'But the holy catholic, that is, universal, church is the totality of the predestinate ...'[44] With this foundation, the visible institution cannot be given its proper weight, and so it was that both Wyclif and Hus were condemned at the Council of Constance in 1415.

Luther believed in and loved the Church, like Wyclif and Hus before him, and indeed as every Christian must do. As one Luther scholar puts it: 'Luther is as sure and confident as his opponents are

---

[40] L'Infaillibilité de l'Église, ed. Olivier Rousseau (Éditions de Chevetogne, 1962), 8.
[41] Leff, Heresy, 516.
[42] Ibid, 518.
[43] The Church by John Huss, translated, with notes and introduction by David S. Schaff, D.D. (Westport, Connecticut: Greenwood Press, 1915, 1974). § 1.
[44] Ibid, § 3.

that Christ remains with his church through his Holy Spirit and that he guides and leads it into all truth. He can say, "We, too, confess that the church does everything right."[45] He had a spiritual view of the Church. For him the Church is simply and solely the assembly of true believers in Christ.[46] According to Congar, 'Luther says constantly that the Church is formed by the adherence of faith in Christ, hidden in God and thus invisible: it is the reign completely spiritual and invisible, in our faith, of Christ spiritual and invisible.'[47] He says that such a completely interior and spiritual community cannot be discerned, it is itself the object of faith, we profess to *believe* it, and therefore not to *see* it, in the Creed: *Credo sanctam Ecclesiam (id est) Sanctorum communionem.* ... It is in this sense that Luther speaks of the 'invisible Church'.[48] This notion of the invisible Church became standard in Reformation theology, though Luther's preferred word was 'hidden' (*abscondita*).[49] 'In the Reformed thinking on the Church, one consideration is always at work, ... that regardless of the visible Church, there exists a *hidden Church*, an *Ecclesia spiritualis, abscondita*, that is known only to God who searches hearts: "The Church is hidden, the saints are unknown."'[50]

And yet, unlike Wyclif, he continued to believe that the Church is visible to some extent. The signs by which one can see externally where the Church on earth is to be found are Baptism, Eucharist and the Gospel.[51] All three of these were to be found in the Church of his day, and Luther accepted that the true Church was externally visible in the Catholic Church. As Althaus puts it: 'In spite of all his heart-felt criticism of the Roman Church, Luther remained certain

---

[45] Althaus, The Theology of Martin Luther, 342.
[46] On this see Congar, Vraie et fausse réforme dans l'Église, 350ff.
[47] Ibid, 350.
[48] Ibid. Congar gives references for the inner Luther quotation, but I was not able to check them.
[49] Ibid, 351.
[50] Heinrich Fries, 'Wandel des Kirchenbilds und dogmengeschichtliche Entfaltung', in Mysterium Salutis: Band IV/I Das Heilsgeschehen in der Gemeinde edd. Johannes Feiner, Magnus Löhrer (Einsiedeln / Zürich / Köln: Benzinger Verlag, 1972), 223-286 at 255.
[51] Congar, Vraie et fausse réforme dans l'Église, 351.

that God had, in spite of everything, miraculously preserved the true church even in the midst of its Babylonian captivity.'[52] Obviously, however, the Catholic Church had ceased to be the true Church. For Luther 'the true church of Christ and historical Christendom are not identical. The true church is hidden ("The church is hidden away, the saints are out of sight.") and not to be identified with the official church and its history. ... This true and hidden church is ruled by Christ's Spirit; it cannot err, even in the smallest article of faith. ... His promise is, however, not automatically valid for the entire organization of the church and for the official church.'[53] Luther believed that the official and the secret church are identical in the central institutions, the Gospel, the sacraments, the apostolic authority, and he finds these in the official Church, even though, for him, it had fallen into irremediable error. According to Luther, 'God has always preserved his church, even under a church organization such as the papacy which erred in many ways. He has done this by marvellously preserving the text of the gospel and the sacraments; and through these many have lived and died in the true faith. This remains true even though they were only a weak and hidden minority within the official church. Luther repeatedly says this.'[54] Luther is clearly an improvement on Wyclif and Hus. He sees the need for a concrete manifestation of the Church on earth. However, his willingness to reject essential elements of the Church means that the end result is the same; the concrete institution has lost its validity. The Catholic (and Orthodox) position is that Christ's guarantee and the presence of the Holy Spirit are to be found in the concrete Catholic Church, with her fundamental institutions of teaching, worship and government, most obviously in the College of Bishops, whose ultimate adherence to Christ is forever guaranteed.

---

[52] Althaus, The Theology of Martin Luther, 333.
[53] Ibid, 342. (The inner quotation is to WA 18, 652.
[54] Ibid, 343.

The Catholic Reaction

The most famous and influential Catholic treatment of the theology of the Church from this period was that of St Robert Bellarmine. In one of his Controversies he takes up the question of the meaning of the word 'church'. He considers five opinions among the Reformers, but the one of most interest here is the one he attributes to Melanchton and Brentius. 'These separate two churches. One is the true church, to which pertain the privileges spoken of in Scripture, and it is the congregation of the saints who believe truly and obey God. This church is not visible, except to the eyes of faith. The other is the external church, which is the church only in name. This is the congregation of men who are one in the doctrine of faith and the use of the sacraments, and both the good and the evil are found in it.'[55] And Bellarmine responds:

> Our position, however, is that there is only one church, not two, and that the one, true Church is the community of people joined in the profession of the same Christian faith and the communion of the same sacraments, under the government of the legitimate pastors, especially the one vicar of Christ on earth, the Roman Pontiff. From this definition it is easy to ascertain who belongs to the Church and who does not. ... What distinguishes our position from all the rest is that all the others require the internal virtues to constitute a person in the Church, and they thus make the true Church invisible. We, however, also believe that all the virtues, faith, hope and charity and so on, are to be found in the Church, and yet, in order that a person can be said to be a part of the true Church, of which the Scriptures speak, we do not consider any internal virtue to be necessary, but only the public profession

---

[55] De conciliis, lib. 3, ca 2, De definitione Ecclesiae in Opera Omnia, Vol. 2 (Neapoli: Josepho Giuliano, 1857), 74.

of faith and the communion in the sacraments which can be perceived by the senses. The Church, then, is a group of men as visible and palpable as is the group of the Roman people, or the kingdom of France, or the Republic of Venice.[56]

Bellarmine goes on to gloss St. Augustine on the Church as a living body, of which the soul is the internal gifts of the Holy Spirit, faith, hope, and charity etc., and the body is defined according to his rule. Therefore people can be distinguished according as they belong to the soul of the Church alone, the body alone, or both. He admits that his definition concerns those who belong to the body of the Church alone, since this is the minimum necessary required for membership of the visible Church, where his interest is focussed.[57]

The inadequacy of Bellarmine's definition is now universally recognised. He was over-reacting to the Reformed denial of the visible Church in affirming the visible Church as alone significant. The Reformers were wrong to affirm two churches, separating the invisible mystery from the visible institution, and in the process evacuating the institution of practically all salvific significance. The appropriate response on the Catholic side, however, was not formulated until the Second Vatican Council, in *Lumen gentium* § 8, which declared: 'This society, however, equipped with hierarchical structures, and the mystical body of Christ, the visible assembly and the spiritual community, the earthly Church and the Church enriched with heavenly gifts, must not be considered as two things, but as forming one complex reality comprising a human and a divine element.' Catholic theology, therefore, must maintain that there are not 'two things', but 'one complex reality.' At the same time, as Congar holds, some duality in our concept of the Church is unavoidable. Giving the background to the notion of the Church of the Reformers, Congar draws attention to the Augustinian ideas underlying it and observes:

---

[56] Ibid, 75.
[57] Ibid.

> One cannot deny that there is a certain duality in this way of thinking; without a doubt it has to be recognized that no ecclesiology can succeed without a certain duality. One always finds oneself, in effect, brought back to two moments, which are so related – and without which there can be no ecclesiology at all – they cannot be completely dissociated. There is the reality of salvation which is fundamentally spiritual and eschatological, and there are the means of salvation, which are visible, social and have an earthly existence.[58]

That some duality has to be recognised is clear. The problem is drawing the distinction properly. Situating the duality between the 'reality of salvation' and the 'means of salvation' does not solve the problem. This is the distinction that St Augustine made and it does not work, as the efforts of Wyclif, Hus and Luther make clear. When the reality of salvation, the life of grace, is separated from the means, the institution, then the institution loses its proper position. A distinction has to be made, but it must be made accurately. Otherwise it becomes a separation, with the 'visible' pole essentially evaporating and the value of the Incarnation being lost. The challenge is to formulate the duality without falling into dualism.

---

[58] Congar, Vraie et fausse réforme dans l'Église, 333-34.

Chapter 4

A Theandric Church and a Human Church

The flaw in the concepts of the Church-mystery so far proposed is that they have been so spiritual or invisible or hidden that the apostolic institutions, and most notably the College of Bishops, have lost their effectiveness. An essential quality of an orthodox conception of the Church-mystery is that it retains the apostolic institutions as an essential component and upholds the authority of the College of Bishops in its full vigour. Distinguishing the human reality of the Church from a spiritual, invisible, or hidden reality accessible only to faith has not worked. The human reality of the visible Church is and must be seen to be an essential part of the Church-mystery, so the distinction must be drawn along some other line.

The fundamental ground requiring a distinction within the Church is the reality of sin within her. There is no doubt that, in order to solve this problem, a distinction must be made. The fact of sin in the Church is obvious. It is a matter of our own personal experience every day, and it is also Catholic dogma. It is an article of faith that sinners are members of the Church. And by sinners here is meant those who are in mortal sin, who have lost the state of grace, and in whom the Holy Spirit no longer dwells. 'This is a truth of our faith which the Church has constantly taught, in patristic times against Montanism, Novatianism and Donatism, in the Middle Ages against the Albigenses, against the Fraticelli, against Wyclif and Hus, and in modern times against the Reformers, against Jansenism and the Synod of Pistoia.'[1] The problem arises from the fact that it is also a dogma of faith that the Church is holy. After belief in the Trinity, it was the first doctrine of faith to become established in the Creeds of the Church. The first short profession of faith in Denzinger's collection has just five clauses, expressing belief in the Father, the Son, the Holy Spirit and then 'in the holy Church.' This fundamental point of faith has retained its central position in the Creed ever since. How can the Church be holy and sinful at the same time? An adequate ecclesiology has to provide a satisfactory answer to this question.

There is a long-standing position of the Magisterium of the Church asserting that the Church is perfectly holy and that the sins of her members do not undermine that truth. According to Congar a decisive development in ecclesiology took place in the West in the wake of the Donatist crisis, namely the idea of an objective sanctity of the ecclesial institution itself, independent of the persons who live in it. The error of the Donatists was precisely in viewing sanctity as purely personal. Against this the Catholic theologians showed that there is an incorruptible sanctity which comes to the Church by faith, the sacraments and the hierarchical powers of the priesthood.[2] St. Ambrose coined a formula which sums the matter up: 'Not in herself daughters, not in herself, but in us is the Church wounded.'[3] This was the general patristic doctrine. The Church herself is holy, and though there are sinners in the Church, they do not fully belong, and so do not compromise her fundamental holiness. Pope Pius XII presented the traditional resolution of the difficulty in the encyclical *Mystici corporis*. 'There is no doubt that there are sinners among the members of the Church,' he said. At the same time we can still say:

---

[1] 'The Church of Sinners,' <u>Theological Investigations 6</u> (Baltimore/London: Helicon Press/Darton, Longman & Todd, 1969), 253-269 at 256.
[2] Congar, <u>Vraie et fausse réforme dans l'Église</u>, 82-83.
[3] <u>De Virginitate</u> 8, 48; PL 16, 292C.

> Certainly the loving Mother is spotless in the Sacraments, by which she gives birth to and nourishes her children; in the faith which she has always preserved inviolate; in her sacred laws imposed on all; in the evangelical counsels which she recommends; in those heavenly gifts and extraordinary graces through which, with inexhaustible fecundity, she generates hosts of martyrs, virgins and confessors. But it cannot be laid to her charge if some members fall, weak or wounded. In their name she prays to God daily: 'Forgive us our trespasses'; and with the brave heart of a mother she applies herself at once to the work of nursing them back to health.[4]

The ecclesial elements in the Church, the deposit of faith, the sacraments, the counsels, the gifts of the Holy Spirit are all pure and without sin. But can it be said that the Church is thereby spotless? The holiness of the constitutive principles does not guarantee the holiness of the visible Church, because we, the members, remain sinful human beings, and our sin must affect the Church, in some way. So, more is required to resolve the difficulty.

In the introduction to his treatise on the Church, Monsignor (later Cardinal) Charles Journet proposed a different approach to this issue. In order to deal with the problem of sin in the Church, he made the distinction between the Church understood 'in its *formal*, or *ontological*, or *theological* sense,' and the Church understood 'in a *material* manner.'[5] The material understanding of the Church refers to the visible Church with which we are familiar. It embraces sinners along with the just, so that 'sinners are regarded as entirely within the Church, their sins included, and the Church herself is seen as a mingling

---

[4] Mystici corporis § 66.
[5] Charles Journet, The Church of the Word Incarnate, Volume One: The Apostolic Hierarchy, London and New York, 1955, xxvii. [Emphasis in the original.]

of sanctity and sin. Evil has penetrated within her boundaries.'[6] The theological understanding of the Church he explains as follows:

> The Church contains sinners. But she does not contain sin. It is only in virtue of what remains pure and holy in them, that sinners belong to her - that is to say in virtue of the sacramental characters of Baptism and Confirmation, and of the theological habits of faith and hope if they still have them. That is the part of their being by which they still cleave to the Church and are still within her. But in virtue of the mortal sin which has found its way into them and fills their hearts, they belong chiefly to the world and to the devil. 'He who commits sin is of the devil' (1 John 3:8). ... Thus the frontier of the Church passes through each one of those who call themselves her members, enclosing within her bounds all that is pure and holy, leaving outside all that is sin and stain, 'more piercing than any two-edged sword and reaching even the division of the soul and the spirit, of the joints also and the marrow, and discerning the thoughts and intents of the heart' (cf. Heb. 4:12). So that even here below, in the days of her pilgrimage, in the midst of the evil and sin at war in each one of her children, the Church herself remains immaculate; and we can apply to her quite fully and without any restriction the passage of the Epistle to the Ephesians (5:25-28). It is therefore always in this formal and theological sense that we take the word 'Church' when we call her One, Holy, Catholic, Apostolic, the Bride and Body of Christ, the temple and dwelling-place of the Trinity. The sins of her members are not to be identified with the Church, or the imperfections of Christians with Christianity. It

---

[6] Ibid, xxviii.

is not these that constitute her, or make her visible; but rather her true body, always illuminated by her soul - though the intensity of the illumination may vary from one age to another.'[7]

The key difference between the 'theological' and the 'material' visions of the Church lies in the attitude adopted to the reality of sin. On the 'material' approach, which is effectively the ordinary common-sense approach which we all adopt without thinking much about it, we accept the reality of the Church as we find it, with the reality of sin a matter of every-day experience. Journet suggests, on the other hand, that in order to understand the true mystery of the Church properly, we must exclude sin from our concept. To do so may seem, at first sight, a pure abstraction, and the procedure is widely challenged. Journet's definition of the Church in its theological sense is grounded in the exclusion of sin. It can appear somewhat like a piece of legerdemain to resolve the problem of sin in the Church simply by postulating a concept of the Church without sin! If it is to be of any practical use, this sinless 'theological' concept must be shown to correspond to reality. Pope Paul VI has made a remark which points a way forward. 'The Church is therefore holy, though having sinners in her midst, because she herself has no life but the life of grace: it is by living by her life that her members are sanctified; it is by removing themselves from her life that they fall into sins and disorders that prevent the radiation of her sanctity.'[8] What is this Church that 'has no life but the life of grace'?

A clue as to the way forward can be taken from a text of St Thomas in which he formulates a distinction between two concepts of the Church.

> The word 'Church' is understood in two ways. For sometimes it designates only the Body which is joined to Christ as its Head, and only in this acceptation does the Church have the nature of a bride; and in this context

---

[7] Ibid, xxvii-xxviii.
[8] Pope Paul VI, <u>Credo of the People of God</u> (1968) § 19.

> Christ is not a member of the Church, but the Head exerting influence on all the members of the Church. In another way, 'Church' is understood as indicating the head and the members joined ... But when the Church is spoken of in this way, 'Church' means not only bride, but bridegroom and bride, as being made one by a spiritual union.[9]

The difference between the two concepts turns on the place of Christ in the Church; in one Christ is a member of the Church, its Head, and in the other the Church is considered apart from him. And that is the distinction to be developed here. No one has presented the concept of the Whole Church, Christ and his Body joined inseparably, better than St Augustine. Emile Mersch summarizes his teaching in a marvellous text:

> He repeats again and again, on countless occasions, that Christ and the Church are one and the same thing, one soul, one man, one person, one just man, one Christ, one Son of God. Hence the whole Christ is not the Saviour alone, but the Head plus the members, Christ united with the Church. The members of Christ are one with Him: He is they and they are He. All are gathered together into this unity, and in God's eyes they are but one well-beloved Son.[10]

And the other divine persons also belong to this Church-mystery. A number of the Fathers have spoken of the place of the Holy Spirit in the Church. Tertullian identifies the Church in a special way with the Holy Spirit. For the Church herself is properly and principally the Spirit Himself, in whom is the trinity of the one divinity, the Father, the Son

---

[9] IV Sent., d. 49, q. 4, a. 3, ad 4.
[10] Emile Mersch, S. J., The Whole Christ : The Historical Development of the Doctrine of the Mystical Body in Scripture and Tradition, trans. John R. Kelly, S. J. (Milwaukee: The Bruce Publishing Company, 1938), 414.

and the Holy Spirit. He gathers that Church which the Lord founded on three.'[11] This identification with the Holy Spirit would be repeated often in the Tradition. There is the familiar text of St. Irenaeus: 'For where the Church is there is the Spirit of God; and where the Spirit of God is, there is the Church …'[12] And St. John Chrysostom says almost exactly the same thing: 'If the Spirit is not present, then the Church does not subsist; if, however, the Church does subsist, it is clear that the Spirit is present.'[13] And St. Augustine also: 'Therefore, whoever has the Holy Spirit is in the Church, … Whoever is outside this Church, does not have the Holy Spirit.'[14] Tertullian it was who best summed up the Trinitarian nature of the divine presence in the Church, when he said: 'But after both the attestation of our faith and the promise of salvation have been pledged under the sanction of three witnesses, it is necessary to add mention of the Church, for where the three are, that is the Father, the Son, and the Holy Spirit, there is the Church, which is the body of these three.'[15] And St Cyprian wrote that the Church is 'a unity proceeding from the divine immutability, and of the same nature as the heavenly mysteries.'[16]

Despite their stress on the divine nature of the Church, the Fathers maintained a solid grasp on the integrity of its human dimension. As Congar tells us: 'The patristic tradition had a very mystical notion of the Church. It saw in the Church a descent of heavenly realities, a passage of humanity and the world into the "spiritual" quality of the Kingdom of God and the Body of Christ, realities of which the true condition

---

[11] 'nam et ipsa ecclesia proprie et principaliter ipse est spiritus, in quo est trinitas unius divinitatis, pater et filius et spiritus sanctus. illam ecclesiam congregat quam dominus in tribus posuit.' De pudicitia 21, 17; CSEL 20, 271.3-6.

[12] AH, III, 24, 1: « Ubi enim Ecclesia, ibi et Spiritus Dei; et ubi Spiritus Dei, illic Ecclesia et omnis gratia: Spiritus autem Veritas. » SC 34, 400.9-10.

[13] De sancta Pentecoste, hom. 1, § 4; « ei mh Pneuma parhn, ouk an sunesth h Ekklhsia;; ei de sunistatai h Ekklhsia, eudhlon oti to Pneuma paresti. » ; PG 50, 459.

[14] Sermo 268, 1; « Qui ergo habet Spiritum Sanctum, in Ecclesia est, … Quicumque praeter hanc Ecclesiam est, non habet Spiritum Sanctum. » ; PL 38, 1232.

[15] 'Necessario adjicitur Ecclesiae mentio, quoniam ubi tres, id est, Pater et Filius et Spiritus Sanctus, ibi Ecclesia, quae trium corpus est.'(De Baptismo, 6; CCL 1, 282.)

[16] De Unitate, ch. 6. CCL 3, 254.158-59.

is heavenly. … at the same time, it does not separate the external and social aspect from the internal and mystical aspect.'[17] And again:

> All through the writings of the apostolic age and the earliest period of Christianity, we see treated as identical, without the slightest separation between the two, the community life in Christ and the mystical Body, on the one hand, and the actual community of Christians, on the other.[18] … The same single Church is declared to be both visible and invisible, to be a hierarchically constituted society and a mystery of heavenly life. The texts are so many and so unanimous that the burden of proof of any dissociation rests on those who assert it.[19]

This patristic vision has continued uninterrupted in the Eastern Church. The Orthodox theologian, Vladimir Lossky tells us that 'Eastern theology never thinks of the Church apart from Christ and from the Holy Spirit.'[20] For them the Church is 'founded on a twofold divine economy: the work of Christ and the work of the Holy Spirit, the two persons of the Trinity sent into the world. The work of both persons forms the foundation of the Church.'[21] Congar shares Lossky's assessment of the ecclesiology of the Eastern Church, and also observes that there is a corresponding lack of development of the institutional aspect of the Church. He tells us that 'from the first, eastern ecclesiological thought envisaged the divine realities at the heart of the mystery of the Church rather than its earthly aspect and human implications. It saw the inward unity of faith and love more clearly than the concrete demands of ecclesiastical communion. The relatively feeble development of ecclesiology by the Greek Fathers has often been

---

[17] Congar, Vraie et fausse réforme dans l'Église, 63.
[18] Congar, The Mystery of the Church, 73.
[19] Congar, Lay People in the Church (Geoffrey Chapman: London, 1957), 26-27.
[20] Vladimir Lossky, The Mystical Theology of the Eastern Church, (Crestwood, New York: St Vladimir's Seminary Press, 2002), 175.
[21] Ibid, 156.

remarked, the fact being that their emphasis was rather on Christology and still more on pneumatology; seeing the Church in Christ and in the Holy Spirit rather than in its ecclesiastical being as such.'[22] The problem is to make this high mystical vision work concretely, and to make it match with the concrete reality of our life in the Church. An examination of three basic analogies used to explain the mystery of the Church can help to focus the difficulty.

---

[22] <u>Divided Christendom</u>, London, 1939, 12; <u>Chrétiens désunis. Principes d'un 'oecuménisme' catholique</u>, Paris, 1937, 14.

Chapter 5

The Incorporation of the Holy Spirit in the Church

There are a number of theological affirmations made concerning the Church which go beyond the scriptural images and use metaphysical categories. We believe that the relationship between the Holy Spirit and the Church is analogous to the relationship between the Word and his human nature in Christ. We believe that the Holy Spirit is the soul of the Church. We believe that in the reality of the Church we experience a mysterious continuation of the reality of the Incarnation. And, finally, we believe that Christ and the Church together form one mystical person. By considering each of these analogies it is hoped to clarify the reality of the Church-mystery underlying the visible institution.

The Holy Spirit is the Soul of the Church

It is appropriate to begin with the doctrine that the Holy Spirit is the soul of the Church. St. Augustine was the first to state the position clearly: 'What the soul is to the human body, that is the Holy Spirit to Christ's body, which is the Church.'[1] And St. Thomas followed him:

---

[1] 'Quod autem est anima corpori hominis, hoc est Spiritus Sanctus corpori Christi, quod est Ecclesia.' (Sermo 267, 4 ; PL 38, 1231.)

'Just as a body is made one by the unity of the soul, so is the Church by the unity of the Spirit.'[2] The Magisterium took up the doctrine with Pope Leo XIII. In his encyclical on the Holy Spirit, he wrote: 'Let it suffice to state that, as Christ is the Head of the Church, so is the Holy Spirit her soul.'[3] In *Mystici corporis*, Pius XII repeated the teaching of Leo XIII and developed it:

> If we examine closely this divine principle of life and power given by Christ, insofar as it constitutes the very source of every gift and created grace, we easily perceive that it is nothing else than the Holy Spirit.[4] ... To this Spirit of Christ, also, as to an invisible principle is to be ascribed the fact that all the parts of the Body are joined one with the other and with their exalted Head; for He is entire in the Head, entire in the Body, and entire in each of the members. ... It is He who, through His heavenly grace, is the principle of every supernatural act in all parts of the Body. ... This presence and activity of the Spirit of Jesus Christ is tersely and vigorously described by Our predecessor of immortal memory Leo XIII in his Encyclical Letter *Divinum Illud* in these words: 'Let it suffice to say that, as Christ is the Head of the Church, so is the Holy Spirit her soul.'[5]

A small, but significant, change was introduced at the Second Vatican Council. The first draft of the document on the Church had said quite simply that the Holy Spirit <u>is</u> the soul of the Church: 'Just as Christ is the Head of the Body, so the Holy Spirit, dwelling in the Head

---

[2] 'Sicut constituitur unum corpus ex unitate animae, ita ecclesia ex unitate Spiritus ...', <u>In Col.</u>, 1, 18, lect. 5 (ed. Marietti, II, no. 46).
[3] <u>Divinum illud munus</u>, 9 May 1897: ASS 29 (1896-97), 650.]
[4] <u>Mysitici corporis</u>, § 56.
[5] <u>Mysitici corporis</u>, § 57.

and the members, is its soul.'⁶ In the second draft, which remained substantially unchanged thereafter, this was changed to read: 'The Holy Spirit ... so vivifies, unifies and moves the whole body, that the fathers of the Church could compare his task to that which is exercised by the life-principle, or soul, in the human body.'⁷ The commentary explains the change as a better interpretation of the patristic texts underlying the doctrine. This qualified formulation was taken up also by the *Catechism of the Catholic Church* which says: 'The Spirit is the soul, *as it were*, of the Mystical Body, the source of its life, of its unity in diversity, and of the riches of its gifts and charisms.'⁸

How is the hesitation in affirming the Holy Spirit's role as the soul of the Church to be explained? It seems to me that the background to the change can be found expressed most clearly in the writings of Congar. This doctrine is one to which Congar returned on different occasions throughout his career, and his position remained constant all that time. He ever affirmed that while the Holy Spirit can be spoken of as the soul of the Church, the affirmation is not to be taken literally, for the Holy Spirit cannot be called the soul of the Church 'in the strict sense, as some of the Fathers, especially St Augustine, believed could be done.'⁹ In another place he writes: 'We can understand that Tradition gives the Holy Ghost the title of soul of the Church. It is not, however, to be taken in the sense of a soul entering into composition with the body of the Church and being united to it in a physical and substantial union, like our souls and our bodies.'¹⁰ And again: 'The Holy Spirit ...is with [the Church] to guide and assist it, to enable it to perform actions which, while outwardly human, are bearers of a divine virtue, *virtus Spiritus*

---

[6] Francisco Gil Hellín, Constitutio Dogmatica De Ecclesia Lumen Gentium (Città del Vaticano: Libreria Editrice Vaticana, 1995), 36.13.
[7] Ibid, 36.38. and Tanner, 853.44-854.1.
[8] CCC, 809 [Emphasis added].
[9] 'Im strikten Sinn kann man den Heiligen Geist nicht „Seele der Kirche' nennen, wie man dies einigen Vätern, besonders Augustinus, entnehmen zu können glaubte.' in 'Die heilige Kirche,' in Mysterium Salutis: Band IV/I Das Heilsgeschehen in der Gemeinde edd. Johannes Feiner, Magnus Löhrer, Einsiedeln / Zürich / Köln, 1972, 458-77, at 465.
[10] Congar, The Mystery of the Church, 170.

Sancti,'[11] but '[w]e must not, however, imagine ... that He is actually the interior form of unity in the Church.'[12] And I would like to add one final quotation which gives another important aspect of Congar's position: 'For the Holy Ghost is not its soul in the sense of making with it one entity, united to it substantially as Christ's humanity is to the Word; the union is solely one of alliance.'[13]

Congar gives a number of reasons for his stand that the Holy Spirit cannot be considered the soul of the Church in the strict sense. One is because of the presence of sin within her. For the Church 'is not impeccable in the person of its human representatives,' she 'is not even wholly guaranteed against error. ... Along with her essential fidelity, divinely guaranteed by that of God himself, she still has the possibility, in each and all of the smaller details of her life, of falling short of the absolute holiness and truth which is God.'[14] In another place he writes: 'Insofar as the Body is united with the Holy Spirit in such a way that it is made up of concrete and historical people, it is subject to the weakness of the *flesh*. On that account, therefore, not *all* the acts of the ecclesial institution can be presumed to be acts of the Holy Spirit.'[15] This is a valid and a strong objection, for the Holy Spirit can have no part in sin; where the Holy Spirit is, there is no sin, and vice versa.

Presenting another argument against the Holy Spirit being truly the soul of the Church, Congar tells us that 'it is sufficient to point out that the Holy Spirit does not enter into composition with [the Church] as a form with matter, but united himself with it as a subject already constituted in being,'[16] and that the union between the Church and the Holy Spirit 'is more a matter of a union between two realities, the Spirit and the Church, each having its own subsistence - a kind of marriage as if between two persons.'[17]

---

[11] Ibid, 171.
[12] Congar, Divided Christendom, 57.
[13] Congar, Mystery, 40.
[14] Ibid.
[15] Congar, Die heilige Kirche, 466.
[16] Congar, Mystery, 171.
[17] Congar, The Mystery of the Church, Baltimore, 1960, 35.

I suggest that Congar is wrong here. It is not true to say that the Church already exists as 'a subject already constituted in being,' before the Spirit enters into her. The individual human beings who constitute the Church all exist prior to the Spirit's intervention, but they do not exist *as Church*. The new, supernatural, life in the Spirit which makes us Christians constitutes us as a completely new creation, and it is only as a result of this new creation that the Church begins to be. And neither can the matter of the Church, the institutions founded by Christ, be considered to pre-exist the action of the Holy Spirit, for he is involved in the formation of the Church at every stage.

Congar continually compares unfavourably the role of the Holy Spirit as the soul of the Church, with the role of the soul in a physical body, so that there is no 'physical and substantial union' between the soul and the body of the Church. On the other hand, Pope Pius XII, in *Mystici corporis*, reasons in exactly the opposite sense. He is comparing the Church as a mystical body with other moral bodies, or human communities, and, speaking of the role of the Holy Spirit, acting as the internal principle, or soul, of the body, he asserts that its 'excellence is such that of itself it is vastly superior to whatever bonds of union may be found in a physical or moral body.'[18] Which is correct? The contradiction is only apparent, and it depends on the notion of Church at work in each case. Congar is taking it for granted that the Church can simply be identified with the concrete, historical reality of Church which is the object of our daily experience, whereas these faith-affirmations about the Church only make sense if we understand the Church 'theologically,' as Journet put it. Thinking of the concrete Church as we know it, it is clear that the Holy Spirit cannot be said to animate every aspect of its being. If, however, we understand the true Church, the holy Church, to be precisely the reality formed by the Holy Spirit as its soul, no more and no less, a different approach is possible. Any living organism has a soul, and the soul is to be understood precisely as the active principle which is the source of the life and all the actions of the living organism. And this can be true of the Church as

---

[18] *Mystici corporis*, § 62.

a moral organism, once certain conditions are laid down. The Church is the object of our faith, and the way to understand the Church is from faith rather than from experience. If we understand the Church as the high mystical reality spoken of by the Fathers, formed by the joint mission of the Son and the Holy Spirit, then the Holy Spirit can be taken to be the soul of the Church, without need of qualification. Not every action of every Christian belongs to the Church-mystery, the Body of Christ. Remembering Irenaeus's definition of the Church as the presence of the Holy Spirit, we take it that only what comes from the Spirit truly belongs to the Church. Everything else is and must be associated with the Church as a sociological reality, for which we are humanly responsible, but it does not belong to the Body of Christ.

A deeper reason for Congar's unwillingness to recognise the Holy Spirit simply as the soul of the Church comes to light in another point he makes. He tells us that the Holy Spirit 'is the First cause and active principle of the Church and her unity, but the inward or immanent principle of the Church is found in the created gifts of God, the supernatural gifts and virtues: not God Himself, but the realities of grace proceeding from God and assimilating us to Him.'[19] As the reflection on created grace developed in post-Tridentine theology, it became accepted doctrine that created grace and charity form the soul of the Church. Charles Journet presents a summary of post-Tridentine theology on the created soul of the Church, pointing out that, while accepting that the Holy Spirit is the soul of the Church, they also affirm that the supernatural gifts of grace and charity constitute the soul of the Church. From this Journet comes to the conclusion that the Church has two souls, one created and one uncreated.[20] Pope Pius XII, in *Mystici corporis*, takes this line. 'If that vital principle, by which the whole community of Christians is sustained by its Founder, be considered not now in itself, but in the created effects which proceed from it, it consists in those heavenly gifts which our Redeemer, together with His Spirit,

---

[19] Congar, Divided Christendom, 57.
[20] Charles Journet, L'Eglise du Verbe Incarné : II. Sa structure interne et son unité catholique, Desclée de Brouwer & Cie., 1951, 565-69, 572.

bestows on the Church, and which He and His Spirit, from whom come supernatural light and holiness, make operative in the Church.'[21] He presents both the Holy Spirit and the created gifts to be the vital principle of the Church. There is a problem with this, however, since all works of God *ad extra* must be ascribed to the Trinity as a whole and can only be attributed to an individual Person by appropriation, so the created gifts are not properly related to the Holy Spirit in person. Are we only 'imagining' the Holy Spirit to be the soul of the Church, animating the Body in its every part, when in fact it is the whole Trinity causing these supernatural effects which constitute the soul? And does it really make sense to speak of an organism having two souls?

The Holy Spirit becomes Grace and Charity

This raises the question as to the relationship of the Holy Spirit to the created gifts which form the created soul of the Church, and what is required is an explanation of the Indwelling of the Holy Spirit in the Church, and in the souls of individual Christians.

The problem is one of long standing and is basically that of finding an explanation of our divinization. There are few scripture texts more striking than 2 Peter 1:4, where we are told that we 'become sharers in the divine nature'. On the basis of this text especially, our divinization was a theme greatly developed by the Fathers of the Eastern Church. For them, the indwelling of the Holy Spirit was all-important. As Rondet tells us: 'The gift of the Holy Spirit is the notion that governed the whole theology of grace in the early days of Christianity. The Christians of the first centuries were aware of living a new life unknown before their day. For quite a long time, people talked about "receiving the Holy Spirit, losing the Holy Spirit, having the Holy Spirit," where we today speak of "being justified, being in the state of sin, being in the state of grace."'[22] Thought on our divinization has not been nearly so well

---

[21] Mystici corporis, § 58.
[22] Henri Rondet, S.J., The Grace of Christ: A Brief History of the Theology of Grace (Newman Press, 1967), 69.

developed in Western theology, though it was never completely lost to view. St. Thomas, for instance, in his treatise on grace in the *Summa theologiae* could write: 'The gift of grace exceeds every faculty of a created nature, since it is nothing else than a certain participation in the divine nature.'[23] Though, clearly, St. Thomas was aware of the Eastern tradition on our divinization, he did not make use of it when he came to explain the presence of God within the souls of the just. What St. Thomas did was to make the crowning contribution to the development of the theology of created grace, which offered a remarkable explanation of the inner dynamics of the Christian life, and Western theology concentrated more on this mystery of our created participation in the divine life, than on the mystery of our divinization, which continued to fascinate the East.[24]

With the rediscovery of the Fathers of the Church in recent centuries, the Eastern doctrine of divinization was brought to light again, and some serious efforts have been made to understand what is involved. Many theories have been proposed over the years,[25] but one approach in particular leads to a conclusion which helps to solve our problem. In the seventeenth century, Denis Petau (1583-1652),[26] made a very thorough study of the Fathers of the Church, and on the basis of the doctrine of divinization he discovered there, became quite dissatisfied with the current theology on the issue. The common teaching then was that the presence of God in the souls of the just is the work of the

---

[23] ST I-II, q. 112, a. 1: 'Donum gratiae excedit omnem facultatem naturae creatae, cum nihil aliud sit quam quaedam participatio divinae naturae …' cf. I-II, q. 62, a. 1 ad 1; q. 19, a. 7, q. 110, a. 3c.

[24] On this see Piet Fransen, 'Dogmengeschichtliche Entfaltung der Gnadenlehre,' in Mysterium Salutis: Grundriß heilsgeschichtlicher Dogmatik, 4/2 Das Heilsgeschehen in der Bemeinde, Zweiter Halbband, edd. Johannes Feiner, Magnus Löhrer, Einsiedeln / Zürich / Köln, 1973, 631-766.

[25] See Rondet, The Grace of Christ, 365-77 and Maurizio Flick, S. J., Zoltan Alszeghy, S. J. Il vangelo della grazia, Librería Editrice Florentina, 1964, 483-98 and 553-60. Rondet made his own effort to resolve the question in 'La divinisation du chrétien : mystère et problèmes,' in Essais sur la théologie de la grâce, Paris, 1964), 107-54.

[26] Rondet, Grace, 366-70.

whole Trinity as efficient cause and is only attributed to the Holy Spirit by appropriation. Petau was convinced that the Scriptural and Patristic doctrine demanded that in the soul there is not only created grace, but the Holy Spirit himself. He taught that the presence of the Holy Spirit is to be understood on the analogy of the Incarnation. The Holy Spirit is in us in much the same way as the Word is in the humanity of Christ, though he was well aware that the union of the Word with his humanity is not exactly the same as the union of the just with the Holy Spirit. The latter is not a physical union or a hypostatic union; we are not gods by nature, but only by grace. Petau formulated his positions carefully, knowing the likely response they would receive. Even so, his opinion was almost unanimously rejected. The theologians of the day 'clung to the iron law of appropriation,'[27] insisting that created grace is a work of the whole Trinity and can only be related to the Holy Spirit by appropriation. There was even the suggestion of heresy involved, since the Council of Trent had taught that grace is the 'only formal cause of justification.' (DS 1529.) Rondet, however, concludes that 'his thesis nevertheless made some headway. It was not enough to condemn the thesis; the problem itself had to be answered.'[28]

Towards the end of the nineteenth century, Petau's idea was taken up again by Matthias Joseph Scheeben (1835-88).[29] He also stressed the parallel with the Incarnation, and Rondet reports his position as follows: 'The Holy Spirit possesses us in a special way, in much the same way that the Word possesses his sacred humanity. The Holy Spirit is not only the *efficient* cause of our sanctification along with the other divine Persons; he is also its *formal* cause. He does not take the place of created grace, which is at once an effect of his presence and a disposition for receiving him. But it is the gift of the Holy Spirit, and not created grace, which is primary.' Scheeben goes even further than Petau in pressing the analogy with the Incarnation, and postulates a truly hypostatic union proper to the Holy Spirit.

---

[27] Rondet, Grace, 372.
[28] Rondet, Grace, 373.
[29] Rondet, Grace, 373-75.

> Sacred Scripture and especially the Fathers, when they speak of the temple of the Holy Spirit, repeatedly employ such striking expressions that in this connection, if anywhere, we are led to think of a possession of the creature that is truly hypostatic and proper to the Holy Spirit. And, in fact, we are of the opinion that this may readily be conceived. ... As each distinct person possesses the divine nature in a special way, He can possess a created nature in His own personal way, and to this extent exclusively. ... If the Son alone takes physical possession of a created nature, why should not the Holy Spirit be able to take possession of a created being in a way proper to His own person, by means of a less perfect and purely moral possession (by a e;nosij scetikh, in contradistinction to fusikh, kai upostatikh,, i.e., eij upo, stasin mi, an [union according to relationship, in contradistinction to a physical and hypostatic union, i.e., according to hypostasis alone]?[30]

Scheeben's effort met with a certain guarded welcome from some theologians, such as G. B. Franzelin, and, although the theology manuals continued to reject the explanations of Petau and Scheeben, 'the return to tradition had now been definitively accomplished.'[31]

In an influential article[32], Karl Rahner made an important contribution to the discussion. He contended that for Scripture and the early tradition, our union with the Holy Spirit is the basis of his created gifts, and this is the reverse of the perspective normal in Western theology. In the Western tradition, the presence of the Holy Spirit is the consequence of the gift of created graced, whereas Scripture and the Greek tradition would say the opposite, that the created gifts are the

---

[30] Matthias Joseph Scheeben, The Mysteries of Christianity, St. Louis / London, 1946, 165-66.
[31] Rondet, Grace, 376.
[32] 'Some Implications of the Scholastic Concept of Uncreated Grace,' Theological Investigations, Volume I, (London: Darton, Longman & Todd, 1961), 319-346.

consequence of the presence of the Holy Spirit. If this perspective is to be justified theologically, more is required than the efficient causality of created grace which, as we have seen, is the standard explanation in Western theology. Rahner proposes that it must be that 'God communicates himself to the man to whom grace has been shown in the mode of *formal* causality, so that this communication is not then merely the consequence of an efficient causation of created grace.'[33] A similar solution was proposed by Maurice de la Taille, whose theory was most clearly defended and developed by Robert Gleason.[34] He argues that

> Scripture and the Fathers suggest that there is a mysterious kind of formal causality at work in the inhabitation.[35] ...If man is to be deified, the seal imprinting itself must be the very substance of God Himself, for it requires God Himself to communicate divinity to man.[36] ... for created grace alone could not deify man. Since we know that it does precisely this, it is clear that it does so only by the giving of the divinity to our souls.[37] ... This union between the substance of the soul and the substance of the divinity is an immediate, ontological union, but of course not a substantial union. The new and special presence of God is to be conceived as a permanent actuation of one's soul by God Himself. ... The technical description of this theory ... is 'created actuation by Uncreated Act.'[38] ... the Holy Spirit becoming, as it were, the vital principle of the just soul.'[39]

---

[33] Rahner, TI 1, 334.
[34] Robert W. Gleason, S.J., <u>Grace</u> (Sheed and Ward: New York, 1962).
[35] Ibid, 138.
[36] Ibid, 140.
[37] Ibid, 142.
[38] Ibid.
[39] Ibid, 144.

Gleason responds to the objection based on the teaching of Trent by pointing out that 'in stating that there is only one formal cause of justification, the council did not deny that the Holy Spirit may be a quasi-formal cause.'[40] And he further claims: 'An indirect proof of our thesis comes from the Fathers' demonstration of the divinity of the Holy Spirit. Man, they argued, is divinized. Yet only God can divinize. Therefore the Holy Spirit, who divinizes man, is God.'[41]

More recently, Heribert Mühlen has made somewhat similar suggestions. He expresses the view that in the period after the Council of Trent theologians concerned themselves too exclusively with the created reality of sanctifying grace, and that the doctrine of uncreated grace has thereby been completely passed over.[42] He seeks to remedy this lacuna and treats of the mission of the Holy Spirit and its analogy with the mission of the Son. He suggests that the Holy Spirit is truly sent into our hearts, so that just as the Son humbled himself by taking on a human nature (Phil 2:6), so the Holy Spirit humbles himself by entering into our hearts in such a manner that he implicates himself really in the adventure of our human freedom.[43] He goes so far as to suggest that the self-abasement of the Holy Spirit is even greater than that of the Son, since he enters into our *sinful* hearts, while the Son took on a *sinless* human nature.[44] Even sinners can 'possess' the Spirit of Christ, or 'be possessed' by the Spirit of Christ, because and insofar as even sinners can be active for salvation and God does not allow his offer of salvation to be dependent on the sinfulness of the persons he calls to mediate salvation. This radical non-separation of the Spirit of Christ from the ecclesial ministries is a moving and shocking example of the deep *kenosis* of the Spirit of Christ.[45] Mühlen does not explain how all this can be, but it is clear that he wants the presence of the

---

[40] Ibid, 145-46.
[41] Ibid, 240.
[42] Mühlen, <u>Der Heilige Geist als Person</u>, 9-10.
[43] Heribert Mühlen, <u>Una Mystica Persona</u>, (München / Paderborn / Wien: Verlag Ferdinand Schöningh, 1968), § 11.36, 416.
[44] Ibid, § 11.28, 406.
[45] Ibid, § 11.40, 419.

Holy Spirit to be understood in a way that goes beyond the presence by appropriation as it has traditionally been taken.

In his presentation of the history, Mühlen dwells more than most on the contribution of Peter Lombard to the discussion, and develops it in a new direction. He considers the teaching of the Lombard particularly significant, in that it has influenced the subsequent development of the Western theology of grace, and that it still does so.[46] He sees the recent efforts to resolve the question of the relationship between the Holy Spirit and created grace as attempts to settle a question left open since Peter Lombard. He observes that, in this matter, 'the analogy with the hypostatic union of the Word of God with his human nature plays a special role.'[47] He wonders if the indwelling of the Holy Spirit can be understood by analogy with the Incarnation of the Word, and understands in this way the proposals of those theologians who speak of a 'quasi-formal' causality for the Holy Spirit in his relationship with the souls of the just.[48] He develops a theory of his own, based on an inter-personal metaphysics, which is quite distinctive. It is certainly suggestive, but is hard to grasp clearly. It seems to me too far from the theological tradition to be really useful, and its failure to make any real headway in contemporary theology is a strong argument against it.[49] He does, however, make one remarkable suggestion which seems to me to point the way forward. Basing himself on the teaching of the Second Vatican Council, in *Lumen gentium*, § 8, that the relationship of the Holy Spirit and the Church is to be understood on the basis of the analogy with the Incarnation, he proposes that, just as the Word became man, so too the Holy Spirit must 'become' something. On two occasions he has the Holy Spirit 'becoming' the Church,[50] while on a third he 'becomes' '"grace" for us.[51] In order to develop this suggestion

---

[46] Mühlen, <u>Der Heilige Geist als Person</u>, § 1.16, 8.
[47] Ibid, § 1.19, 10.
[48] Ibid, § 1.19, 11.
[49] Ibid, 260-305.
[50] Mühlen, <u>Una Mystica Persona</u>, 396 and 398.
[51] Mühlen, <u>Persona</u>, 416.

further, it is necessary to return and revisit in more detail the earlier teaching of Peter Lombard himself.

Peter Lombard's Theory[52]

In the famous *Distinction 17* of the First Book of his *Sentences*,[53] Peter Lombard deals with the mission of the Holy Spirit in the world. Right at the start he affirms as what he considers to be a necessary presupposition, that the Holy Spirit is the charity by which we love God and neighbour. And he means this quite literally, that the Holy Spirit *is* the charity in our souls. He bases himself on St. Augustine, who in turn is commenting on St. John. The fundamental text, obviously, is 'God is charity' (1 John 4:8, 16). St. Augustine, in his reflecting on these texts, does seem to say that God is the charity by which we love. For the Lombard, he says so 'quite openly' (*apertissime*)[54]. He then uses his trinitarian principles to conclude that 'God is charity' in fact means that the Holy Spirit is our charity, since the Holy Spirit is charity in God. This certainly provides a marvellous foundation for the mission of the Holy Spirit. 'He is therefore said to be sent or given, since he is in us making us love God and neighbour, so that we remain in God and God in us.'[55] To conclude his presentation Lombard responds to a number of objections, one of which was to be crucial. This is the objection, based again on St. Augustine who says elsewhere that charity is a movement, an affection and a virtue in our souls, and Lombard denies this. 'Charity is said to be a movement of the soul, not because it is a movement or

---

[52] The background to this matter is in Johann Auer, Die Entwicklung der Gnadenlehre in der Hochscholastik (Freiburg im Breisgau: Herder & Co., 1942), 86ff., Johann Schupp, Die Gnadenlehre des Petrus Lombardus, Freiburg im Breisgau, 1932, 227ff. and Artur Landgraf, 'Anfänge einer Lehre vom Concursus Simultaneous im XIII. Jahrhundert,' in Recherches de Théologie ancienne et médiévale 1 (1929), 202-28, 338-55. A recent treatment is in Gérard Philips, L'Union personnelle avec le Dieu vivant, Leuven University Press, 1989, 67-75.

[53] Peter Lombard, Sentences, Grottaferata, 1971, 141-52.

[54] c. 1, 3; 143.20.

[55] c. 4, 1; 145.2-4.

affection or virtue of the soul, but because by it, as if it were a virtue (*quasi esset virtus*)[56], the mind is drawn and moved.'

The Lombard had some supporters in this doctrine, though all the major scholastic doctors, with the exception of St. Bonaventure, as we shall see later, were solid opponents. Simon of Tournai (1130-1201) rebutted Lombard's argument by reasoning that if the Holy Spirit is our charity, he is a creature and this is absurd and to say so is impious.[57] A longer and more thorough treatment of the issue is provided by Philip the Chancellor (c. 1160-1236), who introduced Aristotelian categories to the discussion.[58] He challenges the Lombard's interpretation of St. Augustine, but for him, the first and determining issue is to settle the point, taken for granted by Simon of Tournai, whether or not there is a created charity (*An aliquid sit caritas creata*)? He seems simply to presume it too, in fact, and this was to become the fundamental point leading to the rejection of the Lombard's doctrine. St. Thomas, in his Commentary on the Sentences and on each occasion subsequently when he handled the issue, made Philip the Chancellor's his first question, Is charity something created in the soul, or is it the Holy Spirit himself?[59] Each time the answer is the same, that charity must be a created reality in our souls. Our act of loving must be voluntary and meritorious, and for these things to be true, it must come from within our wills, and therefore it must be a created reality. He further argues that for the perfection of our loving, in order that it be prompt and pleasant, it must come from an internal and, therefore, created virtue. The last step in the reasoning, that since charity is a created reality it cannot be the Holy Spirit, doesn't require to be stated, but is simply taken for granted. St. Thomas does not mince his words in the matter. In one place he writes that 'it would be ridiculous to say that the act of charity

---

[56] c. 6, 7; 151.19.
[57] Landgraf, Anfänge, 221.
[58] Ibid, 225-28.
[59] Sent. 1 d. 17 q. 1 a. 1c; De caritate, q. un., a. 1c; STh 2-2, q. 23 a. 2.

which we experience when we love God and neighbour is the Holy Spirit himself.'[60]

This reaction to the Lombard's thesis was common among the scholastic doctors. Around 1250 the masters of Paris, as a group, rejected eight propositions of Peter Lombard, of which the first was, 'that charity, which is the love of God and neighbour, is not something created, but the uncreated Holy Spirit himself,'[61] and this rejection became standard in subsequent theology. As mentioned earlier, St. Bonaventure took a position in this matter somewhat different from the others. He presented the Lombard's position clearly, but did not argue against it, though neither did he support it or make further use of it. What he said was: 'And in all this he spoke the truth and did not err, but he fell short: because as well as this one must put charity according to the common opinion, which is a created habit informing the soul.'[62] What it is exactly that St. Bonaventure had in mind is not completely clear, but the point to be made here was mentioned by one of the other medieval commentators. Richard Fishacre (d. 1248), the Oxford Dominican, in his commentary of the *Sentences*, explicitly raised the possibility of a union between the Holy Spirit and the human mind analogous to the union between the Son and the soul of Christ in the Incarnation. He asked the question if such a union might be possible,[63] and first answered 'I do not know. I assert nothing,' subsequently admitting that as far as he could he would support the Lombard.[64] The presumption from Simon of Tournai onwards has always been that if charity is a

---

[60] « Ridiculum autem fuisset dicere, quod ipse actus dilectionis, quem experimus dum diligimus Deum et proximum, sit ipse Spiritus sanctus. », De caritate, q. un., a. 1c.

[61] H. Denifle, Chartularium Universitatis Parisiensis ed. H. Denifle, O. and E. Chatelain, I, Paris 1889, 220-21, n. 194

[62] « Et in his omnibus verum dixit nec erravit, sed defecit; quia praeter hoc est ponere caritatem secundum communem opinionem, quae sit habitus creatus animam informans. » (In I Sent. dist. 17 1 art. unicus, q. 1 (Opera omnia, Quaracchi (1882), 294.

[63] Landgraf, Anfänge, 352.175-181.

[64] Ibid, 'Nescio. Nichil assero.', 352.184; 'Responsio sine assertione, prout mihi videtur probabilius, quo possum tueor sententiam Magistri.', 353.219-220.

created reality, then it is ridiculous, and even impious, to suggest that it can be the Holy Spirit himself in person, which is what the Lombard says. What of the possibility that both things are true? Following the analogy with the Incarnation, which Fishacre wondered about and Petau, Scheeben and Mühlen have actually attempted, the suggestion to be made is that the Holy Spirit, the third Person of the Trinity, is our charity in a manner analogous to that in which the Word, the second person of the Trinity, is a human being.

Bernard Lonergan's Analysis of the Incarnation

We intend to take a cue here from Bernard Lonergan's analysis of the metaphysics of the Incarnation.[65] He proposes that the best approach to understanding the fact that the Word became man is on the analogy with the general principles governing the affirmation of any contingent truth about God. Lonergan takes it as a given of the theological tradition that 'common contingent truths predicated of God add nothing to the divine essence except a relation of reason, but imply an appropriate created term outside God.'[66] He applies the same logic to the reality of the contingent truths about the individual divine persons, formulating the principle that 'proper contingent truths predicated of a divine person add to the subsistent relation only a relation of reason in the divine person, but imply an appropriate created term outside God that is really related to the divine subsistent relation.'[67] He applies this to the particular case of the Incarnation of the Son as follows:

Incarnation is proper to him, for neither the Father nor the Holy Spirit is incarnate. But the Son's incarnation is also a contingent fact since it was possible for the Word not to become incarnate. That within God nothing apart from a relation of reason is added to the subsistent relation is clear from the fact that a divine subsistent relation is really

---

[65] The Ontological and Psychological Constitution of Christ, Collected Works of Bernard Lonergan, Volume 7, Toronto / Buffalo / London, 2002.
[66] Ibid, § 51, 95.
[67] Ibid,§ 52, 97.

identical with the immutable divine essence. That an appropriate external created term is implied is clear from the fact that a contingent truth, as contingent, can have the correspondence of truth only through some contingent being. That this term is really related to the divine subsistent relation is clear from the fact that otherwise the correspondence of truth between the intellect and reality would be lacking. For example, in the intellect one would be saying that *only* the Son was made flesh while there would be nothing in reality to correspond to this true statement.[68]

How is it that the Word of God can become a man, the question being as to how it is that one thing can ever become another thing at all?

> The only difficulty in this matter is a certain anthropomorphic transfer from finite beings to the infinite God. Because Peter is a being, he exists; but because he is a finite being, he exists only as this human being. But God is not a finite being such as would prevent God being something else besides God; rather, God is an infinite being that by way of eminence includes in itself all the perfection of all beings, both actual and possible. Furthermore, just as God by the same infinite act knows not only necessary but also contingent realities, and just as God by the same infinite act wills not only necessary realities but also contingent ones, so also God by the same infinite act of existence not only is necessarily God but also is what God has contingently become.[69]

Lonergan points out that the usual objection to this position is that if the incarnation is constituted by the divine act of existence, then not only the Son, but all three persons would necessarily be incarnate, since the divine act of existence is not proper to the Son but is common to all three divine persons. He accepts that this argument would hold up if 'the divine act of existence were some kind of material principle that

---

[68] Ibid, § 52, 97.
[69] Ibid, § 57, 103.

always acts the same way by blind necessity in accordance with innate laws under identical conditions.'[70] He then goes on:

> For this reason it must be carefully borne in mind that God is not only 'an agent through intellect' but also 'a being through intellect.' God is an agent through intellect because divine acting or producing is nothing other than divine understanding and willing that something be produced. God is a being through intellect because the divine essence is the divine intellect and will, and the divine act of existence is the divine act of understanding and the divine act of willing. Therefore, if the triune God understands and wills that only the Son should become incarnate and this in such a way that the union should take place in the person and on the basis of the person, then by this understanding and willing (1) everything finite required for the incarnation is produced, since God acts through intellect, and (2) the Son is constituted as hypostatically united through the infinite act of existence, since this act of existence is nothing else than that understanding and willing.[71]

Having analysed the constitution of the Incarnate Word of God, Lonergan, in a further stage of his argument proceeds to put the elements he has analysed together again in a description of the concrete reality of Christ, in his divinity and his humanity. As part of that process, he lays down the principle that 'whatever the triune God in his infinite wisdom and goodness can understand and will about himself, God (1) can be, and (2) can be through the divine act of existence.'[72] And he says it again later in other words, which are worth repeating, 'that the divine persons through their infinite act not only necessarily exist in

---

[70] Ibid, § 69, 133.
[71] Ibid, § 69, 134.
[72] Ibid, § 70, 135.

their divine nature but are also capable of existing in any other nature they might wish to assume.'[73]

Applying these ideas to the temporal mission of the Holy Spirit is a comparatively simple matter, for all we need to know is what is the appropriate created reality. And St. Thomas and Lonergan both state quite clearly that it is sanctifying grace.[74] On Lonergan's principles, therefore, God can become the sanctifying grace which gives life to the world if he chooses to do so. If, then, the analogy of the mission of the second person of the Trinity were to be applied to the third, it would follow that, just as the Son is a human being because the appropriate created term is a concrete human nature, so the Holy Spirit is the sanctifying grace which gives life to our souls, since that is the appropriate created term establishing his temporal mission.

Interestingly enough, Lonergan actually considers the possibility of a divine person being joined to sanctifying grace in this manner. He is deducing the reality of the Incarnation from the principles he has laid down and deals with different alternative possibilities in order to exclude them. He affirms that the union of sanctifying grace with the Holy Spirit would not constitute a hypostatic union.[75] Applying this to the case of the Son, it cannot be accepted because, if the appropriate created term 'is received in the very essence of the soul, it would follow that the human nature is assumed by the Word in the same way as the uncreated gift of the Holy Spirit is conferred upon the just through sanctifying grace; but that could be no more than an accidental union which the Nestorians called *synapheia* or "conjunction."'[76] Now, there is no doubt that a Nestorian union is inadequate to explain the Incarnation of the Son. But would it not be fully adequate to explain the union of the Holy Spirit with the Church and with each of us? Nestorius made no secret of the fact that he understood the presence of the Word of God in the humanity of Christ to be like that of the presence of God

---

[73] Ibid, 151.
[74] Summa theologiae, I, q. 43, a. 3c; Bernard Lonergan, S.J., De Deo Trino, II. Pars Systematica, Rome, 1964, 234.
[75] Lonergan, Constitution, 115.
[76] Ibid, 143.

in a temple. 'The body therefore is the temple of the deity of the Son, a temple which is united to it in a high and divine conjunction (suna, feian).'[77] It is precisely our faith that we are temples of the Holy Spirit, so if this Nestorian union applies to the union of the Holy Spirit with the sanctifying grace in our souls, it fulfills an essential condition of our faith in the matter.

The suggestion being made, then, is that Peter Lombard was right after all, that the Holy Spirit is, indeed, the grace and charity by which we love God and neighbour. The mistake that he made was to assume that affirming that the Holy Spirit is our charity implies that he must deny that charity is a created reality. It seems an obvious enough deduction and St. Thomas even went so far as to say that it is ridiculous to suggest otherwise. But that is exactly what is being suggested. The parallel is with the Incarnation of the Son of God. It can surely seem ridiculous to say of this man Jesus, that he is the very Son of God in person. And yet that 'ridiculous' truth is the central dogma of our faith. When the analogy of the Incarnation is applied to the temporal mission of the Holy Spirit, is there not the likelihood that he, too, will 'become' something, as Mühlen suggested? And is there any better possibility than that the Charity of God within the Trinity should become the divine charity which fills our souls and constitutes the soul of the Church?

If this possibility were to be accepted as reality, it would resolve in an amazingly neat manner the problem from which we began. It provides a solid foundation for the Indwelling of the Holy Spirit in our souls. If the Holy Spirit truly and literally _is_ the sanctifying grace and charity which is the life of our souls, he could hardly be more intimately inserted within us. It also explains our divinization, since a part of our being, the created grace and charity which makes us 'sons in the Son', _is_, in truth, the Holy Spirit of God himself in person, and we are truly made to be divine. And it resolves the difficulty of the 'two souls' of the

---

[77] Second Letter of Nestorius to Cyril, condemned at the Council of Ephesus, in Decrees of the Ecumenical Councils, Volume I (Nicaea I – Lateran V), ed. Norman Tanner, S.J., London / Washington, D. C, 1990, 48.43-49.2.

Church, if the Holy Spirit, the uncreated soul, actually is the created soul, which is grace and charity. It obviously helps to consolidate the concept of the Church being developed, the holy Church, defined on the basis of the divine presence within.

Analogy with Incarnation

The application of the analogy of the Incarnation to the Church is a comparative novelty in the Tradition of the Church. It was first developed in a systematic way by Johann Adam Möhler in the nineteenth century, and was taken up by many theologians subsequently, under his inspiration.[78] It was used by Pope Leo XIII in his encyclical on the Church, *Satis cognitum*,[79] and given an authoritative statement by Vatican II: 'It is by no mean analogy that [the Church] is likened to the mystery of the incarnate Word. For just as the assumed nature serves the divine Word as a living instrument of salvation inseparably joined to him, in a not dissimilar manner the social structure of the Church serves the Spirit of Christ who vivifies her for the growth of the body.'[80] It is easy to state that there is an analogy, but not so easy to explain exactly what is involved and how far it applies. Congar, in fact, is quite sceptical about its application. At the end of a thoroughgoing analysis of the matter, he concludes that the analogy lacks rigour, that it is suggestive, indeed, but not explanatory, standing more in need of explanation itself.[81] And Heribert Mühlen also adopts a hesitant position in regard to it. He says that 'although there is a great similarity between the Incarnation and the Church, the dissimilarity is even greater'.[82]

This precise point concerning the applicability of the analogy was discussed at the Second Vatican Council. Two bishops wanted the

---

[78] Congar, « Dogme christologique et ecclésiologie : vérité et limites d'un parallèle, » in Sainte Église, Paris, 1963, 69-104, at 70-74.
[79] ASS 28 (1896) 710.
[80] Lumen gentium § 8, Tanner, 854.16-20.
[81] Congar, Dogme christologique, 102.
[82] Mühlen, Una Mystica Persona, 407.

mention of the analogy removed from the draft of *Lumen gentium*, on the grounds that it does not properly apply to the relationship between the Holy Spirit and the Church at all.[83] The Theological Commission drafting the decree rejected their suggestion, and accepted rather a suggestion which tended in precisely the opposite direction. In its first formulation, the analogy was expressed using the basic Latin terms of comparison, 'sicut … ita …'. Among their suggested amendments to the draft, the Episcopal Conference of Venezuela wanted the formulation strengthened to make clear that likeness applies 'recte, sed analogice'.[84] In the next draft, the 'Sicut … ita…' was changed to 'Sicut … non dissimili modo …', and it was explained that the change was made in order to satisfy the request of the Venezuelan Bishops who had insisted on the analogy.[85] It could hardly be said on this evidence that the Council teaches in clear terms that the analogy applies strictly, but it is tending in that direction, and it seems to me, in fact, that there is a tension between the hesitancy of Congar and Mühlen in regard to the analogy, and the teaching of the Council, and it is hoped that the distinction to be presented here will resolve that tension.

The crucial test in applying the analogy of the Incarnation to the Church is the application of the communication of properties, the *communicatio idiomatum*. All the actions of Jesus are actions of God, his waking and sleeping, even those that have no obvious divine dimension. The ground for this fact is that, in Christ, the union of the two natures is a union 'in being, *per esse, secundum esse*,' as Congar puts it.[86] That is why there is in every case a transfer of every operation of the human nature to God as the subject of attribution. In Christ it is God himself, the Second Person of the Trinity, who sleeps, speaks, stretches out his hands, suffers, walks, etc. Considering the Church from this point

---

[83] They were Paul Nguyen van Binh, Archbishop of Saigon and Paul Gurpide Beope, Bishop of Bilbao. See Francisco Gil Hellín, <u>Constitutio Dogmatica De Ecclesia Lumen Gentium</u> (Città del Vaticano: Libreria Editrice Vaticana, 1995), 983, 1120.

[84] Hellín, <u>Constitutio Dogmatica</u>, 1148.

[85] Ibid, 60.

[86] Congar, <u>Dogme christologique</u>, 83.

of view, Congar first presents that area of the Church's life where the communication of properties applies. He speaks of divine and human actions of the Church, with their origin in two principles or natures, divine and human. The divine actions of the Church are the major actions of the 'powers' proper to the Church, the priesthood and the Magisterium. The actions she performs in the sacraments, the forgiveness of sins, the celebration of the Eucharist, the ordination of the sacred ministers, and so on, can only come from God. And the definitive, infallible acts of Magisterium must also come from God. In addition to these formal actions of the Church, he adds the exorcism of demons, the spiritual gifts and the supernatural virtues, and the extraordinary graces, such as miracles and prophecy, which the Church has always enjoyed. These divine actions, together with the human actions underlying them, proceed from the same concrete being, the Church, the human actions having their origin in a divine principle of operation or nature.[87] Following on that recognition of a set of theandric actions of the Church, Congar simply assumes that there are actions of the Church which are not actions of God. He recalls that all the actions of Jesus are actions of God, his waking and sleeping, even those that have no obvious divine dimension, and then goes on:

> On the other hand, even though there are actions of the Church which proceed from a divine principle, one cannot say with full rigour that all the actions which belong to the human reality of the Church, belong to a divine subject. The Church is indeed the instrument of God, but it is not, like the humanity of Jesus, joined to God in being, but only for certain operations. The union with God is not hypostatic, but one 'of alliance' Therefore her actions, except in a certain sense those which are properly instrumental, are not actions of a divine person; the law of the communication of

---

[87] Ibid, 76, 78-79.

properties does not apply to her as to the Incarnate Word. *Inconfuse*, yes, *indivise*, no.[88]

These negative assertions are simply assumed without argument or elaboration. He takes it to be obvious that the communication of properties does not apply fully, indivise, in the case of the Church, and that the union is not hypostatic, but only of alliance. There is clearly the assumption at work here that the reality of the Church is somehow obvious to all and needs no elaboration. Assuming that Congar allows that the communication of properties does apply to the theandric actions he lists, the sacraments and so on, he sees no need to spell out the actions of the Church to which the communication does not apply. By analogy with what he says of Our Lord, we must presume that he has in mind the ordinary human actions he mentions in the case of the Incarnation, the waking and sleeping, and walking and talking etc, which have no connection with the formal acts of the Church. And, above all, anything springing from the weakness and sin of members of the Church would obviously be excluded from any participation in the communication of properties, since sin can have no origin in a divine Person. Mühlen makes the same deduction, that the presence of sinful members implies that the Incarnation analogy cannot be strictly applied to the Church.[89]

There is no doubt that the presence of sin in the visible Church is an insurmountable objection to the application of the analogy with the Incarnation to the concrete Church of our everyday experience. However, the situation is different in relation to the Church-mystery, the Church formed from the joint mission of the Son and the Holy Spirit and from which all sin is excluded on principle. This Church is formed by the Holy Spirit and is limited to the actions springing from that source, and so the objection arising from the presence of sin does not apply. And Congar's second, and more fundamental, objection can also be dealt with on the principles developed so far. In the Incarnation

---

[88] Ibid, 78.
[89] Una mystica persona, 407.

there are two natures, divine and human, and this fact is fundamental to the mystery. If the analogy is to apply strictly, or *recte* as the Venezuelan Bishops had it, then the divine nature of the Holy Spirit must belong to the mystery of the Church in a manner analogous to the presence of the divine nature of the Word in Jesus. In his analysis, Congar simply takes it for granted that 'in the Church there is not, strictly speaking, a divine nature.'[90] Grace and its concomitant supernatural virtues constitute a quasi-nature, which is like a divine nature and constitutes our participation in the divine nature of which St. Peter speaks, but it is not, strictly speaking, a divine nature.[91] Congar affirms that there are in the Church as a community of salvation acts which unite us with God. There acts presuppose dispositions which ensure that these acts are truly ours, the supernatural habits of grace and the virtues. To these is added 'the substantial presence of the three divine Persons and, by a special title, the Holy Spirit. This it is which corresponds, in the Church, to the divine nature of Christ.'[92] However, despite this substantial presence of God, because the supernatural actions have their immediate principle in grace and the virtues, which constitute a quasi-nature on the human level, one has 'to say that there is not, strictly speaking, a divine nature in the Church.'[93] That objection falls, however, if the suggestion made earlier is able to stand, that the Holy Spirit himself *becomes* the grace and charity which constitute the quasi-nature of the Church. In that case, there is 'strictly speaking' a divine nature in the Church, the divine nature of the Holy Spirit who has become the grace and charity which constitute the Church, so that the analogy with the Incarnation applies perfectly. It then follows that to the mystery of the Incarnation of the Word there corresponds the mystery of the Incorporation of the Holy Spirit. Just as the Word became incarnate in the humanity of Jesus of Nazareth, so the Holy Spirit becomes 'incorporate' in the Church, the whole Church, which is the Body of Christ, Head and members. The idea that the Holy Spirit is incorporated in the Church is strange indeed,

---

[90] Congar, <u>Dogme christologique</u>, 84.
[91] Ibid, 86-87.
[92] Ibid, 85.
[93] Ibid.

but not a complete novelty, for it was Möhler who first formulated the notion when he wrote that 'the entire constitution of the Church is nothing else than love corporified.'[94] And Cardinal Manning, no doubt basing himself on Möhler, wrote that the Holy Spirit 'has assumed the mystical body as the visible incorporation of His presence.'[95]

In this light, the conclusions Congar drew from his analysis can all be countered. He wrote: 'It has appeared to us that the parallelism lacks rigour. In the Church, there are neither two natures properly speaking nor a divine personality. The inseparability of the divine and human operation is not rigorously verified in her.'[96] ... [And] one would be deceived if one attempted to follow it rigorously and in detail for the construction of an ecclesiology.'[97] On the analysis presented here, it can be affirmed that there are two natures properly speaking in the Church, there is a divine personality. With the proper distinctions made, the inseparability of the divine and human operations is rigorously verified in her and the analogy can be followed rigorously and in detail for the construction of an ecclesiology. It means that one arrives at a significantly different concept of the Church, the true Church, the Whole Church, the holy Church, the Body of Christ and the Temple of the Holy Sprit, which must be carefully distinguished, but not separated, from the visible Church of our experience. If we can say that the Holy Spirit truly becomes the grace and charity which constitute the quasi-nature informing the Church, then Congar's assumption is gainsaid, and we can affirm that, in fact, there is, strictly speaking, a divine nature in the Church, by virtue of the real presence of the Holy Spirit in her. The argument would then be reversed. Instead of assuming the absence of a divine nature in the Church and denying the analogy

---

[94] 'Die gesamte Kirchenverfassung ist darum nichts anders als die verkörperte Liebe.' Johann Adam Möhler, Die Einheit der Kirche, ed. Josel Rupert Geiselmann (Köln & Olten: Jakob Hegner, 1956), § 64, 215.

[95] Henry Edward Manning, The Temporal Mission of the Holy Ghost (London: Longmans, Green, and Co., 1866), 63-64.

[96] Congar, Dogme christologique, 102.

[97] Ibid, 104.

with the Incarnation, we assume the analogy and are pushed to affirm the presence of the divine nature.

A Union of Alliance?

It is clear that Congar is hesitant about the use of these analogies, and regularly puts forward as his preferred alternative the position that the union between the Holy Spirit and the Church is not one 'of actual being,' but one 'of alliance'.[98] This step is easy to understand. Once the strict analogy with the Incarnation is denied, and a union in being is deemed impossible, there really is no alternative to a union of alliance, a purely moral union. Furthermore, the reality of sin in the Church demands the postulation of a certain distance between the Holy Spirit and the Church, and that distance can be accommodated within the analogy of an alliance, whereas it would be impossible if a strict union in being were to be upheld.

A first point to note is that Scripture does not speak of such a thing as a marital union in relation to the Holy Spirit. The Old Testament speaks of a marriage between God and his People, and the New Testament speaks of a marriage between Christ and the Church. In fact, Scripture does not speak of the Holy Spirit in personal terms much at all. He is generally viewed as a force or a power, in images such as the wind, fire and water, and the basic image of Scripture is to speak of the Indwelling of the Holy Spirit as in a temple. As between Christ and the Church the situation is different. The human personality of Christ is clearly defined, and, when the Church is understood as separate from Christ, the distinction of persons between Christ and the Church allows that the image of the marriage is certainly applicable, and is essential for a proper understanding of the relationshi Congar is thinking of the Church apart from Christ when he writes that the Church 'was instituted by Christ as a subject in its own right, a collective person,

---

[98] Ibid, 95, 103. This point became a settled part of Congar's ecclesiological doctrine, repeated elsewhere in his writings, for example, <u>Tradition and Traditions</u>, London, 1966, 173.

which he himself called "my Church", the Church we know too to be his spouse.'[99]

However, a proper understanding must also account for the two other basic images, the Vine and the Branches used by Our Lord in St. John's Gospel, and the image of the Head and the Body used by St. Paul. The union between a husband and his wife is a moral union, and no more than that. Between two persons there can only be a moral union. The union between the head and the body, or between a vine and its branches, is not a moral union, but a physical or organic union. A head is only inadequately distinct from the body to which it belongs, and branches are only inadequately distinct from the vine of which they form parts. These images point to the other concept of the Church, understood as one with Christ, the *Christus totus*, and in this understanding the Church is only inadequately distinct from Christ. We, as individuals, are fully and adequately distinct from Christ, but not as Church. The Church only begins to exist by virtue of the joint mission of the Son and the Holy Spirit, and only continues to exist by their continual action. Every action of the Church, understood theologically, is a joint action of the Son and the Holy Spirit, and that total dependence is expressed by the two organic images. The Church understood in this way is not properly speaking a distinct person at all, with whom a covenant union can be formed. Hans Urs von Balthasar has made this point well: 'The Church, however, is "Christ living on"; she is, to use Paul's great analogy, *Christ's body*. This means, if we allow the full range of meaning that the Church, in regard to her Head, is not a person on her own, a new and second one. The "body", in the sense of the simile, forms, together with the "Head", one being; that is, she is a person only "by grace" of the "Head". ... The entire "organism" that the Church forms, and as which Christ willed her to be and founded her, together with her hierarchical structure and monarchical apex, is, taken by herself, headless, acephalous.'[100] If, therefore, the union between

---

[99] Congar, Mystery, 170-171.
[100] Hans Urs von Balthasar, Explorations in Theology: II: Spouse of the Word (San Francisco: Ignatius Press, 1991), 'Who is the Church?' 143-91 at 144-45.

Christ and the Church is not adequately expressed by the marital image taken on its own, it hardly seems likely that it would suffice to express the union between the Holy Spirit and the Church either.

A further difficulty with this notion arises from the fact that the People of God have been in a covenant relationship with God since the time of the Exodus. Is it possible, therefore, that the notion of an alliance between the Holy Spirit and the Church can suffice to express the novelty of the New Testament? Congar compares the two Covenants and observes that in the Old Testament, the Holy Spirit intervenes 'prophetically,' whereas in the New he dwells in a stable manner.[101] In the old dispensation the alliance was conditional; 'If you obey my law, I will be for you …',[102] whereas in the new dispensation the Christ has come and the Holy Spirit has been given, 'in a way that is still imperfect, but real,' and so 'the regime of the Church is no longer *prophetic* but *apostolic*,'[103] and therefore unconditional. It is certainly true that in the apostolic institutions founded by Christ the Church is definitively established, indefectible and infallible. Can the guarantee of indefectibility be properly established simply on the basis of a covenant union between the Holy Spirit and the Church? The relationship between God and Israel is a covenant union, and we still allow that this covenant relationship is compatible with a fundamental infidelity on the part of the covenanted people. In one place, Congar formulates the foundation of the union of alliance as being that '[i]t is based on the predestining will of God, his plan of grace, his gifts and his faithfulness.'[104] The problem with this is that this basis was already fully available to Israel under the old alliance, and it did not ground an indefectible and infallible relationshi Can it not be argued that this evidence of history shows that a purely moral union simply cannot account for what is new and unique in the New Testament.? Mühlen

---

[101] Congar, Dogme christologique, 95.
[102] Congar, Vraie et fausse réforme dans l'Église, 76.
[103] Ibid, 77.
[104] Congar, Dogme christologique, 93.

adopts this view that a merely moral union is insufficient.[105] It is clear that, since the union between the Holy Spirit and the Church is a union between a divine Person and a multitude of independent human beings, it is, indeed, a moral union. However, this moral union, based on the infusion of supernatural grace and the theological virtues, must somehow be more than merely moral, and there is no doubt that the 'more' does not find expression in Congar's 'union of alliance'.

A further point to be made here is that the relationship between the Holy Spirit and the Church is fundamentally the same relationship as that between the Holy Spirit and Christ. The Holy Spirit descended on Christ at his baptism, filling his human soul with grace and the theological virtues. This is an essential point which is much developed by Heribert Mühlen in his books, that the Church is to be understood as the continuation of the anointing of Christ at his Baptism. It would obviously be inappropriate to speak of a mere union of alliance between the Holy Spirit and Christ, and this suggests that it would be similarly inappropriate in relation to the Church.

Some light can be shed on this point using a consideration traditional in Marian theology. The marriage between Christ and the Church is a perfect virginal marriage, and the bond is unconditional and indissoluble. 'The Church is a virgin who keeps integral and pure the faith she has given to her spouse; and, imitating the mother of her Lord by the power of the Holy Spirit, she preserves virginally intact her faith, solid her hope and sincere her charity.'[106] It is, therefore, certainly true that the union between Christ and the Church, and between the Holy Spirit and the Church, is one of alliance, in this sense of a full and perfect marriage. It is wrong, however, to understand the image of the Bride and the Groom as implying a separation between Christ and the Church, or between the Holy Spirit and the Church. And this is what Congar does by affirming the alliance and denying the unity in being, for both perspectives are necessary to elucidate the fullness

---

[105] Heribert Mühlen also makes the point that a merely moral relationship is insufficient. See Mühlen, Una Mystica Persona, 25, 30.
[106] Lumen gentium § 64, Tanner, 896.24-26.

of the mystery. The suggestion being developed here is that the strict union in being applies fully and rigorously only to the Church-mystery, which is effectively defined by the relationship to Christ and the Holy Spirit. When we consider the concrete visible Church of our everyday experience, the analogies do not strictly apply, as Congar makes clear. However, it is questionable if the solution here is to revert to the Old Testament analogy of the covenant, for the full union between Christ and the Church is partially fulfilled even in the visible Church. There is the guaranteed presence of Christ in the sacraments, the guarantee of infallibility in definitive statements of the College of Bishops, and the general promise that Christ will remain with the Church forever. Our sins obscure the union of Christ and the Church, but they do not undermine it completely so that we are somehow on our own again, as a mere covenant union might imply.

Continuing the Incarnation

It will be helpful to further clarify the points being made to consider another of Möhler's distinctive contributions to ecclesiology, the notion of the Church as the continuation of the Incarnation. In his *Symbolik*, first published in 1832, he formulated the idea in this way:

> By the Church on earth, Catholics understand the visible community of all the faithful in Christ in which the actions performed by him during his earthly life for the redemption and sanctification of humanity are mediated under the direction of his Spirit until the end of the world by means of an apostolate founded by him and continued uninterruptedly, and in which all peoples are, over the course of the ages, led back to God. ... So from the point of view advanced here, the visible Church is the Son of God appearing within humanity in human form in a continuous fashion, constantly renewed, eternally rejuvenated, his ongoing incarnation,

just as the faithful are also called in Holy Scripture the Body of Christ.[107]

This concept of the Church as a continuation of the Incarnation was much used after Möhler, but was subject to misunderstanding. For instance, '[t]he relationship between Christ as head and the Church as body was actually misunderstood as a new hypostatic union or simply as an extension of it.'[108] According to Grillmeier, the notion was deliberately avoided by the Second Vatican Council for this reason. It is certainly wrong to understand this notion as if the union between the Word and the human nature of Jesus is extended to each member of the Church. That cannot be what is meant. The continuation of the Incarnation, in the strict sense, is the living incarnate Christ, now in glory, but active and ever-present in the Church. He is, himself, the continuation of the Incarnation and needs no other, but he wants to remain active on earth and this he does in and through the Church, and that this is what Möhler had in mind is clear from the quotation given. As Mühlen remarks: 'Möhler ... ultimately only wishes to emphasise that the saving activity of Christ is continued unbroken in the Church and that in the Church the divine and the human are joined in a similar undivided manner as in the incarnate Son.'[109] The Church is involved in a different hypostatic, in the sense of personal, union, a union with the Holy Spirit, not with the Son, as we have already suggested, better called Incorporation rather than Incarnation. The Church is the continuation of the human manifestation of God, begun in Christ and continued in his Body which is the Church.

---

[107] Johann Adam Möhler, Symbolik, Vol. 1, ed. Geiselmann (Köln & Olten: Jakob Hegner, 1958), 387, 389. Translation helped by Symbolism, Trans. James Burton Robertson (London: Gibbings & Company, 1906) and Michael J. Himes, Ongoing Incarnation: Johann Adam Möhler and the Beginnings of Modern Ecclesiology (New York: The Crossroad Publishing Company, 1997).

[108] Aloys Grillmeier, 'The Mystery of the Church,' in Commentary on the Documents of Vatican II, Volume I, ed. Herbert Vorgrimler (London/New York: Burs Oates/Herder and Herder, 1967), 138-152, at 145.

[109] Mühlen, Una Mystica Persona, § 7.05, 176.

Continuing the Incarnation can be thought of in different ways. If we think of the Incarnation as the action of the Word joining himself hypostatically to his human nature, then it is a mistake to speak of that action continuing. It is a once and for all act which brings the mysterious Man-God into being, and it cannot be continued. If we think of the Incarnation as the result of this action, as the mystery of Christ, God and man, then the continuation of the Incarnation in this sense is the living, risen Jesus, sitting at God's right hand interceding for us and guiding his Church. It is not the Church which is the continuation of the Incarnation in this sense, but Christ himself. Finally, if we think of the Incarnation as the saving mystery of Christ's preaching and miraculous intervention during his public ministry and his death on the Cross, then we can properly speak of the continuation of the Incarnation in the Church. For that is what the Church is. It is Christ continuing his saving mission in the world. As *Lumen gentium* teaches, 'the saving mystery of salvation is revealed to us and continued in the Church, which the Lord constituted as his Body.'[110]

Congar has different objections to speaking of a continuation of the Incarnation, which are already familiar to us from other contexts. He says that the relationship between the Holy Spirit and the Church 'is not an Incarnation, for the Church and the Spirit are only united by a covenant link.'[111] He expands on the point by explaining that '[i]n the first case *all* the actions of the Man-God may be predicated of God and thus bear an absolute guarantee. In the second we have a "mystical" body, which is also the Bride and keeps its own individual subjectivity before Christ its Lord; the human subject is left to its own freedom and responsibility within a framework of weaknesses and graces, efforts and up-and-downs in fidelity; only the ultimate decisions about the reality of the covenant are guaranteed.'[112] We have already considered this view, and found that it is not enough to speak of a covenant link between the Holy Spirit and the Church, and that

---

[110] Lumen gentium § 52, Tanner, 892.3-5.
[111] Congar, Tradition and Traditions, 345.
[112] Ibid, 312-313.

neither is it appropriate to speak of the Incarnation of the Holy Spirit, but that the word for the relationship is Incorporation. On this basis, when the Church is understood theologically, the 'human subject' is not separated from Christ or the Spirit, but is identified as the fruit of their joint mission, and so all weaknesses and infidelities are excluded. It is then untrue to speak of the Church being 'left to its own freedom and responsibility,' or that 'only the ultimate decisions about the reality of the covenant are guaranteed.' The freedom and responsibility of the Church, the Body and the Bride of Christ, are intrinsically joined to the freedom and responsibility of the Word and the Holy Spirit, and this Holy Church is thus fully guaranteed in each and all of her judgements and decisions, for these are the judgements and decisions of God. This does not mean that every act of every ordained minister is guaranteed by God. It does mean that there is an ongoing action of God in the Church which fundamentally guarantees the worship and teaching of the Church despite the many flaws to which these realities are subject.

Mühlen argues that the fact that the Second Vatican Council chose not to use the notions of the 'continuation of the Incarnation,' or 'Christ living on' to characterise the Church indicates an indirect taking of a position in regard to them, so that they must thereby appear to be less useful for the future development of ecclesiology.[113] Mühlen's position is that 'the Incarnation is strictly and as such a completely unique historical event,'[114] and that it is not the Incarnation *as such* which is continued in the Church. The 'Christ' means literally the 'Anointed One', and so the Church can be properly characterised as the continuation of the anointing of Jesus. 'In *this* sense, one can quite reasonably ... characterise the Church as "Christ living on".'[115] And he formulates it as his 'fundamental thesis' that: 'The Church is not the continuation of the Incarnation as such, but the salvific continuation of the anointing of Jesus with the Holy Spirit.'[116] Speaking of the sacraments he points out that they 'have a similarity with Christ himself,

---

[113] Mühlen, Una Mystica Persona, § 10.12, 366.
[114] Ibid, § 10.13, 367.
[115] Ibid, § 7.06, 176.
[116] Ibid, § 8.01, 216.

insofar as the grace of God comes to us "bodily" in them, and that they have thus an "incarnational" structure, but that the self-communication of God in the sacramental rites is ultimately the self-communication of the Spirit of Christ ...'[117] The sacraments, in this perspective, are not simply *instrumenta separata* of the Word as a 'continuation' of the humanity of Jesus, his *instrumentum coniunctum*, but rather they are ... the *instrumenta coniuncta* of the *Spirit of Christ*. In any event this aspect follows from the statement of the Second Vatican Council, that the Church is likewise the *organum* of the Spirit of Christ.[118] 'This does not prevent one describing the Church as the permanent presence of Christ the sacrament through his Spirit.'[119] This point was formulated by Pope St Leo the Great: '*Quod itaque Redemptoris nostri conspicuum fuit in sacramenta transivit,*'[120] which can be translated as 'What was visible in our Redeemer has passed over into the liturgy.'[121] And the other fundamental point is that Christ acts in and through the Church. Ordained ministers act 'in the person of' Christ ... When a minister celebrates a sacrament, it is Christ who celebrates. The 'ongoing Incarnation' idea does not mean that we have become Christ, strictly speaking, but that in the liturgy Christ is really present here and now and acts in and through us.

With these points in place it is now possible to respond to some more of Congar's difficulties with this analogy. He presents what he considers to be exaggerated uses of the notion. 'Certain presentations of the idea of a 'continued Incarnation', according to which, as the Church is Christ's body so its mouth would be Christ's own, and all that it says would come from Christ, fail to take sufficient account of the difference that exists between a hypostatic union and a covenant union.' He quotes an argument used by Perrone grounding the infallibility of the Church in

---

[117] Ibid, § 11.66, 440-41.
[118] Ibid, § 11.66, 441.
[119] Ibid, § 11.68, 442.
[120] Sermo 74 (De ascensione 2) 2, PL 54, 398.
[121] For the argument that 'sacramenta' means the liturgy, see Robert Taft, S. J. in Liturgy in a Postmodern World ed. Keith F. Pecklers, (Continuum: London / New York, 2003), 186, footnote 19.

the image of the continuing incarnation. 'The Church is infallible, just as Christ is infallible, because He willed her to be a living and perfect image of Himself. Indeed, He constituted her to perpetuate Himself on earth in a certain fashion (*quodammodo*), such that, what Christ had and has by His own nature, he communicates by grace and privilege to this His daughter or spouse.'[122] Congar offers his, now familiar, contrast between a union in being and a covenant union, and argues: 'In the first case *all* the actions of the Man-God may be predicated of God and thus bear an absolute guarantee. In the second we have a "mystical" body, which is also the Bride and keeps its own individual subjectivity before Christ its Lord; the human subject is left to its own freedom and responsibility within a framework of weaknesses and graces, efforts and up-and-downs in fidelity; only the ultimate decisions about the reality of the covenant are guaranteed. ... A certain number of the Church's *acts*, or acts of the pope who personifies it, are infallible. It cannot be said, without qualification, of the pope and the Church that they just *are* infallible.'[123] The response to be made to this objection is now obvious enough. It is clear that Congar has the concrete visible Church in mind, especially when he can identify the Church's acts with the 'acts of the pope who personifies it'. The acts of this concrete Church are not all infallibly guaranteed, but the acts of the Church-mystery are, and this is the Church which is the continuation of the anointing of Jesus as the Christ. Congar himself makes a remark elsewhere which apples here most appropriately. 'As Christians, we are only Christ mystically, by a communion, not in his being, but in his messianic operations: dying with, buried with, rising with, sitting with, glorified with.'[124] This is Mühlen's point and it justifies Perrone's argument. Christ did not found the Church to continue his whole being on earth, but to continue his mission. His messianic operations include more than simply the actions of his New Passover mentioned by Congar. Included also are the actions of his public life, his teaching and his healing miracles which

---

[122] Congar, Tradition and Traditions, 312. (Congar gives as the reference for Perrone Praelect., VII, 30.)
[123] Ibid, 312-13.
[124] Congar, Dogme christologique, 87-88.

are continued in the liturgy of the Church. It is on this basis that the Church-mystery is infallible without any qualification.

A Single Mystical Person

The last and most profound of the metaphysical analogies for the Church is the one which asserts that Christ and the Church form one single mystical person. This teaching was proposed and elaborated by Pope Pius XII in *Mystici corporis*. He wrote that Christ 'so sustains the Church, and so, in a certain sense, lives in the Church, that she is, as it were, another Christ.'[125] And that

> our Saviour shares prerogatives peculiarly His own with the Church in such a way that she may portray, in her whole life, both exterior and interior, a most faithful image of Christ. For ... it is He who through the Church baptizes, teaches, rules, looses, binds, offers, sacrifices.[126] ... Thus the Church becomes, as it were, the filling out and the complement of the Redeemer, while Christ in a sense attains through the Church a fullness in all things. Herein we find the reason why, according to the opinion of Augustine already referred to, the mystical Head, which is Christ, and the Church, which here below as another Christ shows forth His person, constitute one new man, in whom heaven and earth are joined together in perpetuating the saving work of the Cross: Christ We mean, the Head and the Body, the whole Christ.[127]

It is clear from the texts that, for the Tradition, in speaking of the Church as one single mystical person, what is being referred to is the

---

[125] Mysitici corporis, § 53.
[126] Ibid, § 54.
[127] Ibid, § 77.

Christus totus, Christ and the Church together forming one person. As Pope St. Gregory the Great put it: 'Our redeemer has shown himself to be one person with the holy Church whom he has taken to himself.'[128] Mersch on Augustine has been referred to already, and Congar's summary of St Augustine makes the same point. 'Saint Augustine explains ... mostly using the same texts, his theology of *Christus et Ecclesia, Caput et corpus = una caro, unus homo, Christus integer (totus), una persona*. He even goes so far as to say *Christus sumus, Corpus Christi, quod est Ecclesia dicitur Christus*, and, placing the words on the lips of Christ, he say of Christians: *Ipsi sunt ego*.'[129] And St. Thomas says basically the same thing: 'Head and members form as it were one and the same mystical person.'[130] The *Catechism of the Catholic Church* gives a good summary: 'A reply of St. Joan of Arc to her judges sums up the faith of the holy doctors and the good sense of the believer: "About Jesus Christ and the Church, I simply know they're just one thing, and we shouldn't complicate the matter."'[131] And this is a fundamental part of the value of this manner of thinking about the Church, to keep our minds focussed on the unity between Christ and the Church. The danger of naturalism is always there, and one of its symptoms is thinking about the Church apart from Christ, as a self-standing human society in the world, related to Christ certainly, but conceived of as essentially separate from him.

Hans Urs von Balthasar has written well on the Church from this perspective.

> It is true that, externally, it seems to have a pronounced monarchic and aristocratic constitution that attributes all initiative to the Pope and the bishops holding office *jure divino* and is by no means representative of the 'will of the people'. At the same time, however, these

---

[128] Moralia in Job, praef., 14: PL 75, 525A.
[129] Congar, 'La personne « Église »,' Revue Thomiste 71 (1971) 613-640 at 615.
[130] St. Thomas Aquinas, ST 3, 48, 2. See also ST 3, 19, 4c; 3, 49, 1c; In Col 1, 24; l. 6, n. 61.
[131] CCC 795, footnote 233; Acts of the Trial of Joan of Arc.

rulers are 'believers' equally and in the same sense as all the rest. They do not follow their own will, not even representing anything like a spiritual *'raison d'état'*, but discharge their office in absolute dependence on the real supreme Head of the Church. This Head is the glorified Christ, his Person transcendent over the whole Church, sovereign and unaccountable. For him it is no sort of hubris but a simple statement of fact to make the equation: *L'Eglise c'est moi*. If we take this literally, we already have the answer to the question 'Who is the Church?' The subject of the Church is, then, simply Christ; he posits and is responsible for her acts in the sense of St. Augustine's reiteration against the Donatists: it is not Peter who baptizes, nor Paul, nor Judas, but Christ alone.[132]

Congar recognises the validity of this vision of the Church. He speaks with approval of the 'mystical subsistence' of the Church, as formulated by Journet, as follows: 'It simply involves recognising that grace does not have its own proper, adequate, connatural and final ontological ground in us but in Christ and the Holy Spirit. It is they who, under the conditions recognised by classical theology and well explained by Charles Journet, form the acting *subject*. It is precisely Charles Journet who has shown with most depth and force how, for every operation of grace which is produced in her, the Church is completely dependent on her divine causes, and she has her existence and consistency from them. That it is, and nothing else, which constitutes the mystical subsistence.'[133] It is in this sense that one can take up the traditional themes of the *una persona, Christus et Ecclesia*, and say, with many modern authors: 'Christ the Lord is properly speaking the Ego of the Church.' The principle of unity is placed *in God*, not properly in the Church herself, where it is only derived and consequent. However, the gifts which form her,

---

[132] Hans Urs von Balthasar, <u>Explorations in Theology: II: Spouse of the Word</u> (San Francisco: Ignatius Press, 1991), 'Who is the Church?' 143-91 at 144.
[133] 'La personne « Église »,' <u>Revue Thomiste</u> 71 (1971) 613-640, at 635-36.

although they only have a specific unity in the Church, find, in their divine or Christic cause, a principle of personalisation.[134] 'The Church is not a person, she does not have a created "subsistence" or a *hypostasis*. However, she does have a title of personality which surpasses the moral personality of a natural society.'[135]

The question must finally be posed, as to whether it is realistic to consider the Church purely as the action of the divine Persons and systematically exclude the effects of our sins. A helpful pointer to the way forward is to consider the meaning of the word 'church'. The Church cannot be properly conceived of simply as a society, a group of persons. The function is essential. According to Ratzinger, the simplest and most straightforward manner of uncovering the New Testament's understanding of the Church is to begin from the word ekklhsi, a.[136] The *Reallexikon* explains the point: 'In the OT the word lh'(Q', assembly, takes its primary meaning from the experience of gathering under Mount Sinai to receive the law, and it always refers to the act of assembling at the Lord's command. It does not refer primarily to the gathered people, but to the act of gathering. ... This grammatical nuance is significant for our point, that it is the Lord gathering his people which is primary in the meaning of evkklhsi, a ... not the group of people assembled.'[137] The holiness of the constitutive principles does not automatically make the people holy, but it makes the structure holy, and, in a certain sense, the Church is more the structure than the people being sanctified by it. Still, if the Church is to be an organism and have life, there must be persons behind the structure. The point to be argued here is that the persons we should look to for the life of the Church are the divine persons at its heart more than the human persons who come first to mind.

---

[134] Ibid, 636.
[135] Ibid, 638.
[136] Joseph Cardinal Ratzinger, <u>Das neue Volk Gottes: Entwürfe zur Ekklesiologie</u> (Düsseldorf: Patmos-Verlag, 1969), 96.
[137] O. Linton, 'Ekklesia' in <u>Reallexikon für Antike und Christentum</u> IV, 905-21 at 907-8.

The suggestion is to view the Church as the earthly manifestation of the joint mission of the Son and the Holy Spirit. As Lossky has formulated it: 'A new reality came into the world, a body more perfect than the world – the Church, founded on a two-fold divine economy: the work of Christ and the work of the Holy Spirit, the two persons of the Trinity sent into the world. The work of both persons forms the foundation of the Church.'[138] The idea is obviously not original or new. Pope Pius XII taught in *Mystici corporis*:

> Although the juridical principles, on which the Church rests and is established, derive from the divine constitution given to it by Christ and contribute to the attaining of its supernatural end, nevertheless that which lifts the Society of Christians far above the whole natural order is the Spirit of our Redeemer who penetrates and fills every part of the Church's being and is active within it until the end of time as the source of every grace and every gift and every miraculous power.[139]

And Congar develops the point:

> The institutional Church, the Church in its outward structure, is wholly dependent on, and continuous with, the Incarnate Word and the messianic energies which the apostolic powers share. The Holy Spirit, the Spirit of the Son, sent by him and proceeding from him, gives force and efficacy to these powers both when exercised in proclaiming the faith and in celebrating the sacraments of faith, as is affirmed in countless passages of Scripture.[140]

---

[138] Vladimir Lossky, The Mystical Theology of the Eastern Church, (Crestwood, New York: St Vladimir's Seminary Press, 2002), Page 156.
[139] Mysitici corporis, § 63.
[140] Congar, The Mystery of the Church, 182.

In a series of conferences on the Church which Congar gave at a very early stage in his career, he formulated a principle which can be of great value to us here.

> The various shortcomings of the Church in history are familiar enough. . . . Today, however, we are to try to view with the eye of faith the Church sprung from that first Pentecost, to perceive the truly divine sublimity of the Church which then received for its soul, its source of life and activity, no other and no less than the Spirit of God himself. . . . If, as St. Paul says, no one can say from the heart 'Jesus is the Lord', otherwise than in the Holy Spirit (1 Cor 12:3; cf. 1 John 4:2-3), that is to say without a communication of grace freely and specifically made by the Holy Ghost, the same is true of every act of faith, of every true witness to God, of every act of love, of every true prayer, of all growth in holiness, of every act of virtue, of every act which the Church performs in communicating the grace of God. So it is that the eye of faith sees a divine history everywhere in process of becoming, within and concurrently with the world's earthly course, the history, indeed, of the people of God. We realize, too, that not a letter of it is spelt out, not a word formed, that the Holy Spirit, from the bosom of the Trinity, has not, secretly but sovereignly, written or uttered. . . . Nothing that is holy ever takes place in the world except by participation in a power from the Holy Ghost, who gives it freely, in love.[141]

Arguing with the Donatists in favour of the validity of heretical baptism, St. Augustine formulated a principle which can be applied here. He kept repeating that baptism retains its holiness, despite the sin of the minister or the recipient, because baptism belongs to Christ and

---

[141] Ibid, 40-41.

not to us.[142] This same argument can be applied, *caeteris paribus*, to all the institutions of the Church and to the visible Church as a whole. A valid sacrament is an action of Christ despite the sinfulness of the minister and any abuses there may be in the celebration. Consideration need not be confined to individual sacraments, taken one at a time. The same principle can be applied to the whole set of sacraments taken together, the liturgy as a whole. This set of actions of Christ, animated by the Holy Spirit, forms the Holy Church. The Church belongs to God, the Father, the Son, and the Holy Spirit, and it follows that there is a holiness in the Church which our sins cannot destroy. This sinless Church is not immediately accessible to everyday experience, but only to faith. It is nonetheless a reality and is our link with God and the basis of our faith.

Applying the metaphysical analogies in their full rigour, as that has been defended in this chapter, we can say that the Holy Spirit, by becoming in person the grace and charity in the souls of believers, truly is the soul of the Holy Church. Likewise, the Holy Spirit is truly incorporated in the Holy Church in a manner strictly analogous with the Incarnation of the Son, so that the union of the Holy Spirit and the Holy Church is one of being and not just of alliance, as the Son is joined in a union of being with the human nature of Jesus. The Holy Spirit and the Holy Church together form, then, a single theandric organism, one single mystical divine person, not just 'as it were' in a qualified manner, but really and truly, where every single act of the Holy Church is the act immediately of the Holy Spirit in person. When the Church is understood in this way, all the acts of the Church are, by definition, acts of the Holy Spirit, and there is no tension between the Holy Spirit and the Church we believe in. This Church of our faith, which is completely filled and ruled by the Holy Spirit, does not have to strive after fidelity in any way; its fidelity is guaranteed by its divine Author and Governor. On the basis of this theological concept of the Holy Church, all Congar's different denials can be rebutted. Contrary to what he says, it can be asserted that the Holy Spirit is 'the interior

---

[142] On this see DTC, II, 224-5.

form of unity of the Church,' that he enters 'into composition with the body of the Church,' and is 'united to it in a physical and substantial union,' thus forming 'a single substantial being which is both divine and human'.

Chapter 6

From the Theandric Organism to the Human Corporation

In the early centuries the spontaneous notion of the Church was that of the Holy Church, and there was a strong awareness of the role of the divine persons within it. Over the centuries different factors led to a stronger and stronger emphasis on the human reality, and a corresponding weakening in the awareness of the divine dimension. It is necessary now to review the process which underlies this change and which has brought us to our present position.

The dominant influence in this, as in so many things, has been St. Augustine, for he had a strong and accurate sense of the Church in both its dimensions. He, like all the Fathers, had a marvellous sense of the mystery of the Church, and he has some of the most beautiful doctrine about Christ and the Church in his Sermons and his Psalm commentaries. However, despite all that, it is another point of his teaching which has been more influential among us in the West, his ideas on the holiness of the Church, on which point he wavered Against the Donatists St. Augustine claimed that the Catholic Church is 'the bride without spot or stain' mentioned in Eph. 5:27, and that the holiness of the Church on earth is real. To explain that real holiness in the face of the obvious sinfulness, he postulated that the holiness is focussed upon a small group of holy ones within the Church. Subsequently, against the Pelagians he had to change that tune. They claimed that they had the group of sinless ones, and so now St. Augustine made the counter claim that there is no such inner group, that we are all sinners, and that 'the bride without spot or stain' will only be revealed in heaven, and that the sinfulness of the earthly Church is an obvious fact of common observation. That became his final position and the one which has stuck with us in the West.[1] Sure enough, the sinfulness of the earthly Church is plain to all, but in making that assertion, the concept of the Church being applied can only be the human corporation of our everyday experience, so that the deeper concept of the theandric organism must be, to some extent at least, overlooked. Affirming this obvious sinfulness in the human dimension of the Church puts pressure on our sense of the divine dimension, unless we make a clear distinction which can protect the Holy Church.

A further significant change in the Western sense of the Church took place during the trinitarian controversies of the second half of the fourth century. Closely related to the Arian denial of the divinity of the Son, there was a corresponding denial of the divinity of the Holy Spirit. One of the arguments used by the defenders of this thesis, known as Macedonians or *pneumatomachoi*, was based on the final clause of the Apostles' Creed: 'I believe in the Holy Spirit, the holy Catholic Church, the forgiveness of sins etc.' On the basis that all the elements of that final clause are governed grammatically by the preposition 'in', the opponents of the divinity of the Holy Spirit argued that the Holy Spirit is placed here on the same level as the Church, and so the Holy Spirit cannot be divine, since the Church is only human. The orthodox answer to this argument, in the West at least, was to reject the grammatical point, and to deny the divinity of the Church, saying that we don't believe <u>in</u> the Church, because the Church is only human, not divine. The position first appears in an explanation of the Apostles' Creed of Rufinus of Aquileia (345-410), which was written around the year 400.[2] Commenting on these last three phrases of the Creed, 'Holy

---

[1] On this see Faul, 'Sinners in the Holy Church,' 404-415.
[2] <u>Expositio symboli</u>, § 34.1, CChrSerLat, 169.1-16.

Church, the remission of sins, the resurrection of this flesh', he says: 'For the rest, where it is not dealing with the divinity but with creatures and mysteries, the preposition "in" is not added, as if to say we are not to believe *in* the holy Church, but the holy Church, not as God, but as the Church gathered together to God ... By this single preposition, therefore, the Creator is distinguished from the creatures, and things divine are separated from things human.'[3] This has remained standard doctrine in the West, repeated most recently in the *Catechism of the Catholic Church*, § 750.[4] This point is important for the argument being made and we will return to the notion of believing 'in' the Church at a later stage. For now, however, we note the separation that has occurred between the Church and God. The earlier patristic tradition, followed always by the East, never thought of the Church as separate from the Son and the Holy Spirit. Here, on the contrary, at this early stage of the Western theological tradition, the Church is strictly and forcefully separated from the Holy Spirit because of the danger of the Holy Spirit's divinity being undermined by association with the Church. The Church is taken to be a purely human reality, a creature to be understood apart from God.

An important symptom of the change in the concept of the Church is a correlative change which took place in the meaning of the phrase the 'Body of Christ.' The phrase, the 'mystical body' was a novelty of the medieval period. It 'does not appear in any author of Christian antiquity nor of the early middle ages.'[5] In the long discussion aroused by Paschase Radbert's treatise *De Corpore et sanguine Domini*, published in 844, 'the *corpus* par excellence, the one which first sprang to mind

---

[3] 'In ceteris vero, ubi non de divinitate sed de creaturis et de mysteriis sermo est, 'in' praepositio non additur, ut dicatur: in sancta ecclesia, sed sanctam ecclesiam credendam esse, non ut Deum, sed ut ecclesiam Deo congregatam. ... Hac itaque praepositionis syllaba creator a creaturis secernitur et divina separantur ab humanis.' CChrSerLat. 169.9-16.

[4] On all this see de Lubac, The Splendour of the Church (New York: Sheed and Ward, 1956), 13-28.

[5] Jerome Hamer O., The Church is a Communion (Geoffrey Chapman: London, 1964), 68-69.

and which it was not necessary to designate in any other way was the Church. *Corpus mysticum*, on the contrary, was used for a fairly long time of the eucharistic body in contrast to *corpus Christi quod est Ecclesia*, which was pre-eminently the *verum corpus*'.[6] It was in the second half of the twelfth century, the Church began to be called *corpus mysticum*. According to Hamer, the inversion of the two formulae resulted from the controversy against Berengarius (1000-1088). Hamer mentions different factors at work, but the one of interest here is this: 'Others might be tempted to over-identify Christ and his Church, the Head and the members of the body; Berengarius, on the contrary, had not even retained the feeling of their mutual immanence.'[7] Berengarius, it seems to me, is the harbinger of the future in the West in this regard. To counter Berengarius, theology proceeded henceforth to emphasize the substantial identity of the body present in the sacrament with the body born of Mary, and to reserve to them the term *corpus verum*, while carefully distinguishing them from the body of the Church or the communion which were shortly to be designated *corpus mysticum*. In Hamer's opinion 'the application of the expression *corpus mysticum* to the Church denotes the homogeneity of the theology of the medieval Church with that of the Fathers and of St. Paul.'[8] I cannot agree with this. The change from the 'true body' to the 'mystical body' marks a loss of the reality of the presence of Christ in the Church, and is not a sign of continuity. It is of a piece with the other changes being noted and is a sign of the loss of the sense of the divinity of the Church and the constitutive role of Christ and the Holy Spirit in the Holy Church.

A crucial moment in this story is what has been called either the reformation or the revolution of the eleventh century, when a number of excellent German Popes were appointed and proceeded to use the office of the papacy for the reform of the Church. There thus began a new pro-active form of papal government which has been the dominant influence in the Western Church ever since. Congar situates here what he

---

[6] Ibid, 69.
[7] Ibid.
[8] Ibid.

considers to be 'the most important event in the history of ecclesiological doctrines,'[9] and which he describes at length. According to him, in the course of tradition in the West, there have been two distinct manners of understanding how God acts in the Church. He wrote: 'God acts in the Church, and thus what is there legitimately done is from him. This is the conviction of the whole Catholic tradition. It has nevertheless been conceived of in two ways, roughly spread over two periods which, in the West, hinge at the twelfth century.'[10] He then goes on to explain that

> the Gregorian Reform and its influence ... marked a definite turning-point: the transition from an appreciation of the ever active *presence of God* to that of *juridical powers* put at the free disposal of, and perhaps even handed over as its property to, 'the Church', i.e. the hierarchy. For the Fathers and the early Middle Ages, the sacred actions are performed *in* the Church, according to the forms of the Church, and are rigorously sacred as such. But their *subject* is *God*, in an actual and direct way. Ecclesiastical structures are much more the manifestation and form of *God's* action than a subject whose internal quality or power could constitute an adequate basis for the certain production of the expected effect. The categories of thought are less those of (efficient) causality than those of the manifestation of the invisible via the visible, and a symphony of the two - the invisible retaining a primacy of presence and operation.[11]

The two ways of conceiving the action of God in the Church Congar describes here, correspond exactly to the two notions of the Church, the Holy Church whose mystery we having been attempting to portray,

---

[9] Congar, « Apostolicité de ministère et apostolicité de doctrine, » in <u>Ministères et communion ecclésiale</u> (Paris : Cerf, 1971), 51-94 at 83.
[10] Congar, <u>Tradition and Traditions</u>, 134.
[11] Ibid, 135.

and the concrete Catholic Church. During the first millennium the sense of the mystery of the Holy Church dominated and the action of Christ and the Holy Spirit was understood to be direct and immediate. During the second millennium the emphasis has been on the human reality of the Church, so that the awareness of the action of God has become weakened and the role of the human intermediaries has come to dominate in our thinking. For when we come to the modern period of Catholic theology, we find the word 'church' being defined as the visible Church, pure and simple. In Melchior Cano's book on method, *De locis theologicis*, he introduces his treatment of the issue as follows: 'Although the society of angels and men is sometimes called the Church, and sometimes the kingdom of heaven, which is made up of the *comprehensores* and the *viatores*, in this present work our intention is to speak only of the Church militant, which is the group of the faithful *viatores*.'[12] This choice to focus on the visible Church has been the policy of the treatise *De ecclesia* ever since.

The weakening of the sense of the mystery of the Church and the corresponding emphasis on the human dimension was intensified by the currents of Deism and Naturalism which emanated from the Enlightenment.[13] Deism primarily involves a tendency to see God as separate from the world he has created and active in it only from a distance, and it inevitably leads to a strong anthropocentrism in theology.[14] According to Mühlen, in the 17th and 18th centuries, this Deism and Anthropocentrism exercised a strong influence on theology: 'It was under the influence of deistic thinking, which even today still has a large influence on our religious experience, that there developed that popular naturalism which the encyclical *Mystici Corporis* sharply rejected.'[15] In relation to the doctrine of the Church this meant that God was active only in the beginning, when he established the hierarchy,

---

[12] Melchior Cano, De locis theologicis, l. 4, c. 2, § 1; Opera Omnia: Vol. 1, (Rome, 1890), 199.
[13] On this see Mühlen, Una Mystica Persona, 5-10, 374, 591.
[14] Ibid, § 1.11, 6.
[15] Ibid, § 1.13, 7.

and then handed the Church over to man. This was the situation which Johann Adam Möhler encountered and against which he reacted. Möhler was reacting against what he saw as the naturalism of the ecclesiology dominant around him, which put all the emphasis on the role of the hierarchy and especially the Pope. The Church was seen as a human society like any other and a strong College of Bishops faithful to the Pope was all that was required for its life and work. 'God created the hierarchy, and so provided more than adequately for the needs of the Church right to the end of the world', was how he summarized the position.[16] The mystery of the Church was overlooked and the need for the continual action of God in the Church disregarded. According to Congar, writing in 1960, this is still an approach which is in evidence in 'many catechisms and expositors of our own time.'[17] The Church is seen and defined, not as an organism animated by the Holy Spirit, but as a society or rather an organisation in which Christ intervened in the beginning as its founder and the Holy Spirit is the guarantor of its authority. 'The very word "Church" often, and more and more, has as its real content not the *congregatio fidelium*, the disciples of Christ, but rather, either the juridical person or institution as the ensemble of the means and prescriptions bringing salvation, or the hierarchical persons who bear the responsibility and the privilege of applying these means of salvation and these rules of conduct. The "Church" designates then the government of the Church, and principally the Roman government and magisterium.'[18] The active subject of the salvific action of the Church is no longer the glorified Christ and his Spirit, but rather man as the holder of ecclesial authority. The deistic separation of God and man became in theology a separation of the Holy Spirit from office in the Church. Because the function of the Holy Spirit in the Church was forgotten, office came to be misunderstood in a one-sided and anthropocentric manner. The human actors in the Church now take centre stage, and in this perspective all the emphasis is on the bishops and on the Pope

---

[16] 'Gott schuf die Hierarchie, und für die Kirche ist nun bis zum Weltende mehr als genug gesorgt.' ThQ 5 (1823), 497.
[17] Congar, The Mystery of the Church, 184.
[18] Congar, L'Église: De saint Augustin à l'époque moderne, 382-83.

in particular: 'Instead of Christ acting *through* the office-holder, the office-holder understands the office as *his* function.'[19] I am suggesting that this problem has not been fully overcome and accept Mühlen's diagnosis, mirroring that of Congar, that 'only a conscious recourse to the Spirit of Jesus can bring about an effective and thorough-going remedy.'[20]

Recovery of Mystery

Möhler's work marked the beginning of the process of recovering the mystery of the Church, and a key concept in his synthesis was, once again, the Body of Christ. Earlier the concept of the Body of Christ was applied to the Church by the Reformers in order to bring out the hiddenness of the Church and the essential spiritual dimension. Now, Ratzinger tells us that 'it was only three hundred years later, in the Catholic Romanticism, that the concept of the mystical Body was newly discovered in Catholic theology.'[21] It was not universally welcomed and was resisted by the theologians who held to the anti-Protestant and anti-Gallican concept which had become traditional since Trent. According to Ratzinger, writing before the Second Vatican Council, two distinct ecclesiological tendencies then opposed one another. One, from the Roman Catechism and Bellarmine, thought of the Church on the basis of the concept of the People, understood primarily hierarchologically and institutionally. And the other, a new organic and mystical conception, was developed which is presented as coming from the Fathers of the Church. The ecclesiological Schema laid before the Fathers of the First Vatican Council made use of the concept of the Body of Christ and met with grave difficulties for that very reason. Pope Leo XIII made the project his own in his encyclical on the Church, *Satis cognitum*, but the resistance was not overcome. In the new theological

---

[19] Mühlen, <u>Una Mystica Persona</u>, § 1.12, 6.
[20] Ibid, § 13.37, 591.
[21] Joseph Cardinal Ratzinger, <u>Das neue Volk Gottes: Entwürfe zur Ekklesiologie</u> (Düsseldorf: Patmos-Verlag, 1969), 92.

breakthrough which followed the First World War, the promising beginnings of Romanticism finally became noticeable. Ratzinger tells that 'with elemental force there came a breach in the centuries-long resistances, and it was experienced as a great achievement that this new vision of the Church found its endorsement by the Magisterium in the encyclical *Mystici corporis*, for one could see in this, at the same time, the overcoming of the one-sided hierarchical understanding of the Church and the acceptance of all the new ideas that had grown in theology since Möhler.'[22] Ratzinger expressed himself somewhat critical of aspects of this development. As he saw it, 'all the marvels of the supernatural were placed in the concept of the mystical Body and a quite unreal concept created, which inevitably appeared as a dreamlike image (ein Traumgebilde) over against the all too human reality of the Church.' He saw it as a problem that a division in ecclesiology had come about. He granted the need of a theology which would treat of the mystical glory of the inner reality of the Church. 'But who could long overlook the fact that the mystical glory would remain an empty word which communicated little, while the concrete Church remains so completely other.' And he concluded that 'the setting beside each other of a dual ecclesiology (zweierlei Ekklesiologie) can be no solution, where it is precisely the intermingling of glory and lowliness which is the problem.'[23] He presented a number of critics who reacted to the theology of the encyclical *Mystici corporis*, and noted, with apparent approval that 'in different ways they all brought out the fact that one cannot construct the Church from a mystical idea, because her visibility cannot be dealt with from this perspective.'[24]

The aim of all that has been written here so far has been to provide a basis for the argument that Ratzinger is wrong in these positions he adopted. The Church is founded on the dual mission of the Son and the Holy Spirit, and there is therefore no alternative but to construct a concept of the Church from this mystical starting-point. From this

---

[22] Ibid, 93-94.
[23] Ibid, 94.
[24] Ibid, 95.

there springs the reality of the theandric organism which continues the divine missions until the end of the age. The Church is also, at the same time, a human corporation, interacting with the other corporations in the human world, and that human reality must be recognised and respected. There is, quite simply, no escaping a 'dual ecclesiology'. It is built into the very nature of the Church, and it is only a clear recognition of this 'duality' which will solve the problems which have been dogging ecclesiology from the very beginning, and which were clearly in evidence at the Second Vatican Council.

The two over-lapping ecclesial realities, the theandric organism which is the Holy Church and the human corporation which is the Catholic Church became attached to the two biblical images the Body of Christ and the People of God. The tension between the Holy Church and the Catholic Church became a tension between the two images, and it came to a head twice in two completely different contexts. At the time of the Reformation, the Reformers used the image of the Body of Christ as a way of expressing their emphasis on the hiddenness of the Church.[25] In the Augsburg Confession we find the following: 'Although in the present the wicked and the godless hypocrites have fellowship with the just in outward signs, in names and offices, still when one will truly speak of what the Church is, one must say of this Church which is called the Body of Christ and implies fellowship not only in outward signs, but has the goods in the heart, the Holy Spirit and faith.'[26] The concept of the Body of Christ becomes here an expression of the invisible inwardness of the Church, and the Catholic theologians recognised the force of the point and so the word appeared dangerous to them. In this way the idea of the Body of Christ disappeared from Catholic ecclesiology and the post-Tridentine definitions of the Church no longer even mention the image. Their starting-point now lay in the idea of the People of God, which more easily permitted an institutional understanding.[27]

---

[25] On this see Ibid, 90-92.
[26] Quoted in Ibid, 91-92.
[27] For more on this see Bonaventure Kloppenburg O.F.M., The Ecclesiology of Vatican II (Franciscan Herald Press: Chicago, 1974), 3-4.

With recovery of the mystery of the Church, beginning with Möhler and the Tübingen school, the image of the Body of Christ was recovered and was now used to bring out the mystical quality of the Church. The problem now lay in the fact that, when the glories of the mystical Church, the Holy Church, the Body of Christ, are applied indiscriminately to the concrete Catholic Church a false glorification is the result. Where the Reformers were using the image of the Body of Christ against the institution, the Catholic Romantics were using it too much in favour of the institution. When Pope Pius XII applied the image of the Mystical Body of Christ directly to the Catholic Church in the encyclical *Mystici corporis*, the problem it leads to was quickly noticed. The critics wanted a return to the concept of the People of God as the more comprehensive and closer to reality. For 'it was feared that the Body of Christ idea gave a false glorification to the Church of the cross and there was concern that the earthly lowliness of the pilgrim Church would be hidden beneath the shining of a false halo.'[28] So, the 'People of God' and the 'Body of Christ' stood over against each other once again as two starting-points for the understanding of the Church and this tension was highly influential in the discussion at the Second Vatican Council.

Ratzinger tells us how the debate began. 'During the discussion of the first Schema on the Church, which came before the Council in December 1962, something, at first sight quite amazing, happened. Twenty years earlier, in 1943, the encyclical <u>Mystici corporis</u> appeared, which was joyfully received by all, not least because it taught that the Church should be understood as the Body of the Lord. The new schema on the Church was constructed similarly on this foundation, but this was precisely the principal starting-point of the criticism.'[29] The most dramatic intervention, one which made a great impact at the time for the surprise it caused, was that of Bishop de Smedt of Bruges in his famous speech in the 31st General Congregation, criticising the first draft of the document on the Church for its triumphalism. He

---

[28] Ratzinger, <u>Das neue Volk Gottes</u>, 95.
[29] Ibid, 90.

quoted one statement from the document: 'Thus the new people goes forward ... not as a disparate crowd but as a well-ordered group, which, nourished by spiritual food and drinking spiritually from the rock, standing strong against the gates of hell and the snares of the devil, it will endure until the end of the age in the unity of faith, in the communion of the sacraments and in the apostolicity of government, remaining always one in the spirit and in charity.'[30] He pointed out that this style is not congruent with reality, with the real state of the people of God,[31] and the upshot of his intervention is well known. The original first draft was abandoned completely and a new document drawn u A new first chapter was drafted on the mystery of the Church and a new second chapter gave pride of place to the image of the People of God. The image of the Body of Christ was downgraded and was now treated as one among a number of biblical images in the third chapter. The document, therefore, witnesses to the tension involved in this matter, between the mystery and the institution, but it does not resolve it.

The same tension was evident when the Council Fathers discussed the place of sin in the Church and the related issue of the need of reform. These issues arose right from the very beginning of the conciliar discussions. Bishop Hurley of Durban, commenting on the proposed Profession of Faith at the meeting of the Central Commission on 9 November 1961, pointed out that 'in the Church, there appear not only unity, holiness, fruitfulness and stability, but also much that springs from human stupidity and weakness. Does it not create a false image when we only propose those considerations which demonstrate the divine face of the Church, and are absolutely silent about those human defects which obscure that face – and are often the reason why many do not come to the Church?'[32] And the points were raised often during the debates. Bishop Lorscheider, speaking on his own behalf and others, said that the holiness of the Church is not total, there exist not only the imperfections of the members, but also of the

---

[30] AS I/IV, 13, also in Gil-Hellín, 16.
[31] AS I/IV, 142.
[32] AP II-II, Pars I, 510-11.

Church as a community. He insisted that all of the limitations inherent in the human and historical element of the Church should be clearly recognized and denounced.[33] Bishop László of Eisenstadt in Austria said that 'if we speak of the pilgrim Church in the public sense, in all the difficulties and miseries of this life, it is not without fault, it is not without sin. ... The people of this world often perceive that the concrete Church is very different from that which the theologians and preachers describe. Theology appears to describe a Church of saints, whereas the life itself of the Church appears to demonstrate a Church of sinners.'[34]

Many calls for the recognition of sin in the Church were made during the discussions on the decree on ecumenism.[35] A number of bishops spoke of the recognition of the faults of individual Catholics[36], while others went so far as to attribute fault to the Church herself. M. Théas, bishop of Tarbes and Lourdes proposed that 'it should be humbly and sincerely confessed that the Catholic Church failed to act or speak rightly in many things, and that she does not lack defects.'[37] R. Masnou Boixeda, bishop of Vich, wanted a confession of the faults of the 'human part of the Catholic Church.'[38] Some bishops suggested that the Church admit her guilt in the processes of division which occurred with the East in the eleventh century, and with the Reformed Churches in the sixteenth. In this line, E. M. O'Brien, archbishop of Canberra and Goulburn, together with his auxiliary I. Cullinane, argued that 'since the Church has never professed herself impeccable ... we can, and indeed must ... publicly assume part of the

---

[33] AS II, 5, 801-02.
[34] Gil Hellín, Constitutio, 1607-08.
[35] On this see Giovanni Cereti, Riforma della chiesa e unitá dei cristiani (Verona: Edizioni ecumeniche, 1985).
[36] R. Tschudy, abbott of Einsiedeln, AS I, II, 1, 423; A. Nierman, bishop of Groninga, AS I, II, 2, 486; B. J. Alfrink, archbishop of Utrecht, AS I, II, 2, 513; A. M. Charue, bishop of Namur, AS I, II, 1, 115.
[37] 'Humilter et sincere confitendum, Ecclesiam catholicam in nonnullis rebus non recte egisse aut dixisse, eamque adhuc non carere defectibus.' AS I, II, 1, 423.
[38] 'Maxime caritas habeatur necnon aliqua confession culparum si quae extarunt ex parte humana Eccesiae Catholicae.' AS I, II, 2, 373. All these texts are reproduced in Cereti, 32-33.

culpability for the divisions of the eleventh and sixteenth centuries.'[39] These contributions, however, made no impact on the redaction of the conciliar text of *Unitatis redintegratio*. The breakthrough in the matter came with two addresses of Pope Paul VI in 1963.[40] In an address to the members of the Roman Curia on 21 September he called them to be at the forefront of 'that perennial reform, of which the Church herself, insofar as she is a human and earthly institution, has perpetual need.'[41] On 29 September, in his opening address at the Second Session of the Council, Pope Paul spoke of the recognition of culpability on the part of the Catholic Church for the division of Christendom. 'If any fault is imputable to us for the separation, we humbly ask pardon of God and beg forgiveness from our brothers who feel offended by us.'[42] This call for a reciprocal confession of faults and forgiveness met with a widespread acceptance in the conciliar discussions[43]

There was, however, a strong current of resistance to this line of thought. There were many Fathers who believed that the admission of fault was against our faith in the holiness of the Church. In his little book on the reform of the Church, published just before the Council, Hans Küng presented well the case against any talk of reform of the Church, when he wrote:

> In the ultimate ground of her being, the life of the Holy Spirit of Jesus Christ, the Church is actually invisible, or, we might also say, visible only to the believer. She lives wholly by the grace of God; she is

---

[39] 'Cum Ecclesia numquam impeccabilem se professa sit …possumus, imo debemus … publice assumere partem culpabilitatis pro divisionibus saeculis undecimo et decimo sexto exortis …' AS I, II, 7, 588-89.
[40] Analysed by Cereti, 65-68.
[41] '… quella perenne riforma, di cui la Chiesa stessa, in quanto istituzione umana e terrene, ha perpetuo bisogno.' AAS 55 (1963), 793-800. This formula appears verbatim in UR 6.
[42] 'Se alcuna colpa fosse a noi imputabile per tale separazione, noi ne chiediamo a Dio umilmente perdono e domandiamo venia altresì ai fratelli che si sentissero da noi offesi…', AS II, I, 183-200.
[43] Cereti, 80-81.

God's spiritual temple, the mysterious reality of the Body of Jesus Christ. The power that gives her her form and structure is the Holy Spirit. It is he, the invisible, who founds the Church each day anew, who awakens and animates and enlightens her, makes her active and effective. It is he who causes her to lead her spiritual life as the community of grace and faith and love. What is there here for human beings to reform?[44]

A typical magisterial statement along this line, often quoted, was that of Pope Gregory XVI who wrote in *Mirari vos* (August 15, 1832), that 'to use the words of the fathers of Trent, it is certain that the Church "was instructed by Jesus Christ and His Apostles and that all truth was daily taught it by the inspiration of the Holy Spirit." (session 13 on the Eucharist, proemium) Therefore, it is obviously absurd and injurious to propose a certain "restoration and regeneration" for her as though necessary for her safety and growth, as if she could be considered subject to defect or obscuration or other misfortune.'[45] Many Fathers, therefore, who did not want the holiness of the Church to be compromised in any way, were unhappy with the efforts to attribute sin to the Church, and the struggle continued until the very end.[46]

In the event the Council formulated the apparent paradox of holiness and sin in the Church in a number of important texts. The holiness of the Church is clearly affirmed: 'The Church ... is believed to be indefectibly holy.'[47]; 'She herself is a virgin, who keeps whole and pure the faith she pledged to her spouse, and imitating the mother of her Lord, in the power of the Holy Spirit, she virginally preserves an integral faith, firm hope and sincere charity.'[48] In one text, the traditional thesis

---

[44] Hans Küng, The Council, Reform and Reunion (Image Books: New York, 1965), 25.
[45] The Papal Encyclicals 1740-1878, Claudia Carlen IHM, The Pierian Press, 1990, 237.
[46] The final stages are reported in Cereti, 86-96.
[47] 'Ecclesia ... indefectibiliter sancta creditur.': Lumen gentium, § 39.
[48] Lumen gentium, § 48.

is formulated that the holiness of the Church survives the presence of sinners in her midst: 'Although the Church, by the power of the Holy Spirit, has remained the faithful spouse of her Lord ...still she is by no means unaware that there have been among her members, both clerics and laity, those who have been unfaithful to the Spirit of God, during the course of many centuries.'[49] The holiness of the Church, however, is characterised as imperfect: '... already on earth the Church is marked with a true, although imperfect, holiness.'[50] The holiness is said to co-exist with a need for purification: 'The Church, embracing sinners in her bosom, at once holy and always in need of purification ...'[51] In another place, perfect fidelity is placed beside a need for continual renewal: 'The Church is strengthened by God's grace ... so that she may not waver from perfect fidelity, but remain the worthy bride of her Lord; that under the action of the Holy Spirit she may never cease to renew herself ...'[52] And it is accepted that the Church stands in need of continual reformation: 'The Church is called by Christ ... to that continual reformation of which she always has need, insofar as she is an institution of men here on earth.'[53]

The suggestion being developed here is that the tension evident in these texts, almost bordering on contradiction, is completely resolved when the distinction between the Holy Church and the Catholic Church is clearly made. When we are thinking of the Church as 'us', the human community which makes up the group on pilgrimage, then, Yes, of course, we are sinners and corporately we are sinful, and we bear a corporate responsibility for the obscuring of the face of Christ. But when we are thinking of the Church as Christ, the Whole Christ, Head and members, incorporated and indwelt by the Holy Spirit, the situation is totally different. All the positive affirmations, which appear triumphalist when applied to the concrete Catholic Church, can be applied without reserve to the Holy Church. It is 'indefectibly holy,'

---

[49] Gaudium et spes, § 43.
[50] Lumen gentium, § 48.
[51] Lumen gentium, § 8.
[52] Lumen gentium, § 9.
[53] Unitatis redintegratio, § 3.

it 'preserves an integral faith, firm hope and sincere charity,' and will never 'waver from perfect fidelity'. The Catholic Church, on the other hand, understood as 'an institution of men here on earth,' is 'marked with a true, although imperfect, holiness,' and is 'always in need of purification.' The distinction between these two concepts of the Church can be brought out by considering the great medieval call for reform of the Church 'in head and members'. This formula is always understood as referring to the Pope and the rest of the Church, so there can be no doubt that it is the human institution which is meant. The same formula has another, higher, reference, which changes its meaning completely. If we take 'head and members' as referring to Christ and his Body, what right have we to presume to reform this Church? This is the Holy Church which is Christ himself, active in the world through the institutions he established, animating them with his Holy Spirit, and that Church stands completely beyond our competence to judge or reform. When the distinction is clearly made between the Holy Church and the Catholic Church, the unresolved tension at the Council is resolved, for our sense of the mystery can be given a free rein in our admiration for the Holy Church, while our sense of realism can be applied carefully to the concrete Catholic Church.

It is worthwhile to return now to a quotation from the early Joseph Ratzinger given at a previous stage of the argument. He said that 'it is ... wrong to consider the incarnation the whole, the total quintessence, and therefore the end, thus decreeing the Church to be the perfected kingdom promised by God, which in effect would be a denial of her great eschatological future, her transformation into judgment and end, as well as an attempt to foist her off as spotless and unimpeachable in this present world.'[54] There are two points being made here which can usefully be considered. One is the definitive nature of the Incarnation, and the other is the exegesis of Ephesians 5:25-27. Contrary to what Ratzinger says here, the Incarnation can and must be considered, in an important and essential sense, the end, the whole, the total quintessence.

---

[54] Joseph Ratzinger, 'Free Expression and Obedience in the Church,' in The Church readings in theology (New York: J. Kenedy & Sons, 1963), 194-217 at 203.

With the Incarnation the Word of God entered human history fully and definitively and remains in its fullness incarnate in the Holy Church until the end of the age. The Word is not fully manifested, so it is true to say that a great eschatological future awaits us. However, this incompleteness must not undermine the more fundamental fact that the Word is fully present already. The Holy Church is the kingdom of God already present among us by the indwelling of the Holy Spirit.

And, furthermore, the Holy Church can and must be recognised as 'spotless and unimpeachable', even in this present world. A key point at issue here, though referred to only indirectly, is the interpretation of Ephesians 5:27, where the Church is described as being 'without spot or wrinkle or any such thing'. Is there a legitimate sense in which the Church can be considered to be truly holy now, in the present age, or must the sinlessness of the Church await the eschatological future? Ratzinger is following St. Augustine's final position as formulated in his *Retractions*, and if one understands the Church to be simply the human reality we all experience, that position is obviously correct. The question at issue, however, is whether or not it is legitimate to view the Church from a different perspective which excludes sin even now, without having to await the Resurrection. What St Paul wrote was this:

> Husbands, love your wives, as Christ loved the church and gave himself up for her, that he might sanctify her, having cleansed her by the washing of water with the word, so that he might present the church to himself in splendor, without spot or wrinkle or any such thing, that she might be holy and without blemish. (Eph 5:25-27, ESV)

The eschatological interpretation is easy, but is not necessarily the only one. The Church which springs from the side of Christ on the Cross, as Eve was taken from the side of Adam in the Garden, and which is symbolised by the blood and water that flowed from his side, is holy in a way that can never fail. This is the Holy Church, the theandric organism which is the continuation in the world of the joint mission of the Son and the Holy Spirit, and she is holy and without blemish now, as she was on the day of Pentecost. The Holy Spirit inhabits her and guarantees her perfection always. There is obviously a sense in which a great eschatological future awaits the Church. But there is this less obvious sense in which the eschaton has already arrived, and that is the present reality of the Holy Church. On this point Hans Küng seems to be a better guide. He wrote:

> We can indeed call the Church, even on earth, a Church 'not having spot or wrinkle ... holy and without blemish' (Eph. 5:27); we are then speaking of the glory with which, by God's grace, she is endowed from above, in her innermost depths, even in this world: the 'pledge' of holiness. But the daily experience of the Church in the concrete will never allow us to forget that the Church 'not having spot or wrinkle' is on this earth a *hidden* reality, not seen but, in the teeth of all her human wretchedness, believed. Her glory shines only for the believer: 'Credo ... sanctam ecclesiam.' Only at the end of time ... will the Church without spot or wrinkle be an actual, total, manifest reality.[55]

The Holy Church is a present reality, and she is perfectly holy. The sin in the Church has its effect in the concrete manifestation where the Church is divided, and the question arises as to where the Holy Church is concretely to be found on earth. And this raises the question as to the relationship between the Holy Church and the Catholic Church.

---

[55] Küng, The Council, Reform and Reunion, 38.

Chapter 7

Believing In the Church

The distinction between the Holy Church and the concrete Catholic Church can be further illuminated by considering the issue of the attribution of divinity to the Church. Congar has difficulty with the application of the adjective 'theandric' to the Church. He writes: 'This conception of the Church has sometimes been called "theandric"; but this is a word that always needs to be explained and is better avoided; "mysteric" or sacramental would, I think, be more suitable.'[1] Congar's hesitation about recognising the theandric nature of the Church is consistent with the difficulty he had with all the metaphysical analogies, and his denial of the strict divinity of the Church. However, on the basis of the ideas presented here, I suggest that the word should be used, and insisted upon, to keep the idea of the Church-mystery at the forefront of our minds. Certainly, the word will always need to be explained, but that is precisely the function of catechesis to explain the special words which communicate the truths of our faith. Interestingly enough, an eminent Eastern theologian, Vladimir Lossky, has no difficulty with the word at all.

---

[1] Congar, <u>Tradition and Traditions</u>, 344.

> The Church ... is a theandric organism, both divine and human.² ... United to Christ ... it is a theandric being having two natures and two wills inseparably united; a union of the creature with God, fulfilled in the person of Christ. ... The divine hypostasis of the Son descended to us and reunited in Himself the created nature and uncreated nature in order that it might be possible for human hypostases to rise to God, reuniting in themselves, in their turn, uncreated grace and created nature, in the Holy Spirit.³

Hans Küng also has difficulty with the divinity of the Church. In his book, *The Church*, Küng develops an argument on the basis that *'Christ is not wholly contained in the Church.'*[4] He concludes that '[i]t is mistaken and misleading, therefore, to talk of the Church as a "divine-human" being, a "divine-human" reality, phrases which stress the unity but overlook the difference between Christ and the Church, and suggest that Christ is simply a part of the Church rather than its Lord, the head of the body. Christ is not wholly contained in the Church.'[5] But the point is precisely that Christ *is* wholly contained in the Church, when the Church is conceived of as the *Christus totus*, Christ and us together forming a unity, the Church in its fullest sense. Of course Christ is the Lord, the Head of the Body, but as a member of the complete Body, not as someone separated and apart. Could we even follow an argument of St Augustine in regard to Our Lady which would lead to a remarkable conclusion? He wrote: 'Mary is holy, Mary is blessed, but the Church is better than the Virgin Mary. Why? Because Mary is part of the Church, a holy member, an excellent member, the most eminent member, but still a member of the whole body. If she is a member of

---

[2] Lossky, The Mystical Theology of the Eastern Church, 184.
[3] Ibid, 185.
[4] Küng, The Church, 236, emphasis in the original as the heading of a section.
[5] Ibid, 237.

the whole body, clearly the body is greater than the member.'[6] On this argument, that the whole is greater than the part, we could argue that the Whole Church is greater than Christ himself? Christ is the Head of the Church, but the head is but one member of the whole body, and so the body is greater than the head alone.

Küng also argues against the divinity of the Church by separating it from the Holy Spirit. He writes:

> For all the links between them there is no identity, but rather a fundamental distinction between the Spirit of God and the human structure of the Church. This difference is not merely a general and abstract one, but the ontic difference between the divine and the human.[7]... To avoid confusing the Spirit and the Church, it would be better not to speak of the Church as a 'divine' reality. The individual believer, after all, does not become a 'divine' reality because he is filled with and governed by the Spirit.[8]

There is a distinction between the Spirit of God and the human structure of the Church. But there is no separation between them. The Spirit has become the grace and charity which form the soul of the Church and is inseparably linked to the body thus formed. And, contrary to Küng's affirmation, the individual believer does become divine, by becoming a sharer in the divine nature as St Peter tells us. If we understand the Church as separate from God, then, obviously, our concept of the Church implies separation from God! But if we

---

[6] Sermo 25 on Matthew 12:41-50, VII: PL 46, 938: 'Sancta Maria, beata Maria, sed melior est Ecclesia, quam Virgo Maria. Quare? Quia Maria portio est Ecclesiae, sanctum membrum, excellens membrum, supermeinens membrum, sed tamen totius corporis membrum. Si totius corporis, plus est profecto corpus, quam membrum. Caput Dominus, et totus Christus caput et corpus. Quid dicam? Divinum caput habemus, Deum caput habemus.
[7] Küng, The Church, 174.
[8] Ibid.

understand the Church in its union with God, then this Church has God within and is, thus, divine.

The tension between the divinity and the humanity of the Church is at the root of an important doctrine of Western Catholic theology. For, as was mentioned in passing earlier, there is what almost amounts to an official teaching of the Catholic Church that the Church is *not* divine! The word 'in' was dropped from the Nicene-Constantinopolitan creed in the Latin translation in order to enshrine the doctrine that the Church is not divine, and in the *Catechism of the Catholic Church*, § 750, we are taught that '[i]n the Apostles' Creed we profess "one Holy Church" (*Credo ... Ecclesiam*), and not to believe *in* the Church, so as not to confuse God with his works.' A footnote refers us to the *Catechism of the Council of Trent* from which this doctrine was taken, so it is clear that this is a position of long standing in the Western theological tradition.[9] This is a doctrine which de Lubac made very much his own. According to him, in the creeds, 'it is not said that we believe "in" the Church, any more than it is said that we believe "in" any other of the works of God. ... In saying "I believe [in] the Holy Catholic Church", we proclaim our faith not "in" the Church but "about" the Church - that is, in her existence, her supernatural reality, her unity, and her essential prerogatives.'[10] And he stresses what he sees as the importance of the distinction. 'Here we are dealing with something more than a matter of detail or a mere *nuance*. In the full sense of the words we can in fact "believe in" - that is to say, have faith in - God and God alone, Father, Son and Holy Spirit.'[11]

The doctrine emerged during the trinitarian controversies of the second half of the fourth century. Closely related to the Arian denial of the divinity of the Son, there was a corresponding denial of the divinity of the Holy Spirit. One of the arguments used by the defenders of this thesis, known as Macedonians or *pneumatomachoi*, was based on the

---

[9] The matter is treated by Henri de Lubac in Méditation sur l'Église : Œuvres Complètes VIII (Paris: Les Éditions du Cerf, 2003), 22-36. The English translation is in The Splendour of the Church (New York: Sheed and Ward, 1956), 13-28.

[10] Ibid, 13.

[11] Ibid, 14.

final clause of the Apostles' Creed: 'I believe in the Holy Spirit, the holy Catholic Church, the forgiveness of sins etc.' On the basis that all the elements of that final clause are governed grammatically by the preposition 'in', the opponents of the divinity of the Holy Spirit argued that the Holy Spirit is placed here on the same level as the Church, and is therefore not divine. The orthodox answer to this argument, in the West at least, was to deny the grammatical point, and to separate the Church from the Holy Spirit. The position first appears in an explanation of the Apostles' Creed of Rufinus of Aquileia (345-410), which was written around the year 400.[12] Commenting on these last three phrases of the Creed, 'Holy Church, the remission of sins, the resurrection of this flesh', he says: 'For the rest, where it is not dealing with the divinity but with creatures and mysteries, the preposition "in" is not added, as if to say we are not to believe *in* the holy Church, but the holy Church, not as God, but as the Church gathered together to God ... By this single preposition, therefore, the Creator is distinguished from the creatures, and things divine are separated from things human.'[13] Rufinus does not mention the polemical background of his argument, which is to be found in the only other independent treatment of the matter, that proposed by Faustus of Riez (400-490/95). The discussion appears in a treatise on the Holy Spirit, written precisely to defend the divinity of the Third Person of the Trinity against the Macedonians.[14] He presents the argument of the opponents of the Holy Spirit's divinity in order to rebut it. For him, the verb 'credere in' can apply only to God and he says: 'We believe the Church as the mother of our regeneration, not in the Church as the author of our salvation. ... Whoever believes in the Church believes in man. Abandon, therefore, the blasphemous notion that you ought to believe in any human creature, seeing that there should be no

---

[12] Expositio symboli, § 34.1, CChrSerLat, 169.1-16.
[13] 'In ceteris vero, ubi non de divinitate sed de creaturis et de mysteriis sermo est, 'in' praepositio non additur, ut dicatur: in sancta ecclesia, sed sanctam ecclesiam credendam esse, non ut Deum, sed ut ecclesiam Deo congregatam. ... Hac itaque praepositionis syllaba creator a creaturis secernitur et divina separantur ab humanis.' CChrSerLat, 169.9-16.
[14] De Spiritu sancto, I, II, CSEL 21, 103.25-105.11.

such thing as believing in even an angel or archangel.'[15] This doctrine becomes standard in the Western theological tradition, and de Lubac gives a long list of texts which all repeat the same point that we do not believe 'in' the Church, because the Church is not God.[16] It becomes so well established that it practically reaches the position of being Catholic doctrine, appearing in both the official catechisms of the Councils of Trent and Vatican II, as we have seen.

Before entering into the substance of the argument, it is necessary to settle in advance the grammatical point at issue. De Lubac insists as strongly as could be on the significance of this point of grammar. He tells that 'we cannot ponder this point too much; the Christian novelty of the formula 'believe *in*' is something more that a mere item of information without any particular significance.'[17] There is no doubt that the formula to 'believe in', 'pisteu, ein eivj', was novelty in St. John's gospel. However, it is doubtful indeed that St. John gave the phrase such a special meaning that it can be properly designated as a *Christian* novelty. De Lubac is simply following a long tradition in this matter, so we return to the sources and make our grammatical argument from there.

The basis of the argument for both Rufinus of Aquileia and Faustus of Riez was indeed their conviction that the verb '*credere*' with the preposition '*in*' applies only to God. Their authority in this is St. Augustine, who, in different places in his writings, distinguishes different kinds of faith in God and in Christ.[18] His fundamental distinction is between '*credere in Deum*' which includes loving adherence to God

---

[15] 'Credimus ecclesiam quasi regenerationis matrem, non in ecclesiam credimus quasi in salutis auctorem.... qui in ecclesiam credit in hominem credit. Recede itaque ab hac blaspheiae persausione, ut in aliquam humanam credere te debere aestimes creaturam, cum omnino nec in angelum nec in archangelum sit credendum.', CSEL 21, 104.6-7, 19-22.

[16] An even fuller list of references is given in de Lubac, Catholicisme: Œuvres completes VII (Paris: Les editions du Cerf, 2003), 49, n. 6.

[17] De Lubac, The Splendour of the Church, 14.

[18] The standard reference in the matter remains Th. Camelot, O., 'Credere Deo, Credere Deum, Credere in Deum: Pour l'histoire d'une formule traditionnelle,' Revue de Sciences Philosophiques et Théologiques 30 (1941-42) 149-155.

as Saviour, and '*credere Deo*' which is simply accepting God's word as true. The second type can be applied to a human being, but the first applies only to God. Now, St. Augustine may have been making a good analysis of faith, but was he providing an accurate grammatical analysis? It would seem not. '*Credere in*' is not a traditional Latin expression at all. It is a neologism which was introduced to translate the 'pisteu, ein eivj' of the New Testament, so that Latin has no inherent usage of this construction on which to base an argument. And the Greek original gives no basis for a special meaning to the verbal usage. After examining the New Testament usage, Camelot concludes that 'it is difficult to find a basis in the text of St. John on which to base the distinction which St. Augustine draws between *credere Christo*, and *credere in Christum*.'[19] And according to Bultmann, in the *Theological Dictionary of the New Testament*, pisteuein eij, although not found in classical Greek or in the LXX, has no special connotation in the New Testament. 'In Jn. es *pisteuein eij and pisteuein o, ti* are constantly used interchangeably in the same sense.'[20] For instance, in John 12:36, Our Lord says, 'pisteu, ete eivj to. fw/j', 'believe in the light', which the Latin translates as '*credite in lucem*' without any difficulty about using the verb with reference to a thing which is not even a person, much less God; the fact that Christ is the Light does not affect the grammatical point. In the New Testament, and in subsequent Greek usage as we shall see in due course, 'pisteu, ein eivj' is used in much the same general way as 'believing in' is used in English and most modern languages, and there is no good reason to attribute anything different to Latin.

A further argument against the special usage of 'credere in' is to be found in a text of St. Ambrose dealing with the same clause of the Apostles' Creed as Rufinus and Faustus, which runs: 'But it has also in *the Church*; but it has also in *the forgiveness of sins*; but it has also in *the resurrection*. What then? The reason is one and the same: we so believe in Christ, we so believe in the Father, even as we believe in *the Church*

---

[19] Ibid, 150.
[20] Theological Dictionary of the New Testament, Vol. VI, ed. Friedrich (Grand Rapids, Michigan: Eerdmanns, 1968), 203.

and in *the forgiveness of sins* and in *the resurection of the flesh*. What is the reason? Because he who believes in the Author believes also in the work of the Author.'[21] What is notable here is that, although the basic theological point is not that much different, for St. Ambrose is also distinguishing believing in God and believing in the Church etc., he has no trouble whatever in applying the verbal form '*credere in*' to the different objects.

A final argument in this matter is to consider what happens when the '*in*' is removed, and we are left with '*credere ecclesiam*', '*credere remissionem peccatorum*', '*credere resurrectionem carnis*', '*credere vitam eternam*'. These are quite obviously nonsense expressions in any language. What can it possibly mean 'to believe the remission of sins', or 'to believe the resurrection of the body', or 'to believe eternal life'? The verb, 'to believe' can only have one of two objects, either the person believed or the proposition he communicates, and the objects in these cases are neither of these. Of course what is meant is that one believes that there is remission of sins, or a resurrection of the body or eternal life, but *credere* with the object in the accusative does not have that meaning. In fact, in these cases, it has no valid meaning at all. It is to be noted that St. Augustine, in his analysis, did not make any reference to a usage of '*credere*' with a direct accusative. That notion appeared subsequently in a conflation of Augustinian texts which passed into the tradition as genuine St. Augustine.[22] The text runs: '*Non dicit, Credo Deum, vel credo Deo, quamvis et haec saluti necessaria sint. Aliud enim est credere illi, aliud credere illum, aliud credere in illum. Credere illi est credere vera esse quae loquitur; credere illum, credere quia ipse est Deus; credere in illum, diligere illum.*' We are interested here in the usage of '*credere*' with the

---

[21] "Sed habet et in ecclesiam, sed habet et in remissionem peccatorum, sed habet et in resurrectionem!' - Quid ergo? Par causa est: Sic credimus in Christum, sic credimus in patrem, quemadmodum credimus et in 'ecclesiam' et in 'remissionem peccatorum' et in 'carnis resurrectionem'. Quae ratio est? Quia, qui credit in auctorem, creddit et in opus auctoris.' Explanatio Symboli, § 6, CSEL 73, 8.2-9.8. The translation is from The 'Explanatio Symboli ad Initiandos': A Work of St. Ambrose, ed. Dom R. H. Connolly, Texts & Studies 10 (Cambridge University Press, 1932), 24.

[22] See Camelot, 152.

direct accusative, and what is said simply does not make sense, wherever it came from. '*Credo Deum*' does not mean '*Credo quia ipse est Deus*', whatever it means. The second sentence makes good sense, 'I believe that He is God,' but what does '*Credo Deum*' mean? The only thing it might reasonably mean is to believe on God's authority, but for Latin that meaning is carried by '*Credo Deo*'. If there is an acceptable sense, it certainly cannot apply to the other cases mentioned above where the object in the accusative is a thing and not a person.

We conclude from all this that the grammatical argument against the notion of 'believing in the Church' is not well founded. However, grammar is not our real concern, obviously. Of greater interest is the theological implication of the grammatical argument. It seems to be quite clear that Faustus of Riez was involved in a polemical argument against a heretical sect and he was led to extreme statements in making his case. In order to affirm the divinity of the Holy Spirit, he felt it necessary to separate the Church completely from the sphere of the divine, and to consider the possibility of 'believing in' the Church as blasphemy. This assigning of the Church to the purely human level is an indication that in these two writers the sense of the msytery of the Church was already on the wane and the acceptance of this doctrine ever after in the Western Church is also symptomatic of our sad lack in this matter. There are no doubt good historical reasons why the emphasis on the human reality has been stronger in the West; the on-going struggle between Church and State which has marked the whole of the second millennium being essential here. With all excuses made, it has to be recognised that the sense of the mystery has waned among us, and has not yet been properly restored.

We find a better guide to appropriate usage here from the East. The Eastern Church has never had any difficulty with applying 'pisteu, ein eivj' quite generally. St. Cyril of Jerusalem (315-87), in his catechetical sermons, deals with this same clause of the Apostles' Creed and he has no difficulty in speaking of believing eivj mi, an a`gi, an kaqolikh.n

evkklhsi,an, kai. eivj sarko.j avna, stasin, kai. eivj zwh.n aivw, nion.²³
The same freedom is to be found in a work of Epiphanius of Salamis (365-403).²⁴ The most important text in this whole matter, of course, is the formula of the Nicene-Constantinopolitan Creed, which remains the fundamental Symbol of faith for the whole Church. In it the eivj is used before the mi, an a`gi, an kaqolikh.n evkklhsi, an, but for the subsequent articles of faith different verbs are used, 'we confess one baptism for the remission of sins and await the resurrection of the body and life everlasting.' Although the Greek usage does not exclude speaking of 'believing in' baptism and the resurrection and life everlasting, still it is better to make the distinction between believing in God and believing in such doctrines. And yet the Creed chooses to retain the 'believing in' for the Church, allowing us to interpret that the Church is a special case. It is not simply a doctrine like the others, but has a special relationship to our faith which will have to be analysed.

As we know, the '*in*' has been removed from the clause dealing with the Church in the Latin translation of the Creed, and the story of how it happened is not without interest. It turns out that when the singing of the Creed was first introduced into the Mass in the West under Charlemagne, the author of the translation used was a friend of Alcuin, Charlemagne's chief advisor in Church matters, Paulinus, bishop of Aquileia.²⁵ Paulinus obviously made his translation according to the Aquileian tradition, and, of course, the eivj before the mi, an a`gi, an kaqolikh.n evkklhsi, an was omitted. Hence it is that what became the Creed for the whole Western Church, when Charlemagne's version entered Rome, was the local translation of the Church in Aquileia, the

---

[23] See Hans Lietzmann, <u>Symbole der alten Kirche</u> (Bonn: 1914), 19 and <u>Catechesis 18</u>,
§ 22, PL 33, 1043.

[24] Ancoratus 119, 11 in <u>Die griechischen christlichen Schriftsteller der ersten drei Jahrhundert 25</u>, (Leipzig, 1951), 149.1-4 has eis before each phrase.

[25] The story is told in D. B. Capelle, 'L'origine antiadoptianiste de notre texte du symbole de la messe,' in <u>Recherches de théologie ancienne et médiévale</u> 1 (1929), 7-20.

very diocese in which the polemic against believing *in* the Church first took its rise.

The tradition upheld by the Catechisms and so vigorously proposed by De Lubac is not the only tradition in this matter. Congar finds an interpretation more consonant with the position being proposed in this book in the work of the medieval theologians. In their commentaries on the Creed they never separated the Holy Spirit from the Church. They understood the whole of the final section of the Creed as dealing with the work of the Holy Spirit. They took the 'I believe in the Holy Spirit, the holy Catholic Church' as one single article, and interpreted it to mean 'I believe in the Holy Spirit unifying, sanctifying and vivifying the Church.'[26] Congar records the fact that in the West 'the preposition *eis* or *in* has usually been omitted before *ecclesiam* and this fact has often been accorded a religious or theological significance,'[27] but it would appear that he does not share the common view.

The dropping of the '*in*' from the Latin creed has not made that much impact on the ground. Latin has long since ceased to be a living language, and the modern translations of the Creed rarely follow the Latin pattern. I was able to check ten European languages, French, Italian, Spanish, Portuguese, English, Irish, German, Dutch, Polish and Hungarian. Only two follow the Latin in dropping the preposition and in both cases, German and Italian, the construction is forced, with no basis in common usage, as is also true of all the others. I also checked four Asian languages, Hindi, Tamil, Marathi and Japanese. None of these languages uses a preposition with the verb to believe, but exactly the same construction is used of the Church as of God the Father, the Son and the Holy Spirit. It goes without saying that the four Eastern languages I checked, Russian, Armenian, Chaldean and Syriac, all retain the preposition, following the Greek. It is clear from this that the grammatical foundation for the argument of Rufinus of

---

[26] Congar, Divided Christendom, 56; Congar, The Mystery of the Church, 36; Congar, Tradition and Traditions, 170; Yves M. J. Congar, I Believe in the Holy Spirit, Volume 2 (London/New York: Geoffrey Chapman/The Seabury Press, 1983), 5.

[27] Congar, I Believe in the Holy Spirit, 5.

Aquileia and Faustus of Riez is to be found in no European language, and this provides another argument weighing against the possibility of its existing in Latin either.

Ultimately the presence or absence of the preposition is not of great significance. 'I believe the holy Church' has a perfectly acceptable meaning. I believe her when she speaks, as she always does infallibly. 'I believe in the holy Church' also has perfectly acceptable meanings. The verbal phrase, 'believing in' takes its meaning from its object. I believe in God. I believe in angels. I believe in miracles. I believe in human rights. I believe in the future of humanity. I believe in exercise and a balanced diet. I believe in lots of things. And I also believe in the Church. I believe 'in the Church', within the Church as a member. I believe 'in the Church', in all that I know and believe *about* her, as I believe in all the other doctrines of the faith. What is important is the theological argument based on the faulty grammar.

Rahner makes a case against believing 'in' the Church based on the lack of personality in the Church. He writes:

> The personal entrusting of each other to each other, which is included in the *'credere in Deum'*, cannot be applied to the Church. However much we may and must 'personify' the Church, however much she may be more than just the numerical sum of individual Christians, however much she is a reality which is not only a juridical reality or fiction, an ideological structure, or a 'moral unity' – the Church as such is not a person, i.e. the Church, in so far as she must be distinguished from real individual persons, cannot be conscious of herself, cannot justify herself, cannot decide, nor is she eternal. The Church, therefore, cannot give herself in that personal surrender of which a real,

self-disposing person is capable, and as such she also cannot receive such a surrender.[28]

Certainly, the Church, taken on its own apart from Christ, is not a person. One would not speak in these personalist terms of the Catholic Church, the social grou It would be wrong to think of entrusting oneself to the Catholic Church or the Anglican Church or any other Christian denomination. However, the Church, the Body of Christ, taken with her Head, is the Whole Christ, and believing in Christ means having a special relationship with the Holy Church which is his presence in the world, the Incorporation of his Holy Spirit. There is, therefore, a special sense of 'believing in' which is unique to the Church, and which is closely related to believing in God. So it is wrong to exaggerate the difference, for the Holy Church is not simply a creature like any other, totally separate from God. The Church is the visibility of God's saving activity in the world, and the two must not be separated, ever. It is possible to think of the Church as separate from God, and all of us do most of the time. However, that purely human manner of thinking of the Church must not be allowed to dominate our theology of the Church, and in our prayer and our spirituality, we must always ensure that our thinking can reach to the holy Church, the true Church, the Christus totus, the mystery that shapes our lives.

There is an interesting moment in Church history which gives evidence that the sense of the divinity of the Church never fully disappeared in the West, and which touches directly on the topic of this book. It emerged in the current of ideas associated with the conciliar movement in the fifteenth century, and has to do with their approach to this clause of the creed and believing 'in' the Church. In order to find a resolution of the profound difficulty created by the election of two, and then three, Popes, it was obvious that some form of a relativisation of the position of the Pope in the Church was required. The Conciliarists turned to the only viable alternative appealed to by every dissident from

---

[28] 'Dogmatic Notes on Ecclesiological Piety,' in Karl Rahner, Theological Investigations, Vol. V (London / New York: Darton, Longman & Todd / The Seabury Press, 1966), 336-65 at 349.

papal authority in every era, the *ecclesia universalis*. Where this led them is reported by one of the ablest of their papalist opponents, Cardinal Juan de Torquemada. He speaks of how perversely some interpret the clause in the creed, 'et in unam sanctam Ecclesiam', and goes on: 'We ourselves saw among those gathered at the universal Council in Basel, some who were so crazy about the authority of the Church that they genuflected at this phrase and venerated that article with profound humility, just as the faithful and devout Christian people normally do at the phrase: "et homo factus est."'[29] Cardinal Torquemada found the Conciliarist enthusiasm for the authority of the Church 'crazy' because it was being used to undermine, as he saw it, the authority of the Pope. And it certainly was being used to place papal authority in a wider context, since it was the uncontrollable papal authority which was pulling the Church apart during the Schism. This point was made explicitly by another Cardinal, Cesarini, in his major address given in the refectory of the Dominican convent in Basel on 16th October, 1433. He said that the Church is not there for the Pope, but rather the Pope is there for the Church. 'And so the Creed does not say *Credo in papam*, but *Credo in sanctam ecclesiam*.'[30] On the understanding of things being proposed here, there is much to be said in favour of the Conciliarist attitude in this matter. For, as I will be arguing in due course, there remains in place an exaggeration of papal authority which needs to be moderated. It is not that papal authority is to be undermined, but it does need to be understood in its full context, which is the whole Church. And the Conciliarist genuflection at the article on the Church in the Creed is also attractive, as it emphasises the crucial point about the Holy Church, its divinity. It is significant that the analogy with the Incarnation implied has since become official teaching

---

[29] Summa de Ecclesia, 1448 (Venice, 1615), bk. i, ch. xx. (Quoted in Lubac, The Splendour of the Church, 21, footnote 3.)

[30] Karl Binder, Wesen und Eigenschaften der Kirche bei Kardinal Juan de Torquemada O., (Innsbruck-Wien-München: Kommissionsverlag Verlagsanstalt Tyrolia, 1955), 99-100.

in *Lumen gentium*. The logic here would lead to a possible addition to the creed, rather than the current removal of the 'in'. This clause might say of the Holy Spirit: 'et *incorporatus est* in unam, sanctam, catholicam Ecclesiam,' in which case the genuflection would be fully justified!

Chapter 8

The Holy Church 'Subsists in' the Catholic Church

Arguments have been made so far to present and justify a concept of the Holy Church distinct from the Catholic Church. If the two are distinct, how then are they related? The answer can only be the one given by the Second Vatican Council; that the Holy Church 'subsists in' the Catholic Church, and a review of the discussion at the Council helps to corroborate the ideas being presented here. According to Sebastian Tromp, the theologian responsible for the drafting of Pope Pius XII's encyclical *Mystici Corporis*, from which the discussion at the Council took its rise, the letter had two goals, to establish the identity of the Mystical Body of Christ and the Catholic Church, and to propose the Pauline doctrine of our being in Christ and his being in us, using the formula of the single mystical person.[1] Both of these goals became part of the dialectic of the Second Vatican Council. The proper formulation of the identity of the Mystical Body of Christ and the Catholic Church was changed in a significant manner, and the formula of the single mystical person was not used at all. These two issues are closely related, and bear on the point being made here. If the Mystical Body of Christ is simply and fully identified with the Catholic Church, there is really

---

[1] Mystici Corporis, U. G., Textus et Documenta, series theologica 26, 1948, ed. S. Tromp, S.J., 3.

no way of avoiding the triumphalism which was condemned at the Council. And the same result arises if the notion of the single mystical person is used without qualification for the concrete Catholic Church. It has been argued here that it is only the Holy Church, with Christ as the founding member, which can be properly and accurately designated as a single mystical person, and to apply that concept to the concrete Catholic Church needs careful qualification. These facts demand that a distinction must be made between the Mystical Body of Christ, which I am calling the Holy Church, and the Catholic Church, and the conciliar discussion reveals how just such a distinction was made by the Second Vatican Council.

Introducing the first two chapters of the Schema on the Church to the Central Commission on 8 May 1962, the Relator, who was Fr. Tromp, explained that the Theological Commission was operating on two principles, the second of which, alone relevant here, was that there is no real distinction between the visible Roman Catholic Church and the Mystical Body of Christ which is the Church.[2] The first to speak in response was Cardinal Liénart, Bishop of Lille. After expressing his firm faith that the Catholic Church is the true Church, he goes on: 'However, it seems to me that we cannot "solemnly profess" (as it is proposed in the text) that the Roman Church and the mystical Body of Christ are one and the same, as if the mystical Body were completely included within the boundaries of the Roman Church. Whereas, the Mystical Body of Christ extends much more widely than the Roman Catholic Church militant. It also embraces the Church suffering in Purgatory and Church triumphant in heaven. It is clear, therefore, that our Church, although it is the visible aspect of the Mystical Body of Jesus Christ, cannot be identified with it absolutely.'[3] When his turn came, Cardinal Ottaviani responded to Cardinal Liénart, expressing his displeasure at his remarks and suggesting that the problem is a possible ambiguity. He said that Cardinal Liénart presumes that by the Roman Catholic Church is meant the Church militant, whereas '[w]hen we say

---

[2] Acta Praeparatoris, II, 2, 3, 994.
[3] AP, II, 2, 3, 998.

that the Mystical Body of Christ is the Catholic Church, the Catholic Church is understood in its integrity, the Church militant, or better, as has been well said, "on pilgrimage", and being purified and the Church triumphant ...'[4] In response to these remarks of Cardinals Liénart and Ottaviani, the Theological Commission conceded that there was dissension on the issue of the identity between the Roman Catholic Church and the Mystical Body on earth, and then continued: 'The Theological Commission considers that this matter has been decided by Pius XII in the Encyclical *Humani Generis* (Denz. 2319), where the doctrine was rejected which denies that the Mystical Body of Christ and the Roman Church are one and the same. Therefore, the Theological Commission can ... admit no weakening in the incorporation of the Mystical Body of Christ on earth, such that it extends beyond the incorporation in the Roman Catholic Church.'[5]

Already in this first exchange at the Council, the duality in the notion of the Church being developed here is well brought out. Cardinal Ottaviani is quite right in saying that the problem underlying the discussion is an ambiguity in the meaning of the word 'Church'. There is no doubt that Cardinal Liénart had the concrete Catholic Church in his mind, as we all do quite spontaneously. On the other hand, Cardinal Ottaviani is correct in pointing out that the affirmation of the identity between the Mystical Body and the Catholic Church is true only when the Catholic Church is understood 'in its integrity' to mean what we are calling the Holy Church, and, in that case, the statement is simply a tautology! When the Catholic Church is understood to be the Mystical Body of Christ, then, obviously, the Mystical Body of Christ is the Catholic Church! However, this distinction between the theandric 'incorporation of the Mystical Body of Christ on earth,' and the human 'incorporation in the Roman Catholic Church,' to quote the Theological Commission, is the fruit of a very long and fraught development, and its implications must be clearly recognised, so that we can settle these questions once and for all.

---

[4] AP II, 2, 3, 1023-24.
[5] AP II, IV, 3, 2, 189.

On Saturday 1 December 1962 the discussion in the Aula began. Bishop Franic introduced the text, explaining 'that it intended to show in clear words that there is no real distinction between the Mystical Body of Christ and the visible Church, between the juridical Church and the spiritual Church, as they say, or the Church of charity, but that these terms signify different aspects of one and the same thing.'[6] Yet again Cardinal Liénart is first to speak, and he repeats his point in Council chamber: 'The Mystical Body extends well beyond the Roman Church militant ... The Roman Church is the .true Body of Christ without however exhausting its reality.'[7] Speaking of other Christians he says: 'I would not dare to say that they in no way adhere to the Mystical Body of Christ, although they are not incorporated into the Catholic Church. It is therefore clear that our Church, although it is the visible manifestation of the Mystical Body of Jesus Christ, cannot be absolutely identified with it.'[8] In his speech on October 3, 1963, Cardinal Lercaro provided a helpful clarification:

> The Church as a society and the Mystical Body express two distinct aspects which are fully and perfectly co-extensive as far as the essential order of things and the constitutive norm set by the divine Founder are concerned, but they cannot be similarly identified in the existential, historical order. In the latter order the two aspects do not always have the same extension; there is now a tension between them, and that tension will last until the end of history, when the identity and equivalence of Church and Mystical Body are finally effected and manifested.[9]

Useful also is the commentary provided by the drafters of *Lumen gentium* § 8 in the third Schema. They wrote:

---

[6] AS I, 4, 122.
[7] AS I, 4, 126.
[8] AS I, 4, 127.
[9] Gil Hellín, Constitutio, 1088.

> The intention is to show that the Church, whose intimate and mysterious nature is described, and which is united with Christ and his work in perpetuity, is concretely to be found on this earth in the Catholic Church. However, this empirical Church reveals the mystery, but not without shadows, until it comes to the fullness of light, just as Christ the Lord came to glory through his self-emptying. Thus the impression is avoided as if the description which the Council gives of the Church were merely idealistic and unreal.[10]

It seems to me that the distinction being developed in this book fits perfectly with the ideas presented here. The Holy Church, as it has been conceived here, bears a certain family likeness to heterodox notions developed by Wyclif, Hus, Luther and other Reformers. However, it is not conceived to be a purely spiritual reality separate from the concrete Catholic Church, for the two concepts overlap in the one essential way; that the apostolic institutions founded by Christ are essential to both. This was what Cardinal Lercaro insisted on, that the two must be 'fully and perfectly co-extensive as far as the essential order of things and the constitutive norm set by the divine Founder are concerned'. The Holy Church is constituted by the deposit of faith, the sacraments and the apostolic hierarchy made alive and active by the Holy Spirit, but with sin and the effects of sin excluded. Its essential characteristic is that the presence of God is kept firmly at the forefront of attention. Christ our Lord himself is a member of this Church and the Holy Spirit is its soul, inseparably united to it, and always thought of as alive and active within it, operative in every single action performed. It is a theandric reality in which the divine and human elements are inextricably conjoined. Sin and its effects cannot, however, be excluded from the concrete Catholic Church, so that 'this empirical Church reveals the mystery, but not without shadows.' And the Catholic Church does not exhaust the reality of the Holy Church, for this latter includes every reality of

---

[10] Ibid, 58.

salvation wherever it is to be found, even outside the visible confines of the Catholic Church. The situation is different for each element of Christ's institution. The Holy Church is present wherever the influence of the Holy Spirit is operative and that covers the whole world. It is present every time the Scriptures are read with faith. It is present in the celebration of every valid sacrament in all the Christian confessions which have them. It is present in the preaching and ruling of every validly ordained minister. The full system is accessible as intended only in the Catholic Church, so it 'subsists in' the Catholic Church, for there alone are full certainty of doctrine and all the means of sanctification and of government to be found.

The distinction between the Church of Christ and the Catholic Church implied in the change from 'is' to 'subsists in' was, in my view, the single most important development achieved at the Second Vatican Council. The foundation for that opinion has, however, recently been challenged at the highest level in the Church. In a recent document, *Responses to some questions regarding certain aspects of the doctrine on the Church* (June 29, 2007), the Congregation for the Doctrine of the Faith answered the question in regard to *Lumen gentium*, § 8, 'Why was the expression "*subsists in*" adopted instead of the simple word "*is*"?,' and replied: 'The use of this expression, which indicates the full identity of the Church of Christ with the Catholic Church, does not change the doctrine on the Church.' The Congregation is here rejecting the interpretation held generally in the Church and asserting that the change from the 'is' of *Mystici corporis* to the 'subsists in' of *Lumen gentium* was not really a change at all!

In order to understand the background to this position we can refer to an article published in *L'Osservatore Romano* in 2006 by a consultor of the Congregation for the Doctrine of the Faith, Fr. Karl Becker, S.J., and emeritus professor at the Gregorian.[11] Fr. Becker explains

---

[11] Karl Josef Becker, S.J., "An examination of 'subsistit in': A profound theological perspective," L'Osservatore Romano (Eng. ed.) 14 December 2005, 11-14. A detailed and useful response to this article can be found in F. A. Sullivan, S. J., 'A Response to Karl Becker, S. J. on the Meaning of *Subsistit in*', *Theological Studies* 67 (2006), 395-409.

that he is writing to correct certain misunderstandings regarding the meaning of the phrase *subsistit in*. He notes that 'there is now a widely held view that the expression *subsistit in* was introduced because of the recognition of *elementa veritatis et sanctificationis* ... present in other Christian communities and therefore with the intention of weakening the identification of the Church of Christ with the Catholic Church.'[12] He sets about rebutting this position, basing himself principally on a book pubished by a doctoral student of his own, Alexandra von Teuffenbach.[13] The thesis consists in a very thorough analysis of the contribution of Fr. Sebastian Tromp to the discussion of this issue at the Council. The interesting and rather remarkable discovery that von Teuffenbach made, and on which she and Becker make their stand, is that it was Fr. Tromp who first made the suggestion to replace 'is' with 'subsists in' in the council document.[14]

Now, Fr. Tromp's position on this matter is well known. He was a stalwart defender of the full identity of the Church of Christ and the Catholic Church and the author of *Mystici corporis*. Congar tells an interesting little story in this regard. In his journal he records a visit he made to Rome in 1946 and speaks of a meeting he had with Fr. Trom He writes: "Tromp is in reaction against anything which would limit, from the more theological point of view, Christological or pneumatological, the perfect identity with the visible institution. ... He is also for a very strong identity between the mystical Body and the visible Church. I put it to him that it is not possible to avoid a certain separation (décalage) between the two, from whatever side one approaches the question."[15] Tromp, as we know, was not persuaded by Congar. He it was who explained as Relator to Central Commission in 1962 that there can be no real distinction between the visible Roman Catholic Church and the Mystical Body of Christ which is the Church, since this point

---

[12] Ibid, 11.
[13] Alexandra von Teuffenbach, Die Bedeutung des Subsistit in (LG 8): Zum Selbstverständnis der Katholischen Kirche (München: Herbert Utz Verlag, 2002).
[14] Ibid, 381-82, 388.
[15] Yves Congar, Journal d'un théologien (1946-1956) (Paris: Les Éditions du Cerf, 2000), 100.

had already been authoritatively decided by Pope Pius XII in *Mystici corporis* and *Humanae generis*.¹⁶ We saw earlier the reaction to this at the Central Commission and to this evidence von Teuffenbach adds a quotation from an unpublished journal of Fr. Tromp to the effect that 'Cardinal Liénart has his opinion: but the Theological Commission did not enjoy the freedom to draw back from the words of Pius XII writing in the Encyclic *Humani generis*.'¹⁷ We have already told the story of what happened subsequently at the Council, and how those events and the doctrine produced are normally interpreted as implying precisely the qualification of the doctrine of Pope Pius XII which Fr. Tromp believed to be impossible. Against all that von Teuffenbach, followed by Becker, places her point of evidence that it was the same Fr. Tromp who first suggested the use of the expression 'subsists in', and deduces that this phrase must mean what Fr. Tromp believed all along, namely that there is a full identity between the Church of Christ and the Catholic Church. On this basis Becker makes his case and concludes: "The Catholic Church has always defended her total identity with the Church of Christ and she has continued to do so since the Council."¹⁸ He expresses his position in a ringing peroration: "The Church of Christ in all its fullness is and remains for ever the Catholic Church. Before, during and after the Council this was, is and will remain the teaching of the Catholic Church."¹⁹

Obviously, I must disagree completely with Fr. Becker. I cannot accept this hermeneutic of conciliar interpretation, that the meaning of a conciliar decree is to be decided on the evidence of the private and unpublished journal of a conciliar *peritus* rather on the published evidence of the conciliar discussions themselves and on the substance of the issue. And I therefore continue to maintain the standard interpretation

---

[16] See above footnote XX.
[17] Tromp's unpublished Observationes (10/2/63). Tromp then gives a long list of Popes upholding the position. For this see Alexandra von Teuffenbach, Die Bedeutung des *Subsistit in* (LG 8): Zum Selbstverständnis der Katholischen Kirche (München: Herbert Utz Verlag, 2002), 309, footnote 93.
[18] Becker, 13.
[19] Ibid, 14.

of the facts available. And I cannot accept Becker's argument on the substantive issue. Becker asserts that to interpret 'subsists in' as implying any distinction between the Catholic Church and the Church of Christ would involve a 'weakening' of the identification between the two. 'Weakening' might have a strong sense and imply something like 'breaking' the identification, and that would be wrong. It could also mean something more like 'qualifying' or 'correcting,' and that is indeed what most of us hold. There is an identity which must be upheld, but there is a *total* identification which must be qualified! Pope Pius XII did indeed claim the *total* identity of the Church of Christ and the Catholic Church, and I continue to believe that the teaching of the Second Vatican Council marks the abandonment of that claim. The Catholic Church, however, continues to claim her *real* identity with the Church of Christ, but she now recognises that the identity is not *total*. The fact that elements of the Church of Christ exist outside the Catholic Church implies as much, and that is the fact of the matter. What the Catholic Church has always claimed and continues to claim is that she is the one true Church. I had an occasion to clarify these matters some time ago,[20] and I quote the key paragraph from those earlier writings.

> Notice that the council chose not to say that 'The Church of Christ is the Catholic Church'. It did not reject the formula; 'The Catholic Church is the Church of Christ' which is a different thing entirely. In the first case the goal is definition. Where is the Church of Christ to be found? Is it exhausted by what we can see of the Catholic Church? We are now clear that it is not, that the Church of Christ 'subsists in' the Catholic Church and elements of Christ's Church are to be found outside it. The second formula is answering a question about the Catholic Church. Is it the true Church of Christ? And the answer is; Yes, it is. The

---

[20] "The Catholic Church's Claim," <u>Doctrine and Life</u> 38 (1988), 421-27 and "Does the Catholic Church claim to be 'the one true church'?" <u>The Furrow</u> 39 (1988), 666-68.

Catholic Church does not exhaust the reality of Christ's Church, but it *is* His Church. The context is the reality of divided Christendom and the existence of the different Christian communities making their several claims to allegiance. Which is true? Is any one of them true, or are they all simply parts of a larger reality which has to be called the Church of Christ? Can any one of them truly claim to be the Church Christ founded? The Catholic Church does make that claim, and the simplest and most unambiguous formulation of it is simply to say that the Catholic Church is 'the one true Church'.[21]

The Congregation spells out the identification of the Church of Christ and the Catholic Church in the response to the previous question in the list. The document first of all affirms that 'Christ "established here on earth" only one Church and instituted it as a "visible and spiritual community", that from its beginning and throughout the centuries has always existed and will always exist, and in which alone are found all the elements that Christ himself instituted.' It states further: 'This Church, constituted and organised in this world as a society, subsists in the Catholic Church, governed by the successor of Peter and the Bishops in communion with him.' It then concludes: 'In number 8 of the Dogmatic Constitution *Lumen gentium* 'subsistence' means this perduring, historical continuity and the permanence of all the elements instituted by Christ in the Catholic Church, in which the Church of Christ is concretely found on this earth.' This is the identification between the Church of Christ and the Catholic Church which the Church has always claimed and must continue to claim always.

There is no doubting the fact that we Roman Catholic theologians have a real difficulty in making any distinction between the Church of Christ and the Catholic Church, and the closer one is to the Holy See the more difficult it seems to be. Congar has registered a heartfelt complaint in this regard in the privacy of his journal. Writing in 1954,

---

[21] "Does the Catholic Church claim to be 'the one true church'?", 667.

when his work was under criticism by the Roman authorities, he had this to say on his disagreements with his Roman critics:

> ... to limit myself to the essentials, profound disagreement about the assessment of the Reformation, of the person of Luther, and of a profound blindness, considering the profound spiritual motives of it all and accepting the smallest putting into question. On the contrary, the affirmation of the complete justice of Rome and the historical Church. And this is absolutely false and unacceptable. Rome has refused every putting into question, every occasion for an examination of conscience, and has enclosed itself in a fabric, patiently woven over the centuries, of its own self-justification, its own glorification, of a totalitarian affirmation of its own absolute authority. On all these points, my disagreement is profound. It has been developed bit by bit, nourishing itself in me with every acquisition of truth and the knowledge of the historical or objective reality of things.[22]

These comments are not on the precise point of the identity of the Church of Christ and the Catholic Church, but I suggest that the identity of the Catholic Church with the Church of Christ is the fundamental intuition underpinning the exalted self-opinion of the Roman Catholic Church.

It is in this context that I must dispute Fr Becker's claim that the Catholic Church has always claimed a *full* identification with the Church of Christ, taking this to mean that there can be no real distinction between the two. I submit that the Catholic Church has never claimed to exhaust the reality of the Church of Christ. I offer in support of this submission a piece of evidence concerning the genuine interpretation of the traditional formula that 'Outside the Church there

---

[22] Congar, Journal d'un théologien, 304.

is no salvation.' This formula can be applied strictly, literally and fully to the Holy Church of Christ which embraces the whole reality of salvation wherever it is to be found. It cannot, on the other hand, be applied in the same way to the concrete Catholic Church, and the first Catholic theologian who made that *full* identification, Fr. Leonard Feeney, S.J., was condemned as a heretic for doing so in 1949.

With these points in mind we return to the declaration of the Congregation for the Doctrine of the Faith, that there is a *full* identity between the Church of Christ and the Catholic Church, and that the change from 'is' to 'subsists in' is no real change at all. I have already said enough to indicate that I cannot accept the Congregation's assertion of full synonymity of 'is' and 'subsists in' or the full identity of the teaching of *Mysitici orporis* and *Lumen gentium*, but I make one last effort to tackle the issue of the *full* identity of the Church of Christ, the Holy Church, and the Catholic Church. The affirmation of a *full* identity can only be achieved at a price in one or other of two directions. In one direction the mystery and the divinity of the Holy Church have to be qualified to fit the confines of the concrete reality of the Catholic Church and we have seen how that process has been part of the experience of the Western Church for more than a thousand years. The alternative, in the other direction is to exalt the concrete Catholic Church to aspire to the glories of the mystery of the Body of Christ, and that leads to the triumphalism so roundly condemned at the Council. It is my firm conviction that neither of these alternatives is acceptable and that the *full* identity must be denied. There must be recognised a distinction without separation between the Holy Church and the Catholic Church, a *real* identity between the two which is not a *full* identity. As the matter is formulated in *Lumen gentium* § 8, the Holy Church and the Catholic Church must not be thought of as two distinct realities, but as forming one complex reality such that the Holy Church organised on earth as an institution subsists in the Catholic Church. It is clear, therefore, that I cannot accept the position enunciated by the Congregation for the Doctrine of the Faith on this matter. The thesis being developed here is geared precisely to explain a situation like this, where a member of the Church is convinced that an official teaching of the Catholic Church, such as this assertion of a *full* identity between the Church of Christ and the Catholic Church by the Congregation for the Doctrine of the Faith, is not, in fact, the genuine teaching of the Church of Christ. There is logic in the fact that there should be a difference of opinon on this point, for this very doctrine of the distinction without separation between the Holy Church and the Catholic Church is the foundation on which the thesis will ultimately rest. Whether the thesis stands or falls, of course, only time and the judgment of the Church will tell.

Chapter 9

The Magisterium of the Holy Church

The last five chapters have been an effort to make the distinction between the Holy Church and the Catholic Church, without falling into the separation of the two which was the mistake made by Wyclif and Hus, and notably by Luther. I have stated my case that the doctrine of *Lumen gentium* § 8, that the Holy Church subsists in the Catholic Church, provides the formula which ensures that the very real danger of separation is avoided when the distinction between the Holy Church and the concrete Catholic Church is clearly made. A further test of the success of the effort will be provided by the next step, which is to work out what the implications of the distinction are for the process of teaching in the Church. The crisis we are currently facing focusses on the teaching authority of the bishops in the Church, and in a special way on the ordinary magisterium of the Pope. In order to resolve the difficulty it is necessary to have a clear idea of the deeper reality which is the ordinary magisterium of the Holy Church, and then to make the connection with the process of episcopal teaching where the problems arise in practice. Placing the teaching role of the bishops in context means bringing out, first of all, the primordial role of the teaching of God in the Church and then, secondly, clarifying the role of the whole Church, clergy and laity, the *ecclesia universalis*. When those two preliminary points are covered, the role of the bishops can be tackled.

Ultimately all the teaching in the Church is done by the divine persons. Christ our Lord continues his role as teacher from his place at the right hand of the Father, and the Holy Spirit teaches the Church from within the hearts of believers, and together they teach everything that is taught in the Church. In St Matthew's Gospel Our Lord says: 'Neither be called teachers, for you have one teacher, the Christ.' (Matt 23:10). And this text was taken traditionally, not as a rhetorical exuberance, but as describing the reality of the situation. St. Augustine quotes Matt 23:10 and says that 'the one who teaches hearts has his chair in heaven.'[1] And again: 'We have one teacher, whose school is on earth and his chair in heaven.'[2] The doctrine was admirably expressed in the first schema of the document of the Church presented at the Second Vatican Council: 'Christ the Lord himself, existing always in heaven as Head of his mystical body, illuminates the whole Church, sending the Spirit of truth which he promised into all its members, into the pastors that they might teach, into the faithful that they might accept and properly understand the word of God.'[3]

The basic texts describing the role of the Holy Spirit are those in St John. 'The Helper, the Holy Spirit, whom the Father will send in my name, he will teach you all things and bring to your remembrance all that I have said to you.' (John 14:26) 'When the Spirit of truth comes, he will guide you into all the truth' (John 16:13) 'You have been anointed by the Holy One, and you all have knowledge. ... The anointing that you received from him abides in you, and you have no need that anyone should teach you. His anointing teaches you about everything- and is true and is no lie...' (1 John 2:20, 27) On this basis, Catholic theologians have constantly referred to the inspiration of the

---

[1] In epistolam Joannis ad Parthos, Tractatus IV, caput II, § 13. (PL 35, 2004.)
[2] Sermo 292, In Natali Joannis Baptistae (PL 38, 1319.)
[3] De Ecclesia (Schema propositum a Commissione Theologica), Caput VII: De Ecclesiae magisterio; Acta et documenta Concilio Oecumenico Vaticano II apparando, Series II (Praeparatoria), Volumen II (Acta pontificiae commissionis centralis praeparatoriae Concilii Oecumenicic Vaticani II), Pars IV (Sessio septima: 12-19 Iunii 1962) (Typis polyglottis Vaticanis, MCMLXVIII). (AP II-II, pars IV.), 622.

Church by the Holy Spirit. He inspired the councils, the Fathers, the popes, or anyone else involved in deciding rules of belief and conduct in the Church. 'This conviction is one of the most certain and unanimous to be found in the course of history, both of the East and of the West.'[4] Beginning with the Council of Jerusalem, 'For it has seemed good to the Holy Spirit and to us' (Acts 15:28), the councils of the Church have ever been convinced of the presence of the Holy Spirit. The Second Council of Nicaea (787) introduced its definition of the veneration to be paid to images with this declaration: 'Following as it were the king's highway and the divinely inspired teaching of our holy Fathers and the tradition of the Catholic Church - because we know it derives from the Holy Spirit, who has his dwelling in the Church ...' (DS 600). And the Council of Trent continually refers to the indwelling of the Holy Spirit in the Church as a guide in establishing the authority of traditions. 'Any legitimate council is *in Spiritu Sancto congregata*, and any dogmatic statement is made with the benefit of the assistance of the Holy Spirit who inhabits, directs, guards and instructs the Church.'[5] At the Council of Trent, Cardinal Cervini, one of the Presidents, spoke of the three foundations of our faith. The first two are Scripture and the Gospel spoken by Our Lord,. And he goes on: 'Thirdly, since the Son of God was not to remain always physically among us, he sent the Holy Spirit, who is to reveal the mysteries of God in the hearts of the faithful and daily, until the end of time, instruct the Church in all truth and settle all doubts that may arise in the minds of men.'[6] All this implies that '[t]he time of the Church and the time of the prophets and the apostles cannot be put in opposition to one another; they cannot even be dissociated, since the principle operating in both is the same: the Holy Spirit.'[7] This direct and immediate action of God in the Church is the foundation of her infallibility. Cardinal Manning, commenting on 1 Jn 2:20-27, made the point well when he wrote:

---

[4] Congar, Tradition and Traditions, 169.
[5] Ibid, 172.
[6] CT V, 1, 11.24-27.
[7] Congar, Tradition and Traditions, 169.

> I do not know in what words the infallibility of the Church and the immutability of its doctrines can be more amply affirmed. For they declare – that by virtue of the perpetual presence of this unction which is the Holy Ghost, the Church possesses the whole revelation of God; that it is preserved by Divine assistance, unmixed, and in all its purity; and, that it is enunciated perpetually through the same guidance by a voice that cannot lie.[8]

On this foundation of the teaching of Christ from heaven and the Holy Spirit teaching the hearts of the faithful, the Church teaches the full Gospel truth always and everywhere. St Irenaeus expressed this point well: 'Having received this preaching and this faith, the Church, though dispersed throughout the whole world, guards them diligently, as if occupying but one house, and believes them just as if she had but one soul, and one and the same heart, and she proclaims them, and teaches them, and hands them down, with perfect harmony, as if she possessed only one mouth.'[9] And St Cyril of Jerusalem said the same: 'The Church, Catholic or universal, gets her name from the fact that she is scattered through the whole world from one end of earth to the other, and also because she teaches universally and without omission all the doctrines which are to be made known to mankind ...'[10] Of more modern theologians, again the best expression I could find was in Cardinal Manning: 'And the mind and voice of the Church are supernatural. I mean the world-wide and continuous intelligence of the Church of all nations and in all ages, which testifies as a witness both natural and supernatural, to the facts of the Incarnation and of Pentecost; and decides as a judge with a supernatural discernment, and enunciates the whole revelation of God as a teacher having authority

---

[8] Manning, The Temporal Mission of the Holy Ghost, 217-18.

[9] Adversus Haereseos I, 10, 2; SC ?, 158.24-31. (English translation helped by ANF, 330.)

[10] Cat. 18, 23; PG 33, 1044A. English translation from Office of Readings, Wednesday Week 17, The Divine Office, Volume 3, 361.

because of the divine illumination, the divine certainty, and the divine assistance which abides with it.'[11] This conviction that the full truth is proclaimed always and everywhere is expressed in the liturgy in the *Rite of Ordination of a Bishop*: 'Are you resolved to maintain the deposit of faith, entire and incorrupt, as handed down by the apostles and professed by the Church everywhere and at all times?'[12] How can it be that the Church proclaims the whole of the Word of God always and everywhere? There is a mystery of faith involved here, and some effort will have to be made in due course to deal with the modalities of teaching in the Church. But, for now, it will suffice to notice the foundation of the hearing of the Word in the Church which is the indwelling of the Holy Spirit.

It is the teaching of the Council of Orange, repeated by the Council of Trent, that our justification takes place 'by the illumination and inspiration of the Holy Spirit'.[13] And the illumination and inspiration of the Holy Spirit is just as much required in maintaining faith in the heart of a Christian as it is in creating it in the first place.[14] St Thomas taught that the work of the Holy Spirit within is the more important part of the divine activity leading to faith. The public ministry of Jesus, his preaching, teaching, and miracles, and the activity of the Church which continues his work, are all essential in inducing faith in believers. But even more important is the action of the Holy Spirit in the depths of the human soul inducing a new internal and spontaneous inclination towards faith and the supernatural life of grace.[15] The implications of this for the process of believing and teaching in the Church have been well brought out by Hans Urs von Balthasar:

---

[11] Manning, The Temporal Mission of the Holy Ghost), 222.
[12] Rite of Ordination of a Bishop: Examination of the Candidate.
[13] Canon 7, DS 377. See also Canon 4, DS 374 and Canon 6, DS 376. Trent, Decree on Justification, Chapter 5, DS 1525 and Canon 3, DS 1553.
[14] St Thomas, ST 2-2 q. 4, a. 4 ad 3m.
[15] Juan Alfaro, S.J., 'Supernaturalitas fidei iuxta S. Thomas; I. Functio 'Luminis fidei',' Gregorianum 54 (1963) 501-42; 'II. Functio 'Interioris instinctus',' 731-87. at 755 and 781-82.

> As the Spirit 'receives' the Word, so, and no otherwise, in just that form, with that shape, with that emphasis, he causes it to be written for the Church. And since that which he has heard in truth is infinitely richer and deeper than what can be composed in a body made of letters, he has also undertaken, as the Spirit, to explain to the Church that which he has heard, in the Church's *tradition*. Because letter cannot of its very nature be the same thing as spirit, and because what is written is necessarily fragmentary (Jn 20:30; 21:25), the Church is the interpreter of what has already been uttered in revelation, but is continually being illuminated in new ways as the meditation of the Church, guided by the Holy Spirit, presents it to the light of conscious faith. Ultimately, the continuity of this interpretation does not reside in the human consciousness of believers or of the Church, but in the Holy Spirit.[16]

This continuing presence and action of the Holy Spirit is at the root of the sense of the faith of the people which is the foundation of the infallibility of the Church in believing, according to *Lumen Gentium*, § 12: 'The body of the faithful as a whole, anointed as they are by the Holy One (cf. 1 Jn. 2:20, 27), cannot err in matters of belief. Thanks to a supernatural sense of the faith which characterises the People as a whole, it manifests this unerring quality when, "from the bishops down to the last member of the laity," it shows universal agreement in matters of faith and morals.' The sense of the faith appears under different terms throughout the documents of the Council[17], and has been well described as follows:

---

[16] Hans Urs von Balthasar, A Theology of History (London / New York: Sheed and Ward, 1963), 101.
[17] Sensus fidei, LG 12; PO 9. Sensus catholicus, AA 30. Sensus christianus fidelium, GS 52. Sensus christianus, GS 62. Sensus religiosus, NA 2; DH 4; GS 59. Sensus Christi et Ecclesiae, AG 19. Instinctus, SC 24; PC 12; GS 18.

> The believer is grafted into Christ like a shoot into the vine, and thus shares in Christ's thoughts (*nous*, 1 Cor. 2:16) and sentiments (*ennoia*, 1 Pet. 4:1), and all this entails a structure of beliefs, opinions, affective attractions, and behavioral tendencies that he considers valid because it is testified to by the Spirit as a requirement and way of following Christ. When the believer meets outside elements or doctrines, he measures them against this interior picture, and 'judges' them (1 Cor. 2:15) with a spontaneous, intuitive, and analytical judgment, brought about and accompanied by strong affective elements, as a necessity for the life of faith, or as reconcilable with faith or irreconcilable with it.[18]

It is brought about by the presence and action of the Holy Spirit and is part of the set of habits of intellect and will which constitute the reality of sanctifying grace, whereby we participate in the knowledge of God Himself. St. John of the Cross speaks of it.

> There is no need to wonder that the soul should be capable of aught so high; for since God grants her the favour of attaining to be deiform and united in the Most Holy Trinity, wherein she becomes God by participation, how is it a thing incredible that she should perform her work of understanding, knowledge and love in the Trinity, together with it, like the Trinity itself, by a mode of participation, which God effects in the soul herself?[19]

---

[18] Zoltán Alszeghy, S.J., 'The Sensus Fidei and the Development of Dogma,' in René Latourelle ed., Vatican II: Assessment and Perspecives, Volume One (New York/ Mahwah: Paulist Press, 1988), 138-156, at 147.

[19] A reading from The Spiritual Canticle of St John of the Cross, Second Reading, Friday Week 18, The Divine Office?, Volume 3, 397-398.

This sense of the faith is the subjective correlative of the indwelling of the Holy Spirit in the Church and in the individual soul. It constitutes the inner light which illuminates every object of investigation in the area of faith and morals. Newman speaks of it as 'a certain ethical character, one and the same, a system of first principles, sentiments and tastes, a mode of viewing the question and of arguing, which is formally and normally, naturally and divinely, the *organum investigandi* given to us for gaining religious truth …'[20] The teaching of the Holy Church takes this form, with Christ, the One Teacher, acting from his seat in heaven, and the Holy Spirit at work in the hearts of believers, inspiring the intellectual gifts which ensure that the word of the Father is heard always and everywhere.

The Whole Church (*Ecclesia universalis*)

While giving priority to the role of the divine persons in the process of teaching in the Holy Church, it also needs to be brought out that, on the human level, it is the *whole* Church, clergy and laity together, which is the appropriate organ of teaching. Our ultimate goal in this argument is to conceive properly the role of the bishops in teaching in the Church, and to do that we must first of all establish the role of the whole Church, the *Ecclesia universalis*, in teaching, within which alone the specific role of the bishops can be properly understood. Congar makes the basic point here, when he writes: 'If there is one truth which is universally affirmed from Antiquity to Vatican II, it is that the faith and tradition are carried by the whole Church, that the universal Church is the only adequate subject, under the sovereignty of the Spirit who has been promised to her and dwells within her: *Ecclesia universalis non*

---

[20] John Henry Newman, A Grammar of Assent (Notre Dame/London: University of Notre Dame Press, 1979), 386.

potest errare.[21] Part of the renewal in theology in the early part of the twentieth century was a reaction against and one-sided emphasis on the role of the clergy in the Church, and an effort to re-empower the laity in their essential ecclesial role. This movement bore its fruit at the Second Vatican Council, and the point is well accepted in the Church, but it is good to review the key points briefly here.

Congar give a good summary of the Scriptural teaching:

> The Old Testament heraldings of a new dispensation in the messianic age are so many promises of knowledge and inwardness addressed to the new people as a whole.[22] ... The Lord repeated these promises to the apostles with an eye to the whole Church: cf. John 14:16-17, 25-26; 14:13-14; 17:26. And see what apostolic testimony says about their fulfilment. ... The faithful are established in light and are themselves a light (John 3:19, etc.). All know the things of faith (1 John 2:20, 27, etc.); all are taught by God (1 Thess 4:9, etc.); all drink of one Spirit (1 Cor 12:13); all have received the gifts of understanding and wisdom abundantly (ibid. 1:4-5, etc.). They must be children in faith, but grown men in understanding (Eph 4:14, etc.); and again it is St. Paul who wants all to be filled with knowledge (Coll 1:4-9, etc.) ... the faithful recognize Christ's voice (John 10:4; 1 John 4:6), they discern Christ and antichrist (1 John 2:18-27; 4:1-6), they have the capacity to make a judgement (1 Cor 2:10-16, etc.).[23]

---

[21] Cardinal Yves Congar, Église et Papauté (Paris: Cerf, 2002), 241. Walter (later Cardinal) Kasper makes the same point: 'It is a universal Christian conviction, to be found in the medieval and the Reformed tradition, that the ecclesia universalis cannot err in faith.' Theologie und Kirche (Mainz: Grünewald, 1987), 56.

[22] Congar, Lay People in the Church, 272, with abundant Scripture references.

[23] Ibid, 273.

And further scriptural evidence is available. St. Paul is confident that Christians in general are filled with 'all knowledge,' (Rom 15:14; 1 Cor 1:4) and that they are 'able to instruct one another.' (Rom 15:14) And he is speaking of us all when he writes that 'we have the mind of Christ.' (1 Cor 2:16). He is writing to the whole Church at Corinth when he instructs them to 'maintain the traditions even as I delivered them to you.' (1 Cor 11:2) It is 'all the saints' who comprehend 'what is the breadth and length and height and depth,' (Eph 3:18) He prays for the Colossians that they would 'reach all the riches of full assurance of understanding and the knowledge of God's mystery, which is Christ' (Coll 2:2). That they would 'Let the word of Christ dwell in you richly, teaching and admonishing one another in all wisdom' (Coll 3:16). The Thessalonians are told to 'stand firm and hold to the traditions that you were taught by us,' (2 Thess 2:15) St. Peter also recognizes that Christians know the truth of the Gospel: 'Therefore I intend always to remind you of these qualities, though you know them and are established in the truth that you have.' (2 Peter 1:12) And St. John: 'But you have been anointed by the Holy One, and you all have knowledge. I write to you, not because you do not know the truth, but because you know it, (1 John 2:20-21) ... But the anointing that you received from him abides in you, and you have no need that anyone should teach you. But as his anointing teaches you about everything- and is true and is no lie, just as it has taught you- abide in him.' (1 John 2:27).[24]

This role of the whole Church in the three messianic functions of teaching, worship and ruling was a major theme of the Second Vatican Council. Chapter 2 of *Lumen gentium*, on the People of God, was introduced to emphasise the priority of the whole Church in fulfilling the mission given by the Lord, and the point in regard to teaching is made explicitly in two places. The infallibility of the Church in

---

[24] More on this can be found in Bertulf van Leeuwen, O. F. M., 'La participation universelle à la fonction prophétique du Christ » in L'Église de Vatican II, ed. G. Baraúna, O. F. M and Y. M.-J. Congar, O., vol. 2 (Paris: Cerf, 1966), 425-55. Fondement biblique 429-40. Jer 31 :31-34 ; 1 Jn 2 :18-27, 4:1ff ; 2 Cor 1 :21-22 ; Heb 6:4, 8 :11 ; John 6 :45, 10:4 ; 1 Thess 4:9; 1 Cor 1:5, 2:10ff, 12:13; Eph 1:8; Coll 1:9; Acts 2.

believing is desribed in *Lumen gentium* 12: 'The universal body of the faithful who have an anointing from the Holy One (cf. 1 Jn 2:20, 27) cannot err in believing, and manifests this special quality through the supernatural sense of the faith of the whole people when "from the bishops to the last of the faithful laity" it manifests its universal consensus in matters of faith and morals. By this sense of the faith, which is aroused and sustained by the Spirit of truth, the people of God, under the guidance of the Sacred Magisterium, which it faithfully obeys, accepts not the word of men but truly the word of God (cf. 1 Th 2:13); it adheres indefectibly to "the faith once delivered to the saints" (Jude 3), penetrates it more deeply with right judgement and applies it more fully to life.' Some bishops wanted more to be said about the sense of faith in this text, but the request was refused, and the official relation explains that the text already suffices since it gives an objective analysis of the sense of faith: 'It is, as it were, a faculty of the *whole* Church, by which she perceives in faith the revelation given, discerning between true and false in the things of faith, and at the same time enters into it more deeply and applies it more fully in life.'[25] And in *Dei Verbum* 10 we are told: 'Sacred Tradition and Sacred Scripture constitute a single sacred deposit of the word of God entrusted to the Church. Adhering to it, the entire holy people, united with its pastors, perseveres perpetually in the teaching and communion of the apostles, in the breaking of the bread and the prayers, so that in holding to, practicing and professing the faith handed down, there is brought about a marvellous harmony of Bishops and faithful.' (DV 10) The Relator for this text, Archbishop Florit, emphasised the role of the whole Church in his remarks: 'Since the revealed deposit is a divine gift made to the *whole* Church, it is to the *whole* Church, therefore, that the task falls to conserve it, to enter into it, and to transmit it to every generation.'[26] In the preparation of both these texts the Council rejected earlier drafts structured on a descending hierarchical model: 'God – Christ – Peter and the apostles – the Pope and the bishops – the clergy – the laity', deliberately choosing

---

[25] AS III/I, 199 (Italics in the original.)
[26] AS III/3, 139 (Italics mine.)

to make clear how the messianic functions of prophet and priest are related to all members of the Church, including the ordained, before the modes of the messianic functions proper to the clergy are dealt with.[27] Some of the strongest statements in this line are to found in the chapter on the laity, and what is said there applies to any member of the Church who is not a bishop, whether priest, deacon or religious. *Lumen gentium*, § 35 says: 'Christ ... fulfils his prophetic office, not only by the hierarchy ... but also by the laity, whom he therefore constitutes as witnesses and instructs by the sense of faith and grace of the word, so that the power of the gospel may shine in daily life, in the family and in society.' And *Lumen gentium*, § 37 asserts their right to speak out on matters of concern to them. 'By reason of their knowledge, competence and excellence, the laity have the right, and even sometimes the duty, to manifest their opinion on matters which concern the good of the Church.' This conciliar teaching is now fully accepted doctrine in the Church. In his first encyclical, *Redemptor hominis*, Pope John Paul II summarised this teaching on the various roles that all the members of the Church are called on to play.

> In the light of the sacred teaching of the Second Vatican Council, the Church thus appears before us as the social subject of responsibility for divine truth. ... The sharing in the prophetic office of Christ himself shapes the life of the whole of the Church in her fundamental dimension. A particular share in this office belongs to the Pastors of the Church, who teach and continually and in various ways proclaim and transmit the doctrine concerning the Christian faith and morals. ... Catechesis certainly constitutes a permanent and also fundamental form of activity by the Church, one in which her prophetic charism is manifested: witnessing and teaching go hand in hand. ... Linked with this fact,

---

[27] Robert Murray, S. J., 'The human capacity for God, and God's initiative,' in <u>Commentary on the Catechism of the Catholic Church</u>, ed. Michael J. Walsh (London: Geoffrey Chapman, 1994), 6-33 at 11-12.

the Church's responsibility for divine truth must be increasingly shared in various ways by all. ... mentions different experts ... As members of the People of God, they all have their own part to play in Christ's prophetic mission and service of divine truth ...[28]

The doctrine is well summed up, yet again by Congar: 'It is the whole Church, believing, loving, penitent and praying, but also teaching, assisted in order that it may teach and, when necessary, define the revealed truth. So there is only one fully adequate "order" where tradition can be known or known for what it is as forming part of the economy of revelation, and that order is the faith of the Church, an organic body, the communion of the faithful and the hierarchy.'[29] And lest there be any misunderstanding, it should be made clear that in highlighting the role of the rest of the Church, there is no intention of denying the essential role of the bishops. As Schillebeeckx put it: 'The subject of the Church's active tradition is certainly the whole of the Church's believing community, but this according to its inner, hierarchical structure.'[30]

The Whole Church Teaching with the Liturgy at the Centre

How does the whole Church teach, and how does the teaching role of the bishops fit within that totality? Cardinal Newman gave one of his broad views of the whole situation.

> I think I am right in saying that the tradition of the Apostles, committed to the whole Church in its various constituents and functions *per modum unius*,

---

[28] Redemptor hominis, § 19.
[29] Congar, Tradition and Traditions, 219.
[30] Edward Schillebeeckx, O., Revelation and Theology (London and Melbourne: Sheed and Ward, 1967), 90.

manifests itself variously at various times: sometimes by the mouth of the episcopacy, sometimes by the doctors, sometimes by the people, sometimes by liturgies, rites, ceremonies, and customs, by events, disputes, movements, and all those other phenomena which are comprised under the name of history. It follows that none of these channels of tradition may be treated with disrespect; granting at the same time fully, that the gift of discerning, discriminating, defining, promulgating, and enforcing any portion of that tradition resides in the *Ecclesia docens*.[31]

In one place, Congar gives a similar summary of the situation, comparing the ordinary manner of teaching with the extraordinary teaching of dogmatic definitions. 'The Church teaches in a variety of ways, by catechisms, preaching, the liturgy, ecclesiastical life and practice; and it is in this ordinary teaching that her thought is chiefly to be looked for. Solemn definitions were nearly always made in opposition to particular errors and put forward only one aspect, sometimes not even the deepest or most significant, of the truth.'[32] And in another place, he makes clear that at the centre of the whole complex of teaching in the Church, there stands the liturgy. He explained that 'the liturgy is a privileged custodian and dispenser of Tradition, for it is by far the principal and primary thing among all the actions of the Church. It is, indeed, the active celebration of the Christian mystery, and as it celebrates and contains the mystery in its fullness, it transmits all the essential elements of this mystery.'[33]

This fits well with the concept of the Church-mystery, the Holy Church. Christ is the one teacher, and in order to teach he is always present to his Church, especially in the liturgy (*Sacrosanctum concilium*, § 7). The teaching of *Sacrosanctum concilium*, § 10 applies to teaching

---

[31] On Consulting the Faithful in Matters of Doctrine, 1871 version, edited and introduced by John Coulson, Sheed and Ward, N. Y., 1961, 63.
[32] Congar, The Mystery of the Church), 92.
[33] Congar, Tradition and Traditions, 354.

as to every aspect of the Christian life: 'The liturgy is the apex towards which the action of the Church tends and at the same time the source from which all her power flows.' The Word of God has been formulated in definitive form in Sacred Scripture and this word is placed before the people continuously in the liturgy. The liturgy transmits the whole of the word of God, whereas only certain aspects 'have been formulated by our theological understanding and in dogmas.'[34] It is in living the faith and witnessing to it in the liturgy that the word lives in the Church. Congar again: 'Not the voice of the magisterium teaching, defining, reproving, condemning or refuting, but the voice of the loving, praying Church, doing more than merely expressing its faith: hymning it, practising it, in a living celebration, wherein too, it makes a complete self-giving. For this reason, the liturgy is assured of a character and a place without parallel as an instrument of tradition, as much because of its style or characteristic forms, as because of its content.'[35] The whole truth can be proclaimed in the liturgy in a way that is not possible in documents, because it also embodies the truth in symbol and action. In the liturgy we can even be witnessing to truth we do not understand! As Congar says: 'I have pointed out a number of times already that it is the special property of action, as also of symbols and rites, to embody the whole of a reality in a more complete way than the mind can grasp, even confusedly. Likewise, it is the special prerogative of the faithful carrying out of the Church's worship to be able to retain and pass on again its heritage, in its entirety, no matter how fragmentary may be our awareness of its actual content.'[36] And so Congar concludes: 'A large part of the Church's belief has become known to it through the holy living out of its faith, hope and love. Thus the liturgy is the privileged *locus* of Tradition, not only from the point of view of conservation and preservation, but also from that of progress and development.'[37] Dom Guéranger, in his *Institutions liturgiques*, also called the liturgy the principal instrument of the Church's tradition:

---

[34] Ibid, 355.
[35] Ibid, 427-28.
[36] Ibid, 433.
[37] Ibid, 429.

'It is in the liturgy that the Spirit who inspired the Scriptures still speaks to us; the liturgy is tradition itself, at its highest degree of power and solemnity.'[38] Archbishop Edelby speaking on the document on revelation at the Second Vatican Council made the same point: 'From this it is clear that Tradition, or the Church, in transmitting the riches of the economy of the Word, is essentially the liturgy.'[39] And Pope Pius XII, speaking to the congress on the Liturgy at Assisi in the early 1950s, said: 'the whole deposit of faith and the whole truth of Christ contained in the Scripture and in tradition is found in the liturgy.'[40]

Putting the liturgy first does not undermine the central role that must be accorded to Sacred Scripture. Scripture is a liturgical book, and the word it contains is proclaimed continuously in the liturgy. This point was also made by Archbishop Edelby: 'Sacred Scripture is a liturgical and prophetic reality. It is proclamation more than a written book. It is the witness of the Holy Spirit about Christ, whose special and privileged time is the celebration of the Eucharistic Liturgy.'[41] It is in the liturgy that the Scriptures are broken down and explained to the people on an on-going basis. The Second Vatican Council teaches that Sacred Scripture, together with Sacred Tradition, constitutes the supreme rule of faith. (DV 21.) It is an interesting formulation, affirming the central importance of Scripture as the rule of faith, but avoiding the *sola scriptura*. For its proper understanding, though, it requires us to get clear what exactly 'Sacred Scripture, together with Sacred Tradition' is. When the two are joined as one, what do we have? It seems to me that what we have is the Sacred Liturgy, and this it is which constitutes, in fact, the supreme rule of faith. The Bible is not a book, but a library of books. It is not any kind of a library of books, but is really a liturgical lectionary. Scripture has its true home in the liturgy. Not only is it in the liturgy that the Scriptures are proclaimed in the Church, but the whole of the liturgy is the Bible made real and

---

[38] Quoted in Ibid, 434-35.
[39] General Congregation 94, on 5 October 1964, Acta Synodalia III/III, 306.
[40] The Assisi Papers, 225, 233-234. The same ideas are expressed in the Allocution Vous Nous avez demandé, 22 September 1956; AAS 38 (1956), 713.
[41] General Congregation 94, on 5 October 1964, Acta Synodalia III/III, 306-307.

practical in the present day. All the sacraments and other liturgical actions are biblical events, and they are constituted principally from biblical sources. The language used and all the references come from the Bible. Tradition is principally liturgical tradition, and the primary role of the Bishops is to safeguard the liturgy. Even the teaching function of the Bishops is for the protection of the liturgy, for it is in the liturgy that the faith is professed and lived. All three poles of the living Word, Scripture, Tradition and Magisterium come together to constitute the Liturgy, and the Liturgy stands as the supreme and living rule of faith. It is not being suggested that the liturgy is indefectible in all its forms. The massive reform of the Catholic liturgy in the wake of the Second Vatican Council gives the lie to such a notion. However, the liturgy contains the whole word of God, in word and in action. It is not perfectly formulated in all its details but, in principle, everything is there. And there is no Christian life without active participation in the liturgy, so that every Christian has access on a continual basis to the whole word of God in the liturgy. In a fundamental way, in the power of the Holy Spirit, Christ guarantees that 'the Gospel is properly taught and the sacraments are rightly administered' in the Catholic liturgy, and it is in the liturgy that the full truth of the Gospel is proclaimed always and everywhere.

In the liturgy the word of God comes alive in such a way that it is not inappropriate to see what is happening there as, in a certain sense, revelation taking place there as an event in the present, and this is implied in the liturgical use of biblical texts. In the liturgy, they are taken out of their historical setting and divorced from their strictly exegetical meaning so that they may have contemporary relevance as God's revelation and communication of himself. Congar recalls that St. Bernard justified this use of the Bible by insisting that the Bride of Christ enjoyed the Spirit of Christ. He concedes that the disadvantage of Thomas Aquinas' more precise use of the term 'revelation' was that it came to be seen as a completed event which had simply to be interpreted and elaborated by theologians, and states that theologians and the Magisterium state now as in the past that the Holy Spirit is active in the Church, enlightening and guiding it, in accordance with the Lord's promise.[42] As he says, in another place:

> Alongside God's revelatory action and intervention in Scripture there exists another action and intervention, namely, God's communication of the meaning of Scripture and its content to men, by his Spirit. This action is sometimes called 'inspiration', or even 'revelation, disclosure' in the wider sense of the term, ... and sometimes 'the Gospel in the heart'. The active subject is God, through his Holy Spirit, and the beneficiaries of this activity are the souls of the individual faithful or the Church.[43]

Neither is there any suggestion that the liturgy stands in any way in opposition to the overall authority of the bishops in the Church. The role of the liturgy in the proclamation of the faith was discussed by Pope Pius XII in the encyclical *Mediator Dei*. The fundamental principle was recognised, that 'the entire liturgy ... has the Catholic faith for its content, inasmuch as it bears public witness to the faith of the Church.'[44] But the liturgy, like Scripture, needs to be interpreted, and it is clear that 'the sacred liturgy ... does not decide or determine independently and of itself what is of Catholic faith,' for it is 'subject ... to the supreme teaching authority of the Church.'[45] The supreme teaching authority of the Church must be upheld inviolate. That is not in question. The last word always falls to the College of Bishops. But the large body of teaching in the Church, day by day, over the centuries is not carried on by the Bishops issuing statements, but in the living liturgy and the regular catechesis associated with it. The priority of the liturgy over magisterial pronouncements was accepted by Pope Pius XI,

---

[42] Yves M. J. Congar, I Believe in the Holy Spirit, Volume 2 (London/New York: Geoffrey Chapman/The Seabury Press, 1983), 30.
[43] Congar, Tradition and Traditions, 504.
[44] Mediator Dei, § 47.
[45] Ibid, § 48.

in the encyclical *Quas primas* establishing the feast of Christ the King: 'People are instructed in the truths of faith, and brought to appreciate the inner joys of religion far more effectually by the annual celebration of our sacred mysteries than by any official pronouncements of the teaching of the Church. Such pronouncements usually reach only a few and the more learned among the faithful; feasts reach them all; the former speak but once, the latter speak every year - in fact, forever.'[46]

Gathered around the liturgy there is a range of people who fulfill teaching functions in the Church, all of which are preparatory to the liturgy. There are the initial preachers of the Gospel who establish churches. There are teachers of theology who prepare the ministers who will celebrate the liturgy. There are the catechists who prepare Christians for their participation in the liturgy. There are parents who prepare their children for participation in the liturgy. And overseeing all of this teaching there are the bishops. In the present context, it is essential to make clear that the bishops are not the only teachers in the Church, they are not necessarily the first teachers. Christ our Lord did entrust his truth to the Apostles and he sent them out to preach the gospel to all the nations. However, that short summary does not at all give a complete picture of what happened. And if that incomplete picture is mistakenly taken for the whole, it becomes a serious distortion. Christ began his mission by preaching the gospel to all in the towns and villages of Galilee. He had gathered many disciples before he chose the Twelve, and on Pentecost day when the Holy Spirit came down on the assembly, no one there had learned the truth from the Apostles, but from the Lord himself. And the early preaching of the Gospel was not done by the Apostles alone. One writer has made a useful list of all the different communicators of the message mentioned in the New Testament.

> A fairly comprehensive inventory can be made from the frequent lists of gifts, ministries, and offices

---

[46] Pope Pius XI, Quas Primas, December 11, 1925, AAS 17 (1925), 603. (Eng. Trans. Claudia Carlen IHM, The Papal Encyclicals, 1903-1939 (The Pierian Press, 1990), 275.)

in the New Testament. Thus, Ephesians (4:11) mentions apostles, prophets, evangelizers, ... pastors, and teachers. Other lists and supplementary passages enable us to add the following: speakers, ecstatics and their interpreters, discerners (1 Cor. 12:8-10), administrators (deacons), leaders (Rom. 12:7-8), catechists (Gal. 6:6), counsellors (1 Thess. 5:12), sages (Mt. 23:34), witnesses (Acts 1:22 and passim), and heralds (1 Tim. 2:7; 2 Tim. 1:11).[47]

And the early Church had no difficulty in recognising a multiplicity of teaching roles in the Church. St Irenaeus wrote: 'For in the Church,' it is said, 'God hath set apostles, prophets, teachers, (1 Cor 12:28) and all the other means through which the Spirit works.'[48] This broader picture of the relationship between Christ and the Church holds to this day. Christ our Lord speaks most directly to those whom he calls in the liturgy, and the extra-liturgical teaching is carried on by a variety of ministers. Bishop Dupanloup of Orleans gave a short summary in a speech he made on *Dei Filius*: 'The magisterium by which the faithful are taught, the ordinary magisterium, is exercised in the Catholic Church, under the universal authority of the Supreme Pontiff, by pastors and doctors, by bishops and parish priests, by preachers of the divine word, by orthodox theologians, by approved books, but mainly by liturgical and catechetical books.'[49] The fact of the matter is that the vast majority of Catholics never meet a Bishop until the day of their confirmation, and then never after. And only a very few of them read the more serious episcopal statements. The oversight by the Bishops of the liturgy and preaching of the Church is caricatured by the 'one-sided' picture with which we are familiar. The Bishops have a key role in the Church, but it is limited in important ways. Most importantly, from the point of view of the topic being discussed here, the preaching and teaching of the Bishops is not the only, or even the principal, channel

---

[47] Frederick E. Crowe, S.J., Theology of the Christian Word: A Study in History (New York, N.Y./Ramsey, N.J./Toronto: Paulist Press, 1978), 11.
[48] AH, III, 24, 1, Ante-Nicene Fathers, 458.
[49] Mansi 51, 229D.

of communication of truth to the Christian. The central channel is the liturgy, where Christ our Lord speaks directly to his people.

The co-ordinated assimilation of the Word of God by the whole Church, hierarchically constituted, is clearly to be seen in the liturgy. All the ordained, priests and deacons as well as bishops, have the function of teaching in the Church by divine right, which they fulfil in the liturgy. And the people exercise their active function of receiving the word by the manner in which they listen and accept it. An Orthodox theologian has written of this: 'The Holy Spirit rests on the entire Church. The ministry of the celebrant is preaching and teaching. The ministry of the people of God is in accepting this teaching. But both these ministries are of the Holy Spirit, both are accomplished by him and in him. One can neither accept nor proclaim the truth without the gift of the Holy Spirit, and this gift is given to the entire assembly.'[50] The role of the assembly is not to be underestimated because it takes place mostly in silence. Every preacher knows well the effect of the congregation's reaction on what he can say, and the power the people exercise as they respond spontaneously to what is set before them. Schmemann says of this: 'In antiquity, the assembly responded to the celebrant's sermon with a triumphal *amen*, testifying by this to the acceptance of the word, sealing their unity in the Spirit with the celebrant. Here, in this *amen* of the people of God, is the source and principle of that 'reception' of teaching by church consciousness, of which Orthodox theologians speak so often, contraposing it to the Roman division of the Church into the *learning* Church and the *teaching* Church, and also to Protestant individualism.'[51]

In the light of this exposition of the full process of teaching in the Church, it is possible to give its full meaning to the title, 'the ordinary Magisterium of the Church'. The Magisterium of the Church is the function of teaching in the Holy Church, in which Christ is the One teacher and he ensures that his word is heard by the illumination of the

---

[50] Alexander Schmemann, The Eucharist: Sacrament of the Kingdom (Crestwood, New York: St Vladimir's Seminary Press, 2003), 79.
[51] Ibid, 80.

Interior Teacher, the Holy Spirit, working in the minds of believers. This Magisterium operates in the manner that has been described, teaching the whole truth infallibly always and everywhere through all the actions of the Church, with the liturgy at the centre, surrounded by the full panoply of teachers, and all under the supervision of the College of Bishops. This Magisterium is the teaching function of the divine persons, Christ and the Holy Spirit, and it is to be identified with them and never separated from them. This distinction between the ordinary and the extraordinary magisterium of the Church was made by Johannes Kleutgen at the end of the nineteenth century. He coined the term 'ordinary magisterium' to correct an erroneous position advocated by a German moral theologian, Johannes B. Hirscher (1788-1865). Hirscher wrote a book on moral theology and, in a chapter on 'heresy', he suggested that, except for what has been dogmatically defined, everyone is free to follow whatever opinion seems best to him. Heresy for Hirscher meant only the failure to accept defined doctrine. Against this Kleutgen argued that the everyday teaching authority of the Church dispersed throughout the world (*ecclesia per orbem dispersa*) enjoys the same assurance of infallibility in proposing revealed doctrine for belief that a solemn council (*ecclesia in concilio congregata*) does, and in matters of faith it demands the same assent. Kleutgen made the distinction in this way. 'The Church exercises a twofold magisterium. The one is ordinary and perpetual (*ordentliche und immerwährende*) and consists in that continuing apostolate of which Hirscher speaks ... The other is *extraordinary* and has been used only at particular times when erroneous doctrines are disturbing the peace of the Church.'[52] He then elaborates on the ordinary magisterium. 'The Church has, in the beginning through her continual, ordinary magisterium, and subsequently also through explicit conciliar judgments, explained the Sacred Scripture as we have it now, as the genuine and unadulterated Word of God. She has thus laid before us the whole content of the same as the revelation of God. As soon as we can no longer doubt that

---

[52] Johannes Kleutgen, Die Theologie der Vorzeit, 5 vols, 2nd ed. (Münster: Theissing, 1867-74), 1.98.

something is contained in Scripture, so we are also certain that it is taught by the Church as revealed truth.'[53] I consider it reasonable to take it that Kleutgen is here speaking of the mystery of teaching in the Holy Church. It is the process which was described earlier by which the One Teacher, Christ, communicates his truth in and through the Church by the power of the Interior Teacher, the Holy Spirit, to all who believe in him. Christ teaches the full Gospel always and everywhere, and every believer has access to this truth in the power of the Holy Spirit illuminating their minds. He has in mind the process of teaching by which the whole Church teaches, not just the bishops. He writes: 'In the principle we are considering, it is not only the general teaching of the pastors of the Church, but also the general faith of Catholic Christianity which is established as an infallible guide to dogmatic truth.'[54]

This position was formulated as Church teaching, with Kleutgen's help in both cases, by Pope Pius IX in *Tuas libenter* and the First Vatican Council in *Dei Filius*. In his letter to the Archbishop of Munich, December 21, 1863 expressing concern about a meeting of Catholic theologians organized by Ignaz von Döllinger earlier that year, at which Hirscher's position had met with approval, the Pope wrote: 'For even if it is a matter of that subjection which must be given in the act of divine faith, it must not be limited to those things which have been defined by the express decrees of councils or of the Roman pontiffs and of this apostolic see, but must also be extended to those things which are handed on by the ordinary Magisterium of the whole Church dispersed throughout the world as divinely revealed ...' (DS 2879). And the same point was made subsequently at the First Vatican Council. In *Dei Filius* we read that 'all those things are to be believed with divine and Catholic faith, which are contained in the word of God, written or handed down, and which, either in solemn judgment or through her ordinary and universal Magisterium, are proposed by the Church for belief as having been divinely revealed.' (DS 3011)

---

[53] Ibid, 1.100-01.
[54] Ibid, 1.104-05.

Every Christian has equal access to this ordinary and universal teaching of the Church, by the illumination of the Holy Spirit given in Baptism. Kleutgen has a useful set of remarks in this connection. He speaks of the different sources of revelation available in Scripture and Tradition and goes on:

> Now we ask here whether one cannot achieve complete certainty from such sources, prior to any express decision of the Church, about what the Catholic Church teaches not only about many other truths, but especially about those articles of belief which have an intimate relationship with the Christian and ecclesial life: ... If not, then, one could not believe with full assurance those truths, which mesh so deeply and in so many ways in one's life, before the councils or popes issued dogmatic decrees about all those articles in later centuries. And it is just this possibility that we lay down in broad opposition to the view we dispute. If nothing pertains to faith except what the Church has stipulated by an express decision, then members of the Church could go for centuries without eliciting an act of faith in the most important mysteries and moral teachings of religion. Then everyone could follow the view which seemed to him to be most correct at the time.[55]

It follows that this ordinary and universal Magisterium is equally and absolutely binding on everyone in the Church, and dissent from any point of it is heresy.[56] Heresy only becomes formal after a definition, but the reality is there beforehand. Kleutgen declares Hirscher's view unheard of in the ancient tradition, which always held the the rule of faith to include all those things which are taught and believed in the

---

[55] Ibid, 1.51-52
[56] Francis A. Sullivan, S.J. has a good chapter on this matter, 'Undefined Dogmas', in Creative Fidelity: Weighing and Interpreting Documents of the Magisterium (Dublin: Gill & Macmillan Ltd, 1996), 100-108.

Church generally as revealed truth. As he makes clear: 'Even when the Church establishes a point of doctrine through a formal judgment, one must be careful to say that she does not make a dogma, but clarifies what is already dogma, and so we repeat that a teaching is dogma because and as soon as it is established by the Church.'[57] The Fathers did not hesitate to label as heresy doctrines which departed from the faith generally held by the Church - even before a conciliar condemnation. The standard example referred to in this connection is the situation in the early Church prior to the Council of Nicaea. St. Irenaeus wrote his book *Against the Heresies*, and described and refuted a long list of heresies prior to any definition. St. Athanasius makes the same point: 'The fathers at Nicaea speaking of the Easter feast say "We have decided as follows." But about the faith they do not say "We have decided," but "This is what the universal Church believes." And immediately they proclaim how they believe, in order to declare, not some novelty, but that their belief is apostolic, and that what they write down is not something they have discovered, but those very things which the Apostles taught.'[58] And Newman follows him, observing that: 'it must be borne in mind that the great Council at Nicaea was summoned, not to decide for the first time what was to be held concerning our Lord's divine nature, but, as far as inquiry came into its work, to determine the fact whether Arius did or did not contradict the Church's teaching.'[59]

The Proximate and Universal Norm

In later centuries, the role of this ordinary and universal teaching began to be formulated as an epistemological principle, which would become, and continues to be, much disputed. Gratian had collected a text which would be much referred to: 'It is obvious that in a doubtful matter regarding the faith, the authority of the universal Church holds, which is supported by the consensus of the succession of bishops and

---

[57] Kleutgen, Die Theologie, 1.105.
[58] Epistola de Synodis, par. 5, RJ 785.
[59] Apostolical Tradition in Essays, Critical and Historical (1871), vol. I, 125.

all peoples from the founding sees of the Apostles to the present day.'[60] On this basis, Ockham formulated the principle that in order to believe anything, the basis must be that *Omne revelatum a Deo est verum* or its equivalent *credat omnia quae credit Ecclesia*.[61] In his time, Cano formulated the same principle: 'Since the Church cannot err in faith, the faithful must accept, that whatever the Church holds as a dogma of faith is true, and nothing is false which it believes and teaches as to be believed.'[62] In the next century, there is the much quoted syllogism of Juan de Lugo who said: 'What the Catholic Church teaches with the assistance of the Holy Spirit must be true; But the Catholic Church teaches X. Therefore X must be true.'[63] In the eighteenth century, another Jesuit, Isaac Berruyer (1681-1758), made the same argument against the Gallicans. He argued that the ground of certainty cannot be an appeal to historical tradition, a Gallican proclamation of the doctrines of the Fathers. How do we judge the consensus of the Fathers? To ask such a question is to deliver ourselves to uncertainty and to probability, to hold the faith as the judgment of a discursive reason and not as assent to a divinely revealed truth. The ground of certainty, therefore, can only be the infallible teaching of the present Church.[64] It follows that no evidence drawn from the past can ever control the present, so that, for Berruyer, the present is supreme, and historical

---

[60] Decretum Gratiani d. 11, c. 9; ed. Friedberg, I, 25. Gratian introduced this text as being 'Augustine "Against the Manichees"'. Friedberg, in his apparatus, gives as a quotation from St Augustine Contra Faustum Manichaeum, l. 2, c. 2: "Et vides in hac re quid ecclesiae catholicae valeat auctoritas …" I wasn't able to find this sentence, however, in CSEL 25, 254-56. It seems clear, therefore, that Gratian's text is very much a paraphrase of St. Augustine's teaching, but it is none the less valuable for that.

[61] A. van Leeuwen, L'Église règle de foi dans les écrits de Guillaume d'Occam, ETL 11 (1934) 249-288, 263.

[62] Melchior Cano, De locis theologicis, l. 4, c. 4, § 4; Opera Omnia: Vol. 1, (Rome, 1890), 199.

[63] Quoted in Owen Chadwick, From Bossuet to Newman 2nd edition (Cambridge University Press, 1957, 1987), 41. (I was unable to consult the original.)

[64] Ibid, 72.

records fundamentally irrelevant.[65] Then, in the nineteenth century, beginning the exposition of his defence of Catholic theology, Kleutgen lays down the principles, and the first is: 'Accordingly, we can formulate the norm of our faith in this way: *All that, and only that, belongs to the Catholic faith, which the Church proclaims as the truth revealed to her by God.*'[66] And not long after, Bainvel: 'Thus we understand how it is rightly said in our formula for the act of faith: 'I believe whatever the holy Church believes and teaches.'[67]

Another way of expressing this point of our total dependence on the Church for the faith is to speak of our having 'implicit faith' in her word. Cardinal Newman was a great exponent of the notion. For him the duty of 'implicit faith' is a consequence of the dogma of the Church's infallibility. 'The "One Holy Catholic and Apostolic Church" is an article of the Creed, and an article which, inclusive of her infallibility, all men, high and low, can easily master and accept with a real and operative assent. It stands in the place of all abstruse propositions in a Catholic's mind, for to believe in her word is virtually to believe in them all. Even what he cannot understand, at least he can believe to be true; and he believes it to be true because he believes in the Church.'[68] Speaking for himself he wrote that 'I believe whatever the Church teaches as the voice of God - and this or that particular inclusively, *if* she teaches this - it is this *fides implicita* which is our comfort in these irritating times.'[69] As Manning says: 'The voice of the living Church, of this hour, when it declares what God has revealed is no other than the voice of the Holy Spirit, and therefore generates divine faith in those who believe.'[70] The doctrine is taught definitively by the First Vatican

---

[65] Ibid, 73.
[66] Kleutgen, Die Theologie der Vorzeit, 46.
[67] J. V. Bainvel, De Magisterio vivo et Traditione (Paris: Beauchesne, 1905), 45. 2, 56-57.
[68] An Essay in Aid of a Grammar of Assent, (Notre Dame/London: University of Notre Dame Press, 1979), 129.
[69] To Henry Wilberforce, July 21st, 1867 in Wilfrid Ward The Life of John Henry Cardinal Newman, Volume 2 (New York: Longman's, Green, and Co., 1913), 234.
[70] Manning, The Temporal Mission of the Holy Ghost, 81.

Council: 'Wherefore, by divine and Catholic faith all those things are to be believed which are contained in the Word of God written or handed down, and which are proposed by the Church to be believed as divinely revealed ...' (DS 3011.) And: 'What holy mother Church has held and holds is to be taken as the true meaning of Sacred Scripture, for hers it is to judge the true meaning and interpretation of Sacred Scripture.' (DS 3007.) The Catholic rule of faith places the Church at its centre. St. Ignatius of Loyola summarized the tradition in his Rules for Thinking with the Church:

> We must put aside all judgment of our own, and keep the mind ever ready and prompt to obey in all things the true spouse of Christ, our holy Mother, the hierarchical Church.[71] ... If we wish to proceed securely in all things, we must hold fast to the following principle: What seems to me white, I will believe black if the hierarchical Church so defines. For I must be convinced that in Christ our Lord, the Bridegroom, and in His spouse the Church, only one Spirit holds sway, which governs and rules for the salvation of souls. For it is by the same Spirit and Lord who gave the Ten Commandments that our holy Mother Church is ruled and governed.[72]

Ever since the Protestant Reformation challenged the Catholic Church in its very foundations, the basic task has been the clear formulation of the rule of faith.[73] In response to the Protestants, who made Scripture the ultimate norm, the Catholic theologians spoke of a 'living rule', sometimes called 'living tradition' or a 'living Gospel'.

---

[71] Rules for Thinking with the Church, § 1; The Spiritual Exercises of St. Ignatius, ed. Louis J. Puhl, S.J. (Chicago: Loyola University Press, 1952), § 353, 157.
[72] Ibid, § 13.
[73] Y. Congar, 'L'ecclésiologie, de la Révolution française au Concile du Vatican, sous le signe de l'affirmation de l'autorité,' in L'Ecclésiologie au XIXᵉ siècle: Unam Sanctam 34 (Paris : Les Éditions du Cerf, 1960), 77-114, at 85-86.

One way of putting the matter was to argue that there must be a living judge who can decide what is of faith and what is not. Cano, for instance said: 'The definition of doubts which arise in regard to the faith pertains to the present Church. There must therefore be a living judge in the Church who can decide controversies about the faith, because God cannot fail provide all that is necessary to his Church. ... Judgment about such things will pertain to the Church of the present time.'[74] Again, Franzelin, still arguing with the Protestants at the end of the nineteenth century, concedes that Scripture is the one objective norm of faith, in that it contains the whole of revelation and the adequate material object of the faith, but Scripture cannot be the *judge* of faith. The judge can only be the visible and living authority which judges what is consonant with the objective rule of faith and what is alien to it.[75] Without a living judge, the only alternative is that each one is judge of doctrine for himself,[76] and the Church is the living judge.[77] There was proposed the concept of a proximate rule of faith. Scripture and Tradition must obviously be recognised as rules of faith, in some sense, but they are called 'remote' in the sense that they come to us in documents from the past which must be interpreted. What Catholic theology is looking for as the rule is access to the truth without the need of my interpretation, an authority which does the interpreting for me and tells me the truth. It is the Church which fulfils this function. Suarez wrote that 'as far as we are concerned, it is the Church which is proposed to us, as ruled by the Holy Spirit, as the proximate and sufficient rule of faith, because all the faithful cannot judge the doctrine of faith, or always resort to the divine authority expressly considered, for it is too high and spiritual...'[78] Perrone followed Suarez and wrote that 'theologians must refer to the word of God whether written or

---

[74] Melchior Cano, De locis theologicis, Lib. II, Ca VII, § 13; Opera Omnia: Vol. 1, (Rome, 1890), 40. Refers, a bit vaguely, to proximate and remote principles of faith in § 17, also on 40.
[75] J. B. Franzelin, S.J., De Divina Traditione et Scriptura (Rome, 1875), 8.
[76] Ibid, 9.
[77] Ibid, 10.
[78] De Fide, d. 3, s. 10, n. 10; Opera, Vivès ed., Paris, 1858, Vol. XII, 94.

handed down, which constitutes what they call the *remote* rule of our faith. Since, however, we cannot establish with certainty the genuine and authentic word of God and its meaning, which is the object of revelation, without a secure and infallible means, which is the Church, which constitutes the so-called *proximate* rule of faith …'[79]

The infallibility of the Church is foundational, and yet much disputed in practice, and must be dwelt upon. The sampling of texts just given makes clear that the conviction pervades Catholic tradition, and the precise import of the doctrine needs to be grasped. Consider at a bit more length some of the key texts. Cano elaborates on the principle he laid down:

> That the Church cannot err in faith is to be believed by the faithful in this way, that whatever the Church holds as a dogma of faith is true, and nothing is false which she either believes or teaches to be believed. Since she is the Body of Christ, as the Apostle teaches the Ephesians, she is certainly moved and governed by her head. And error of the Church would be referred to Christ as its author. In no way, therefore, can she err in faith. For the Spirit of truth is the soul of this body: 'One Spirit and one body' (Eph 4:4). If the Church acts in the Spirit of truth, she cannot be moved to any error or ignorance. The Church has an excellent promise, that she will never be deserted by Christ, but that she will be led into all truth by his Spirit. (Jn 14:1, 26.)[80]

Cano bases his argument on the complete identity of the Church with Christ and the Holy Spirit; no margin of error is entertained. And Cardinal Manning says the same thing:

---

[79] Johannes Perrone, Praelectiones theologicae (editio vigesimaquinta) (Mediolani / Genuae: Carolus Turati et soc. / Darius Josephus Rossi, 1857), § 6, 248.
[80] Melchior Cano, De locis theologicis, l. 4, c. 4, § 4; Opera Omnia: Vol. 1, (Rome, 1890), 199.

> As soon as I perceived the Divine fact that the Holy Spirit of God has united Himself indissolubly to the mystical body, or Church of Jesus Christ, I saw at once that the interpretations or doctrines of the living Church are true because Divine, and that the voice of the living Church in all ages is the sole rule of faith, and infallible, because it is the voice of a Divine Person.[81] ... The Holy Spirit, through the Church, enunciates to this day the original revelation with an articulate voice, which never varies or falters. Its voice to-day is identical with the voice of every age, and is therefore identical with the voice of Jesus Christ.[82]

Suarez also makes the same point:

> The Church is the infallible rule of our faith. However it is so insofar as it is a kind of organ or instrument through which the Holy Spirit speaks, and so cannot be the formal ground of faith (ratio formalis credendi). This is rather the authority of the Holy Spirit ruling her, since in an instrument the whole ground and power of action is from the motion of the principal agent.[83]

And Möhler:

> If it is the divine element, the living Christ and his Spirit in her, which is infallible, eternally unerring, so also the human element is infallible and unerring, for the divine element does not exist for us without the human element, and yet the human element is not

---

[81] Manning, The Temporal Mission of the Holy Ghost, 28.
[82] Ibid, 78.
[83] De Fide, d. 3, s. 10, n. 10; Opera, Vivès ed., Paris, 1858, Vol. XII, 94.

infallible and unerring in itself, but only as the organ and the manifestation of the divine.[84]

And this has implications for the manner in which theology is to be done, how one is to enter concretely into the mysteries of the faith. Humbert Clerissac had some good things to say about the role of the Church.

> Since revelation is present in the living Church, the theologian must place himself within the mystery of the Church, in personal contact by his living faith with the word of revelation. He must incorporate himself into her, living in communion with the whole Church, so that he can assimilate the experience of the faith accumulated in her womb through all the ages of her life. In this way, the theologian becomes aware of the development of revelation in the totality of the mystical Body, from the beginning to the present moment.[85] ... The Church is not only a society and an administration, even supernatural. She is the living Body of Christ; she is the Christ-Church. To have the sense of the Church, the *sensus Ecclesiae*, is to have the sense of Christ, the *sensus Christi*.[86]

Hugo Rahner:

> The teaching, believing and praying Church as a whole is herself the final instance for what is her 'tradition' ... and the Spirit, who leads her, ensures that what he himself conceived and worked in the hiddenness of his mysteries of salvation, he slowly

---

[84] Johann Adam Möhler, Symbolik, Vol. 1, ed. Geiselmann (Köln & Olten: Jakob Hegner, 1958), 389.
[85] L. Charlier, O. Essai sur le Problème Théologique (Thuillies: Ramgal, 1938), 76.
[86] Ibid, 158.

proclaims through the living Church and *he* (not the historical research of theologians alone) ensures that nothing enters into the faith-awareness of the Church which is not a development of the apostolic deposit, so that the final certainty, that a given truth is of the apostolic faith, does not come from history, philology and logic alone (however much these are useful, even necessary and obligatory), but from the single fact, that this truth is what is, in fact, believed.[87]

And, finally, Congar:

> The Church ... witnesses to what it is, to what it lives from, to what it believes, to the very content of its 'tradition', which is the uninterrupted presence in her, over time, of her principles and of her principle, the Holy Spirit. ... The Church is the very Christian reality itself, it is the Body of Christ and has the meaning, the voice and the word of Christ in her. She must obey this word and the meaning of Christ, for Christ is her Lord and her Head, as the husband is the head of the wife. But this meaning and this word of Christ are the interior law, a law which she examines in herself and does not only rule her life, but animates it.[88]

It is being taken here that all these texts are referring to the Holy Church, and they can be accepted as applying fully and completely. Difficulties arise if this qualification is not kept in mind, and the infallibility of the Holy Church is applied indiscriminately to the concrete Catholic Church. Consider, for instance, an explanation of the infallibility of the Church presented towards the end of the last century by one of the theologians of the Roman School, Giovanni Perrone, in

---

[87] Hugo Rahner, S. J., 'Noch ein neues Dogma?' Orientierung 13 (1949) 13-16, at 15.

[88] Congar, Vraie et fausse réforme dans l'Église, 468.

the following terms: 'The Church is infallible, just as Christ is infallible, because He willed her to be a living and perfect image of Himself. Indeed, He constituted her to perpetuate Himself on earth in a certain fashion (quodammodo), such that, what Christ had and has by His own nature, he communicates by grace and privilege to this His daughter or spouse.'[89] Congar is critical of this logic on grounds, familiar from an earlier part of our discussion, that it fails to take sufficient account of the difference that exists between a hypostatic union and a covenant union.

> In the first case *all* the actions of the Man-God may be predicated of God and thus bear an absolute guarantee. In the second we have a 'mystical' body, which is also the Bride and keeps its own individual subjectivity before Christ its Lord; the human subject is left to its own freedom and responsibility within a framework of weaknesses and graces, efforts and up-and-downs in fidelity; only the ultimate decisions about the reality of the covenant are guaranteed. ... A certain number of the Church's *acts*, or acts of the pope who personifies it, are infallible. It cannot be said, without qualification, of the pope and the Church that they just *are* infallible.[90]

So, despite the universal tradition of the infallibility of the Church, Congar expresses the opinion here that it cannot be said, without qualification, that the Church simply *is* infallible. This difficulty of Congar disappears, I suggest, once the distinction between the Holy Church and the Catholic Church is clearly drawn. Congar is thinking of the concrete Catholic Church, and in that case the qualifications he makes are necessary. However, in the case of the Holy Church Perrone's logic works perfectly, and one can truly say that the infallibility of the Church is identically the infallibility of Christ himself.

---

[89] Praelect., VII, 30, quoted in Congar, Tradition and Traditions, 312.
[90] Congar, Tradition and Traditions, 312-13.

Congar also has difficulties with the line of argument being pursued here, from the point of view of the role of the Holy Spirit in the Church. He speaks of 'a sort of ecclesiological positivism or fideism' which made itself felt at the turn of the thirteenth and fourteenth centuries. He says that 'Nominalism and the Scotist criticism both came to the conclusion that all the articles of faith depend upon this one article, the first of all: *Credo Ecclesiam regi a Spiritu Sancto*,' but that 'those trained in the Thomist school reacted against this.'[91] This approach he sees continued by the Jesuit theologians, following the spirituality of St Ignatius of Loyola, to whom he attributes a very close identification between the kingdom of God and the Church militant, between the discernment of what is of the Spirit of God and the judgement of 'the hierarchic Church'.[92] He says that 'such a position, staking heavily on the actuality of divine causality, was too naïvely "divinistic".' In his view 'this ecclesiological pneumatology led to an excessive tendency to situate at the same level the apostolic moment of constitutive revelation and the historical moment of assistance. The former ran the risk of not appearing fully and supremely "situating", *normans*, the latter of not being sufficiently "situated", *normatum*.'[93] He credits the Thomists with being the most faithful to the normative primacy of Scripture, and distinguishing between the various stages of the economy, between inspiration and Inspiration, between spiritual writings and the Scriptures. Apparently it was Dominic Bañez who first 'made use of the word *assistentia*, a more precise and happier choice than the admittedly ambiguous *revelatio* or *inspiratio*.'[94] He doesn't dispute 'the thoroughly incontestable principle of an action of the Holy Spirit coextensive with the duration of the Church,' but points out that it 'was liable, *in actual practice*, to render such a distinction precarious. The movement to exalt the authority of the Church, and even, in fact, papal authority, continued and was even strengthened by the theology of the Counter-Reformation. This theology is characterized by the affirmation of the

---

[91] Ibid, 183.
[92] Ibid, 176, footnote 3.
[93] Ibid, 174.
[94] Ibid, 175.

principle of authority, that is to say the formal principle or *quo*, in a way which hardly allows for its conditioning by the content, the objective datum or *quod*.'[95] He speaks of Suárez comparing the definitions of the Church to new revelations. He allows that 'Suárez held that revelation is closed, but said that the infallibility which this *assistentia Spiritus Sancti* assures to the Church "aequivalet revelationi vel consummat illam, ut ita dicam", so that the force of the decisions taken by authority appears as unconditioned and truly divine. Instead of seeing tradition as having its reference to the past, there is a tendency to see it in reference to the current magisterium of the Church expressing itself in the passing of time.'[96] In another place he says: 'It is clear that the preference given to the consideration of the transcendent, and real, cause of a truth, envisaged in itself and apart from time, tended, perhaps not to abolish, but at least to diminish the difference between the Church of the time, or of the post-apostolic period, and the Church of the apostles.'[97] Against this he cites the teaching of St Thomas completely subordinating the whole post-apostolic Church to the given fact of the prophets, Christ and the apostles.[98]

The Assistance or the Illumination of the Holy Spirit?

So, what precisely is the role of the Holy Spirit in the present-day Church? Congar speaks of 'the risk of putting two qualitatively different stages on the same level - the time of the apostles and the time of the Church.'[99] He points out that they are different not only in that the time of the apostles is constitutive of revelation, whereas that of the

---

[95] Ibid, 176.
[96] Ibid, 176. He refers to De Fide, Dis III, Sect. 2, n. 11 (Opera, ed. Vivès, Vol. XII, 100); In IIIam Partem, q. 27, a. 2, Dis III, Sect. 6, n. 4 (Vol. XIX, 48).
[97] Ibid, 93.
[98] In IV Sent., d. 17, q. 3, a. 1, sol. 5; d. 27, q. 3, a. 3, ad 2; ST, III, q. 64, a. 2, ad 3: 'Apostoli, et eorum successores, sunt vicarii Dei quantum ad regimen Ecclesiae instituae per fidem et fidei sacramenta. Unde, sicut not licet eis constituere aliam Ecclesiam, ita non licet eis tradere aliam fidem, neque instituere alia sacramenta'.
[99] Congar, Tradition and Traditions, 208.

Church is not, but they are different in that 'the apostles were *inspired*, receiving the grace of revelation, whereas the Church is only *assisted* in transmitting and announcing it. Certainly it is the same Holy Spirit at work in each case, hence the fundamental homogeneity of the two stages. But he does not intervene in the same way.'[100] Congar speaks of the 'fundamental homogeneity' of the 'two qualitatively different stages'! And yet putting them on the same level constitutes a risk. Which is more important, the similarity or the difference?

There is no doubt that the situation for the Church changed at the end of the apostolic era, when revelation ceased. However, it is wrong, I suggest, to exaggerate the importance of the moment. Congar makes much of the choice of the word 'assistance' to describe the role of the Holy Spirit maintaining the Church in the truth. The word was chosen so as to avoid any suggestion of new revelation since the close of the apostolic age. The assistance is understood to be *per se negative*,[101] and Congar explains this by observing that 'it is necessary to distinguish between an immediate impulse bestowed by the Holy Spirit on the authors of Scripture, in virtue of which they were inspired in everything, and an assistance given to the *human work* of the councils and popes, which is only guaranteed in so far as it relates to what is necessary for salvation.'[102] Cardinal Newman dealt with this question at the time of the First Vatican Council, and gave a useful account of the standard teaching. He compares the two eras, that of the apostles and that of the Church:

> To the Apostles the whole revelation was given, by the Church it is transmitted; no simply new truth has been given to us since St. John's death; the one office of the Church is to guard 'that noble deposit' of truth, as St. Paul speaks to Timothy, which the Apostles bequeathed to her, in its fullness and integrity. Hence

---
[100] Ibid, 208-9.
[101] See John Boyle, Church Teaching Authority; Historical and Theological Studies, (Notre Dame/London: Notre Dame University Press, 1995), 49 for references.
[102] Congar, Tradition and Traditions, 136. (Emphasis in the original.)

the infallibility of the Apostles was of a far more positive and wide character than that needed by and granted to the Church. We call it, in the case of the Apostles, inspiration; in the case of the Church *assistentia*.[103]

There are points which need to be disputed in these accounts. Newman says that the infallibility of the apostles was of a far more positive and wide character than that needed by and granted to the Church. This is not so. The Church preaches exactly the same message as the apostles did, and shares fully the same infallibility. There is no distinction between the two eras on that basis. The difference is simply in the fact that the Gospel was new to the apostles, whereas it is traditional for the Church. Everything else is the same. Congar speaks of the assistance being given to the *human* work of the Church authorities and that the assistance only operates insofar as it relates to what is necessary for salvation. These points do not mark a difference from the apostles. They engaged in a *human* work in their preaching and writing, and the inspiration they received related only to what was necessary for salvation, and not to *everything* as Congar says. It is this emphasis on the *human* work in Congar's reflections which points up the flaw in what he says. The work of the Holy Spirit inspiring the apostles in the process of revelation was primary, even though the apostles had much human work to do. The same is true of the Church. The Church needs the inspiration of the Holy Spirit to accept and grasp the word of revelation. The Gospel is a supernatural message, completely beyond the power of the human mind to grasp, and no human effort is adequate for its assimilation. The Holy Spirit is as close to and active in the Church today as he was on the day of Pentecost. There is no distinction at the fundamental level whatsoever. It is necessary to distinguish the period of revelation from the subsequent period of tradition, but not in such a way as to sideline the Holy Spirit from this ongoing task. One could distinguish between revelatory inspiration and illuminative inspiration,

---

[103] Letter to the Duke of Norfolk in Certain Difficulties felt by Anglicans in Catholic Teaching, (London / New York / Bombay: Longmans, Green, and Co.: 1900), Volume 2, 327.

in order to distinguish the effect of the Holy Spirit's action in the two cases, though the action itself is essentially the same. Or one might simply distinguish inspiration and illumination.[104] One thing is sure is that 'assistance' does not do justice to the reality. The word 'assistance' denotes a secondary cooperation in a function in which the primary actor is basically competent. This, however, is not true in the case of Christians coming to understand the truths of revelation, for the role of the Holy Spirit is absolutely fundamental. I therefore dispute Congar's claim that a strong emphasis on the actuality of divine causality is too naively 'divinistic', and I make the counter claim that any failure to place this emphasis properly is too humanistic, and looses sight of the essential and immediate role of the Holy Spirit in the Church. And I further argue that the time of the apostles and the time of the Church are basically on the same level. The Indwelling of the Holy Spirit in the Church has been a reality since the day of Pentecost, and this Indwelling is at a level and of such importance that the difference between the era of revelation and the era of tradition is a matter of relative triviality. Divinely revealed truth is supernatural and completely beyond any human power to judge. Only divine wisdom can judge its truth, and so God must be immediately active in any infallible judgement, assistance not enough. It is not a matter of the Holy Spirit helping human beings in a task they are basically qualified for, but need assistance. Infallible judgment belongs to God alone, and it is therefore the Holy Spirit who is judging in and through the human instruments.

Focussing on the role of the Holy Spirit as the source of the Church's faith and her infallibility allows sense to be made of a manner of speaking which emerged at the end of the nineteenth century, which Pope Pius XII made his own, namely, that the Church can be considered as, herself, the 'source' of truth. The Pope wrote: 'The Church, by the command of God the interpreter and guardian of the Sacred Scriptures and herself the depositary of the living Sacred Tradition, is the gateway

---

[104] The use of this word was suggested to me by an excellent chapter entitled 'Inspiration and Illumination' in Paul C. McGlasson, *Invitation to Dogmatic Theology: A Canonical Approach* (Grand Rapids, Michigan: Brazos Press, 2006), 55-72.

to salvation and is herself, under the guidance and leading of the Holy Spirit, the source of truth. (*ipsa ... sibi fons est veritatis.*)'[105] If the Church is taken as the human corporation considered apart from God, in the Deistic manner which comes to us all so easily, then the notion that it might be the source of supernatural truth is unacceptable. If, however, the Holy Church is kept in mind, then it can be seen that the source of truth is the Holy Spirit, the soul of the Church, and the attribution can be made of the Church herself as well. Congar made this same point also: 'The Word of God is not a rule external to the Church, to which she must conform *from outside*, having equally the possibility of diverging from it and required to be brought back by the experts, even the experts of Sacred Scripture. ... The Church reads her faith in the monuments of tradition and above all in the first and incomparable monument of the divine Scriptures. But she reads these monuments *in herself*, possessing them as the archives of her conscience.'[106] And it is the Holy Spirit who governs the Church and ensures that everything is done in her according to the mind and will of Christ. Congar again: 'The Church, in effect, cannot act at any moment as an arbitrary authority, which could decree and impose anything at all (ST III, 64, 2, ad 3 etc.) She has the deposit within her, she does not receive it from outside. But she is subject to this deposit and must maintain it within its objective limits.'[107] This *must* of Congar is first of all an inner necessity, and only in the second place a criterion or a norm for the human ministers, and this point will need to be addressed also. In the meantime, it can be seen how the absolute identification of the Holy Church with God answers a problem posed by John Calvin. He wrote: 'This final inference of theirs that the Church cannot err in those matters which are necessary for salvation, we do not contradict. But we are very much against what these words imply. We consider that she cannot fail to the extent that, setting aside her own sagacity, she suffers herself to be taught of the Holy Spirit, *by the Word of God*. They, on the contrary, incline to this: that since

---

[105] 'Animus noster', Address for the fourth centenary of the Gregorian, 17 October, 1953. AAS 45 [1953] 685.
[106] Congar, <u>Vraie et fausse réforme dans l'Église</u>, 468.
[107] Ibid, 470.

the Church is governed by the Spirit of God, she can surely proceed without the word; and that, whatever she does, she can neither think nor speak other than truth.'[108] Calvin's mistake is to separate the Word and the Spirit and the Church. These are all intimately conjoined, and there can be no separation between them. The Church cannot 'proceed without the word'; she does not exist without the word. The Word and the Spirit and the Church are the one reality, inseparably. This is true, of course, fully, only of the Holy Church. The Word of God has entered fully into the Church he founded and the Holy Spirit he sent guarantees its indefectible permanence. This Holy Church, formed by the Word and the Spirit, subsists in the Catholic Church and is available there in its fullness, but to a certain degree hidden by the effects of our sins. The Holy Church is completely under the control of Christ and his Spirit and is not subject to our control in any way whatever, so that the danger posed by an erring human authority does not arise. A certain degree of separation is possible when the concrete Catholic Church is meant, and here John Calvin was reacting, to some extent with justification, against an over-hasty identification of the concrete Catholic Church and her authorities with the Holy Church of God. And that problem has to be faced.

Hans Küng has attacked an over-identification of the Church with the Holy Spirit. He wrote: 'A Church which identifies itself with the Holy Spirit has no need to listen, to believe, to obey. It turns itself into a revelation, it knows and does everything. It needs only to listen to itself, to obey itself and believe in itself and urge others outside the Church to listen, believe and obey. In short, it will fall prey to a self-glorifying and egocentric conception of the Church…'[109] Küng is both right and wrong in what he says here, and his critique can only be resolved by the use of the distinction between the Holy Church and the Catholic Church. The Holy Church is completely identified with the Holy Spirit. It is the Incorporation of the Holy Spirit on earth, the Holy Spirit is its

---

[108] Institutions, Ch.15 . . . also Inst. (1560); IV, viii, 13; quoted in Congar, Tradition and Traditions, 173-74.
[109] Küng, The Church, 175.

soul and each and every act of this Church comes from the Holy Spirit. It is true, then, that this Church reveals the Word of God, and it knows and does everything. But it listens, believes and obeys Christ, for that is what the Spirit was sent for. And it is not self-glorifying or egocentric. The Holy Church is the Mystical Body of Christ and does everything for his glory. We, in the Catholic Church, recognise the mystery of the Holy Church as something which constitutes us, but not fully. We believe that the Holy Church subsists in the Catholic Church, but is obscured in many ways by our sins, without losing her fundamental identity. The kind of self-glory which Küng condemns may be possible as sin to which we are prone, but avoiding it must not cause us to lose sight of the glory of the Holy Church which is present in the world, subsisting in the Catholic Church.

An interesting witness in this matter is Cardinal Newman. As an Anglican he protested against the Catholics that 'they supersede the appeal to Scripture and Antiquity by putting forward the infallibility of the Church, thus solving the whole question by a summary and final interpretation both of Antiquity and of Scripture,'[110] and that 'the Church of Rome … exalts the will and pleasure of the existing Church above all authority, whether of Scripture or Antiquity.'[111] Then, as a Catholic, he entered enthusiastically into the Catholic claim. Now, for him '[t]he word of the Church is the word of revelation.'[112] 'I believe with all my heart and soul all that the Holy Roman Church teaches and never had one single doubt about any portion of her teaching whatever, ever since I became a Catholic.'[113] 'I absolutely submit my mind with an inward assent to the Church, as the teacher of the whole faith.'[114] He writes that 'we must ever hold … that the object of faith is … the whole

---

[110] Lectures on the Prophetical Office of the Church (London, 1837), 60.
[111] Ibid, 100.
[112] An Essay in Aid of a Grammar of Assent, (Notre Dame/London: University of Notre Dame Press, 1979), 231.
[113] Meriol Trevor, Newman Light in Winter (New York: Doubleday & Company, 1963), 266.
[114] Letter to Dr. Pusey, March 22nd 1867 in Wilfrid Ward The Life of John Henry Cardinal Newman, Volume 2 (New York: Longman's, Green, and Co., 1913), 219-20.

word of God, explicit and implicit, as dispensed by His living Church.'[115] And finally: 'I say there is only one Oracle of God, the Holy Catholic Church and the Pope as her head. To her teaching I have ever desired all my thoughts, all my words to be conformed; to her judgment I submit what I have now written, what I have ever written, not only as regards its truth, but as to its prudence, its suitableness, and its expedience.'[116] This is not such a *volte face* as it might appear, for, already as an Anglican, Newman had believed fully in the Holy Church as the source of truth. He wrote that '[b]oth we and Roman Catholics hold that the Church Catholic is unerring in its declarations of faith, or saving doctrine; but we differ from each other as to what is the faith, and what is the Church Catholic.'[117] And in the Introduction to this work he quoted, and made his own, a profession of faith by John Bramhall (1594-1663), Anglican Archbishop of Armagh: 'I submit myself and my poor endeavours, first to the judgment of the Catholic Ecumenical essential Church … And if I should mistake the right Catholic Church out of human frailty or ignorance …, I do implicitly and in the preparation of my mind submit myself to the True Catholic Church, the Spouse of Christ, the Mother of Saints, the Pillar of Truth.'[118] These great Anglican theologians had a profound sense of the mystery of the Church, the Holy Church, and that faith is a point that every Christian can share, while honest differences arise as to the identification of the Holy Church in concrete experience. Newman's conversion to Catholicism meant simply that he finally identified where the Holy Church is concretely to be found, subsisting in the Catholic Church.

To complete this presentation on the infallibility of the Church, we can note how the distinction between the Holy Church and the Catholic Church resolves difficulties raised by two recent theologians. Hans Küng, in his book on infallibility, struggled with the mixture of truth and error in the Church, and his problem, as for Luther, it is

---

[115] Ibid, 221-22.
[116] John Henry Newman, Letter to the Duke of Norfolk (London, 1875), 147.
[117] Newman, Lectures on the Prophetical Office of the Church, 1877 edition, in The Via Media of the Anglican Church, Volume 1, 212.
[118] Quoted in Ibid, xiii.

being suggested here was his lack of a proper distinction in the concept of the Church. He criticises the standard Catholic theology in this way:

> Identification of the 'Church' (it would be better to say the 'hierarchy') with the Holy Spirit had become so habitual that it was assumed that admitting certain errors, aberrations, deviations and mistakes by the Church would be attributing them to the Holy Spirit. ... True, God acts on the Church through the Holy Spirit, is testified to by the Church, he founded, maintains and rules it, it is he who is *Deus qui nec fallere nec falli potest*, God who can neither deceive nor be deceived. But the human beings who constitute the Church can err, miscalculate and blunder, mishear, misunderstand and go astray; they are *homines qui fallere et falli possunt*. He who has faith in God will ... distinguish between the Spirit of God and the Church, and not identify them.[119]

Küng insists that the possibility of the failure of Our Lord's promise is absolutely unacceptable to the Christian believer. However, he also rejects the traditionally acceptable alternative 'that there are at any rate some errors that must never be admitted, which is the line taken by a triumphalist Church and is likewise unacceptable to the believer.'[120] He states as his conclusion: 'The dilemma can be resolved only by raising the alternatives to a higher level and asserting that the Church will remain in truth in spite of all the errors that are always possible.'[121] It is being suggested here, that the higher level alternatives which resolve the problem are to be found in the two ways of understanding the 'Church'. If we focus exclusively on the empirical Catholic Church, as Küng is doing here, the dilemma cannot be resolved. A resolution is possible, however, once we concede that there is a real and existing,

---

[119] Küng, Infallible?, 145-46.
[120] Ibid, 144.
[121] Ibid.

holy and infallible Church, subsisting in the Catholic Church but not identical with it without remainder, and that the infallibility of God belongs to this Church fully but not to the concrete Catholic Church. It does not make sense to speak of remaining in truth in spite of errors. Truth and error are contradictories, and cannot coexist in the same subject, under the same aspect, at the same time. The Church which remains permanently in the truth is the Holy Church. Error can indeed be found in the Catholic Church at different levels because of our sins, and it needs to be challenged and removed, while underneath the veils the Holy Church continues to teach the truth infallibly, always and everywhere. However, the subsistence of the Holy Church in the Catholic Church means that, under certain circumstances infallible propositions can be made. Conciliar and Papal definitions must be accepted as true, because in them Christ and his Holy Spirit have spoken definitively. The infallibility of God is engaged here. In a fundamental sense, despite all and any abuses, there is a limit to how far these abuses can go, for we believe that the Gospel is being properly proclaimed and the sacraments rightly administered in the Catholic Church. That is a basic article of the Catholic faith, and is what is meant by the claim that the Holy Church subsists in the Catholic Church.

The distinction between the Holy Church and the Catholic Church permits a resolution of the problem as formulated by Rahner. In his early article on sin in the Church, Rahner had a section on *The Fallible Church*.[122] He recalls the doctrine on the infallibility of the Church and its power to give peace in the midst of uncertainty, and goes on: 'However, in the middle of this glory it still remains true (and must therefore be said), that the Church is a fallible Church because it is a Church of sinners.'[123] There is sin in the Church and, therefore, darkening of the intellects of all believers and 'it follows that this darkening and narrowing of the concrete faith of the believing members of the Church must be an erring of the concrete Church (for

---

[122] Karl Rahner Sämtliche Werke 10 (Freiburg / Basel / Wien: Herder, 2003), 96-98. On page 701 we are told that this section, omitted from earlier German editions, appeared in Dutch translation in 1951.
[123] Ibid, 96.

there is no other). ... And so it is that, in cases which do not involve an authoritative and definitive proclamation, the teaching Church is fallible.'[124] It is not surprising that this section of Rahner's article was censored out of his original publication. It is a fundamental article of Catholic faith that the Church is infallible. Rahner is wrong, therefore, to say without qualification that the Church is fallible. He is correct that there can be error in the concrete Church, but he is wrong to say that 'there is no other'. The concrete Catholic Church can be recognized to be fallible, within certain limits and with the obvious qualifications made. The Church, however, with no qualifying adjective, refers to the Holy Church, the mystery of the divine presence on earth, and this Church is infallible fully and unequivocally. It follows that if one is going to speak of *The Fallible Church*, one must do so cautiously and with a clear recognition of the more fundamental truth of the Church's real infallibility.

A final point might be made before leaving this aspect of the matter. The Catholic apologetic has insisted that the teaching of the Church must be taken as the proximate norm and that Scripture must be considered to be remote. But surely calling Scripture a 'remote' norm is not good. If one thinks of the Bible as a set of ancient documents, relaying ancient events in ancient languages, and needing training and expertise for their interpretation, then maybe it can be considered 'remote'. If, however, Scripture is understood as the living word proclaimed continuously in the liturgy, there is nothing remote about it at all. Seeing Scripture as remote and the Magisterium of the Church as proximate misconstrues both. Scripture and the Magisterium are not two separate realities, for Scripture is at the centre of the Church's Magisterium, taking its privileged place in the liturgy. And it is Scripture, proclaimed in the liturgy, which is the 'proximate' source of our growth in faith.

---

[124] Ibid, 97.

Chapter 10

A Secondary Object of Infallibility?

The concern here is with the Pope's authority to teach in the Church, and the first set of limits of papal teaching must be sought from the side of the object to be taught. All the long line of dissidents who fill the second millennium wanted the Gospel to set the limit to papal teaching, and this point remains at issue under the heading of the secondary object of infallibility. The doctrine of the secondary object of infallibility claims that the Church, and therefore the Pope, has the authority to teaching infallibly outside the ambit of revealed truth. The dissidents were always complaining that the Pope was teaching outside the ambit of the Gospel and, to begin with at least, the Popes never claimed that they could. It was always presumed that the Church only taught what Christ had revealed, until the seventeenth century, when the idea was mooted that definitive judgments could be made outside of revelation. In the wake of this development, the doctrine of a secondary object of infallibility was proposed and began to gain ground.

The Origin of the Doctrine

The doctrine of the secondary object of infallibility is unusual in that its emergence can be dated, almost to the hour! It took place during the controversy between the Jesuits and the Jansenists over the famous

Five Propositions, whose relationship to Cornelius Jansen's book, the *Augustinus*, became the point at issue.[1] The propositions first appeared at the monthly meeting of the doctors of the Sorbonne, when the syndic, Nicolas Cornet, called for the examination of seven propositions which he claimed to have found in the recent baccalaureate theses. At the time he denied that he was making any reference to the *Augustinus*. The university was divided on the issue and the (now) Five Propositions were subsequently sent to Rome for judgement, still without any clear reference to the *Augustinus*. The Propositions were condemned by Pope Innocent X in the apostolic constitution, *Cum occasione* (1653), bearing the *incipit*, *Cum occasione libri Cornelii Jansenii*, so still in only a general relationship to the *Augustinus*.

In 1654 Antoine Arnauld argued that of the five propositions, only the first could be found, almost literally, in the *Augustinus*, and in a context which rendered it perfectly orthodox. And he also produced from the book five sentences which were clearly contrary to the propositions condemned. He concluded that the bull condemned the five propositions in a heretical sense, but that this sense was not that of Jansen himself. Arnauld was making the famous distinction between the point of principle '*point de droit*' (the five propositions are to be condemned) and the point of fact '*point de fait*' (but they are not to be found in the work of Jansen). The French clergy met in March and lamented the fact that this distinction opened the way to a continuing and interminable controversy. On 2 September 1656, the Bishops of France, gathered in a general assembly, wrote to the new Pope, Alexander VII, asking him to settle the matter. And this the Pope did by issuing the Constitution *Ad sacram Petri sedem* (16 October 1656), in which he 'declares and defines' that the propositions are to be found in the *Augustinus* in the sense condemned.[2] Thus was established the dogmatic fact of Jansenism which will become the founding item of the secondary object of infallibility.

---

[1] This account is taken from Jean-François Chiron, L'infaillibilité et son objet, (Les Éditions du Cerf: Paris, 1999), 41-72.
[2] DS 2012.

On the basis of this declaration, the French Bishops and clergy drew up a Profession of Faith to which all had to subscribe, including the following formula:

> I submit sincerely to the constitution of Pope Innocent X of 31 March 1653, in its true sense which was determined by the constitution of our Holy Father the Pope Alexander VII of 16 October 1656. I recognise that I am obliged in conscience to obey these constitutions, and I condemn with heart and mouth the doctrine of the Five Propositions of Cornelius Jansen, contained in his book *Augustinus*, which these two Popes and the Bishops have condemned, which doctrine is not that of St. Augustine, which Jansen has badly explained against the true meaning of the holy Doctor.[3]

This was deemed to be a true Profession of Faith and those who refused to subscribe were deemed to be 'heretics'. The Jansenists, still holding that the Five Propositions did not represent a correct interpretation of Jansen's work, and refusing to concede that the full adherence of divine faith can be invoked for a question of fact of this kind, could only offer to observe a 'respectful silence'.

On the 12th of December 1661, a Flemish Jesuit, Fr. Coret, defended a thesis at the College of Clermont proposing that Christ had accorded to Peter and his successors the same infallibility which he himself enjoyed, and that there thus exists in the Church, even apart from a Council, an infallible judge in controversies about the faith, both in matters of principle and in matters of fact. Fr. Annat, the Jesuit Provincial of Paris and confessor to King Louis XIV drew up a summary of the thesis containing three central points. These are that the Popes enjoy a personal infallibility which is the same as that of Christ, that this infallibility extends to matters of fact, and that it is possible to adhere with divine faith to the heretical character of the *Augustinus*, on the

---

[3]   Chiron, L'infaillibilité, 50-51.

basis that the Five Propositions are taken from it and are condemned in the sense of Jansen. This constitutes the first clear statement of the doctrine of the secondary object of infallibility, and its precise dating was proclaimed, with some irony, by Antoine Arnauld:

> Let the whole Church understand and notice that it was on 12th of December 1661 that the Jesuits have published this monstrous opinion, considered for some time; that it was on this day that they proposed as a Catholic assertion, that the Pope, when he speaks *ex cathedra*, *has the same infallibility as Jesus Christ* not only in matters of principle, *but also in matters of fact*; and that therefore one can believe, *with divine faith*, that the Five Propositions are Jansen's.[4]

What Arnauld rejects, is that an assent of divine faith can be demanded in a matter which does not belong to Revelation, Scripture or Tradition, and he responds to the accusation of heresy with one of his own, 'that whoever demands the signature of the Formula under pain of heresy, without making or allowing the distinction between principle and fact, falls into heresy.'[5] On this basis he vehemently rejects the secondary object: 'What you propose ... that a fact of the 17th century, and consequently not revealed, is inseparably connected to the essence (*au droit*) and to the dogmas of faith, is a ... ridiculous ... impertinence. The dogmas of faith are nothing other than the truths revealed by Jesus Christ to his Apostles, and conserved in Scripture and Tradition, such that anything which is not revealed in this way cannot belong to the Faith.' Arnauld denounces vigorously this novelty that a fact not revealed, 'which is only of the 17th century, can become an object of divine faith, ... and that one can oblige all the faithful to believe it and to recognise it as an article of Catholic faith newly revealed by God to his Church.'[6]

---

[4] Ibid, 54. (Emphasis in the original.)
[5] Ibid, 55.
[6] Ibid, 56.

A new Archbishop Péréfixe of Paris, trying to find a compromise to resolve the dispute, declared, in an ordinance of 8 June 1664, that in signing the Formula, divine faith is not required in regard to the fact, but only 'a human and ecclesiastical faith, which obliges one to submit his judgement sincerely to that of his legitimate superiors.'[7] The Jansenists were happy that the Archbishop accepted the basic distinction between principle and fact, but note the novelty of this new type of faith: 'It is not a matter of divine faith …, but of another sort of faith which is called a human and ecclesiastical faith.'[8] It is without precedent in history. 'For 1600 years there has been liberty not to believe such defined facts,' and the new obligation was characterised as 'a new dogma contrary to the opinion of all Catholic theologians.'[9] In the discussions about the 'human and ecclesiastical faith,' it was understood that it was the authority of the Church which is involved, since submission was demanded, not to God himself, but to the authorities which represent him legitimately. At the time of its origin, therefore, the ecclesiastical faith was not openly linked to the infallibility of the Church. But, in practice, the result was very much the same. At least that is how it was taken by the Jansenists, for the 'human and ecclesiastical faith,' imposing belief in a matter of fact, usurped in practice the characteristics of infallibility. Infallibility in fact, practical infallibility, an infallibility that dare not speak its name, transferring to the Church prerogatives belonging to God alone: these were the accusations of the Jansenists, who refused to be bound by it.[10] At the time, therefore, the concept of an ecclesiastical faith, having served no useful purpose, was quickly set aside.[11]

There was a short period of truce in the stand-off under Clement IX, who was prepared to tolerate the 'respectful silence' of the Jansenists in the interest of peace. The situation changed again under Clement XI. Although the Jansenists were prepared to condemn the five propositions

---

[7] Ibid, 58.
[8] Ibid, 59.
[9] Ibid, 60.
[10] Ibid, 64-66.
[11] Ibid, 66-68.

'in their natural sense,' their opponents insisted that, through the propositions, the book, its author and his meaning must be implicated. Pope Clement XI supported the anti-Jansenist faction and, in *Vineam Domini Sabaoth* (1705), refused to accept the 'respectful silence'; 'Rather the meaning condemned in the five propositions aforementioned of the book of Jansen, which meaning is exhibited in the words of the propositions as they are in the propositions, must be condemned and rejected as heretical by all the Christian faithful not with the mouth only but with the heart.' (DS 2390)

The first person to set about the task of developing a thorough foundation for the notion of a secondary object of infallibility was François Fénelon (1651-1715), Archbishop of Cambrai.[12] The basic issue at stake for him was the defence of the papal judgment of the Jansenist fact, so his whole effort was devoted to the task of breaking down what he called 'the fundamental principle of the [Jansenist] party,' according to which 'the infallibility of the Church does not extend beyond the limits of Revelation.'[13] He himself basically accepted the same principle, while seeking to prove that the principle itself demanded its own extension beyond the limits of Revelation strictly understood. The infallibility in regard to the interpretation of texts, he argued, is necessary for the protection of the revealed deposit, and 'it is clear that the second type of infallibility is much wider than the first, and beyond the revealed meaning, it also includes the choice of all the means essential for the conservation of this meaning in its integrity.'[14] Fénelon's efforts met with very little acceptance in his lifetime. He was completely isolated among the French Bishops, for not a single French Bishop accepted his positions and many contested them.[15] And even in Rome the reception of his ideas was, according to Chiron, quite 'reserved.'[16] All that was to change in due course, however, for his basic idea that the safeguarding of the deposit of revelation required

---

[12] Ibid, 17.
[13] Ibid, 99.
[14] Ibid, 96-97.
[15] Ibid, 107.
[16] Ibid, 109.

the extension of infallibility beyond its limits, was to be the pivot of all reflection on the object of infallibility in the 19th and 20th centuries.[17]

The First Vatican Council

Fénelon's new doctrine made little headway at the time, but it gradually became the standard teaching of the theological schools during the nineteenth century.[18] It had achieved so high a status that, when it came up for discussion at the First Vatican Council, the Council was 'agitated by this question from the preparatory phase to its conclusion.'[19] The first Schema *De Ecclesia Christi*, distributed on 21 January 1870, in Chapter 9, *De ecclesiae infallibilitate*, contained the following: 'We teach that the object of infallibility extends as far as the deposit of faith and requires its own protection. Therefore the prerogative of infallibility which the Church of Christ enjoys includes within its ambit, both the whole revealed Word of God, as well as everything, which even if it is not in itself revealed, is however such that, without it the deposit could not be safely conserved, certainly and definitively proposed for belief and explained, or validly asserted and defended against the errors of men and the opposition of falsely so-called knowledge.'[20] And a canon was attached which would condemn anyone who refused to accept the secondary object of infallibility as a heretic. 'If anyone says that the infallibility of the Church is restricted only to those things contained in divine revelation, and that it does not extend to those truths which are by necessity required that the deposit of revelation can be integrally guarded; anathema sit.'[21] It is noteworthy that the doctrine was presented as a definable teaching of the Church.

---

[17] Ibid, 97.
[18] Ibid, 121-150.
[19] Umberto Betti, La Costituzione Dommatica 'Pastor Aeternus' del Concilio Vaticano I (Roma: Pontificio Ateneo 'Antonianum', 1961), 641.
[20] Primum Schema De Ecclesia Christi, Caput IX De ecclesiae infallibilitate; Mansi 51, 543A. (Italics mine.)
[21] Canon IX; Mansi 51, 552A.

Chiron gives a full account of the discussion which ensued, with opinions on all sides being expressed.[22] There were Bishops who argued for the extension of the object of infallibility to include matters that had not been revealed, there were those arguing in the opposite sense that the object of infallibility was quite simply restricted to the deposit of revelation, and there were those who argued that it could be extended to matters necessary for its defence, but that these matters were so closely connected to the deposit that they were themselves implicitly revealed. Bishop Rogers of Chatham asked for the suppression of the passage specifying the object of infallibility, on the grounds that the doctrine is uncertain, and made a point which seems to me of considerable importance and to which we will return, that it implies that Christ's work of revelation is imperfect in that it does not contain all that is required to achieve its goal and requires the assistance of men.[23] The document on the Church was never finalised, and so this discussion was never resolved.

The issue did come up, however, in the discussion of the document on papal infallibility. Before dealing with that it is useful to recall something that happened earlier in the Council's work, in connection with a paragraph in the constitution *Dei Filius*, defining the object of faith.[24] Just prior to the Council, Pope Pius IX had condemned the opinion that Christians are only obliged to believe doctrines which have been formally defined, and that they are otherwise free to form their own opinion. In the letter *Tuas libenter*, he wrote that our belief must not be limited only to what has been defined 'but must also be extended to those things which are handed on by the ordinary Magisterium of the whole Church dispersed throughout the world *as divinely revealed* …'[25] It is to be noted that, in his letter, Pope Pius IX takes it for granted that faith has revelation as its object.

---

[22] Ibid, 214-273. See also Roger Auber, Vatican I (Histoire des Conciles Oecuméniques, vol. 12, Paris: Éd. De l'Orante, 1964) 211, 225-25, and Betti, Pastor Aeternus',175, 389-404.
[23] M51, 817A-B.
[24] See Chiron, L'infaillibilité, 207-09.
[25] DS 2879 (Italics mine.)

The Council decided to reiterate this doctrine of Pope Pius IX and taught that 'all those things are to be believed by divine and Catholic faith, which are contained in the Word of God, written and handed down, and which are proposed by the Church *for belief as divinely revealed* either by a solemn judgment or the ordinary and universal magisterium.'[26] What is notable here again is that, when the issue of a secondary object was not raised explicitly, the Bishops taught spontaneously that faith and revelation are correlative, just as the Pope had done before them.

In the preparation of the document on papal infallibility by the drafting committee, the *Deputatio de Fide*, the issue of the secondary object did come up, and the committee was divided on this issue. Some members wanted to limit the object of infallibility to revealed truth, and their voice had prevailed in the formula presented to the council on May 9th, 1870, which spoke of the pope defining what was 'to be held as of faith' (*tamquam de fide tenendum*) by the universal Church, following the pattern of *Dei Filius*. However, as a result of the insistence of some members, notably Bishops Manning and Senestrey, who objected to the limitation of infallibility to what was 'of faith,' the final text of the definition was changed so as to allow for the possibility of infallible definition of matter that was not revealed. For this purpose, the words *de fide* were dropped, leaving only 'doctrine about faith or morals to be held (*tenendam*) by the universal Church.'[27] An authoritative statement of the implications of this for the teaching of the Council in this matter is given in Bishop Gasser's famous *Relatio* at the end of the debate.

> However, other truths ... are more or less strictly connected to revealed dogmas which, although not in themselves revealed, are required that the deposit itself can be retained intact, properly expounded and effectively defined. Such truths, for instance dogmatic facts without which the deposit of faith could not be

---

[26] DS 3011. (Italics mine.)
[27] Francis A. Sullivan, S.J., 'The 'Secondary Object' of Infallibility,' TS 54 (1993) 536-550 at 538.

safeguarded and expounded, are not part of the deposit of faith but required for its custody. All Catholic theologians are agreed that in the authentic proposal and definition of such truths the Church is infallible, so that to deny this infallibility would be a grave error. But opinions vary only about the degree of certainty, whether the proposal of such truths or in proscribing errors with a note less than heresy should be considered a dogma of faith, so that to deny this infallibility of the Church would be heretical; or whether it is only a truth in itself not revealed, but deduced from a revealed dogma, and so only theologically certain. …The question, therefore, is whether papal infallibility in defining these truths is only theologically certain or is a dogma of faith in the same way as is said of the infallibility of the Church. Since the Fathers of the Deputation unanimously agreed that this question should not be defined, but left in its present state …[28]

Bishop Gasser presents it as something about which 'all Catholic theologians are agreed,' that there exist truths 'not in themselves revealed,' which 'are not part of the deposit of faith but required for its custody' and 'that in the authentic proposal and definition of such truths the Church is infallible, so that to deny this infallibility would be a grave error.' For him the only question was as to the status of this affirmation, whether it is only theologically certain or a dogma of faith, and the bishops chose not to decide the issue. 'The choice of the Council was to opt for the non-exclusion of doctrines of a lesser weight and opted for the norm that the object of papal infallibility was the same as that of the Church.'[29]

---

[28] Mansi, 52, 1226B-C.
[29] Betti, Pastor Aeternus, 643.

The Second Vatican Council

At the Second Vatican Council the issue was raised again, with exactly the same result.[30] Just as at the First Vatican Council, the first draft of the document on the Church, prepared before the Council, explicitly taught the existence of the secondary object of infallibility. The paragraph on the object of the magisterium runs as follows: 'The authoritative magisterium of the Church regards primarily the preaching, guarding and interpreting of the Word of God written and handed down. But it also extends, by the same authority, to all those things, not in express words or implicitly revealed, but which are so connected with revealed truths that they are necessary so that the deposit of faith can be integrally guarded, correctly explained and effectively maintained.' A footnote points out that the text is declaring the primary and secondary objects of the infallibility of the Magisterium, adopting a formula used by Bishop Gasser for that purpose at the First Vatican Council.[31] This draft was badly received by the Council Fathers, for reasons that had nothing to do with this issue, and was withdrawn without a vote.

A new schema was prepared and presented to the Fathers in May 1963. In the oral and written reactions to the schema, the dominant issue was collegiality, though the question of the object of the Magisterium was dealt with. The most striking intervention on the issue was that by Fidelis Garcia Martinez, titular bishop of Sululitanus,[32] who submitted a little treatise on the matter. He attacked the notion of ecclesiastical faith, saying that 'no kind of faith was acknowledged in traditional theology but divine or divine-Catholic faith.' He went on: 'The so-called *ecclesiastical* faith is first invented by some theologians in the year 1664 on the occasion of the Jansenist heresy, and in the whole series of dogmatic documents of the Magisterium up to the present day, there has been no mention of such a supposed ecclesiastical faith.'[33] He then recalled the

---

[30] The only full account of the discussion at the Second Vatican Council is in Chiron, L'infaillibilité, 280-317.
[31] Gil Hellín, Lumen Gentium, 627.
[32] AS 2/1,664-668.
[33] AS 2/1,664-668 at 664, footnote 5.

debates at Vatican I and, quoting a number of the interventions made there, aligned himself with the view that the object of infallibility is restricted to the deposit of revelation and those things necessary for its defence which are so closely connected with revelation that they are themselves implicitly revealed.[34] Nothing else of any significance was said on this question, and the result was, as mentioned already, that the doctrine was not taught, but its supporters made sure that nothing was said which would be incompatible with it. In *Lumen Gentium*, § 25, the Council declared that the 'infallibility ... with which the divine redeemer wished to endow his Church in defining doctrine pertaining to faith and morals, is coextensive with the deposit of revelation, which must be religiously guarded and loyally and courageously expounded.'[35] The official explanation of this text by the Theological Commission says: 'The object of the infallibility of the Church thus explained, has the same extension as the revealed deposit; hence it extends to all those things, and only to those, which either directly pertain to the revealed deposit itself, or are required in order that the same deposit may be religiously safeguarded and faithfully expounded.'[36] So far there is no mention of truths that are not revealed. The possibility of teaching on matters outside revelation does get explicit mention in one connection with a significant parallel to what happened at the First Vatican Council. In dealing with the ordinary magisterium of the bishops a text was formulated which seemed to exclude the possibility of the secondary object, and this text was changed 'lest the infallibility of the episcopal body seem to be restricted to that only which is proposed to be believed as divinely revealed.'[37] As Sullivan points out: 'Clearly, the intention of this emendation was to avoid using an expression which might have seemed to exclude the secondary object of infallibility.' [38] Just as at the First Vatican Council, the Theological Commission at the Second Vatican Council is clearly of the opinion that the Church can

---

[34] AS 2/1, 664-668 at 668.
[35] Tanner, 869.27-30.
[36] AS, III/1, 251.
[37] AS, III/1, 251.
[38] Sullivan, Magisterium, 132.

teach infallibly beyond the revealed deposit, but the actual conciliar text does not make that opinion explicitly its own. So, after both Councils the view that the Magisterium can teach infallibly truths which are not revealed remained a theological opinion, not an official teaching of the Church. According to Umberto Betti, a well-qualified commentator on both the Vatican Councils, 'Vatican I wished to remain with the negative position of non-exclusion, and Vatican II added nothing in this regard.'[39] Rahner's interpretation is worth quoting for the interesting remarks he makes about the secondary object. 'On LG25; The words "to be inviolably preserved" imply that the object of infallible authority includes truths which form a safeguard for the deposit of revelation strictly speaking, even though these truths are not formally revealed (implicitly or explicitly) – that is, if there are such truths: if there really is a *fides ecclesiastica* and if it really has a proper object, a point on which theologians do not agree.'[40]

Cardinal Ratzinger has disputed this careful interpretation of the teaching of the Second Vatican Council and defended the existence of the secondary object of infallibility in strong terms. He responded to an earlier critic of the notion as follows:

> Hünermann directs his criticism at the so-called second level of the profession of faith, which distinguishes teaching that is valid and indissolubly linked with Revelation from true and proper Revelation. It is utterly false to say that the Fathers of the First and Second Vatican Councils expressly reject this distinction. On the contrary, precisely the opposite is true. ... The separation of the two levels took conceptual form at the First Vatican Council through the distinction made between 'credenda' (to be believed) and 'tenenda' (to

---

[39] Betti, L'Ossequio, 452.
[40] Commentary on the Documents of Vatican II, Volume I, ed. Herbert Vorgrimler (London/New York: Burns Oates/Herder and Herder, 1967), 212. Rahner expressed these doubts about the existence of the secondary object in Sacramentum Mundi III, 355.

be held). ... Moreover, it is enough to leaf through any theology book from the pre-conciliar period to see that this is what was precisely written, even if details in elaborating the second level were debated and still are today. The Second Vatican Council naturally accepted the distinction formulated by the First Vatican Council and strengthened it. I fail to understand how one can assert the contrary.'[41]

It is indeed false to say that the Fathers of the First and Second Vatican Councils expressly reject the secondary object of infallibility. It is clear that many of the Fathers of the First Vatican Council accepted the secondary object, but it is equally clear that many of them rejected it, and it is manifest that the Council chose not to take a position on the matter, though the distinction between the primary and secondary object did take conceptual form in the distinction made between *credenda* and *tenenda*. It is not clear what the bulk of the Fathers of the Second Vatican Council thought about this issue. What is clear is that the drafters of *Lumen gentium* held to the distinction and formulated certain sentences in order that the distinction would not be excluded, but is not clear that what they did in this regard can be considered as strengthening the distinction.

The Catechism of the Catholic Church

In the drafting of the *Catechism of the Catholic Church*, the issue of the secondary object arose in a manner which has been observed already at both the Vatican Councils. Just as at the First Vatican Council and the Second Vatican Council, the drafters of the *Catechism of the Catholic Church* got into trouble by using language which failed to maintain the distinct secondary object of infallibility and the special type of faith response it requires. In its first version the *Catechism* said:

---

[41] Cardinal Ratzinger, interview with the Frankfurter Allgemeine, OssRom, 29 November 2000, 6.

'The Church's Magisterium exercises the authority it holds from Christ to the fullest extent when it defines dogmas, that is, when it proposes truths contained in divine Revelation or *having a necessary connection with them*, in a form obliging the Christian people to an irrevocable adherence of faith.'[42] Commenting on the *Catechism*, Francis Sullivan noted that '[i]t is obvious that the italicized clause refers to truths which are not contained in divine revelation',[43] and protested at what was implied. 'Here the Catechism has espoused an opinion that has been held by a number of prominent Catholic theologians (among them, F. Marin-Sola, Charles Journet and Yves Congar) to the effect that the proper response to infallibly defined doctrine would be an act of divine faith, even though the matter in itself was not revealed. However, this opinion has been strongly contested by a great many Catholic theologians, who insist that only divinely revealed truth can be defined as dogma calling for an assent of divine faith.'[44] On the basis of this objection, the text of the *Catechism* was changed, and now reads: 'The Church's Magisterium exercises the authority it holds from Christ to the fullest extent when it defines dogmas, that is, when it proposes, in a form obliging the Christian to an irrevocable adherence of faith, truths contained in divine Revelation or also when it proposes, in a definitive way, truths having a necessary connection with these.'

It is to be noted that this text, like the others we have met, does not explicitly affirm the existence of a secondary object, but is formulated so as not to exclude it. What I suggest is of significance in this little fracas, and what it has in common with the similar incidents at the two Vatican Councils, is that when the Bishops of the Church are drafting a text on this matter, the spontaneous assumption that faith and revelation are correlative first arises and then has to be corrected by the adamant adherents of the secondary object.

---

[42] CCC 88 (Emphasis added.)
[43] TS (1993) 536.
[44] Creative Fidelity, 17.

The Profession of Faith of 1989

The cautious exegesis of the two Vatican Councils being advocated here has not been universally shared. The Congregation for the Doctrine of the Faith has chosen to interpret the teaching of *Lumen gentium* § 25 as if it actually taught the existence of the secondary object, and has made significant interventions in that sense. In its document *Mysterium Ecclesiae* (1973) the Congregation states: 'According to Catholic doctrine, the infallibility of the Church's Magisterium extends *not only* to the deposit of faith *but also* to those matters without which that deposit cannot be rightly preserved and expounded. (LG 25)'[45] The Council said that the ambit of infallibility 'is coextensive with the deposit of revelation, which must be religiously guarded and loyally and courageously expounded'. *Mysterium Ecclesiae* says that infallibility extends *not only* to the deposit of faith *but also* to other matters. The implication that these others matters do not belong to the deposit of faith, to revelation, is there to be drawn. The same tendency is to be observed in the wording of a new formula for the Profession of Faith promulgated in 1989. After the Profession of the Creed, the text continues:

> With firm faith I believe as well everything contained in the Word of God, written or handed down in tradition and proposed by the Church -whether by a solemn judgment or by the ordinary and universal Magisterium - to be believed as divinely revealed. I also firmly accept and hold each and every thing that is proposed by that same Church definitively with regard to teaching concerning faith and morals.[46]

What is of interest here is that the matters to be accepted are placed in two categories. In the first sentence we believe what is contained in

---

[45] More Postconciliar Documents, ed. Austin Flannery, O. (Dominican Publications: Dublin, 1982.), 432. (Emphasis added.)
[46] ND 41.

the Word of God and proposed by the Church as divinely revealed. In the second sentence we affirm our acceptance of all that is proposed definitively, and there is the hidden implication that these things are not divinely revealed. This hidden implication was first mentioned explicitly in the Instruction on the Ecclesial Vocation of the Theologian, *Donum Veritatis* (1992). In discussing the competence of the Magisterium and its extent, the document says: 'By its nature, the task of religiously guarding and loyally expounding the deposit of divine Revelation (in all its integrity and purity), implies that the Magisterium can make a pronouncement 'in a definitive way' on propositions which, *even if not contained among the truths of faith*, are nonetheless intimately connected with them, in such a way, that the definitive character of such affirmations derives in the final analysis from revelation itself.'[47] The point is made again a little later in the document as follows: 'When the Magisterium proposes 'in a definitive way' truths concerning faith and morals, which, *even if not divinely revealed*, are nevertheless strictly and intimately connected with Revelation, these must be firmly accepted and held.'[48] What is new in these statements is the specification that what is being taught is 'not contained among the truths of faith,' 'not divinely revealed.' In adding these specifications, the Instruction goes beyond what has been officially taught by either of the Vatican Councils.

In 1998 Pope John Paul II issued an Apostolic Letter, *Ad tuendam fidem*, on this issue, introducing certain additions to the Code of Canon Law to deal specifically with this second category of truths introduced into the Profession of Faith of 1989. The introduction to the letter indicates that these changes are deemed necessary 'given the compelling need to forestall and refute the theological opinions being raised against this second category of truths.'[49] In the letter, in § 3, Pope John Paul says that the 'second paragraph of the *Profession of Faith* is of utmost importance since it refers to truths that are necessarily connected with divine revelation,'[50] and in the new text of Canon 750,

---

[47] Donum Veritatis, § 16. (Emphasis added.)
[48] Ibid, § 23. (Ephasis added.)
[49] L'Osservatore Romano (Eng. ed.), 15 July 1998, 1.
[50] Ibid.

§ 2 the equivalent formula is used, that the second paragraph refers to 'those things required for the holy keeping and faithful exposition of the deposit of faith.'[51] Yet again, it is to be noted that neither the Pope nor the Canon Law says that these truths are *not* revealed, though the presumption is obviously hidden under the text. Accompanying *Ad tuendam fidem*, the Congregation for the Doctrine of the Faith published a *Commentary on the Concluding Formula of the 'Profession of Faith'*, and the definition of the secondary object given there is of interest. It says: 'The object taught by this formula includes all those teachings belonging to the dogmatic or moral area, which are necessary for faithfully keeping and expounding the deposit of faith, even if they have not been proposed by the Magisterium of the Church as formally revealed.'[52] This is a different qualification from any that has gone before. It is not stated that these truths are *not* revealed, but that they have not been proposed as *formally* revealed. This qualification leaves open the possibility that they are implicitly revealed, which marks an important difference. So, yet again, as at the First Vatican Council and at the Second Vatican Council, when the effort is made to formulate this doctrine at a high enough level, the explicit statement of the non-revealed character of these truths is avoided.

Is there a Secondary Object of Infallibility?

This doctrine of a secondary object of infallibility has been hovering on the verge of Church teaching for a long time now, without yet managing to become official teaching, and it is time now to consider the substance of the issue. There are two questions. Can the Church teach infallibly a doctrine which lies outside the ambit of revelation? And is there a corresponding Christian response of faith which is not divine? These issues are crucial for the position to be adopted in this book, so it is necessary to examine them now and take up a position in

---

[51] Ibid, 2.
[52] Commentary, § 6. Ibid, 3.

regard to them. The essential arguments in the matter were made when the doctrine was first formally proposed in seventeenth-century Paris.

The Clermont Jesuits based their case on the principle 'that the Popes enjoy a personal infallibility which is the same as that of Christ,' and this point was dealt with in a defence of their position written by some leading Jansenists.

> When it is a case of an issue where men are capable of making a mistake, as in that of interpreting an author whose work is controversial, I cannot conclude that a given individual is not mistaken, because he is an archbishop or the Pope, unless I suppose that God has joined to these dignities some supernatural light … or has raised them to a participation in one of the qualities of the Divinity, which is that of never being mistaken in His judgements. … It is not permitted to anyone to attribute to himself, or to anyone else, a privilege of this kind, without undeniable evidence that it has been given by God. It would be necessary, therefore, in order to be able to say that all the decisions of the popes are certain, even on matters of fact, that one can show the basis of this privilege, and show that it is contained in Scripture and recognised by the Fathers and by the whole Church …[53]

The correctness of this argument hardly needs to be elaborated. No one now bases papal infallibility on a personal endowment of the Pope granting him a supernatural light to guarantee the correctness of his judgments in any matter, much less matters outside the ambit of revelation. That the Clermont Jesuits would make such a case is significant, for it is symptomatic of a problem which goes to the heart of the difficulties in this whole matter, the separation of the Church from Christ and the Holy Spirit. The Clermont Jesuits were clearly thinking

---

[53] Chiron, L'infaillibilité, 61, footnote 2.

of the Pope making his judgment on his own, with his own light, and our response being based on the validity of his personal judgment. But this is not the manner in which infallibility works in the Church.

God alone is infallible, and creatures can participate in the infallibility of God only as he arranges it. Christ our Lord was and is infallible in his humanity by virtue of the beatific vision he enjoyed on earth and enjoys still. He has arranged for the infallibility of his Church by the gift of the Holy Spirit who dwells in the Church and leads her into the whole truth. The infallibility of the Church is based on this presence of the two divine persons, by the Incarnation of the Word and the Incorporation of the Holy Spirit, and the Church's infallibility cannot be separated from them. The indwelling of the divine persons forms the basis of the Church's infallibility and establishes its limits. The Holy Spirit only speaks what is Christ's, nothing more and nothing less. The Bishops, when they are teaching in the Church, are speaking in the person of Christ and in the light of the Holy Spirit, and what they say with authority is the word of Christ himself. The light by which they judge is the same light of faith which we all share, to which is joined a special assistance or illumination of the Spirit which ensures that their judgment is true. It is clear that this assistance is not the foundation of a personal infallibility of the Bishops but simply ensuring that the Bishops can judge correctly by participating providentially in the infallibility of God. If these points are valid, then there is no way the Pope can pronounce infallibly on a matter which falls outside the ambit of revelation.

This principle, that the Church can teach infallibly everything necessary for the guarding and propounding of the deposit of faith, is the one which continues to ground the secondary object of infallibility. The principle cannot be disputed, but the conclusion can. And here the strongest argument is the one made by Bishop Rogers of Chatham at the First Vatican Council.[54] The suggestion that the Bishops have to go outside the ambit of revelation in order to protect the deposit of faith implies that Christ our Lord did not provide properly for his Church,

---

[54] See footnote 35.

and that implication cannot be allowed to stand. Anything which is necessary for the guarding and propounding of the deposit of faith, and which is strictly and necessarily connected with it, must *ipso facto* be implicitly revealed, and will hence fall within the ambit of revelation.

One can make another argument against the secondary object of infallibility in the form of a *reduction ad absurdum*. If the Church pronounces infallibly on any matter, it speaks with the authority of God, for only God can grant the gift of infallibility. Anything which God says with infallible authority is, *ipso facto*, revealed. If the Church makes such a statement outside the ambit of what has been revealed already, the statement must be recognized as a new revelation. But that is impossible. There can be no new revelation. It follows that the matter must have been part of the original revelation, and the presupposition of speaking outside the ambit of the original revelation must fall.

I have argued against the secondary object of infallibility on principle. Now, in support of this contention that infallibility applies only to revealed truths, I would like to bring forward some texts from the tradition. Opening his treatment of the virtue of faith in the Summa, St. Thomas tells us that 'the faith of which we speak assents to nothing except what has been revealed by God.'[55] He also makes clear that the teachers in the Church are bound by the deposit of revelation. 'The Apostles and their successors are vicars of God in regard to the regime of the Church constituted by faith and the sacraments of faith. Therefore, just as they are not permitted to found another Church, so they are not permitted to hand on another faith, nor institute other sacraments.'[56] This was standard doctrine, which no one thought to question, until the matter of the secondary object emerged. The consensus on the matter was beginning to break down in the nineteenth century, and the signs are there at the First Vatican Council, as we have seen, but there were still authoritative figures holding to the older conviction. Joseph Kleutgen, for instance, in his large work defending the faith against the

---

[55] STh 2-2, q. 1 a. 1c.
[56] ST, III, q. 64, a. 2, ad 3; cf. II-II, q. 88, a. 11; In IV Sent., d. 17, q. 3, a. 1, sol. 5; d. 27, q. 3, a. 3, ad 2.

errors of the day which would be so influential was quite clear that the authentically Catholic principle asserts that the only object of Christian faith is what the Church teaches as a truth revealed by God. He argues that whatever is proposed by the Church as a matter of faith must be contained in the word of God, for otherwise the Church would err in proposing them - contrary to the divine promise. Therefore, they are matters of divine faith. 'All that (and only that) belongs to the faith, which has been revealed by God, (i.e., what is contained in the Word of God which has been written down or handed on orally,) and which has been proposed as such to all for belief by the Church.'[57]

In reviewing the discussion at the First Vatican Council, we saw how many Bishops remained of the old opinion, and in *Dei Filius*, when the secondary object didn't come up for consideration, a formula was used taking the traditional position for granted. The issue was relevant, for there were Bishops at the Council who were arguing for a completely unlimited scope for papal infallibility. One bishop, Mgr Salas, made a point about the limits to the authority of the Pope which has been much quoted since. 'The power of the Supreme Pontiff is limited by the natural and divine law, it is limited by the precepts and doctrines of Jesus Christ our Lord, it is limited by the common good of the Church, it is limited by conscience, it is limited by right reason and common sense, it is limited by the rule of faith and morals.'[58] The 'precepts and doctrines of Jesus Christ our Lord' and 'the rule of faith and morals' both refer to the deposit of faith as setting the limit of papal infallibility. And even after the First Vatican Council, there were still those who understood that the Pope's authority was unlimited. Archbishop Fessler replied to one such critic and affirmed: 'The Pope, in his doctrinal utterances, only speaks what he finds, under the special divine assistance, to be already part of the truth revealed by God necessary for salvation, which He has given in trust to the Catholic Church (i.e. in the divine *depositum fidei*). The same assistance of God which securely preserves the Pope

---

[57] Joseph Kleutgen, S.J., <u>Die Theologie der Vorzeit verteidigt</u>, 3 vols, 1st ed. (Münster: Theissing, 1853-60). /5 vols, 2nd ed. (Münster: Theissing, 1867-74), Vol. 1, 46-47.

[58] M52, 579D-580A.

from error preserves him with equal security from declaring <u>that</u> to be revealed by God, and entrusted to the keeping of the Catholic Church as a matter of truth or morals, which God has *not* revealed and has *not* deposited in His Church.'[59] And the same point was dealt with in the Joint Pastoral Letter of the Swiss Bishops in 1871: 'It is, then, the revelation given by God which is the domain perfectly traced out and exactly circumscribed, within which the infallible decisions of the Pope are able to extend themselves, and in regard to which the faith of Catholics can be bound to fresh obligations.'[60] Of this letter we are told that '[t]he Pope [Pius IX] wrote to the Swiss bishops that nothing could be more opportune or more worthy of praise, or cause the truth to stand out more clearly, than their pastoral.'[61]

One theologian who was strong on the point, was Cardinal Newman who deals with the matter at some length.

> Infallibility cannot act outside of a definite circle of thought, and it must in all its decisions, or *definitions*, as they are called, profess to be keeping within it. The great truths of the moral law, of natural religion, and of Apostolical faith, are both its boundary and its foundation. It must not go beyond them, and it must ever appeal to them. Both its subject-matter, and its articles in that subject-matter, are fixed. . . . It must ever profess to be guided by Scripture and tradition. It must refer to the particular Apostolic truth which it is enforcing, or (what is called) *defining*. Nothing, then, can be presented to me, in time to come, as part of the faith, but what I ought already to have received, and have not actually received; if not, merely because it has not been told me. Nothing can be imposed upon me

---

[59] Joseph Fessler, <u>The True and the False Infallibility of the Popes</u> (London: Burns and Oates, 1875), 53.
[60] Fessler, <u>The True and the False Infallibility of the Popes</u>, 63.
[61] Cuthbert Butler, <u>The Vatican Council</u> (London: Longmans, Green and Co., 1930), 465.

> different in kind from what I hold already, - much less
> contrary to it. The new truth which is promulgated, if
> it is to be called new, must be at least homogeneous,
> cognate, implicit, viewed relatively to the old truth. It
> must be what I may even have guessed, or wished, to be
> included in the Apostolic revelation; and at least it will
> be of such a character, that my thoughts readily concur
> in it or coalesce with it, as soon as I hear it. Perhaps I
> and others actually have always believed it, and the only
> question which is now decided in my behalf, is that I
> am henceforth to believe that I have only been holding
> what the Apostles held before me.[62]

These are all valuable authorities, and their witness makes it clear that the opinion that infallibility is limited to the truths of revelation is perfectly acceptable within the communion of the faith.

Is there such a thing as Ecclesiastical Faith?

In approaching the issue of ecclesiastical faith, it seems appropriate to give the first word to Antoine Arnauld, who made a trenchant critique of the 'human and ecclesiastical faith' when it was first mooted by Archbishop Péréfixe. He wrote:

> Divine faith is that which is based on the revelation
> of God, who has deigned to speak to men and to reveal
> his mysteries by his prophets, by Jesus Christ and
> the Apostles. This revelation, coming to us through
> Scripture and Tradition, is proposed to us by the
> Church, which is assisted by the Spirit of God so as not
> to deceive us in the points she proposes. It is in this that
> she is infallible, according to the consensus of all the
> theologians, and it is in this that God does not permit

---

[62] Apologia pro Vita Sua (Image Books, New York, 1956), 329-330.

> that she will give us as an article of faith or a principle of morality anything which is not coherent with what the Son of God has revealed by his Apostles. Human faith is that which is not based on the revelation of God, but on the authority of men of whatever dignity to which they have been raised. Therefore, anything which is determined touching a point of particular fact can only be believed with human faith, since it is certain that it cannot be based either on Scripture or Tradition, which are the two channels by which the revelation of God, on which divine faith is based, come to us.[63]

His critique is based on the fundamental principle that there are only two kinds of faith, divine and human, and no other possibility exists. According to Congar, this has been the case ever since, that the critics of the notion regularly base their position on *De veritate*, q. 14, a. 8 that only the authority of God can ground an infallible faith, and this authority is the motive of divine faith. He says that 'there is no doubt that the roots of the debate are found more in ecclesiology than in the theology of faith. For the partisans of divine faith, it is by one and same movement, in the case of an infallible definition, that the believer believes in God witnessing in and through the Church. They clearly cannot hold this position without restricting, one way or another, the definitions in question to direct revelation.'[64] That is the position being adopted here. The infallibility of the Holy Church is based on the fact that there is only one Teacher, Christ, and he teaches the Word of God always and everywhere in the Church through the Holy Spirit. He teaches the whole Word of God and only the Word of God. It is out of the question that he would teach anything else, so infallible declarations by the Church outside the ambit of revelation are simply impossible.

Cardinal Newman was also a strong critic of the very idea of ecclesiastical faith. He wrote: 'This seems to me contrary to the great

---

[63] Chiron, L'infaillibilité, 63.
[64] Congar, 'Fait dogmatique et foi ecclésiastique' in Sainte Église (Paris, 1963) 357-373 at 362.

tradition of teaching in the Church...'[65] And 'I am averse to it, 1. because it does not seem to be the old way. 2. because I do not understand a certainty which is more than moral and less than supernatural, and a faith which is neither divine nor human.'[66] And further: 'I object to this as a novel doctrine, unknown to our great dogmatic writers of whatever school, who teach that that alone has a universal claim on our faith which was given in the beginning. ... I object to it as an unmeaning distinction and an evasion. What do you mean by de fide, but what is necessary to be believed in order to achieve salvation? And is it not absurd to speak of a certainty which is more than moral and less than supernatural? or of a faith which is neither divine nor human, but something between, or mixed up of both?'[67] He was not writing here in a fully formal manner, but his great distaste for the very notion of an ecclesiastical faith is apparent.

The two notions of a secondary object of infallibility and an ecclesiastical faith which is not divine stand or fall together, and the arguments have been presented in defence of the position that there is no such thing as either the one or the other. The thesis of this book demands that that there is no such thing as a secondary object of infallibility. And, correspondingly, there is no such thing as an ecclesiastical faith. There is only one Teacher in the Church, Christ our Lord, who teaches through the Church and enlightens us to receive his teaching by the Holy Spirit. The Holy Church teaches only what Christ teaches, for the two are one mystical Person. The teaching of the Church and the teaching of Christ are, therefore, exactly coterminous. The Church cannot and does not teach anything outside the ambit of revelation, and there is only one response of faith, divine and Catholic faith, which accepts the truth of Christ, the whole truth of Christ, and nothing but the truth of Christ. This principle is foundational for the thesis being proposed here and will appear again in the sequel, but first the implications of this trenchant position must now be considered.

---

[65] J. Derek Holmes, The Theological Papers of John Henry Newman on Biblical Inspiration and on Infallibility (Oxford: Clarendon Press, 1979), 112.
[66] Ibid, 113.
[67] Ibid, 137.

Pope Alexander's (Infallible?) Judgment

This whole theory of a secondary object of infallibility was first elaborated by the Clermont Jesuits and subsequently by Archbishop Fenélon in defence of Pope Alexander VII's judgment on the dogmatic fact of Jansenism, so a stand has to be taken in regard to it. Pope Alexander did say that 'we declare and define' the point, (DS 2012) but does this judgment have to be taken as definitive and binding on the Church? A first question to ask is whether he intended this judgement as one to be held by all the faithful? He had the recalcitrant Jansenists in mind, and not many other people had ever read the book, so one is entitled to doubt it.

A more fundamental question asks if it is possible that the fact that what Jansen meant when he wrote his book is exactly what was condemned in the Five Propositions is a matter fit for infallible definition? On what basis could Pope Alexander make such a judgment, and how could he presume to insist that the whole Church concur in it? The argument that is still given in support of Pope Alexander VII's declaration is that it was deemed necessary for the defence of the truth of the Five Propositions. But it was not necessary for that purpose. The Five Propositions were formally taught and were universally accepted, even by the Jansenists themselves, so nothing further was needed for their defence. There was some confusion between the two sides in this dispute, but it does not seem that anyone has ever successfully discerned what it was, and certainly Pope Alexander's insistence on a particular interpretation of Jansen's book did not solve the problem. So, this definition of Pope Alexander was not necessary for the defence of the deposit of faith, it notably failed in its objective of defending the Five Propositions and, with good reason, no Pope has ever subsequently attempted such a procedure. I suggest that an infallible judgement in such a matter is impossible. To know what Jansen meant exactly one has to read his book carefully, one has to understand his mind exactly and interpret it with precision. If Pope Alexander ever read the book, from where would he get the wisdom required to understand it with any more precision than anyone else? And who could verify his judgement? Why would anyone want to? What difference does it make? Nothing in the teaching of the Church stands or falls by the meaning of an individual work by an individual theologian and it is a mistake to suggest that such a judgement is 'strictly and intimately connected with Revelation.' I do not say that Pope Alexander's judgment was erroneous. I do not know whether it was or not, and nor does anyone else. No one could possibly know with certainty whether or not the Five Propositions represent an accurate interpretation of Jansen's book. But I am certain of the fact that Pope Alexander had no right to make a definitive judgment in the matter, and I join myself with the Jansenists in rejecting his decree. I therefore suggest that it was not an infallible definition, that it was not fit matter for infallible definition, and therefore it should not be deemed part of the object of infallibility at all. If this judgment holds the original foundation of the secondary object of infallibility is removed.

The Position of the Congregation for the Doctrine of the Faith

The Congregation for the Doctrine of the Faith has espoused this doctrine of the secondary object of infallibility in the series of interventions which have been referred to already, and this certainly constitutes a difficulty for anyone arguing against its very existence. The Congregation's concern is to ensure that there will be no diminishing of the full object of the Church's infallibility, and that concern must be fully supported. I dispute, however, the suggestion that establishing a secondary object of infallibility protects the infallibility of the Church. In its Commentary on the Profession of Faith of 1989, the Congregation defines the secondary object of infallibility as follows: 'The object taught by this formula includes *all those teachings belonging to the dogmatic or moral area, which are necessary for faithfully keeping and expounding the deposit of faith, even if they have not been proposed by the Magisterium of the Church as formally revealed.*'[68] Later in the same paragraph the Congregation explains 'that these doctrines may not be proposed as formally revealed, insofar as they add to the data of faith *elements that are not revealed or which are not yet expressly recognized as such,*' and yet 'it cannot be excluded that at a certain point in dogmatic development, the understanding of the realities and the words of the deposit of faith can progress in the life of the Church, and the Magisterium may proclaim some of these doctrines as also dogmas of divine and Catholic faith.'[69] Can these affirmations be taken as constituting a clear affirmation of the secondary object of infallibility? From the point of view being advocated here, the hesitation of the document as to whether these doctrines are revealed or not is significant.

The teaching office of the Church is an organ of Jesus Himself teaching and is, therefore, a mystery of faith. From this follows the extreme difficulty in determining the limits of infallibility. None of us possesses the knowledge on which infallibility is based, for we are all of us believers. Only Jesus with His Beatific Vision grounding a sure and certain grasp of what He knows is fully aware of the extent and limits of His knowledge. Our efforts to formulate limits are *post factum*, after the teaching has been communicated. There are dangers on both sides; a danger of excessive extension and a danger of excessive limitation. On the principle being advocated here, if any doctrine is taught definitively by the Church it is, *ipso facto*, revealed. The Church cannot teach definitively a doctrine which is not revealed. It never has and it never will. The implication of this is that the second group of truths to which the second clause of the new Profession of Faith is empty. All truths taught definitively by the Church are revealed truths. They are to be accepted and held indeed, but with divine and Catholic faith. We have developed our basic criterion that the Church's infallibility belongs only to truths of faith and morals which are divinely revealed. We have

---

[68] Congregation for the Doctrine of the Faith, 'Commentary on the Concluding Formula of the 'Professio fidei',' AAS 90 (1998) 544-551 at 546; (English translation; L'Osservatore Romano (Eng. Ed.), 15 July 1998, 3.) (Emphasis in the original, in both languages.)

[69] Ibid.

argued that if any matter belonging to faith and morals is taught with authority as to be held by all the faithful, it is implicitly being proposed as belonging to the deposit of faith, as being divinely revealed. And the logic works also in reverse. If any matter clearly does not belong to the deposit of faith, is clearly not revealed by God, then it follows that it is not fit matter for infallible definition. The fear that such a principle is unduly restrictive is unfounded when we bear in mind the principle that any truth which is are 'strictly and intimately connected with Revelation' is itself revealed.

The position being advocated here, therefore, in no way undermines the authority of the Church teaching any point which might appear to fall under a putative secondary object of infallibility. In its Commentary on the new Profession of Faith, the Congregation for the Doctrine of the Faith had this to say about matters it takes as belonging to the secondary object of infallibility: 'Every believer, therefore, is required to give *firm and definitive assent* to these truths… Whoever denies these truths would be in a position of *rejecting a truth of Catholic doctrine (Ad tuendam fidem) and would therefore no longer be in full communion with the Catholic Church*.'[70] The position being advocated here turns this argument around and argues that if a doctrine is taught infallibly it must be revealed, and is not secondary at all. The object of infallibility is one, integral, organic whole; not a set of discreet 'truths.' What is taught infallibly is taught on the authority of God revealing and is, therefore, revealed. On this view, it is the Congregation for the Doctrine of the Faith which is undermining the authority of the Church in teaching these doctrines, by categorizing them as secondary and declaring that they have not been revealed, when in fact they must have been, and therefore they have been.

The possible secondary object was discussed in the schools and the bishops were not able to decide the issue. They were not sure whether or not there was, and if so in what it consisted. They were not going to deny the secondary object lest they in some way prematurely limit the object of infallibility. What they were sure of was that the object

---

[70] Ibid.

of infallibility was as extensive as it needed to be for its own proper maintenance and progress. The required extension does not take the object beyond the limits of revelation and hence there is, in fact, no secondary object. In conclusion, therefore, I suggest that invoking this so-called secondary object of infallibility is a mistake. On the one hand it grants excessive weight to secondary matters which are not revealed, and which cannot be proclaimed infallibly at all. But what is more serious is that it undermines the true value of the mystery of the Church's participation in the infallibility of God revealing and lessens the weight of the authority of the Church teaching truths which are clearly revealed and belong by full right to the deposit of faith. If two councils of the Church broach a question on two occasions a full century apart and fail to agree an answer, that fact suggests that there is some flaw in the posing of the question. The standard theology on which all these developments are based has no hesitation in affirming the existence of the secondary object, and yet, every time the doctrine comes close to magisterial formulation, a greater or lesser hesitation emerges, but always the hesitation. It appears that, despite continued efforts, the doctrine cannot get itself magisterially accepted. The position being advocated here is that the explanation for this is that the doctrine is not true, and the Holy Spirit, in his providence, prevents the error coming to magisterial expression. It is my view that the Congregation for the Doctrine of the Faith has gone down a blind alley in beginning to raise the manualist view to the level of doctrine, but it has had the good effect of beginning the process of final clarification of the issue.

Is this dissent?

Does my rejection of a secondary object of infallibility constitute dissent from an official teaching of the Catholic Church? What is the status of this doctrine? It was presented to the First Vatican Council as a doctrine to be defined with an anathema attached convicting anyone who refused it of heresy. In his *Relatio* to the Council, Bishop Gasser considered it at least theologically certain, if not a dogma of faith, and considered rejecting it to be a grave error. Despite these strong statements, the doctrine was not taught by the Council, although a formula was used in *Pastor aeternus* which would not exclude it. The doctrine was presented again to the Second Vatican Council to be taught with conciliar authority, and again it did not appear in any document of the Council, although, as at the First Vatican Council, formulas were used in different places so as not to exclude it. It has been noted how the Congregation for the Doctrine of the Faith takes this to be Catholic doctrine, and formulated the clauses at the end of the Profession of Faith of 1989 so that theologians must promise to accept teachings the Congregation believes to fall within the secondary object. It has been noted too that Pope John Paul II introduced changes into the Code of Canon Law to cover a presumed secondary object of infallibility and issued an Apostolic Letter to explain his action, which indicates that he too believes there is such an object of infallibility.

The only magisterial document to teach this doctrine specifically is the *Commentary* on *Ad tuendam fidem* of the Congregation for the Doctrine of the Faith. Cardinal Ratzinger, then Prefect of the Congregation, had occasion to explain the status of this document. He said that

> its whole text was composed by the Congregation, also, at the successive stages of its preparation, it was submitted to the assembly of the Cardinals, and at the end it was approved by them. It obtained also the approval of the Holy Father. Such approvals notwithstanding, all agreed that the text should not be given a binding force; rather, it should be offered as a help to understanding. It was not, therefore, published as a proper document of the Congregation itself. To show, however, that {the Commentary} is not the private work of the Prefect and the Secretary of the Congregation but an authorized aid for the understanding of the texts, a

specific {extraordinary} manner for its publication was chosen.[71]

It is clear from this explanation that this document of the Congregation has the lowest level of magisterial authority that there can be in a document of the Holy See. So, is this official teaching or not? If it is not, I simply disagree with it. If it is, I dissent from it formally, and will be quite happy to accept any consequences accruing from my dissent. My own interpretation of the marvellous vicissitudes of this doctrine over the two Vatican Councils and after, is that it is a perfect example of how the providence of God ensures that error does not enter into the teaching of the Church. It is true that I may be wrong in this. But, if I am, I will be quite happy to be the 'heretic' whose travails lead to the clear exposition of a genuine teaching of the Church, one way or the other!

---

[71] Cardinal Joseph Ratzinger, 'Infallibility Explored - the Cardinal responds,' in Céide March/April 1999, 28-29.

Chapter 11

The Moral Teaching of the Church

Heresy in the strict sense of the term is the denial of a truth proposed by the church as revealed. Many of the tensions in the life of the church today between the hierarchical magisterium and theologians do not concern the revealed truths of faith, no matter how this term is understood. Discussions about moral issues such as contraception and sterilization or the possibility of dissent from authoritative, noninfallible teachings of the hierarchical magisterium on moral matters do not involve heresy in the strict sense of the term.[1]

According to Charles Curran, an element of the justification for his dissent from some moral teachings of the Church is the claim that such teachings are not revealed truths, and that they are, thus, secondary matters which do not belong to the core of the Christian proclamation. If the moral teaching of the Church is not revealed then it is true to say, with Curran, that dissent from teaching could never be heresy. And the logic also holds in reverse. If the moral doctrines are, in fact, revealed they will then belong by full right to the deposit of faith, and dissent from them would involve heresy. This is obviously a fundamental point of the discussion. If the moral teaching is part of the teaching of the Church, in the full sense, the teaching of the holy Church, then it

---

[1] Charles E. Curran, Moral Theology: A Continuing Journey (Notre Dame - London: University of Notre Dame Press, 1982), 3.

must be revealed. For the holy Church of Christ can only teach what is revealed and taught by Christ himself in and through the Church by the power of the Holy Spirit. In moral matters a difficulty arises from the fact that morality overlaps with reason, since the natural law is the rule of right reason, and every human being has a certain competence here. If the Bishops are considered to be on their own interpreting matters within the competence of human reason, we would then seem to be at a double remove from the divine sources of knowledge in the Church. It is necessary, therefore, to establish clearly the provenance of moral teaching in the Church, and the precise ground of the competence of the bishops of the Church in teaching moral principles. So, a judgment has to be made as to whether or not the specific moral norms are revealed.

It has been the common opinion of theologians in recent centuries that the precepts of the natural law have been revealed, and the scriptural foundation centred on the revelation of the Ten Commandments, the Sermon on the Mount and the moral teaching of St. Paul.[2] The giving of the Law on Mount Sinai is arguably the central text of the Old Testament, and it is hardly necessary to argue a case for the importance there of the moral teaching involved in the giving of the Ten Commandments. Jesus' giving of the New Law in the Sermon on the Mount is not the central text of the New Testament, but it surely carries a great weight, and it has to be granted as a matter of significance that when Jesus began his promulgation of the New Covenant, he proclaimed a set of new commandments; 'But I say to you!' (Matt 5:28 etc.) Consider the prophecy of Isaiah 2:3: 'And many peoples shall come, and say: 'Come, let us go up to the mountain of the Lord, to the house of the God of Jacob, that he may teach us his ways and that we may walk in his paths.' For out of Zion shall go forth the law, and the word of the Lord from Jerusalem.' The people are being called precisely to learn the law of the Lord and to do his will as he has revealed it.

---

[2] Boyle, Church Teaching Authority, 47. Some useful references to the tradition in regard to moral teaching can be found in Germain Grisez, *The Way of the Lord Jesus: Christian Moral Principles* (Chicago: Franciscan Herald Press, 1983), 837-38 and in John Finnis, *Moral Absolutes: Tradition, Revision, and Truth* (Washington, D.C.: The Catholic University of America Press, 1991), 6-9.

Jeremiah's prophecy of the New Covenant: 'This is the covenant that I will make with the house of Israel after those days, says the Lord: I will put my law within them, and I will write it on their hearts.' (31: 33) And Ezekiel's prophecy of the New Covent runs: 'And I will put my Spirit within you, and cause you to walk in my statutes and be careful to obey my rules.' (36:27) The role of the promised Holy Spirit is the keeping of the revealed moral law, even to be the New Law written in our hearts. Our Lord presented himself as the light for our path, that we could live properly: 'I am the light of the world. Whoever follows me will not walk in darkness, but will have the light of life.' (John 8:12) and 'I am the way, and the truth, and the life' (John 14:6). Is it not obvious that morality is central here? And, finally, the Great Commission runs: 'Go therefore and make disciples of all nations, baptizing them in the name of the Father and of the Son and of the Holy Spirit, teaching them to observe all that I have commanded you.'(Matt 28:19-20). The mission of the apostles is summed up as baptising people and teaching them the moral law. This is indeed a very small selection of texts, but they are basic ones, and the matter could easily be elaborated if it were necessary to make the point that Scripture reveals a key, if not central role, for moral teaching. It is hard to imagine a text that might tell in the opposite sense! As Rudolph Schnackenburg said of the New Testament: 'Jesus brought a religious message and it was from that message that his moral demands originated. ... Nowhere in the New Testament is it possible to break the unity between religion and morality.'[3]

A valuable witness in favour of the importance of moral teaching in the Church's witness is Cardinal Newman, and his doctrine is emphatic and clear. He wrote: 'The primary object of Revelation was to recall men from idolizing the creature,'[4] a highly moral goal. And he had the following to say on the role of the Pope: 'His very mission is to proclaim the moral law, and to protect and strengthen that 'Light which

---

[3] Rudolf Schnackenburg, The Moral Teaching of the New Testament (Burns & Oates: London, 1964), 13.
[4] Newman, Lectures on the Prophetical Office of the Church, 1877 edition, in The Via Media of the Anglican Church, Volume 1, Preface to the Third Edition, lxxiii.

enligheneth every man that cometh into the world.' ... It is his claim to come from the Divine Lawgiver, in order to elicit, protect, and enforce those truths which the Lawgiver has sown in our very nature ... The championship of the Moral Law and of conscience is his *raison d'être*.'[5] He could hardly insist any more forcefully on the place of morality in teaching of the Church. And it is not a new morality different from natural morality that he has in mind. He tells us: 'In saying all this, of course, I must not be supposed to be limiting the Revelation of which the Church is the keeper to a mere republication of the Natural Law; but still it is true, that, though Revelation is so distinct from the teaching of nature and beyond it, yet it is not independent of it, nor without relations towards it, but is its complement, reassertion, issue, embodiment, and interpretation.'[6] In a sermon preached at Pentecost on the coming of the Holy Spirit 'who is promised to us as the source of all spiritual knowledge and discernment,' he speaks of the central importance of moral teaching in ringing tones:

> The grace promised us is given, not that we may know more, but that we may do better. It is given to influence, guide, and strengthen us in performing our duty towards God and man; it is given to us as creatures, as sinners, as men, as immortal beings, not as mere reasoners, disputers, or philosophical inquirers. It teaches what we are, whither we are going, what we must do, how we must do it; it enables us to change our fallen nature from evil to good, 'to make ourselves a new heart and a new spirit.' But it tells us nothing for the *sake* of telling it; neither in His Holy Word nor through our consciences, has the Blessed Spirit thought fit so to act. Not that the desire of knowing sacred things for the sake of knowing them is wrong.... But

---

[5] Letter to the Duke of Norfolk in Certain Difficulties felt by Anglicans in Catholic Teaching, (London / New York / Bombay: Longmans, Green, and Co.: 1900), Volume 2, 252.
[6] Ibid, 254.

still God has not given us such knowledge in the Bible, and therefore to look into the Bible for such knowledge, or to expect it in any way from the inward teaching of the Holy Ghost, is a dangerous mistake, and (it may be) a sin. And since men are apt to prize knowledge above holiness, therefore it is most suitably provided, that Trinity Sunday should succeed Whit Sunday; to warn us that the enlightening vouchsafed to us is not an understanding of 'all mysteries and all knowledge,' but that love or charity which is 'the fulfilling of the Law.'[7]

Pope John XXIII, in calling the Second Vatican Council, saw it as having an essentially moral purpose: 'The greatest concern of the Ecumenical Council is this: that the sacred deposit of Christian doctrine should be guarded and taught more efficaciously. That doctrine embraces the whole of man, composed as he is of body and soul. And, since he is a pilgrim on this earth, it commands him to tend always toward heaven. This demonstrates how our mortal life is to be ordered in such a way as to fulfil our duties as citizens of earth and of heaven, and thus to attain the aim of life as established by God.'[8]

Still, modern theology is divided on this issue as to the place of morality in the Church's teaching, in particular the possibility of establishing binding moral norms. There are theologians who follow the traditional line which integrates dogma and moral principles. Ladislas Orsy, for instance, writes: 'There is no doubt that the evangelical message includes particular moral precepts: it tells us about God's mighty deeds and <u>the way</u> to the Father. The church cannot be less competent in proclaiming this way than it is competent in narrating

---

[7] <u>Sermon XVI: The Christian Mysteries</u>; John Henry Newman, <u>Parochial and Plain Sermons, Volume I</u> (London / New York: Longman's Green, and Co., 1891), 203-204.

[8] <u>Pope John XXIII's Opening Address to the Second Vatican Council</u> in <u>The Documents of Vatican II</u> (Abbott edition), 710-719, at 713-14.

the story of our redemption.'[9] And according to the early Rahner, 'the Church teaches these commandments with divine authority exactly as she teaches the other 'truths of the Faith'.'[10] He was then emphatic on the point: 'When the whole Church in her everyday teaching does in fact teach a moral rule everywhere in the world as a commandment of God, she is preserved from error by the assistance of the Holy Ghost, and this rule is therefore really the will of God and is binding on the faithful in conscience, even before it has been expressly confirmed by a solemn definition.'[11] In recent years a change has come about in theological opinion. Curran himself offers an interesting example in this regard in that he has two quite different positions at the earlier and later stages of his career. In the early books he recognises that one can have the impression that the Church has reached its grasp of moral norms by arguing on the basis of the natural law. But, against that, he says: 'The Church teaches a particular point because it seems to be a part of the scriptures and the living tradition of the Church.'[12] And again: 'The basis for all teaching of the Church must be sacred scripture.'[13] He uses the teaching on contraception as an example, and is confident that the teaching did not arise from natural law reasoning, but from the experience of the Christian people. The natural law reasoning came later in order to give reasons for the already existing teachings.[14] In his later writing the situation is different. Now, he is clear that the 'Catholic tradition in moral theology has insisted that its moral teaching is based primarily on natural law and not primarily on faith or the Scripture.'[15]

---

[9] Ladislas Orsy, S.J., The Church: Teaching and Learning (Dublin / Leominster: Dominican Publications / Fowler Wright Books, 1987), 74.
[10] Karl Rahner, Nature and Grace (London and Sydney: Sheed and Ward, 1968), 98.
[11] Ibid, 99.
[12] Charles E. Curran, Christian Morality Today (Notre Dame: Fides Publishers, 1966), 82.
[13] Ibid, 88.
[14] Charles E. Curran, 'Absolute Norms and Medical Ethics' in Absolutes in Moral Theology?, ed. Charles E. Curran (Washington - Cleveland: Corpus Books, 1968),108-153 at 147.
[15] Curran, Faithful Dissent, 61.

And Rahner has undergone a certain change of opinion. He now says that 'apart from wholly universal moral norms of an abstract kind, and apart from a radical orientation of human life towards God as the outcome of a supernatural and grace-given self-commitment, there are hardly any particular or individual norms of Christian morality which could be proclaimed by the ordinary or extraordinary teaching authorities of the Church in such a way that they could be unequivocally and certainly declared to have the force of dogmas.'[16] 'Hardly any' norms is not a very precise opinion, but a new direction of his thinking seems to be indicated.

This later opinion has now become the dominant one among contemporary Catholic theologians, and it is necessary to review some of the arguments.[17] An argument against the revelation of moral norms is made on philosophical grounds, that the very fact that the norms belong to the natural law implies that they cannot be revealed. This is the line taken by Alfons Auer.[18] Auer bases himself on the traditional understanding, best represented by St. Thomas, that natural moral norms have their ultimate foundation in right reason. He quotes St. Thomas saying that 'the human good is to be according to reason, and evil is what is against reason.'[19] On this basis Auer concludes that the fundamental rationality of morality demands its autonomy,[20] and this autonomy holds even in relation to the faith.[21] Bruno Schüller

---

[16] Karl Rahner, 'Basic Observations on the Subject of Changeable and Unchangeable Factors in the Church,' *Theological Investigations* 14 (London: Darton, Longman Todd, 1976), 3-23 at 14.
[17] See Sullivan, Magisterium, 136-152.
[18] Alfons Auer, *Autonome Moral und christlicher Glaube* (Selbstverlag Tübingen, 1977).
[19] '*bonum hominis est secundum rationem esse, malum autem quod est praeter rationem*', Summa Theologiae 1-2, q. 18, a. 5c.
[20] '*Mit der Rationalität des Sittlichen ist seine Autonomie gegeben.*' Alfons Auer, *Autonome Moral und christlicher Glaube* (Selbstverlag Tübingen, 1977), 29.
[21] Auer, *Autonome Moral*, 130.

makes exactly the same argument[22], and his conclusion is even more forcefully expressed: 'This means ... that ... moral goodness ... is, by a primordial logic, revealed only to inner discernment and not to some faith that relies upon the authoritative assurance of another, even if this other person were God himself.'[23] Louis Janssens also takes up this argument as to the 'autonomy' of morality,[24] and presents it as a Thomistic position. According to his interpretation, St. Thomas 'insists to a surprising degree upon the autonomy of the human subject in the elaboration of moral norms.'[25] He paraphsases the prologue of the *Prima secundae* of the *Summa theologica* to say: 'As image of God man is the autonomous subject of his own actions,'[26] when what St. Thomas actually said was that 'man is the principle of his actions, as having free will and the power of his actions.'[27] And he quotes the striking phrase that man is '*ipse sibi lex*' (In III Sent d. 37, aa. 1, 2, 5; ST I, 1, a. 6 ad 3, cf. II/II q. 45, a. 2).[28] At least he appeared to be quoting, but upon examination the phrase was not found in any of the texts cited, and a word search in the *Index Thomisticus* indicated that this phrase is not to be found anywhere in the writings of St. Thomas.

Obviously a full rebuttal of these arguments is impossible here. That would require a treatise in fundamental moral theology. But a response can be offered following the teaching of the First Vatican Council on the necessity of revelation. The Council taught that 'it is indeed thanks to this divine revelation, that those divine things which are not of themselves beyond the scope of human reason, can, even in the present state of the human race, be known by everyone,

---

[22] Bruno Schüller, *Wholly Human: Essays on the Theory and Language of Morality* (Dublin / Washington, D.C.: Gill and Macmillan / Georgetown University Press, 1986), 2-3, 26-27.
[23] Ibid, 27.
[24] Louis Janssens, 'Considerations on "Humanae Vitae",' *Louvain Studies* 2 (1968-69), 231-53 at 237.
[25] Ibid, 238.
[26] Ibid, 238.
[27] '*ipse est suorum operum principium, quasi liberum arbitrium habens et suorum operum potestatem.*'
[28] Janssens, "Considerations on "Humanae Vitae"", 239.

without difficulty, with firm certitude and with no intermingling of error.'[29] There can be no serious doubt that the Council intended this affirmation to apply to the whole scope of divine revelation, faith *and morals*. The fact that the moral norms taught by the Church belong to the natural law does indeed mean that they are true to human nature and according to right reason. This means that, in principle, the norms are accessible to human reason, but it does not mean, however, that the norms have to be 'discoverable by human reasoning' *in practice*, much less that they '*has* to be *discovered* by human intelligence reflecting on experience'. It is the same situation in regard to proving the existence of God, his omnipotence, eternity, immensity, incomprehensibility and infinite perfection, all of which are taught in the previous chapter of *Dei Filius*. All these truths about God belong to natural theology and are, in principle, accessible to human reason. Not many of us could prove these things for ourselves, or even find the arguments for God's existence compelling, but we can believe them without any trouble at all as a fundamental part of the faith of the Church. In just the same way, the concrete norms of morality can be very hard to prove and sometimes hard to see at all, but we can believe them on the word of the Church teaching, without infringing their fundamental rationality. The rationality of morality does not imply its 'autonomy' in relation to God and to faith. The genuine Thomistic sense of autonomy is simple enough. It means that we have free will and are the sources of our own actions by our own free choices. We are not puppets controlled from outside or pure automatons whose every action is determined. It does mean that morality is suitable to the human being in the sense that it truly fits his nature, but it does not render us independent of God or self-sufficient so that we have no need of faith or revelation to know with certainty what God is asking of us.

Janssens has another argument in favour of the 'autonomy' of morality and its foundation in human reason. Basing himself on the teaching of *Gaudium et spes*, he refers to the principles which apply when the light of revelation is applied to the discernment on the concrete

---

[29] DS 3005.

moral problems which arise in human affairs. This reflection must be based upon the data of human experience, and it is linked, therefore, with the historical evolution of the laws and values of earthly affairs. This is a human endeavor and its autonomy was upheld by the council in *Gaudium et spes* § 36. In this connection he writes: 'The help of the Holy Spirit promised to the magisterium does not imply, on the level of concrete natural values, any secret fund of knowledge, nor any information inaccessible to human reason.'[30] He then concludes that

> in the domain of concrete moral norms, it is not the argument of authority but the intrinsic value of the evidence which is decisive; such norms remain valid only as long as they continue to express the human values inherent in current historical acquisitions and possibilities. As soon as the magisterium makes a statement concerning concrete moral norms, it is placing itself within the domain of the legitimate autonomy of men and it is opening itself to dialogue with all men of good will (GS 33, 46).[31]

As an example of how this discernment of moral norms works in practice, he instances the the development of moral teaching in the social encyclicals, from *Rerum Novarum* to *Populorum Progressio*.[32] As he understands it, the process begins from the data of human experience and the concrete moral norms are developed gradually in the community in response to the situations which arise. Systematic moral science comes later and discerns the validity of the norms which have emerged from the community. 'The magisterium can intervene only after the fact, to compile the norms which have developed in the life of the community and to communicate them universally.'[33] In Janssens's view, 'historical progress in the morality lived by men and societies is

---

[30] Janssens, 'Considerations on "Humanae Vitae",' 244.
[31] Ibid, 243-44.
[32] Ibid, 244.
[33] Ibid.

the source of all the statements of the magisterium. Thus, dialogue is indispensable, especially since the gospels offer no specific solutions to current moral problems; these solutions can only be discovered through human experience (GS 33, 43, 46).'[34]

There is no doubt that everything Janssens says here is true, as far as it goes. The Council did affirm the legitimate autonomy of earthly affairs and the fact that the Church does not have answers to all the questions that arise. But there is hardly any doubt that *Gaudium et spes* had no intention of denying the existence of the discreet number of absolute moral norms which have been part of the patrimony of the Church always. At issue in these affirmations are the many particular questions which arise in regard to different social and cultural situations where decisions have to be made on practical matters. Differences of opinion will inevitably arise as to the best manner of proceeding in regard to social and political matters, and the Church is careful not to prejudge issues precipitately. However, despite this clear avowal of the legitimate autonomy of earthly affairs, the traditional teaching in regard to the revelation of a deposit of moral doctrine and the role of the absolute moral norms which have ever formed a part of it is completely unchanged.

According to Francis Sullivan, 'the strong trend in current moral thinking is to deny that the particular norms of the natural law are virtually revealed. To say that they are virtually revealed is to claim that they can be somehow deduced from revealed principles, and most theologians do not agree that we can arrive at the concrete determinations of the natural law by such a process of deduction from revealed principles.'[35] The reasoning is that such determinations have to be worked out by reflection on human experience, which is complex and it is, therefore, difficult to determine moral norms in a way which could lead to an irreversible norm.[36] Along this line Richard Gaillardetz writes:

---

[34] Ibid, 244-45.
[35] Ibid, 137.
[36] Francis A. Sullivan, <u>Magisterium: Teaching Authority in the Catholic Church</u>, (Paulist Press: New York/Ramsey, 1983), 150-52.

> Concrete moral norms, concerned as they are with guiding one in objectively right behaviour, do not pertain directly to salvation and the conversion of human attitudes, intentions, and dispositions. At the same time, these concrete norms often depend on changeable empirical data, making it difficult to attribute to them the kind of continuity in their fundamental meaning that can be attributed to Church dogma. Consequently, it is the conclusion of many theologians that while it is legitimate and necessary for the pastoral teaching office of the Church to propose concrete moral norms for the guidance of the faithful, these concrete moral norms are not divinely revealed and cannot be taught as dogma.[37]

It is difficult to grant any force to Gaillardetz's first argument that concrete moral norms do not pertain directly to salvation, although they guide us in objectively right behaviour. Salvation surely involves right behaviour as a basic constituent and guidance along the right path is part of the preaching of the Church. His second point as to the difficulty of clarifying the concrete norms is one that is widely shared. The difficulty is undeniable, in some cases at least, but it does not make the task impossible. Particular norms have been part of revelation from the time of the Sinai Covenant when the Ten Commandments were revealed through Moses, and discerning the content of revelation is a subtle and complex process which is not readily available to reflective consciousness. It is not possible by reflection to be sure exactly how the concrete norms are discerned, but there is no doubt that what precisely constitutes moral theology as opposed to ethical reflection in general is its grounding in Scripture and Tradition. The position of Archbishop (now Cardinal) William Levada seems correct in this, when he writes: 'While we may know that many moral norms are part of the deposit of faith, it can be difficult to arrive at a precise formulation of them (an

---

[37] Richard R. Gaillardetz, <u>Teaching with Authority: A Theology of the Magisterium in the Church</u> (Collegeville, Minnesota: The Liturgical Press, 1997), 114.

infallible 'definition') because of the changing technological data which often affect the human acts in question.'[38] The difficulty is in clarifying the formulation of some concrete moral norms, not in establishing their existence.

It is not always easy for us to judge whether a matter is revealed or not. Sometimes it is obvious in one sense or the other. The divinity of Christ is obviously revealed, and the geo-centricity of the solar system is obviously not. It is especially difficult, understandably, in matters where faith and reason overla We all have access to the natural law, and it is possible for us, in principle to know its demands by reason alone. So how can we be sure whether a given point is revealed or not? Let us first of all deal with the question; How could we be sure that a given point was not revealed? Is that possible? There is no one who disputes the possibility of revelation in moral matters. The argument is against particular norms, for various reasons. Cardinal Newman makes some remarks about the interpretation of Scripture which seem germane to this issue. He writes:

> It is in point to notice also the structure and style of Scripture, a structure so unsystematic and various and a style so figurative and indirect that no one would presume at first sight to say what is in it and what is not. It cannot, as it were, be mapped, or its contents catalogued; but after all our diligence, to the end of our lives and to the end of the Church, it must be an unexplored and unsubdued land, with heights and valleys, forests and streams, on the right and left of our path and close about us, full of concealed wonders and choice treasures. Of no doctrine whatever, which does not actually contradict what has been delivered, can it be peremptorily asserted that it is not in Scripture; of no

---

[38] Archbishop (now Cardinal) William Levada; 'Dissent and the Catholic Religion Teacher', <u>Readings in Moral Theology No. 6; Dissent in the Church</u>, edd. Curran and McCormick, SJ., (NY, 1988), 133ff. at 145-146.

reader, whatever be his study of it, can it be said that he has mastered every doctrine it contains.[39]

It seems to me to be similarly impossible to assert with certainty that any particular moral norm is not revealed. On the other hand, then, can we be certain that a particular norm is revealed? This point has been argued out extensively recently in connection with the issue of contraception. John C. Ford and Germain Grisez worked on the question and concluded: 'Admittedly, it does not seem there is any way to establish *conclusively* that this teaching either pertains to revelation or is connected with it apart from the fact that the ordinary magisterium has proposed the teaching in the manner in which it has, and the faithful as a whole until recently have accepted the norm as binding.'[40] They go on to argue that a similar state of affairs was used as a basis for solemnly defining the Assumption of our Lady.[41] When he defined the dogma of the Assumption, Pius XII argued 'from the universality of the acceptance of the dogma as a matter of faith to its objective status as a truth pertaining to divine revelation.'[42]

Sullivan objects to the use of the parallel with the definition of the Assumption and makes two arguments. He grants the major premise that the whole People of God is infallible in its faith, but questions whether or not the acceptance of the Church's teaching on contraception by the faithful is a matter of *faith*. Their acceptance does not prove that they accepted it as a revealed truth. It seems likely to him that many of them accepted it simply as a binding law of the Church, which they had to observe whether they were convinced of its truth or not. Is that a plausible view? No bishop certainly ever suggested that he was imposing this norm as a law on his own authority. Is it possible that such a thing could happen or that the people would stand for

---

[39] John Henry Cardinal Newman, <u>An Essay on the Development of Christian Doctrine</u>, (New York: Image Books, 1960) with a foreword by Gustave Weigel, S.J.
[40] 'Contraception and the Infallibility of the Ordinary Magisterium', TS 39 (1978) 258-312, at 286-287.
[41] Ibid.
[42] Ibid, 287, footnote 65.

it? I don't really see much light down that tunnel, and, in any case, Sullivan's other argument is more fundamental, and goes to the heart of the matter. He writes:

> My major difficulty with the argument that Ford and Grisez have proposed ... is that it would eliminate the possibility of challenging any magisterial act that was claimed to be infallible by questioning whether the subject-matter of the act fell within the limits of the proper object of infallibility. In other words, the supposition of their argument seems to be: if the magisterium speaks in a definitive way about something, it must necessarily be the case that what they speak about is the proper object of infallible teaching. The question of the object would no longer be an independent criterion by which it could conceivably be judged that the magisterium had not really spoken infallibly, on the grounds that the matter on which it spoke was not a proper object of infallible teaching.[43]

Against this, Sullivan argues that if it were true, there would have been no point at all in the insistence of Vatican I and Vatican II that the Magisterium can speak infallibly only on matters of faith and morals. If a definitive exercise of the Magisterium is guaranteed in itself, there would be no need to specify the limits of its competence. Sullivan concludes: 'It seems to me that the supposition underlying the argument of Ford and Grisez would open the door to absolutism in the exercise of the magisterium'[44] I do not think that Sullivan is correct in this. Declaring that the limit of infallibility and of Church teaching is faith and morals is a statement of fact and a principle to guide the discernment of all of us in our acceptance of the teaching of Christ in the Church. The College of Bishops is never on its own in discerning the teaching of the Church. Their discernment takes place within the

---

[43] Sullivan, Magisterium, 144.
[44] Ibid, 145.

Church, and each of us has our part to play and our influence to bring. The College of Bishops is not just a supreme notary recording what the People think, indeed, for the bishops must make their own discernment. And there is only need of a judgment from the bishops when the rest of the Church is, to some extent at least, divided on the issue at hand. If someone believes that a particular teaching lies outside the ambit of faith and morals, he can make his case in that sense. Galileo was quite right to apply this criterion to the judgment made against him by the Roman Inquisition, as he did at the time, though the validity of his criticism was not officially recognised until very recently. However, the criterion of the limit to faith and morals cannot be applied in judgment after a definitive judgment is made, for then it is too late as well as unnecessary, for the promise of Christ will guarantee such a judgment, and it can be accepted with complete confidence. It is the promise of Christ guaranteeing the definitive judgment which removes the danger of absolutism. Rahner has formulated the point in regard to the supreme authority of the Pope:

> This is clearly to be seen, for example, in the fact that the highest seat of jurisdiction in the Church, the pope, also possesses competence to determine what his competence is. If he invokes his highest and ultimate authority, it is not possible to oppose his decision with the claim that he has exceeded his powers, acted <u>ultra vires</u>, and that his judgment is not binding on that account. For it is not possible to verify that he has kept within the scope of his competence by applying a criterion to him, as though by juridical process, to test his conduct. When he invokes his ultimate authority in making a decision, this action is itself the only guarantee that he has remained within the limits of his competence. But that means that such an office held by a human being, if it is not to be an absolute tyranny, must itself rise into a sphere to which no juridical criteria can be applied. It must necessarily be charismatic. And that means that

it is only conceivable if there is always added to it in fact and in idea a power which is itself indefectible, the assistance of the Spirit of God himself, permanently promised to it, even though this is not something that can be administered or comprised in legal terms.[45]

Another point telling against the revelation of the moral norms is the notion that the moral teachings of the Church are secondary matters. On the basis of his opinion that Church teaching on moral matters is based more on reason than on faith, Curran concludes that 'such teachings are thus somewhat removed from the core of Catholic faith as such,' and that 'the distance of these teachings from the core of faith and the central realities of faith grounds the possibility of legitimate dissent.'[46] This notion that the moral teachings he rejects are peripheral to the Christian faith is one that Curran often repeats,[47] and if he is correct it does provide some basis for his position. He is supported in this point, to a certain extent, by the Congregation for the Doctrine of the Faith itself. In its commentary on the concluding formula of the Profession of Faith of 1989, the Congregation for the Doctrine of the Faith gives the moral norms forbidding euthanasia, prostitution and fornication as examples of truths contained in what is known as the secondary object of infallibility.[48] The secondary object of infallibility refers to truths taught by the Church, which are

---

[45] Karl Rahner, The Dynamic Element in the Church (Freiburg / London: Herder / Burns & Oates, 1964), 45.
[46] Curran, Faithful Dissent, 61.
[47] 'Peripheral' is Curran's own word in Faithful Dissent, 60. He repeats the point in 'Response of Charles E. Curran, August 20, 1986' in Readings in Moral Theology No. 6; Dissent in the Church, edd. Charles E. Curran and Richard A. McCormick, S.J., (New York/Mahwah: Paulist Press, 1988), 364-369 at 365; Charles Curran; 'Public Dissent in the Church' in Readings in Moral Theology No. 6; Dissent in the Church, edd. Charles E. Curran and Richard A. McCormick, S.J., (New York/Mahwah: Paulist Press, 1988), 387-407 at 399 and 400.
[48] Congregation for the Doctrine of the Faith, 'Commentary on the Concluding Formula of the 'Professio fidei',' AAS 90 (1998) 550; (English translation; L'Osservatore Romano (Eng. Ed.), 15 July 1998, 4.)

closely connected with revelation, but are not themselves revealed. By placing these moral norms in this category, the Congregation is clearly espousing the opinion that these moral norms are not revealed. The Congregation does not hold that none of the moral norms belonging to the natural law are revealed, for it places the the condemnation of the killing of the innocent in the first category, among the revealed truths of faith. [49] However, if any of these moral norms are not revealed, how can we be sure which are, and which are not?

The doubt as to the revealed quality of the moral norms has even entered into certain official episcopal formulations. The Congregation for the Doctrine of the Faith taught: 'What concerns morality can also be the object of the authentic Magisterium because the Gospel, being the Word of Life, inspires and guides the whole sphere of human behaviour. ... By reason of the connection between the orders of creation and redemption and by reason of the necessity, in view of salvation, of knowing and observing the whole moral law, the competence of the Magisterium also extends to that which concerns the natural law.'[50] This is the line of reasoning which developed in the theology manuals during the eighteenth and nineteenth centuries.[51] Its presupposition would seem to be that the natural law is not revealed and that, therefore, some other explanation is required for its teaching in the Church. Interestingly, the Congregation goes on in the next sentence to say that 'Revelation also contains moral teachings which per se could be known by natural reason. Access to them, however, is made difficulty by man's sinful condition. It is a doctrine of faith that these moral norms can be infallibly taught by the Magisterium.'[52] But, if the norms are revealed, why the need of the earlier syllogism to defend the competence of the Magisterium in regard to them? If the norms are revealed, the Church would teach them, not because of the connection between the orders of creation and redemption, but simply because they are revealed by God.

---

[49] Ibid, 549.
[50] Donum veritatis, n. 16.
[51] See Chiron, L'infaillibilité, 196, footnote 2.
[52] Donum veritatis, n. 16. [ND 180c.]

Similarly, the Popes have taught that the whole of the natural law falls under the authority of the Magisterium, since the observance of the natural law is necessary for salvation.[53] Pope Paul VI, in *Humanae vitae*, summed up this tradition when he wrote:

> No member of the faithful could possibly deny that the Church is competent in her magisterium to interpret the natural moral law. It is in fact indisputable ... that Jesus Christ, when He communicated His divine power to Peter and the other Apostles and sent them to teach all nations His commandments, constituted them as the authentic guardians and interpreters of the whole moral law, not only, that is, of the law of the Gospel but also of the natural law. For the natural law, too, declares the will of God, and its faithful observance is necessary for men's eternal salvation. (*Humanae vitae*, § 4.)

The key question here is as to what is meant by the competence of the Bishops to 'interpret' the natural law. In order to answer that question, it is necessary first of all to resolve this question as to how the natural law relates to the law of the Gospel. The formulation in *Humanae vitae* seems to suggest that the natural law is a separate thing from the law of the Gospel, and somehow added to it. That would then seem to lead to the notion that the Bishops have an authority to 'interpret' the natural law even though it falls outside the ambit of revelation. And that is how this doctrine seems to be interpreted by many theologians. Consider, for instance, the view of two authoritative moral theologians writing just before the publication of the encyclical. They reviewed the magisterial documents dealing with this question

---

[53] Pius X Singulari quadam, AAS 4 (1912), 638; Pius XI Divini illius Magistri, AAS 22 (1930), 54; Pius XII, Magnificate Dominum, AAS 46 (1954), 671-673; Paul VI *Humanae vitae*, AAS 60 (1968), 483. The doctrine appeared in the draft of the Constitution on the Church by Preparatory Commission 1962; Acta Synodalia Conc. Vat. II, I/4, 48, and is also to be found in the Catechism of the Catholic Church, § 2036.

and concluded: 'It seems to us that the real purpose of such assertions is to vindicate the Church's power to teach and to apply the natural law, whether it is revealed or not.'[54]

If it were accepted that the particular moral norms taught by the Church were not revealed, then it would have to follow that this interpretation of the moral law is an original function of the Catholic bishops, who interpret the natural law and pass on their interpretation to the rest of the Church and the world at large. John Boyle asks the pertinent question about the Catholic bishops; '[D]o they know about the natural law in a way not open to other members of the Church, or for that matter, to men and women generally?'[55] Speaking of Church teaching on social and sexual ethics, he writes that 'for the most part the warrant for this teaching is explicitly the natural law, not revelation as transmitted by scripture or tradition,'[56] and that 'if such insights are logically independent of revelation, it remains to be explained to what extent the moral insights of bishops differ from and are more authoritative than those of others.'[57] Indeed it does. As far as I can see, nothing in Scripture or Tradition, or the experience of history, begins to explain how the Catholic bishops can, by their own gifts, be experts in morality in such a way that they can interpret it for the rest of humanity. The notion of the Pope claiming to be the interpreter of the natural law, somehow standing on his own making a judgment on these most complex moral matters simply does not make sense. It seems to me that the matter is really much more simple. Surely the presumption rather must be that, since these mattes are necessary for salvation, they must have been revealed by Christ as part of his saving work!

According to the thesis being developed in this book, if there is to be a moral teaching of the Church in the full sense, the Holy Church, the Body of Christ and the Temple of the Holy Spirit, then that moral teaching must form part of the deposit of faith; it must be revealed.

---

[54] J. C. Ford, S.J. and G. Kelly, S.J., *Contemporary Moral Theology: II. Marriage Questions* (Cork: The Mercier Press, 1963), 273.
[55] Boyle, <u>Church Teaching Authority</u>, 44.
[56] Ibid, 58.
[57] Ibid, 59.

Christ is the One Teacher and he only teaches by way of revelation. Apart from the deposit of faith, the bishops are one and all fallible men, and there is no question of their being experts in the natural law on any other basis. If the Church is to teach moral doctrine at all, it can only be because it is revealed. The only thing that can make sense of the Catholic bishops being experts in the natural law, is that it is revealed, and to the extent that it is revealed. The bishops are experts in revelation, and they can only be experts in the natural law, if it is revealed and to the extent that it is revealed. The bishops only have authority to teach in Christ's name on the basis of what he has communicated to them by revelation. The revealed Word of God forms a unified whole which includes the natural moral law as a constituent part. It is called the natural law because it is, in principle, accessible to human reason and is common to all human beings, but it is none the less revealed for all that. The bishops, therefore, do not 'interpret' the natural law by some power granted to them to work out its dictates with a greater wisdom than other people. Their authority is to declare the content of revelation, including those norms of natural morality accessible to all. It is in this sense that they can be called 'interpreters' of the natural law. They can declare it with authority on the basis of revelation.

An implicit argument against the revelation of moral norms lies behind a demand, often repeated, that, in proposing a concrete moral norm, clear and convincing reasons must be given in support of the teaching. It is especially necessary 'when the magisterium pronounces its judgment on an issue like birth control, about which a great many people already had formed their opinion, and many were competent to judge the question on its merits.'[58] He considers that it would be inconsistent to propose a moral norm as a requirement of the natural law without offering convincing reasons in its favour. For Sullivan a norm belonging to the natural law is a 'law which has to be discovered by human intelligence reflecting on experience,' and because such a norm 'is said to be discoverable by human reasoning,' convincing reasons

---

[58] Sullivan, Magisterium, 165.

must be given.[59] If the thesis were to stand that natural law morality is not part of revelation, then all that Sullivan says here would follow. If, on the other hand, this norm has been revealed by God, the situation is quite different. On this premise, there is no inconsistency in the norm being proposed by the Church, even when convincing reasons are lacking. For the situation within the faith is unique. Bishops do not speak with any authority of their own. They speak as witnesses to the faith of the Church which is the revelation of Christ. They cannot claim to be experts in married life or the technicalities of procreation. They will have a certain competence in moral reasoning, but not necessarily a great expertise. They are experts in the teaching of the Church to some extent, but their real authority is, in fact, the formal authority that comes with their valid ordination. So, they can offer what reasons they can, within the faith, and mainly to support the contention that such and such a position is of faith, more than for its inherent reasonableness. The presumption is that we are unable by our unaided reason to see clearly and with certainty why the action is wrong, and we need the help of Christ's revelation. All I want from the bishops is the valid exercise of their formal authority. The justifying of the teaching is a task for the theologians and other experts more than for the Bishops, whose special competence is the judging of doctrine, not its explanation.

The issue of the revelation of moral norms needs to be resolved. It has never been faced before in quite the same manner as it is being faced now, and a magisterial judgment is beginning to be formed. In response to the many denials in the contemporary literature, Pope John Paul began to formulate ever more and more clearly the place of the moral teaching in the deposit of faith. In *Reconciliatio et penitentia* (1984) he wrote: 'There is a doctrine, based on the Decalogue and on the preaching of the Old Testament, and assimilated into the kerygma of the Apostles and belonging to the earliest teaching of the Church, and constantly reaffirmed by her to this day.'[60] And he saw the need to make the point in regard to particular absolute moral norms: 'The

---

[59] Ibid.
[60] *Reconciliatio et paenitentia* (1984), § 17.

whole tradition of the Church has lived and lives on the conviction' that 'there exist acts which, *per se* and in themselves, independently of circumstances, are always seriously wrong by reason of their object.'[61] And the Pope saw the need to devote an encyclical precisely to the topic, *Veritatis Splendor* (1993). He makes it clear that '[t]he specific purpose of the present Encyclical is this: to set forth, with regard to the problems being discussed, the principles of a moral teaching based upon Sacred Scripture and the living Apostolic Tradition ...' (VS 5). As a first principle he asserts that 'the decisive answer to every one of man's questions, his religious and moral questions in particular, is given by Jesus Christ, or rather is Jesus Christ himself.' (VS 2) In general this implies that '[t]he Church has faithfully preserved what the Word of God teaches, not only about truths which must be believed but also about moral action, . . . she has achieved a *doctrinal development* analogous to that which has taken place in the realm of the truths of faith.' (VS 28), and in particular that '[i]n teaching the existence of intrinsically evil acts, the Church accepts the teaching of Sacred Scripture.' (VS 81) He makes the point at length in one paragraph.

> Within Tradition, the *authentic interpretation* of the Lord's law develops, with the help of the Holy Spirit. The same Spirit who is at the origin of the Revelation of Jesus' commandments and teachings guarantees that they will be reverently preserved, faithfully expounded and correctly applied in different times and places. This constant 'putting into practice' of the commandments is the sign and fruit of a deeper insight into Revelation and of an understanding in the light of faith of new and historical and cultural situations. Nevertheless, it can only confirm the permanent validity of revelation and follow in the line of the interpretation given to it by the great Tradition of the Church's teaching and life, as witnessed by the teaching of the Fathers, the lives of

---

[61] Ibid.

the Saints, the Church's Liturgy and the teaching of the Magisterium. (VS 25)

Pope John Paul is here clearly teaching that the moral doctrine of the Church is based on Christ, on Scripture and Tradition, and that it is revealed by God. He does not stress the fact that the particular norms of morality are revealed, but surely they must be since they are most obvious content of the moral doctrine of the Church. Furthermore, he makes the point explicitly in regard to one particular norm, the condemnation of artificial contraception.

> The Church teaches this norm, although it is not formally (that is, literally) expressed in Sacred Scripture, and it does this in the conviction that the interpretation of the precepts of the natural law belongs to the competence of the Magisterium. However, we can say more. Even if the moral law, formulated in this way in the Encyclical *Humanae vitae*, is not found literally in Sacred Scripture, nonetheless, from the fact that it is contained in Tradition and - as Pope Paul VI writes - has been 'very often expounded by the Magisterium' (HV, n. 12) to the faithful, it follows that this norm *is in accordance with the sum total of revealed doctrine contained in biblical sources* (cf. HV, n. 4). . . . It is a question here not only of the sum total of the moral doctrine contained in Sacred Scripture, of its essential premises and the general character of its content, but of that fuller context to which we have previously dedicated numerous analyses when speaking about the 'theology of the body'. Precisely against the background of this fuller context it becomes evident that the above-mentioned moral norm belongs not only to the natural moral law, but also to the *moral order revealed by God*: also from this point of view, it could not be different, but solely what is handed down by Tradition and the

Magisterium and, in our days, the Encyclical *Humanae vitae* as a modern document of this Magisterium.[62]

According to Sullivan this is the first official document of the Church to base the authority of the magisterium in moral matters on the grounds that the whole moral law is revealed.[63] Sullivan is wrong to suggest that the document demands the principle that the whole moral law is revealed. What is does demand is that the whole of the moral doctrine taught by the Church is revealed. It may be first time that this point has been made explicitly, but it can be held that it has been made implicitly for a long time in the simple phrase which sums up the object of Church teaching in general, that it deals with matters of 'faith and morals'. One well-qualified commentator on the use of the phrase in *Pastor Aeternus*, the document on papal infallibility of the First Vatican Council, concludes that there is no doubt that the Council understood 'morals' in the phrase 'faith and morals' as referring to revealed morality. He writes: 'In reality, understanding the word exclusively in the sense of points revealed concerning human conduct, is to make it a duplicate of 'faith', for such things, insofar as they are revealed, are the object of faith as much as speculative matters. However, there is no doubt that the Council understood it in this way.'[64] And it can hardly be doubted that the moral teaching of the Church is included within the teaching of *Dei Filius* on revelation which teaches that 'it is to be ascribed to this divine revelation that such truths about things divine which of themselves are not beyond human reason, even in the present condition of the human race, be known by everyone without difficulty, with firm certainty and with no admixture of error.' (DS 3005) During the discussion at the First Vatican Council leading to this paragraph, the Deputation for

---

[62] General Audience on Wednesday, 18 July 1984, L'Osservatore. Romano (Eng. Ed.), 23 July 1984, 1.
[63] Francis A. Sullivan, S. J., 'Infallible Teaching on Moral Issues? Reflections on Veritatis Splendor and Evangelium Vitae' in Choosing Life: A Dialogue on Evangelium Vitae, edd. Kevin Wm. Wildes, S. J., Alan C. Mitchell, (Washington, D.C.: Georgetown University Press, 1997), 77-89 at 81.
[64] Betti, Pastor Aeternus, 640. (Note 1).

the Faith rejected efforts to insert explicit reference to the natural law into the chapter which defined the power of human reason to know of God's existence from creation. The *Relator* for the Deputation, Bishop Vincent Gasser, explained that the amendments were superfluous, since a knowledge of God, 'the beginning and end of all things,' included knowledge of at least one's principal moral duties toward God, and the 'truths about things divine which of themselves are not beyond human reason' included the natural law.[65] The notion that the moral teaching of the Church is revealed is implied in the teaching of the *Catechism of the Catholic Church* which speaks of a 'deposit' of moral teaching, which it is easy to identify with the deposit of faith. It says: 'Thus from generation to generation, under the aegis and vigilance of the pastors, the 'deposit' of Christian moral teaching has been handed on, a deposit composed of a characteristic body of rules, commandments and virtues proceeding from faith in Christ and animated by charity.'[66]

This chapter began with a quotation from Charles Curran denying that the particular norms of morality taught by the Church belong to the deposit of revelation. This point is basic to Curran's justification for his dissent from a number of those norms. He summed up his position in one sentence when he wrote: 'The central issue involved in the controversy between the Congregation for the Doctrine of the Faith and myself is the possibility of public theological dissent from some non-infallible teaching which is quite remote from the core of faith, heavily dependent on support from human reason, and involved in such complexity and specificity that logically one cannot claim absolute certitude.'[67] The last set of clauses all refer to Church's teaching of absolute moral norms. It has been argued here that none of his qualifications apply. Anything taught by the Church must be contained within the deposit of revelation, and this applies also to her moral teaching. Nothing revealed is 'remote from the core of the faith' or 'heavily dependent on human reason'. The

---

[65] Mansi 53, 276D, 279C.
[66] CCC 2033.
[67] Charles Curran; 'Public Dissent in the Church', in <u>Readings in Moral Theology No. 6; Dissent in the Church</u>, edd. Charles E. Curran and Richard A. McCormick, S.J., (New York/Mahwah: Paulist Press, 1988), 387-407 at 401.

revealed norms of Christian morality intersect with human reason and their complexity and specificity has meant that considerable time has been necessary for the implications of the revealed truth to be clarified. The process of clarification was just as difficult, if not more so, in the case of the metaphysics of the Trinity and the Incarnation. And just as in those cases, so also in the area of morality, once the clarification has been achieved, the authority of God revealing renders anything that is taught by the Church acceptable with the full supernatural certainty of divine faith. It follows that the justification of dissent from the official teaching of moral norms, as of any other Church teaching, must be sought elsewhere.

Chapter 12

From the Magisterium of the Church to the Magisterium of the Bishops

Corresponding to the change which took place in Western theology, by which the word 'church' ceased to refer primarily to the Holy Church, the mystery indwelt by God, and came to refer first to the concrete institution, a parallel change occurred in the use of the word 'magisterium'. Traditionally, the Magisterium of the Church was understood as referring to the teaching of the Church-mystery, the Holy Church, as that reality has been presented in the previous chapter. Gradually, however, over the period of the second millennium, the Magisterium of the Church came to refer first to the teaching function of the bishops in the Church, and to that of the Pope in particular.

The identification of the Church and the bishops was already well under way at the time of the Reformation. This fact constitutes an essential part of the background to the Protestant Reformation. Congar tells us: 'The fourteenth and fifteenth centuries had unfortunately bequeathed to an age marked all at once with religious crisis … the false option between the primacy of Scripture and the primacy of "the Church." This option became with the Reformers a choice between submission to God and submission to some human bidding. Put in such a way, the issue was never in doubt. The whole Reformation movement flowed from this.'¹ A key to the Protestant problem here is the fact that the submission to the Church immediately meant for them submission to some *human* bidding, where ultimate submission is possible only to God. If that posing of the problem were correct, then the Reformers were right to rebel. Properly understood, however, there is no need to choose between submission to God and some human authority, for all authority in the Church belongs to God. The notion of the Holy Church which has been developed avoids this dichotomy, because in the Holy Church the human actors are totally subordinated to the divine. Christ and his Holy Spirit have total control of the Holy Church and human sin and fallibility do not enter into the equation. There are human actors, indeed, but their actions only pertain to the Holy Church insofar as they are under the direct and complete influence of the Holy Spirit.

Congar makes a criticism of the Catholic apologists of the time which also turns on this point. He tells us that 'many thought, or at least expressed themselves in such a way as to give the impression, that "the Church", in practice the pope, gave Scripture its "authority" by approving it and declaring it canonical.' And he objects that '[t]his is not the true Catholic tradition. Throughout the Middle Ages, and up to and including the teaching Luther himself had received, the Church affirms the submission of the magisterium, including that of the pope, to God's institution and the apostolic norms.'² Is it not clear that the overhasty identification of the Church with the Pope is at the root of the problem here? The Catholic apologists Congar refers to were basing themselves on St Augustine's famous word on this matter: 'I would not believe the Gospel if the authority of the catholic Church did not move me to do so.'³ There is no question that St Augustine had the Pope of the day, or any other human authority in mind, when he spoke of the authority of the catholic Church. He was thinking of the Holy Church, and of the Holy Church, it can and must be said that it gives Scripture its authority by approving it and making it canonical. The Bible does not

---

¹ Congar, Tradition and Traditions, 142.
² Ibid, 146.
³ Evangelio non crederem nisi me catholicae ecclesiae commoveret auctoritas. C. Epist. Manich. quam vocant fundamenti, 5, 6 (PL, 42, 176).

come to the Christian believer as a book he finds and reads for himself, which has its role in faith established by God in a vacuum. The Bible is the Church's book, or set of liturgical books, and the books were chosen and established as canonical by the Church, and ultimately by an authoritative judgment of the College of Bishops. So, one can truly say that the Church gave the Bible its very being, and hence obviously whatever authority it has. Obviously, it does not mean that the current office-holders in the Church give the Scriptures their authority. That was done long ago, and the Scriptures now stand as a fundamental norm by which all in the Church are bound, but it remains true that the Church gave the Scriptures their authority, and continues to broker that authority to anyone who comes to Christian faith.

A crucial contributor to this process of collapsing the mystery of the Church into the bishops alone was Francisco Suarez. He is considered to be the originator of the distinction between a living rule (*regula animata*) and an inanimate rule (*regula inanimis*),[4] and his originating contribution sets a pattern which would be much followed. He wrote:

> A rule of faith can either be inanimate, and so unable to explain the meaning, or a living and animate rule which can speak. ... A person who is alive and can speak is called a living rule, and a distinction is to be made between a fictive or mystical person and a true one. The first is the Church, which is the mystical Body of Christ, and it can be considered in two ways. It can be considered, in itself and formally, as the congregation of all the faithful under one head, the Vicar of Christ, and is thus properly called the Church. Alternatively, it can be considered insofar as it is gathered together in its leaders, which gathering is called a Council, which, when it is a general and legitimate Council, represents the universal Church. The true person who is the rule of faith, can only be the Supreme Pontiff and Vicar of

---

[4] See DTC 15, 1328.

Christ or the Bishop of Rome.[5] ...although the Church is infallible in its faith, nevertheless, taken formally, so to say, and only as a whole, it is not sufficient as a living rule of faith in its teaching. The reason is that it is impossible for this Church to achieve a definition of faith, and so it is not able to speak and teach as a living rule. Also because the greater part of this Church is not suitable for teaching, which does not pertain to their status, and this is true principally of the laity. Further, another reason is that an <u>ex Cathedra</u> definition belongs to the key of knowledge and is a special act of the power given by Christ to rule the Church in doctrine. Christ did not, however, grant this power to the whole body of the Church, but to its head ...[6]

It seems to me that Suarez makes a number of judgments here which have been determinative of the subsequent discussion in modern Catholic theology. The certainty that no objective norm, whether Scripture or Tradition or both, can suffice is expressed in the conviction that a living rule is necessary, and this can be taken as established. Suarez sees that such a living rule must be a person, and in this again he is correct. But now the problems begin. He distinguishes between a 'fictive or mystical' person and a 'real' one. The Church, for Suarez, is 'fictive or mystical', and the 'real' person who can act as the 'living rule' is the Pope, because he can define doctrine. It cannot be said that Suarez originated this identification of the Church with the Pope, but he gave it a theoretical form, and a fateful turn has been taken here, from which Catholic theology has yet to fully recover. Suarez demonstrates here no awareness of the mystery of the Holy Church. There is no awareness of Christ as the one teacher in the Church. The Church, the mystical Body of Christ, is indeed a mystical person, but not a 'fictive' person. Christ is the real person who teaches in and through the Church and

---

[5] <u>De Fide</u>, d. 5, s. 2, n. 4; <u>Opera</u>, Vivès ed., Paris, 1858, Vol. XII, 141.
[6] <u>De Fide</u>, d. 5, s. 6, n. 9; <u>Opera</u>, 157.

he sends the Holy Spirit to be the 'living rule' who guides the Church into the complete truth. Suarez forgot the marvellous things he had written earlier in his treatise about the essential role of the Holy Spirit, and limited his vision to the human actors in the Church, so that, for him, the Pope is the living rule.

Catholic theology basically followed Suarez in his reasoning. From saying, as Suarez himself had done, that the *Church* constitutes the proximate rule of faith, over the course of recent centuries it came to be said that it is the *Magisterium* of the Church which fulfils that role, and the word 'magisterium' itself gradually changed its meaning. Until the middle of the nineteenth century, the word regularly meant what it means literally, the *function* of teaching the faith, whoever exercises this under the authority of the one Teacher, Christ, as presented in the previous chapter. Since that time the word has come to be used for the special teaching function of the bishops, and this was so strongly emphasised that all other members of the Church were denied any share in Christ's *magisterium* at all.[7] The word then underwent another change and it can now refer, not to the teaching function of the bishops, but quite simply to the College of Bishops itself.[8] There was developed the notion of the *Ecclesia docens*, which was identified with the College of Bishops, and then the whole Church, including the bishops, constituted the *Ecclesia discens*, which received the truth from the bishops. The heavy emphasis on the bishops arose out of the tensions which have been part of the experience of the Western Church for practically the whole of the second millennium. As Congar tells us, in reaction to the new proactive use of papal authority, an important aspect of the ecclesiological thought within the dissident movements from the fourteenth to the seventeenth century was an emphasis on the active role of all the members of the Church and a questioning of the Church's

---

[7] Robert Murray, S. J., 'The human capacity for God, and God's initiative,' in Commentary on the Catechism of the Catholic Church, ed. Michael J. Walsh (London: Geoffrey Chapman, 1994), 6-33 at 16.

[8] Sullivan, Magisterium, 25-26. See also Jean-François Chiron, 'Le Magistère dans l'histoire,' Recherches de Science Religieuse 87/4 (1999) 483-518, at 489ff.

hierarchical structure.[9] Congar has no doubt that, in response to these challenges to the internal principles by which she lived, it was inevitable and right that the Church should reassert and defend those things that she felt were threatened: 'her hierarchical structure, the reality of her institution antecedent to and superior to the faithful and the community that they form.'[10] However, legitimate though the defence of these constitutive elements may have been, the practical result was an over-reaction, placing an undue emphasis on the points which were being challenged and losing sight of other points which are also fundamental for a proper understanding of the whole reality of the Church. So it was that 'Catholics replied in treatises that were apologetical and polemical, … anti-Gallican and anti-Protestant throughout.[11] … The treatise *de Ecclesia* was principally a 'hierarchology', and the two terms between which that mediation comes, the Holy Spirit on one side, the faithful people … on the other, were as it were kept out of ecclesiological consideration.'[12] The fear of any counter-balance to the role of the Bishops as teachers in the Church reached a high point with Pope Benedict XV, who denied that anyone in Church, apart from the Bishops, could act as a teacher, either by publication or public lecture.[13] By the middle of the twentieth-century, the process had reached a term in the doctrine taught by Pope Pius XII, who wrote:

> Christ the Lord entrusted the truth he had brought from heaven to the Apostles and through them to their successors. As he was sent by the Father, so he sent the Apostles that they would teach all nations what they had heard from the Lord. The Apostles, therefore, are established by divine right as true doctors or teachers.

---

[9] Congar, Lay People in the Church, 36.
[10] Ibid, 37.
[11] Ibid, 38.
[12] Ibid, 39.
[13] 'Item nemo privatus, vel libris diariisve vulgandis vel sermonibus publice habendis, se in Ecclesia pro magistro gerat.'; 'Ad beatissimi Apostolorum', 1 Nov. 1914; DS 3625.

> Apart from the legitimate successors of the Apostles, the Roman Pontiff for the universal Church and the Bishops for the faithful committed to their care, there are no other teachers by divine right in the Church of Christ. Those who are called to teach in the Church do so, not in their own name, or by virtue of their theological knowledge, but by virtue of the mission they receive from the legitimate authority.[14]

It is not difficult to see what is happening here. In order to protect the hard core of the *binding* authority of the bishops in teaching, a general theory was developed which gave the bishops *all* authority to teach, and excluded everyone else from any teaching role whatever. On the basis of these developments, the principle which states that the Magisterium is the proximate and universal norm of truth changed its meaning. As Congar reports:

> some argued from 'living tradition' or 'the common and present teaching' of the Church, in the sense that the magisterium, justified and guaranteed once and for all by the institution and promises of Jesus Christ, is the rule of belief. It can not only interpret Scripture and the witness of tradition, which must be read 'with the eyes of the Church', but can also pronounce doctrinal truth and condemn concrete errors throughout the course of history *in the context of history* and its concrete demands.[15] ... (objective) tradition and Holy Scripture were presented as constituting the remote rule of faith, whilst the Church, or more precisely the magisterium of her pastors, was its proximate rule.[16]

---

[14] Allocution Si diligis (To the Cardinals and Bishops at the canonization of Pius X) 31 May 1954; AAS 46 (1954) 314-15.
[15] Congar, Tradition and Traditions, 191.
[16] Ibid, 199.

This was the formula adopted by Pope Pius XII in *Humani generis*, when he taught that 'this sacred Magisterium, ... should be the proximate and universal norm of truth for the theologian, since Christ the Lord has entrusted the whole deposit of faith to it ... to guard, preserve and interpret ...'[17] The Second Vatican Council showed a certain reserve in regard to this way of formulating the matter. The schema of the Constitution on the Church drawn up by the preparatory commission, adding a reference to this place in *Humani generis*, stated that theologians must always look upon the ecclesiastical magisterium as the 'proximate norm of truth'.[18] The first draft of what became *Dei Verbum* also proposed the doctrine of *Humani generis* that the Magisterium is the proximate and universal norm of belief.[19] A further draft stated that the Magisterium is the proximate rule of faith, while the Sacred Deposit is remote.[20] This sentence was removed in the next draft as not being a suitable point to make in the context. A number of Fathers had expressed criticisms of the doctrine. Two Bishops made the point that the Word of God himself, the First Truth, is the sole *regula regulans non regulata*, while the Magisterium is a *regula regulata*, whose function is to judge interpretations given of revealed truth.[21] The Council thus discreetly refrained from repeating Pope Pius XII's teaching in this matter.[22] Congar regarded this refusal of the Council to use this formula as a matter of significance. He considered that 'the Council re-established the traditional relationship of subordination of the pastoral authority to what is given or the object, in brief, the primacy

---

[17] DS 3884.
[18] Schema Constitutionis De Ecclesia, ca VII, n. 32; Acta Synodalia I/4, 52.
[19] Schema I: Constitutio dogmatica de fontibus revelationis, presented in the first Conciliar Session, November 14, 1962, § 6; in Francisco Gil Hellín, Dei Verbum: Concilii Vaticani II Synopsis (Città del Vaticano: Libreria Editrice Vaticana, 1993), 182.
[20] Gil Hellín, Dei Verbum, 78.
[21] Andreas Jacq, Titular Bishop Cerasenus and Paulus Petrus Meouchi, Patriarch of Antioch of the Maronites. E/366 and 375 at 10 G c) in Gil Hellín, Dei Verbum, 403 and 407.
[22] Max Seckler, 'Die Theologie als kirchliche Wissenschaft nach Pius XII. und Paul VI.,' in Theologische Quartalschrift 149 (1969) 209-234 at 211.

of the *quod* over the *quo*, both by affirming that the Magisterium is linked to the Word of God and at its service (LG 25, 4; DV 10, 2), and by refusing to take up the affirmation which the preparatory schema had drawn from *Humani generis*, the idea that the Magisterium is the *proxima veritatis norma*.'[23] However, although no such statement was retained in any document of the Second Vatican Council, Pope Paul VI, on several occasions, returned to Pope Pius XII's formula that the Magisterium is the proximate and universal norm of truth.[24]

There is clearly a tension here. A significant group of bishops at the Second Vatican Council shared Congar's resistance to affirming the Magisterium to be the proximate and universal norm of truth. And, even so, Pope Paul VI insisted on repeating this doctrine of Pope Pius XII. Congar proposes a diagnosis of this problem, and offers guidelines for a solution.

> The narrow view fairly reflects the weakness of a certain ecclesiology ... in which Möhler saw a result of naturalism: the working of the Holy Spirit is overlooked, leaving in the ecclesiological field only a passive mass and a machinery of mediation; and then all there is to be considered is the running of the mass by the machinery. When, however, all infallibility in the Church is expressly referred to the working of the Holy Spirit which Jesus promised should enable his Church to live in the truth, then the prospect widens out. In that case, each is acted on in view of an infallibility (finally one) according to his place in the body, receiving the

---

[23] Cardinal Yves Congar, O., 'Bref historique des formes du 'magistère,' in Église et papauté, (Paris, 1994), 312-13.
[24] 'Ex divina autem Christi voluntate, huius (scil. Revelationis et Evangelii) indefectibilis veritatis norma proxima et universalis nonnisi in authentico Ecclesiae Magisterio invenire poterit ...' (Allocution Libentissimo sane 1 October 1966; AAS 58 (1966) 891. See also 'Siamo particolarmente lieti', 11 July 1966, AAS 58 (1966) 653; 'Praesentia vestra', Sept. 1967, AAS 59 (1967) 962; 'Paterna cum benevolentia' AAS 67 (1975) 14.

> infallibility that belongs to him in function of the infallibility of the total organism, rather as each of man's various powers receives its part and pertinent energy from the soul.[25]

I suggest that Congar's solution finds expression in the distinction which has been developed in this book. If the Magisterium is understood in its full sense as the Magisterium of the Holy Church, then it can and must be recognised as the proximate and universal norm of truth. It is the Magisterium of the One Teacher, Christ, and is the Holy Spirit himself in person, and there can be no objection whatever to the formula being applied. If, on the other hand, one has the narrow vision of the Magisterium in mind, where it is the teaching of the bishops of the Church which is being referred to, then the formula does not apply properly, and the resistance of the Council Fathers is fully justified. The College of Bishops and their teaching do not constitute the proximate and universal norm of truth in the Church. The bishops are bound by the true proximate and universal norm, the teaching of the Holy Church, in the same way as every other Christian is. The bishops have a special role to play which is recognised by all, but it must not be over-exaggerated.

Although the word 'magisterium' is often now taken as a practical equivalent of the College of Bishops, the frequent use of 'Magisterium', with the capital 'M', indicates that somehow more is intended than simply the bishops. It is surely obvious that it would not make sense to say that the College of Bishops constitutes the proximate and universal norm of truth. Of course, no one ever said such a thing! And yet, the suggestion was lurking beneath the surface in the way the words were changing their meaning. Consider, for instance, this excerpt from a document of the International Theological Commission. Speaking of the Magisterium they write:

---

[25] Congar, Lay People in the Church, 290.

> Her mission does not consist in merely ratifying and making definitive, as if she were a supreme 'notary', the process of interpretation in the Church. She must also stimulate it, follow it step by step, and direct it, and to the extent that the process comes to a positive conclusion, give it, by an act of official validation, objective standing, and make it a matter of universal obligation. In this way, the Magisterium will give a sense of direction and certainty to the faithful who find themselves faced with confusing opinions and endless theological disputes: this may take place in various ways and with varying degrees of obligation, beginning with the usual preaching, exhortations and encouragement and on to authentic statements of doctrine, even infallible ones.[26]

It is clear from what is said, that, by the word 'Magisterium', the document is referring to the College of Bishops. And yet it seemed appropriate to personify the Magisterium, and to refer to it as 'she'. Such devotion to the episcopacy seems just a little excessive to me, and I suggest that what is happening is an unconscious identification of the bishops with the Church herself, in which case such personal language is quite acceptable. I further suggest that much of what is said in this paragraph applies better to the Church as a whole, and to the Holy Spirit acting in the Church, and that the whole position becomes clearer if the Magisterium of the Church is understood in the full sense being advocated here, and not at all narrowed to the College of Bishops. And the phrase, the *Ecclesia docens*, takes on a more adequate meaning also. The 'Church teaching' means just what it says, the Church teaching through all the channels available to her, under the direction of the Holy Spirit, and the role of the College of Bishops is to be specified within that totality.

---

[26] International Theological Commission, 'The Interpretation of Dogma,' ITQ 56 (1990) 251-277 at 276.

This perspective on the Magisterium helps to resolve, in theory at least, part of the tension which currently exists between bishops and theologians. A most useful contribution to this discussion was made recently by Max Seckler.[27] He gives a full history of the relationship between these two groups within the Church. During the first millennium, the inevitable tension between theology and the Magisterium did not take the form of a stand-off between bishops and theologians, since most of the important theologians were bishops. In the patristic period, apart from such great exceptions as Clement of Alexandria, Origen, and Tertullian, all the Church Fathers were bishops, and so it continued.[28] The change came in the medieval universities, when the Dominicans and the Franciscans made theology a profession for the first time, and gained an authority in the Church which would last for a long time. As Seckler tells us: 'Thus it was that Thomas conceived of *two magisteria* in the Church; the *magisterium cathedrae pastoralis and the magisterium cathedrae magistralis*. ... The *scientia sacra* is the domain reserved to the *doctores*. On the basis of their *licentia docendi* they take on a genuine *officium docendi*. They are called *magistri* and exercise a *magisterium*.'[29] The bishops exercise their *magisterium* on the foundation of their valid ordination, whereas the theologians exercise theirs on the foundation of their scientific expertise. Another stage was reached when the universities, especially the University of Paris, began taking on the role of judges of the faith. They began to control the content of the doctrine, organising trials and pronouncing judicial censures, behaving in a manner more suited to the *magisterium* of the bishops.[30] Seckler presents an interesting interpretation of Luther's problematic as an attempt for supremacy by the academy over the ecclesiastical institution, and he sees in the experience of the Council of Trent an ideal situation where a strong theology and a strong episcopal Magisterium co-operated in a clear mutual relationshi He writes:

---

[27] Seckler, 'Kirchliches Lehramt,' 17-62.
[28] Ibid, 21-25.
[29] Ibid, 30-31.
[30] Ibid, 37-38.

> In its order of business and its practice, the Council brought the theology of the theologians and the magisterium of the Bishops into a relationship whose form should be significant and in fact was. The two Vatican Councils of the 19th and 20th centuries followed the same pattern in this regard. No doubt these were conciliar processes and contents which, as such, are something extraordinary in the life of the Church. On the other hand, though, in the teaching and pattern followed by an ecumenical council, structures of the Church are formulated and realised which are not meant only for a single day.[31]

Within this serene and objective presentation of the historical background, Seckler has a rather acerbic and polemical section entitled 'The Totalitarian Claim of the Church's Magisterium according to Pope Pius XII and Paul VI'[32]. He protests against the claim, made by both these Popes, that the Magisterium constitutes the proximate and universal norm of faith, and the manner of conceiving the role of the theologian in the Church which follows from this principle. He protests that the theologian is not just a servant of the bishops, and that his role is more than simply justifying the positions taken by them, and he rejects the implication that the theologian has no critical function to perform. He states firmly that the Magisterium is *in* the Church, it is not *the* Church.[33] This is a point which other notable theologians consider it necessary to make. Walter (now Cardinal) Kasper has written: 'The authority of the Magisterium is not situated above the Church. Moreover, it does not have its authority as the authority of the Church simply, but as an authority within the Church. And this is why it can only exercise its specific ministry in communion with the whole community of faith which is the Church and with the other

---

[31] Ibid, 44.
[32] Ibid, 49-53.
[33] Ibid, 60.

Christians ...'³⁴ It is being suggested here that this stand-off would be resolved if the word 'magisterium' were given its fuller and truer sense. The Magisterium of the Church, which constitutes the proximate and universal norm of faith, is the Magisterium of the Holy Church which binds every Christian equally, from the bishops to the last of the lay faithful. Despite the narrow background from which they received it, this is really what Pope Pius XII and Pope Paul VI were teaching, and this is the truth of the matter. The role of the bishops in the Church is narrower and more precise, and does not undermine any of the rights and duties belonging to the rest of the People of God, but has the function of promoting and protecting them all. This is the vision upheld by Pope John Paul II who has written that the 'task of achieving an ever deeper understanding of the content of faith belongs to every member of the Church.'³⁵ And the Congregation for the Doctrine of the Faith has said the same in *Donum veritatis*, when it says: 'Thus thanks to the new birth and the anointing of the Holy Spirit (cf. Jn 3:5; 1 Jn 2:20, 27), we become the one, new People of God whose mission it is, with our different vocations and charisms, to preserve and hand on the truth.³⁶ ... For the sake of this mission, the Spirit of truth distributes among the faithful of every rank special graces "for the common good" (1 Cor 12:7-11).'³⁷

Seckler himself understands the matter in fundamentally the same way as is being proposed here, though his language is different and needs to be slightly adjusted. He has written: 'The *norma proxima* is the faith of whole Church and not only the preaching and teaching of the pastoral Magisterium. Obviously the pastoral Magisterium, in its witness to the *fides catholica*, plays a normative and authoritative role for the whole Church. But the pastoral Magisterium is <u>in</u> the Church,

---

34   Walter Kasper, <u>La théologie et l'Église</u>, trad. Paris, 1990, 82.

35   Address to Bishops of the state of New York (U.S.A. Region II) on Saturday, 15 October in L'Osservatore Romano (Eng. Ed.) 24 October 1988, 22. Also in <u>Origins</u> 18 (1988-89) 347.

36   <u>Donum Veritatis</u>, § 3.

37   Ibid, § 5.

it is not *the* Church.'³⁸ In his view 'the subject of theology is not the individual or even the community of theologians but the Church as such and as a whole, of which theology, *her* theology, forms an original life-function. So theology is in the Church and of the Church.'³⁹ He recognises that the faith witness of the Church is normative, but it is an historical reality, changeable and capable of development. Although the faith of the Church in the power of the Holy Spirit cannot fall from the Word of God, it can, in its actual state in time be the subject of deficiencies, and it is part of the legitimate critical task and prophetic mission of theology to struggle against them.⁴⁰ This is fine, but then Seckler says that the Word of God infinitely transcends the Church, and can be against the Church if necessary, and that from this it follows that the *norma suprema* of theology is not the witness or the doctrine of the Church, but the Word of God. He contends that the 'inherent encouragement and freedom' for the critical function of theology 'are grounded in the insurmountable theological difference between the *Word of God* and the *teaching of the Church*. ... *norma proxima* but not *norma suprema* ...'⁴¹ It is being contended here that Seckler is quite wrong in these last assertions. There is no difference whatever between the Word of God and the teaching of the Holy Church. Ratzinger made this point in a comment on the teaching of the Council of Trent, when he wrote:

> Trent continued to maintain that the word is not a reality standing independently above the Church but that it is delivered by the Lord to the Church. Nor is it thereby exposed to random caprice but precisely in that way remains in his own hands out of reach of

---

³⁸ Max Seckler, 'Die Kirchlichkeit und Freiheit der Theologie,' in <u>Handbuch der Fundamentaltheologie, Band 4: Theologische Erkenntnislehre</u>, edd. Walter Kern, Hemann Josef Pottmeyer, Max Seckler (Tübingen / Basel: A. Francke Verlag, 2000), Ch. 7, § 4, 161-83, at 168.
³⁹ Ibid, 162.
⁴⁰ Ibid, 167.
⁴¹ Ibid.

> human arbitrariness. In the view of the Fathers of Trent it probably seemed fundamentally a form of weakness in faith to be anxious for the word committed to the Church as though the Church might, as it were, outgrow it in such a way that recourse would have to be had to the word against the Church; they were indubitably certain that the Lord who instituted the Church as his Body is also able to preserve it for his word.[42]

The fact of the matter is that the Word of God is made to live in the Church by the Indwelling of the Holy Spirit, and the teaching of this Holy Church is identically the Word of God and, as such, constitutes the *norma proxima, universalis, et suprema* and any other superlative adjective one cares to bring forward. The critical function of theology in relation to magisterial teaching is not based on the difference between the Word of God and the teaching of the Church. It is based on the distinction between the Holy Church and the Catholic Church, whereby it can happen in particular circumstances that the truth is obscured because of human sin.

A point which needs to be addressed is the lack of definition of the teaching of the Holy Church. The Church teaches the whole doctrine of Christ infallibly always and everywhere, but it does so, as Christ himself did, by a process of witness and preaching which, of its nature, lacks precise definition. The Magisterium of the Church teaches, not in clear and definitive statements but in the total manner of which the liturgy is the principal exemplar. Christians can hear this voice of God in the Church, but in a mysterious and indefinite manner, which leaves room for the darkened intellects of fallen men to cause much disarray. This lack of definition is not to be taken as implying that God speaking in this way is to be considered 'fictive', as Suarez put it, and treated thereby as of no account. On the contrary, this remains the fundamental form of the Christian response of faith. The infallibility of the Church is the same

---

[42] Joseph Ratzinger, 'Revelation and Tradition,' in Karl Rahner and Joseph Ratzinger, <u>Revelation and Tradition</u>, <u>Quaestiones Disputatae 17</u> (New York: Herder and Herder, 1965), 26-49 at 30.

reality, in an active mode, as the inerrancy of Scripture. The inerrancy of Scripture implies that, if I properly understand the Scripture, the doctrine I find there is the word of God and is true. The same applies to the teaching of the Holy Church. If I properly understand what the Church teaches, then the doctrine I learn is the word of God and is true. The problem in both cases is being sure that my understanding is correct. The College of Bishops has a central role in this listening to the voice of God in the Church, in supervising every aspect of the life and teaching of the Church, and in making final judgments when they are required. But the bishops are not alone in this matter of listening to God, and it can happen that they are bound to listen to others who, for whatever reason, are closer to the Spirit on a particular point than they are. That can happen, and has happened in the past, and is happening now, and will happen in the future. It is in the nature of the case, where sin is a reality in the Church, that such things must occur. The task of formulating and clarifying and defining doctrine is important in the life of the Church, and that is the task of the bishops and the theologians. However, it is not so central that one should make the mistake of thinking that this is the be all and the end all of all teaching in the Church, as Suarez did. The normal Christian has no particular need for these fine points, and most have no hand, act, or part in the defining of doctrine, but they hear the voice of God speaking in the Church just as clearly as the professionals who devote their lives to such things. God speaks directly to every baptised Christian and this primordial speaking is the fundamental matter.

Congar tells us that from the developments we have been following there has resulted 'the notion that the Church and its present-day teaching are almost autonomous theological sources. Hence has arisen a tendency for the Church to regard itself as a source, although it can only "define" what has been revealed, and despite the fact that its magisterium, far from being identical with Tradition, must refer back to Tradition as to the source of its teaching and, as such, its objective rule.'[43] Congar sees this approach attributing autonomy to the faith

---

[43] Congar, <u>Tradition and Traditions</u>, 336-37. See also 181, 188, 269-70.

of the Church and the living Magisterium, and replacing 'the ancient formula: "The Church believes this because it is to be found in the revealed deposit," with another: "This is to be found in the revealed deposit because the Church believes it."[44]

It is being suggested here that the fundamental flaw in the approach Congar is criticising lies in the tendency to identify the Church with the Pope, or the College of Bishops, the human authorities in the Church. There is a legitimate complaint to be made against an unconditional claim on behalf of the Pope and the bishops, who are fallible human beings, but not against an unconditional claim on behalf of the theandric Church, the Bride and the Body of Christ, the Incorporation of the Holy Spirit. There can be no grounds for and no legitimate demand for any control over the teaching of this Church. It is the teaching of Christ and the Holy Spirit and it must be accorded total implicit faith. It does not make sense to speak of the autonomy of the Holy Church, which is precisely the teaching of Christ himself in the power of the Holy Spirit. Even Christ our Lord is not autonomous in his teaching. As he said himself, he only teaches what he has received from his Father. (John 5:30; 8:26, 28.) The two formulas which Congar places in opposition to each other are not in contradiction. It is true to say that 'the Church believes this because it is to be found in the revealed deposit.' The Church is the depositary of revelation and the Holy Church believes and teaches the whole deposit of revelation always and everywhere; the two are one. It is also true to say that 'this is to be found in the deposit of revelation because the Church believes and teaches it.' This latter is from our point of view, because our only access to the deposit of revelation is through the Church. Once the clear distinction is made between the Holy Church and the Catholic Church Congar's difficulties can be resolved. There is a perfection and a finality about the teaching of the Holy Church which can appear to be 'unconditional' and 'autonomous'. We meet it as something given over which we have no control whatever, and which we must accept with a complete and unreserved submission

---

[44] Y. M. J. Congar, O., La foi et la théologie (Paris: Desclée, 1962), 97. See also Congar, O., 'Bref historique des formes du 'magistère,' 309.

of faith. The same cannot and must not be said about the human teaching within the Catholic Church. This is not unconditional or autonomous in any way whatever.

An authoritative formulation of the special role of the bishops in the formulation of doctrine was made at the Second Vatican Council in connection with the interpretation of Scripture. Traditionally, it was said that the deposit of faith was entrusted to the Church to guard and proclaim, and that it was for the Church to judge the true meaning and interpretation of Scripture. This was the understanding underlying Trent and Vatican I. At the Council of Trent, the decree on the vulgate edition of the Bible and the manner of interpreting Sacred Scripture was directed against those who would distort the meaning of Scripture 'against the meaning which holy mother Church has held and holds, for to the Church belongs the authority to judge the true meaning and interpretation of the Sacred Scriptures' (DS 1507). This formula was quoted verbatim in Vatican I, *Dei Filius*, DS 3007. Later in the same decree it is taught that Christ instituted the Church as the guardian and teacher of the revealed word. (DS 3012, 3018, 3020) In the teaching of Popes Pius XII and Paul VI, it is said that these functions are performed by the Magisterium of the Church, where it is clear that it is the role of the bishops that is meant.[45] The doctrine is stated clearly in *Dei Verbum* 10: 'The task of authentically interpreting the Word of God, written or handed down, has been entrusted to the living Magisterium

---

[45] Pius XII: 'Cui [Magisterio Ecclesiae] Christus Dominus totum depositum fidei – Sacras nempe Litteras ac divinam 'traditionem' – et custodiendum et tuendum et interpretandum concredidit.' – 'Quod quidem depositum nec singulis christifidelibus nec ipsis theologis divinus Redemptor concredidit authentice interpretandum, sed soli Ecclesiae Magisterio.' (Humani generis, 12 August 1950, AAS 42 (1950) 567, 569) ... 'Quod quidem depositum authentice illustrandum atque interpretandum Divinus Redemptor uni concredidit Magisterio Ecclesiae.' (Radio message 'Inter complures', 24 October 1954; AAS 46 (1954) 678.) ... 'Cum enim Revelationis depositum soli Ecclesiae Magisterio authentice interpretandum commissum sit ...' (Apostolic Constitution Sedes Sapientiae 31 May 1956; AAS 48 (1956) 362.) – 'unice' (Allocution Si diligis 31 May 1954; AAS 46 (1954) 316.). - Vatican II: DV 10: 'Munus authentice interpretandi verbum Dei scriptum vel traditum soli vivo Ecclesiae Magisterio concreditum est.'

of the Church alone.'[46] What precise aspect of the task of interpreting Scripture can be said to belong to the bishops 'alone'? They are not the only interpreters of the Bible by any means. Every Christian has the right and the duty to interpret the Scripture as best he can for his own Christian life. And there are experts in exegesis who have a particular function to perform in the Church's interpretation of the Word of God. The episcopal interpretation of Scripture doesn't refer to exegetical interpretation, which has rarely happened and is not a practice likely to be taken up by the bishops. This is not the way the bishops exercise their role. Surely this text can only be referring to judgments of doctrine which are effectively interpretations of Scripture. The crucial point is that it is the 'authentic' or authoritative interpretation of Scripture which belongs to the bishops 'alone'. They alone are entitled to make definitive judgments binding the whole Church, and this is clearly what the text has in mind.

Having offered an approach which may solve Congar's problems here, is it possible that the distinction between the Holy Church and the Catholic Church could resolve Luther's difficulties also? There was occasion earlier to present an account of Luther's full and earnest belief in the infallibility of the Church. In his adherence to this doctrine, Luther clearly has in mind the Church-mystery, what is being called here the Holy Church, but he follows Wyclif and Hus and makes this 'true' Church so spiritual that it does not intersect with the concrete Church at all. And so, his difficulties with the concrete Church can only result in its rejection. And Luther finds plenty of evidence of error in the Church. He cites the examples of David and Nathan in the Old Testament, and St Peter's error as reported in Galatians 2: 11ff. in the New. Luther then argues that, for these Scriptural reasons, and the many examples of error in Church history, a Christian cannot unconditionally obey the Church. We owe Christ unconditional obedience, but we pass judgment on the apostles, the church, and even on angels according to the standard of God's word. For Luther the Church is exempt

---

[46] 'Munus authentice interpretandi verbum Dei scriptum vel traditum soli vivo Ecclesiae Magisterio concreditum est.'

neither from humanity nor sinfulness, and these factors forbid any human Church authority from claiming unconditional authority and demanding unconditional obedience,[47] and he concludes that we must always ask whether the papal and other official decrees and regulations of Rome came from the Holy Ghost or from Satan. (WA 7, 713.) [48] With his customary vehemence, Luther expresses his position in strong terms: 'Let all obedience be damned to the depths of hell which obeys the government, father, mother, or even the church in such a way that it disobeys God. At this point I know neither father, mother, friendship, government, or the Christian church.' (WA 28, 24.)[49] There is much in what Luther is saying that must be taken up into any justification of legitimate dissent in the Church. However, the root of the problem lies in his separation of the Church from God. The concept of the Church as the human corporation separate from God had been developing over the centuries in Western theology and had come to dominate so completely that the sense of the Church-mystery immanent in the concrete Church was weak. Luther does not see that his 'true Church' subsists in the Catholic Church. The two are not fully identical, and this to some extent justifies his protest, for the concrete Catholic Church can err and has erred in its human representatives. However, Christ's promise to be with his Church until the end of the age applies to the Catholic Church, so that the level of error that is possible could never justify its complete rejection.

---

[47] Althaus, The Theology of Martin Luther, 339-40.
[48] Ibid, 343.
[49] Ibid, 339.

Chapter 13

The Ordinary Magisterium of the Bishops

The aim of this book is to clarify the proper response to the ordinary teaching of the bishops in the Church, and of the Pope in particular. The question was focussed in the wake of the First Vatican Council and has not yet been adequately resolved. The First Vatican Council defined that when the Pope defines doctrine, he exercises the infallibility of the Church and the definition is inerrant. That definition of the inerrancy of extraordinary papal definitions focussed the question as to the status of all the rest of papal teaching, his ordinary magisterium. The standard position which developed speaks of the Pope being infallible in his definitions, and the rest of his teaching being non-infallible.

The position has been summarized recently by Avery (later Cardinal) Dulles. Dulles tells us that 'Catholics are required in principle to affirm with certitude the articles of the creed, the defined dogmas of the Church, and doctrines constantly and universally taught in the Church as matters of divine and Catholic faith,' and then he goes on: 'But they are not bound to accept, under pain of infidelity, everything taught by the magisterium. Most of the doctrines of the Church are taught noninfallibly and are, as the phrase goes, reformable.'[1] He elaborates on this last point elsewhere, where he writes: 'In point of

---

[1] Dulles, The Assurance of Things Hope For: A Theology of Christian Faith (New York / Oxford: Oxford University Press, 1994), 234.

fact, theologically educated Catholics have always known that the vast majority of the Church's teaching is fallible and therefore subject to error. In all the thousands of pages of encyclicals issued by the popes of the last hundred years, there is not to my knowledge a single sentence of infallible teaching. In the 800-odd pages of the documents of Vatican II, there is not one new statement for which infallibility is claimed.'[2] This view of the matter is common indeed. The notion of the non-infallibility of ordinary teaching was a key part of Curran's position and was conceded by the Congregation for the Doctrine of the Faith in the course of the discussion between them. The difficulty with the position has, however, been noted on occasion, as, for instance, by Archbishop (now Cardinal) Levada when he wrote: 'Some discussions about dissent fail to recognize that not everything that the Church teaches infallibly has been infallibly defined. … For this reason the use of the simple dichotomy infallible and non-infallible teaching can be misleading. One cannot simply presume that any Church doctrine which has not been infallibly defined … is not in fact contained in the infallible teaching of the Church's universal ordinary Magisterium…'[3] And it will be remembered that Pope Pius XII, when he was discussing the appropriate response to papal encyclicals, pointed out: 'Often, too, what is expounded and inculcated in encyclical letters already appertains to Catholic doctrine for other reasons.'[4]

There is a double confusion involved here which needs to be resolved. There is the ambiguity between the Magisterium of the Church and the Magisterium of the bishops or the Pope, and there is a confusion between definitiveness and infallibility. Unravelling the first ambiguity has been the principal goal of all that has preceded here, and the point

---

[2] Avery Dulles, S. J., The Survival of Dogma (New York: Doubleday & Company, 1971), 144. The point is repeated in 'Faith and Revelation', in Systematic Theology, edd. Francis Schüssler Fiorenza and John Galvin (Minneapolis: Fortress Press, 1991), 89-128 at 125.
[3] Archbishop William Levada; 'Dissent and the Catholic Religion Teacher', Readings in Moral Theology No. 6; Dissent in the Church, edd. Curran and McCormick, SJ., (NY, 1988), 133ff. at 145-146.
[4] Humani generis, AAS, 42 (1950), 568.

needs to be spelled out. In Chapter 9 the structure of the Ordinary Magisterium of the Church was presented, and it was pointed out how this understanding of the Ordinary Magisterium was the one introduced by Johannes Kleutgen and made official in Pope Pius IX's letter, *Tuas libenter*, and in the decree, *Dei Filius*, of the First Vatican Council. Kleutgen's traditional notion of the ordinary Magisterium was not the only one current at the time, however, for a new version, which understands the ordinary Magisterium as referring to the teaching of the bishops, rather than the teaching of the Holy Church, had already begun to make headway. When the matter was being discussed at the First Vatican Council, there was confusion by what was meant by the new term, 'ordinary magisterium'.[5] Some thought it referred to the ordinary teaching of the Pope, though most took it as referring to the ordinary teaching of the bishops spread throughout the world in their day-to-day teaching. An amendment made to the text reveals the general mindset. The first draft did not have the phrase 'as divinely revealed', and some Fathers remarked that one is not obliged to believe with divine faith everything proposed by the Church, but only that which is proposed as divinely revealed, and wished the formulation to be qualified, as it was in the final draft.[6] It is clear from this objection that the bishops had the human corporation of the Church in mind, not the Holy Church, for the Holy Church only teaches what is divinely revealed. In his *Relatio* presenting the document, Archbishop Simor of Strigoniensis speaks of the *ecclesia docens dispersa* preaching and teaching, making it evident that he has the bishops in mind.[7] And Bishop Martin, in a short intervention on behalf of the Deputation of Faith on the text, referring to the situation before the Council of Nicaea, told how 'all the Catholic bishops' believed in the divinity of Christ, making it clear that he also had the bishops in mind, rather than the Church-mystery.[8] And Bishop Felix Dupanloup of Orleans, in his

---

[5] On this see Roger Aubert, Le problème de l'acte de foi (Louvain : Warny, 1945), 185-191.
[6] Mansi 51, 217D, 226A, 230B.
[7] Mansi 51, 47C.
[8] Mansi 51, 225A.

intervention, spoke of 'what is ordinarily and commonly proposed to the faithful by those who exercise the ordinary magisterium of doctrine in the Church.'[9]

This has become the standard meaning of the phrase. Sullivan, for instance, says: 'The term *universal* ordinary magisterium' refers to the concordant teaching of the whole Catholic episcopate together with the Pope, apart from the rather rare occasions when the bishops are gathered in an ecumenical council.'[10] There can be no doubt that this is the meaning of the phrase taken for granted at the Second Vatican Council. In preparing *Lumen gentium*, § 25, on the infallibility of teaching in the Church, there was discussion about the infallibility enjoyed by the bishops spread throughout the world, and it is clear that this is what was understood by the ordinary magisterium of the Church.[11] With this meaning in mind, the question arises as to the infallibility of the ordinary magisterium, and so a qualification had to be added that the bishops spread throughout the world can speak infallibly if they teach a doctrine to be held definitively.[12] On the understanding of the matter being advocated here, there is a confusion involved in this which obscures matters significantly. It is a feature of the teaching of the bishops spread throughout the world, which is very easy to verify from history, that they simply cannot teach anything definitively. The whole reason for ecumenical councils is to make definitive judgments, which are otherwise impossible. If, then, the infallibility of the ordinary magisterium is made conditional on definitiveness, the infallibility is simply lost completely. An uncertain infallibility is no infallibility at all, and the general uncertainty is evidenced by one well qualified commentator who had this to say: 'The question has been raised whether this statement of Vatican I defines the *infallibility* of the ordinary universal magisterium. It certainly does not do so explicitly ... However, it might be said to follow as a theological conclusion from the obligation

---

[9] Mansi 51, 230A.
[10] Sullivan, Magisterium, 122.
[11] See, for example, Karl Rahner in Commentary on the Documents of Vatican II, Vol. 1, New York, 1965, 210-211.
[12] Gil Hellín, Lumen Gentium, 256.

on all the faithful to believe what is taught by this magisterium, in view of the basic principle that the whole Church cannot err in its faith. While the Second Vatican Council did not define the infallibility of the ordinary universal magisterium either ... it did explicitly state the conditions under which it is infallible.'[13] It is being suggested here that this narrowing down of the term 'ordinary magisterium' to the explicit teaching of the bishops is a mistake. If the ordinary magisterium is understood properly, as Kleutgen first proposed it, and as the tradition clearly understands it, the matter takes on a different aspect. The ordinary magisterium *of the Church* is the teaching of Christ, in the power of his Spirit, teaching his truth always and everywhere, and its infallibility is certain. It is not simply a matter of the bishops teaching, whether unanimously or not, or in any other manner to be specified. It is the teaching of the whole Church with the liturgy at its centre, teaching the whole truth always and everywhere. And, interestingly enough, the traditional and correct meaning is retained in Canon 750 of the Code of Canon Law, which gives legal form to the teaching of the First Vatican Council. Here, the object of divine faith includes the teaching of the 'ordinary and universal Magisterium, which is manifested by the common adherence of Christ's faithful under the guidance of the sacred Magisterium.' The ambiguity of the word 'magisterium' is in evidence here. The first use refers to the broad concept, the Magisterium of the Church, and the second to the bishops.[14]

The traditional meaning of the 'ordinary magisterium' continued in use, at least until the Second Vatican Council. It was used 'to describe infallible teaching by ordinary means,' and, as Orsy points out the proper response to its teaching is the assent of faith.[15] Now the term is

---

[13] Sullivan, Magisterium, 123. (Emphasis in the original.)

[14] This ambiguity in the use of the word is discussed by Ladislas Orsy, S.J. in The Church: Teaching and Learning (Dublin / Leominster: Dominican Publications / Fowler Wright Books, 1987), 60-61, and 'Reflections on the Text of a Canon,' in Readings in Moral Theology No. 6: Dissent in the Church, edd. Charles E. Curran and Richard McCormick, S.J. (New York / Mahwah: Paulist Press, 1988), 231-238 at 236-37.

[15] Ibid, 236.

used quite differently. Now it refers to noninfallible teaching which is authentic but not definitive, to which the proper response can only be 'religious respect.'[16] In the manuals, any teaching function of the Pope or the Bishops apart from the definitive declarations is categorized as *merely* authentic magisterium, *mere authenticum*.[17] When the teaching function of the Holy Spirit in the ordinary Magisterium of the Church is unappreciated, and the whole focus is on the bishops as the only teachers, such an odd formulation becomes possible. Since the bishops spread throughout the world cannot speak definitively, it follows, so the logic would have it, that they cannot teach infallibly, and so their teaching is *merely authentic*, and word 'authentic' now loses its force. It now refers to teaching proposed 'authoritatively', in proper form, but not definitively, so that its genuine authenticity remains in doubt, and the assent of faith to such teaching is considered inappropriate.

It is important to make a clear distinction between infallibility and definition. Christ our Lord is the original infallible teacher, and he defined nothing. All his sermons, and the sermons of the Apostles after him, were moments of infallible teaching, without any definitions. The Church passed some of the best days of her life, prior to the Council of Nicaea, without defining any doctrine. And yet the whole faith was passed on, and believed with certainty all this time. Since then, the moments of definition have been few and far between, and still the whole Gospel continues to be proclaimed infallibly and believed with certainty. This mixture of infallibility and indefiniteness is crucial. Every Christian believer hears the Word of God. We all believe God directly; our faith is based immediately in him. And we believe what God teaches with full certainty in his infallible teaching. However, our grasp of God's word is imperfect in many ways, due to the darkness of our intellects as a result of sin. And it is this combination of the certainty of faith, combined with actual error in belief, which makes theological arguments so heated and *odium theologicum* so bitter. And

---

[16] Ibid.
[17] See for example J. Salaverri, 'De Ecclesia Christi,' in <u>Sacrae Theologiae Summa, I</u> (Madrid: BAC, 1962), 704.

still, the fact that any individual Christian's judgment of the faith is not, and cannot be, definitive, does not remove his primordial right to judge the faith. Otherwise he believes very little at all, and that cannot be. The experience of Ecumenical Councils is illustrative in this matter. When the bishops gather to define the faith, it has always been a difficult process. The bishops all have an excellent grasp of the faith in a general way, but they always differ when it comes to details. But those differences do not mean that they are unable to discern and judge what is of faith. It simply means that all of our intellects are darkened and not one of us is personally infallible. But that does not prevent us knowing the faith with certainty and living it fruitfully.

It is in this area that the truth of Hirscher's insight can be located. The ordinary teaching of the Church is infallible but indefinite. The infallibility of the Church as a whole covers everything that the Church teaches. Catholics are required in principle to accept all the doctrines constantly and universally taught in the Church as matters of divine and Catholic faith, whether defined or not, and these are not so much a set of distinct propositions as the organic whole which is the Word of God, the Gospel of Christ. On this understanding all the doctrines of the Church are taught infallibly and are none of them reformable. However, that a doctrine is not taught definitively does not automatically mean that it is not taught infallibly. Most of the doctrines of the Church are taught non-definitively, but they remain part of the Church's faith and are, therefore, taught infallibly and are not reformable. They are taught with the infallibility of the Church, even though that infallibility has not come to definition by the teaching of the Bishops in Council or of the Pope representing the College on his own.

The failure to distinguish between the infallible Church and the fallible ministers leads to a mistake in either of two directions. One can apply the infallibility of the Church to the human minister, and then one gets the exaggerated view of the infallibility of the Pope. This position overlooks the fact that the Pope is and always remains a sinful and fallible human being like the rest of us. The fact of the matter is that the Pope is never infallible. In certain circumstances he can make a definitive judgment which is guaranteed to be inerrant by the infallibility of the Church, but he himself remains always a fallible man. After the First Vatican Council, when this view of papal infallibility was not canonised, the obverse mistake arose. When the fallibility of the Pope's ordinary teaching was recognised, it began to be taken that the ordinary teaching of the Church is fallible in the same way. So it is that Hirscher's mistake, which was rejected in one statement by the First Vatican Council, was implicitly reinstated by another route.

The confusion between definitiveness and infallibility is to be found in the document of the Congregation for the Doctrine of the Faith, *Donum Veritatis*, where it is written:

> More frequently, it is asserted that the theologian is not bound to adhere to any Magisterial teaching unless it is infallible. Thus a kind of theological positivism is adopted, according to which, doctrines proposed without the exercise of the charism of infallibility are said to have no obligatory character about them, leaving the individual completely at liberty to adhere to them or not. The theologian would accordingly be totally free to raise doubts or reject the non-infallible teaching of the Magisterium particularly in the case of specific moral norms. With such critical opposition, he would even be making a contribution to the development of doctrine.[18]

The document is here rejecting Hirscher's mistake, that Christians are only bound to accept definitive teaching, which the Congregation mistakenly calls infallible teaching. Properly understood, it is true to say that the Christian is only bound to accept infallible teaching, because all the teaching of the Church, ordinary and extraordinary, is infallible. The *Instruction* is wrong to make the distinction between doctrines taught infallibly and fallibly, for there is no such thing as 'non-infallible teaching of the Magisterium,' properly understood. All the binding

---

[18] Donum Veritatis, § 33.

teaching of Christ and the Church is taught infallibly. If it is not taught infallibly it is not the teaching of Christ and so is not binding in faith, for Christ can only teach infallibly. The appropriate distinction is between doctrines taught definitively and clearly, and those whose character as properly the teaching of Christ and the Church has not yet been clearly discerned and definitively stated, and this distinction is not of fundamental importance as so many suggest. It is surely helpful to have doctrines clearly defined, when clear definition is called for, but the general infallible teaching of the Church which covers everything the Church teaches *per modum unius*, as Newman liked to say, is what the Christian lives by. Ordinary Christians do not know which doctrines have been taught definitively, and there is no good reason why they should, for it does not affect the living of the Christian life that much. They learn the teaching of the Church as an integrated whole, infallibly proclaimed in its totality, and that is what they live by. The vast mass of undefined doctrine is just as important, and just as infallibly taught, as the discreet number of points which historical circumstances have brought to definition over the centuries.

Returning to the quotation from Avery Dulles given earlier, the flaws in his reasoning can be discerned. Dulles is confusing definition and infallibility, and he shows a weak sense of the infallible Church, the *Ecclesia universalis*, what I am presuming to call the Holy Church. It doesn't make sense to me to claim that 'theologically educated Catholics have always known that the vast majority of the Church's teaching is fallible.' We all know that the vast majority of the Church's teaching is not defined. But we all still believe that the Church is infallible. The 'doctrines constantly and universally taught in the Church as matters of divine and Catholic faith,' which Dulles mentions in his first sentence, cover the whole gamut of Church teaching, and constitute the fundamental teaching of the Church, which is all taught infallibly. Further, while it is true to say that there is no definition to be found in any of the papal encyclicals or the documents of the Second Vatican Council, it is wrong to conclude that none of this teaching is infallible. Taken as a whole, as truly representing the teaching of the Church, this body of teaching is generally infallible. The Fathers of the

Second Vatican Council deliberately chose not to make any dogmatic definitions. However, the long work of formulating the documents led to a teaching which can be taken as representing the mind of the Church in a broad and general way, and in that broad and general way, it is taught infallibly. I submit that the problem in this approach, as represented here by Dulles, is the almost exclusive attention to the teaching of the human ministers in the Church, with a corresponding overlooking of the teaching of the divine principals. When the true theandric vision of the Church is brought to the forefront, the perspective is reversed. When we speak of the 'the teaching of the Church,' there is a first sense of the phrase which refers to the teaching of the Holy Church, which is infallible in its totality. It is only upon reflection that we have to recognise the duality in the meaning of 'the Church,' and recognise that there can be official teachings of the Catholic Church which do not correspond exactly to 'the teaching of the Church,' taken absolutely. It seems to me, therefore, that Dulles has it completely the wrong way round. The 'vast majority' of what the Catholic Church teaches, in matters of faith and morals, is taught infallibly, with the infallibility of the Holy Church which subsists in it. Due to human failings and sin, from which no-one in the Church is exempt, there can be teachings which turn out to be erroneous, and thus reformable, but they will constitute a small part of the whole.

Another version of the flawed perspective which needs to be overcome can be observed in a contribution by Ladislas Orsy. He writes that 'to separate within the "non-infallible" portion of beliefs the incorrupt expressions of our faith from what are human opinions is not easy. To determine if a given point of doctrine is an integral part of revelation or not, it is necessary to examine the precise content of that doctrine, its place in Christian tradition, its connection with other mysteries. Such inquiry is always a slow process, and can be full of pitfalls. It requires a good deal of historical knowledge and training in methodology.'[19] This is not correct. It presumes that what is not defined is a vague

---

[19] Ladislas Orsy, S.J., The Church: Teaching and Learning (Dublin / Leominster: Dominican Publications / Fowler Wright Books, 1987). 59.

conglomerate of ideas among which the 'incorrupt expressions' are embedded, and that the discernment is a matter of scholarshi Both these notions are mistaken. The faith of the Church is an organic whole of the Word of God, within which some erroneous elements are mixed due to the darkness of our human intellects from sin, both original and actual, and the discernment is a matter for the light of faith given to every Christian in Baptism. Orsy is here presenting a mitigated form of Hirscher's position which was refuted by Kleutgen, and it cannot be accepted now any more than it was then. Catholics generally accept the faith of the Church in its totality, and they have a generally workable knowledge of what the faith entails. The detailed defining of doctrine involves the accurate discernment Orsy writes of, but the teaching of the Church can be known in a valid manner without definition, as most Christians have always known it, and will always do so. Consider another formulation of Orsy. He is discussing the problem of dissent, and he wonders: '... could the legitimacy of the dissent be decided by invoking the distinction between infallible and non-infallible teaching and saying that dissent from non-infallibly defined propositions is legitimate? The answer cannot be a simple *yes* because of the complex composition of the *corpus* of non-infallible beliefs and opinions'[20] What Orsy is saying here is basically correct, but the confusion of the language renders the matter most confusing. Here again we have the ordinary teaching of the Church presented as a '*corpus* of non-infallible beliefs and opinions,' and he speaks of a 'non-infallibly defined' proposition. The ordinary teaching of the Church is a *corpus* of teaching which is proclaimed infallibly, but indefinitely, around which there can be all sorts of beliefs and opinions which are not part of the teaching of the Church at all. And, in the technical language of traditional Church usage, there is no such thing as a 'non-infallibly defined' proposition. If a proposition is defined, then it is known clearly to be part of the infallible teaching of the Church.

All of this provides background to the discussion between the Congregation for the Doctrine of the Faith and Charles Curran. As

---

[20] Ibid, 95.

part of the justification for his dissent, Curran writes: 'Within this large area of what is non-infallible and not central to the Christian faith, it is necessary to recognize various degrees and levels of relationship to faith. ... I have recognized this fact by consciously referring to dissent from *some* non-infallible teachings which are somewhat removed from the core and central faith realities.'[21] Curran makes a number of points here, and it will be necessary to deal with them one by one. He argues that he is dissenting from 'some' 'non-infallible' doctrines which are not 'central' to the faith. On the standard theology, what he says makes sense. On the position being developed here, Curran is not entitled to say that the doctrines he is dissenting from are 'non-infallible'. What he actually means, and what is true, is that they are not defined. Whether or not they are infallible needs to be determined; it cannot be taken as given. It must also be recognised that the Congregation for the Doctrine of the Faith is working on the same faulty theology of the ordinary magisterium of the Church, and falls into some of the same mistakes as does Curran. On the first page of the 'Observations' sent to Curran it says that 'Father Curran minimizes or even denies the specific value of the noninfallible magisterium which enjoys the presumption of truth grounded in the ... assistance of the Holy Spirit.' And in one of the later letters to Curran, it was stated that 'the Church does not build its life upon its infallible Magisterium alone but on the teaching of its authentic, ordinary Magisterium as well.'[22] These statements imply that the teaching of authentic, ordinary Magisterium of the Church is not infallible. The Congregation has the manualist notion of the 'merely authentic' teaching of the bishops in mind, and what is said makes a certain kind of sense with that in mind. I would wish to argue that what counts is the ordinary Magisterium *of the Church*, and this

---

[21] Charles Curran; 'Public Dissent in the Church' in Readings in Moral Theology No. 6; Dissent in the Church, edd. Charles E. Curran and Richard A. McCormick, S.J., (New York/Mahwah: Paulist Press, 1988), 387-407 at 400.

[22] Congregation for the Doctrine of the Faith: Cardinal Ratzinger's Letters to Charles Curran, in Readings in Moral Theology No. 6: Dissent in the Church, edd. Charles E. Curran and Richard A. McCormick, S.J. (New York/Mahwah: Paulist Press, 1988), 357-363, September 17, 1985, 361.

Magisterium is not 'merely authentic', but fully authentic and always infallible. Following on that, I would wish to say that the Church does build its life upon its infallible teaching alone. All the teaching of the Church is infallible, for it is the Word of God, and it is upon that Word that the Church builds its life.

In the light of what has now been established it is possible to clarify an ambiguity in what we mean when we speak of the the 'teaching of the Church.' This phrase can refer to the teaching of the Holy Church and, in that case, it means the teaching of Christ speaking through the Holy Spirit in the Church and proclaiming the whole Word of God infallibly always and everywhere. On the other hand, the phrase can refer to the official teaching of the Catholic Church which can now be clearly seen as something quite different. The official teaching of the Church can be affected adversely by the sin which is part of the concrete Catholic Church and is not, therefore, infallible in all its details. Just as the Holy Church subsists in the Catholic Church, so the teaching of the Holy Church subsists in the official teaching of the Catholic Church. There is a real and substantial identity between the two, but, as in the case of the Church, the identity is not full, and it is on the basis of this distinction between the teaching of the Holy Church and the official teaching of the Catholic Church that the theology of dissent must be constructed.

Chapter 14

Religious Submission to the Pope: the Resolution

With these points established, we are now in a position to tackle the issue of the appropriate response to the teaching to the Pope, or any other bishop, or even the College of Bishops as a whole. The resolution of the matter hangs on giving its proper place to the role of Christ, the One Teacher, and the Holy Spirit, the Interior Teacher, in the concrete life of the Church. It is only in this way that the role of the human ministers can be seen in its proper perspective. A place to begin is with a principle proposed in a document produced by the German bishops shortly after the Second Vatican Council to provide some guidelines in this matter, a document which met with a measure of official approval. It was published as semi-private document and distributed to the German dioceses, and an Italian version appeared in the *Osservatore Romano*, in a translation commissioned, apparently, by the Secretariat of State. It marks the first occasion on which this problem has been explicitly tackled at all in a (relatively) official document.[1] The document bases its analysis of the response to an ordinary episcopal teaching on the analogy of the response to an expert opinion in normal human affairs.

---

[1] Karl Rahner S.J., 'The Dispute Concerning the Teaching Office of the Church' in *Theological Investigations, Vol. 14*, (London: Darton, Longman & Todd, 1976), 85-97. at 88.

The document says: 'In such a case the position of the individual Christian in regard to the Church is analogous to that of a man who knows that he is bound to accept the decision of a specialist even while recognizing that it is not infallible.'[2] This is an interesting analogy, but it is more useful as a point of negative comparison, for the example of a specialist in some field, e.g., a doctor, does not properly apply. The issue there is a practical decision and one must operate on the best advice available; the specialist is not a teacher. The comparison with a human teacher was presented more fully by Bruno Schüller, who wrote:

> That the authentic magisterium speaks with genuine authority means that it speaks with the special assistance of the Holy Spirit which Christ has guaranteed, and consequently from a superior insight into Christ's Gospel and law, an insight which protects it in a special way from error. Thus it can vouch for the truth of what it teaches and proclaims, and it deserves to be trusted. ... Make no mistake: teaching authority consists primarily of superior insight. ... Thus by definition a teacher is superior to the student in knowledge and insight. ... Accordingly, the authentic magisterium has binding authority for believers because through the assistance of the Holy Spirit it has superior insight into Christ's truth which is binding upon believers for their salvation.[3]

The analogy of a human teacher is more appropriate than an expert in practical matters, but it still needs to be better adapted to the situation of teaching in the Church. Consider a teacher, e.g. Socrates, Plato or Aristotle, any great original philosopher, giving his opinions. At no stage does he make a claim to infallibility and his listeners are free to accept or

---

[2] Ibid, 87.
[3] Bruno Schüller, S.J., 'Remarks on the Authentic Teaching of the Magisterium of the Church,' in Readings in Moral Theology No. 3: The Magisterium and Morality, edd. Charles E. Curran and Richard McCormick, S.J. (New York / Ramsey: Paulist Press, 1982), 14-33 at 16.

reject his opinions as they wish. A Christian pastor making a judgement in a matter of faith is in a unique position. His personal judgment is in principle fallible as is that of any human specialist. However, he is not speaking on his own authority; he is speaking 'in the person of Christ', who is infallible. Our absolute obedience of faith is owed to Christ, speaking by the illumination of his Holy Spirit in and through the holy Church. That absolute, unconditional, obedience can be offered to no human authority, not even the College of Bishops, except in the case where the conditions are fulfilled which allow one to conclude that God is speaking. When a Christian hears a bishop preaching, or reads an episcopal statement, even a papal encyclical or a decree of an Ecumenical Council, he is not listening to the bishop as the teacher involved, but to Christ. The bishop is a minister of Christ who speaks 'in his person', and the Christian is listening to Christ in the power of the Interior Teacher, the Holy Spirit, who illuminates his mind to hear what is being said. Just as the power of sacraments is not based on the superior holiness of the ministers, no more is the power of the teachers in the Church based on superior understanding, but on the authority of Christ. I listen to my Bishop, not because he has any human gifts to which I do not have access, but because he has been ordained and sent to speak in Christ's name, and for no other reason. The bishop is not, properly speaking, a teacher in relation to the Christian at all, for we have only one Teacher, the Christ. The bishop is a teacher only insofar as he represents Christ, the one and only Teacher. His teaching role is not based on any expertise of his own at all, but only on the authority Christ in whose name he speaks. Pope John Paul had some marvellous things to say to catechists about Christ, the one Teacher: 'Every catechist should be able to apply to himself the mysterious words of Jesus: "My teaching is not mine, but his who sent me." ... What assiduous study of the ---word of God transmitted by the Church's Magisterium, what profound familiarity with Christ and with the Father, what a spirit of prayer, what detachment from self must a catechist have in order that he can say: "My teaching is not mine!"'[4] This doctrine applies equally

---

[4] Catechesi Tradendae, 6.

to a bisho When a bishop teaches, both he and those who are listening to him must remember that it is not he who is speaking, but Christ speaking in him. This, then, is the fundamental principle to be applied in the area of teaching in the Church. There is only one Teacher, the Christ, and everyone who teaches in the Church teaches in his name. This principle also sets the norms which govern the appropriate response to episcopal teaching. It establishes the object that is being taught and gives guidelines for the discernment of the appropriate response.

Furthermore, Christians listening to a bishop are not in the same position as students listening to a teacher. Formed Christians know the faith already. They do not listen to a bishop to learn new things, but to hear the faith of the Church proclaimed. The 'superior insight' in the situation belongs to Christ, the One Teacher, who is speaking through the bisho It is not the bishop that I believe, but God who speaks in and through the bisho The bishop is a fallible man like me. He is not an 'expert' in relation to the believer. He is a messenger who has received a gift of the Holy Spirit to fulfil a task. His supernatural sense of the faith is assisted by the Holy Spirit, but not to the level of infallibility. The Christian listens with his own sense of the faith and judges the congruence of the bishop's statement with his own grasp of God's word. The relationship of expert to the uninitiated is not relevant at all, for every Christian has a direct link to God in faith and has his own supernatural sense of the faith with which to judge what is said.

The formed Christian is, in a fundamental way, the equal of the bishop, even the Pope, who is addressing him. He knows the teaching of the Church in a general way and has the right and the duty to judge what is said by anyone in the Church. St Paul specifically teaches that we all have the right and the duty to judge what is being said, regardless of who is speaking. He tells the Galatians that 'even if we or an angel from heaven should preach to you a gospel contrary to the one we preached to you, let him be anathema.' (Gal 1:8) Who could have a higher authority than St. Paul himself? And yet his Christians are to judge what he says! It is to be recalled that he put his own doctrine into practice in relation to St. Peter; 'when Cephas came to Antioch, I opposed him to his face, because he stood condemned.' (Gal 2:11) St John also makes this same point: 'If anyone comes to you and does not bring this teaching, do not receive him into your house or give him any greeting …' (2 John 1:10) Granted it is only Timothy who is told to 'guard the good deposit' (2 Tim 1:13). Bishops do have a special responsibility in the matter, but it is clear that maintaining the tradition is not their unique preserve, but something which concerns us all in the Church at our different levels of responsibility. St. Ignatius of Antioch provides a witness from tradition who teaches the same doctrine. In his letters to the churches he commends and encourages the Christians to be careful judges of everything that they hear. He commends the Ephesians in the following terms:

> Onesimus spoke personally in the highest terms of your own correct and godly attitude in this respect; he told me that truth is the guiding principle of your lives, and heresy is so far from gaining a foothold among you that any speaker who goes beyond the simple truth about Jesus Christ is refused a hearing.[5] … All the same, I did hear of a visit paid to you by certain men from another place, whose teaching was pernicious. However, you refused to allow its dissemination among you, and stopped your ears against the seed they were sowing.[6]

And he encourages the Trallians to be careful in these words: 'And so I entreat you (not I, though, but the love of Jesus Christ) not to nourish yourselves on anything but Christian fare, and have no truck with the alien herbs of heresy.'[7] And he repeats the same message to the Philadelphians: 'As children of the light of truth, therefore, see that you hold aloof from all disunion and misguided teaching; and where

---

[5] Letter to the Ephesians, § 6 in Early Christian Writings: The Apostolic Fathers, tr. Maxwell Staniforth (London: Penguin Books, 1968), 77.
[6] Ibid, § 9.
[7] The Letter to the Trallians, §6 in Early Christian Writings: The Apostolic Fathers, tr. Maxwell Staniforth (London: Penguin Books, 1968), 96.

your bishop is, there follow him like shee[8] ... Have nothing to do with such poisonous weeds; they are none of the Father's planting, nor have they Jesus Christ for their husbandman.'[9] If all these exhortations are to make sense, then every Christian is called on to make his own judgment of the faith, and to judge every human statement, however exalted, in the its light.

Saint Augustine had no doubt about the real situation involved when he, as a bishop, was teaching his flock. He wrote: 'It is safer, therefore, that both we who speak and you who listen know ourselves to be fellow disciples under one teacher. It is altogether safer and expedient if you listen to us, not as teachers but as fellow disciples.'[10] In another sermon, he expanded on the point.

> Observe, brethren, a great mystery: the sound of our words beat on your ears, the teacher is within. Don't think that you learn anything from a man. We can admonish through the sound of our voice; if there is not the teacher within, our noise is in vain. ... In so far as it pertains to me, I speak to all. However, for those in whom the inner anointing does not speak, if the Holy Spirit does not teach within, they go away untaught. Outward teachings and admonitions are a hel But the one who teaches hearts has his chair in heaven. And so it is that he says himself in the Gospel: 'Call no one on earth your teacher: you have one teacher, the Christ.' (Matt. 23:10.)[11]

---

[8] The Letter to the Philadelphians, § 2 in Early Christian Writings: The Apostolic Fathers, tr. Maxwell Staniforth (London: Penguin Books, 1968), 111.
[9] Ibid, § 3.
[10] Augustine Sermo 23, c. 2, PL 38, 155.
[11] In epistolam Joannis ad Parthos, Tractatus IV, caput II, § 13, PL 35, 2004. He makes the same point in Sermo 292, In Natali Joannis Baptistae, Caput primum, § 1; PL 38, 1319-20 and Sermo 298 § 5 end; PL 38, 1267.

A Christian reading an episcopal statement is not listening only, or even principally, to the bishop speaking or writing. He is listening to Christ speaking through the bishop, and he has the Holy Spirit within to help him in the task. This is a fundamental point which has its defenders right throughout the tradition. In the second century, Hippolytus wrote: 'On those who have a right faith, the Holy Spirit bestows the perfect grace of knowing how those who are at the head of the Church must teach and safeguard all things'[12] St Thomas taught that the knowledge by which we know what to believe is a gift given to all Christians.[13] William of Ockham wrote: 'A question of faith pertains to all Christians and not only to the prelates, indeed also to the laity,'[14] and he spent much effort subsequently arguing that Pope John XXII had fallen into heresy on the poverty question. Congar reports that 'Luther ... makes much of those biblical passages that attribute to the faithful detection of false teachers and deceivers in the order of salvation: Matt 7:15; 24:4; John 10:14, 27, etc. ... Every Christian is anointed, he says, and can interpret the word of God, judging any doctor, bishop or pope in the act of teaching.'[15] And a modern theologian has written:

> The gift of understanding facilitates entry into the revealed deposit, and allows the believer to recognise, even before the Magisterium what is contained in it. The gift of knowledge gives an instinctive judgment on what is to be accepted and rejected in faith, while the gift of wisdom gives a kind of connaturality with the truths of faith. From this point of view theologians and even the holders of magisterial office have no advantage

---

[12] Trad. apost., c. 1; SC 11bis, 40-41.
[13] ST 2-2, q. 9, a. 1, ad 2; In III Sent., d. 24, a. 3, sol. ad 3.
[14] A. van Leeuwen, L'Église règle de foi dans les écrits de Guillaume d'Occam, ETL 11 (1934) 249-288 at 276.
[15] Congar, Lay People in the Church, 278.

over the simple believers. The sense of faith depends on a living faith, and what is decisive here is holiness.[16]

Theologians are the intellectual equals of the bishops, and often their intellectual superiors. What sets the bishop above the theologian is not his expertise but his position in the Church, and his right to speak 'in the person of Christ'. Judgment on a matter of faith is not based on research into arcane or difficult matters, where expertise is required. The doctrine of the Church is a matter of public record, and is based on sources available to all. Any theologian, indeed any well-educated Catholic, has all the resources available to make a judgment. As regards the human judgment required, the bishop is in no better situation than the rest of us. He is not in the position of an expert in relation to some uninitiated laity. We all have equal access to the teaching of the Lord. A bishop is engaged in the same theological reflection to which all Christians are called. It is not theological expertise that counts, but union with God and the development of one's supernatural sense of the faith, so that one can recognise the divine truth when it is formulated. Finding the appropriate formulation is the task of the theologian, and it is hard. However, recognising the truth of a formulation is much easier, and is the right of every Christian, and final judgment in the matter is ultimately the function of the bishops.

This highlighting of the role of God the Holy Spirit at work directly in the soul of the individual Christian receiving an episcopal teaching brings spontaneously to mind the danger of Illuminism. The fundamental truth underlying Illuminism is the undeniable fact that the Holy Spirit illuminates the mind, heart and soul of every believer. The heresy of Illuminism arises when that primordial reality is dislodged from its proper place within the communal reality of the Church. The illumination of the Holy Spirit sheds the light of Christ on the soul and draws the believer to the Church as the objective source of the truth being communicated. If that illumination is taken as a private possession

---

[16] Herbert Hammans, Die neueren katholischen Erklärungen der Dogmenentwicklung (Essen: Ludgerus-Verlag Hubert Wingen KG, 1965), 255.

which dispenses one from the ecclesial control exercised by the whole community under episcopal oversight, then there is Illuminism, and that is wrong. When that illumination is understood within its proper context, it represents the essential foundation of faith, which must never be overlooked or forgotten. It has to be said, on the other hand however, that forgetting this primordial illumination and falling into an episcopal magisterial positivism, which grants all authority to the bishops and forgets the immediate working of God in the Church, is an even greater danger than the easily perceived danger of Illuminism. This episcopal positivism is also a heresy which is just as distorting of the truth as is Illuminism, but it can pass so easily unnoticed because, of its nature, it never rocks the boat.

The implication of these points is that the religious submission of will and intellect being called for has its proper object misplaced, when the human minister is offered a submission that is proper only to God. There is a scriptural background to this suggestion, coming from the word '*obsequium*' which is translated as submission. In the Vulgate translation, the word appears six times. Three times it translates latrei, a (John 16:2, Romans 9:4, 12:1), twice it translates leitourgi, a| (Phil 2:17, 30), and once it translates u'pakoh. (2Cor 10:5). Each time it refers to the submission to be offered to God. *Dei Verbum*, § 5, which deals with our faith response to God revealing, places this last text, 2Cor 10:5, together with Rom 1:5 and 16:26 which both speak of the 'obedience of faith'. The scriptural background, therefore, clearly understands this word, *obsequium*, as referring to our faith response to God. This is the understanding of DV 5: 'In response to God revealing the 'obedience of faith' is to be given, by which a man freely commits his entire self to God, making 'the full submission (*obsequium*) of intellect and will to God revealing,' and willingly assenting to the Revelation given by Him.'[17] The mistake is the separation of the bishop speaking from Christ; considering the Pope, or the Church, as a self-standing independent witness to the truth. This is not the case. As Tertullian pointed out long ago: 'For the Church herself is properly and principally

---

[17] Tanner, 973.8-11.

the Spirit Himself ... It is to the Lord, not to a servant, that authority and decision belong; to God Himself, not to a priest.'[18] It follows, then, that it is a mistake to distinguish the religious submission of intellect and will due to an episcopal teaching from divine faith, for they are one and the same. There is only one Christian response of faith owed to God in the Church, and the precise response due to episcopal teaching within that overall response of faith needs to carefully delineated.

Light can be shed on the matter by considering the appropriate response to the teaching of any bisho *Lumen gentium* § 25 teaches that one must adhere with religious submission to the teaching of one's local Bishop[19], and that this religious submission is to be given 'in a special way' to the ordinary teaching of the Pope.[20] By virtue of his unique role as 'first among equals' in the College of Bishops the Pope has a special authority when he teaches. However, fundamentally, 'the magisterium of the Roman Pontiff ... is of the same nature as the magisterium of the individual bishops.'[21] The practice of religious submission to any bishop is therefore a model for the religious submission due also to the Pope, in his ordinary teaching. That great Father of episcopal obedience, St. Ignatius of Antioch, wrote that 'every man who belongs to God and Jesus Christ stands by his bisho'[22] This clearly doesn't mean that the Christian must stand by his bishop, right or wrong. If he genuinely believes that his bishop is wrong, he must take steps to correct him. Standing by him demands it, and when the bishop corrects himself communion can be full again. If the bishop refuses to correct himself, then he must be replaced because it must be possible to stand by one's bishop in the full faith of the Church. The history of the Church has given many examples of how this works, the most famous probably

---

[18] 'nam et ipsa ecclesia proprie et principaliter ipse est spiritus ... Domini enim, non famuli est ius et arbitrium; dei ipsius, non sacerdotis.' De pudicitia 21, 17 (CSEL 20), 271.2-4; 10-11.
[19] Tanner, 869.11.
[20] Tanner, 869.12.
[21] Betti, 'L'Ossequio,' 448.
[22] The Letter to the Philadelphians, § 3; Early Christian Writings: The Apostolic Fathers, tr. Maxwell Staniforth (London: Penguin Books, 1968), 112.

being the reaction to the teaching of Patriarch Nestorius against the divine motherhood of our Lady. The Christians of Constantinople had the duty of religious submission to their duly ordained bishop, and yet when he strayed from the faith they had to take steps to correct him. In the case of every bishop except the Pope, there is the easy solution of the appeal to Rome. If and when the Pope strays from the faith, there is no simple solution, but the basic problem remains. Within a proper understanding of the religious submission due to papal teaching, allowance must be made for the occasion when the Pope is teaching error.

It is being argued here that the religious submission of will and intellect one gives to ordinary episcopal teaching, is not a different kind of obedience, but simply a particular instance of the one obedience of faith offered to Christ, in whose name the bishop is speaking. It is a mistake to say that the response to ordinary teaching in the Church is different in kind from the extraordinary. The infallibility of the Church, the Holy Church, is universal and perpetual. The Church teaches infallibly always and everywhere; she can only teach infallibly and everything she teaches must be accepted with divine faith. The distinction between teaching which is defined and teaching which is not defined, is not so great that it requires a response which is different in kind. It is necessary to define doctrine in certain circumstances, but the basic teaching of the Church goes on, whether defined or not. It is also wrong to seek for an alternative form of faith which covers the ordinary teaching of the bishops without distinction. It is the one response of faith which accepts the full word of God which is taught by the Church always and everywhere. What belongs to the faith of the Church is accepted with divine faith; what does not belong to the faith of the Church, even though it happens to be taught by a bishop, is not accepted with any faith at all. It can be a considered opinion of the bishop to be treated with the respect it deserves on the human level, or it can be an mistake masquerading as a Christian teaching which needs rather to be resisted as erroneous. Since the bishops are fallible men, it can happen that opinions enter into episcopal teaching which do not belong to the genuine teaching of the Church, and that possibility poses the difficulty for our response to ordinary episcopal teaching. It is wrong, therefore, to consider the mixture of the genuine and the false to constitute a single category which has to be taken as one, to be responded to in a special manner. In considering a particular point of the teaching, everything depends on whether the teaching is that of the Church or not. If it is the teaching of the Church, the appropriate response is the assent of faith. If it is not the teaching of the Church, the appropriate response is to repudiate it as counterfeit. It is in this context that the confusion of the Congregation for the Doctrine of the Faith in regard to the distinction between the assent of faith and the religious submission due to ordinary teaching assumes its significance. We may recall here a confusion which arose in the exchange between the Congregation for the Doctrine of the Faith and Charles Curran. At one point the Congregation spoke of the 'clear doctrine of Vatican Council II regarding the principles for the assent of faith,' and referred to Canon 752, which makes the distinction between the assent of faith and religious submission of will and intellect, as summing up the thought of the Council on this point. Later the Congregation corrected itself, but this 'mistake' of the Congregation, when it spoke of the assent of faith as covering the whole matter of our response to teaching in the Church, would turn out, on the principles being developed here, to have been evidence of the true position breaking through the confusion.

Consider the question as formulated by Francis Sullivan: '... can teaching which does not claim to be infallible, and may be in fact erroneous, still be authoritative? And if so, on what grounds?'[23] Posed in this way, the question cannot be answered until the appropriate distinction is made. The ordinary teaching of the bishops, which contains both truth and error, cannot, for that reason, be considered as a homogeneous set of doctrines and judged as a whole. And, even though it is mixed in this way, the ordinary teaching does claim to be infallible, with the infallibility of the Church. It is not definitive, but the Pope or the bishop is making the claim to speak truly on behalf of the Church, and if he is correct in this judgment the teaching is

---

[23] Sullivan, Magisterium, 158.

infallible with the infallibility of the Church. Either it is the teaching of the Church, and thus infallible, or it is not the teaching of the Church, and thus erroneous or at best a human opinion masquerading as the teaching of the Church. I either accept the teaching with the religious submission of intellect and will which is divine faith as the teaching of the Church, or I recognise it as error or human opinion and, therefore, a misuse of the bishop's authority to teach in the person of Christ. There is no mixed middle ground, of a generally non-infallible body of teaching which is to be judged as a whole. The Pope does not teach, properly speaking. He witnesses to the faith of the Church. The bishop speaks on behalf of an infallible teacher, and if he misjudges the faith of the Church he misuses his office. It is wrong, therefore, to judge episcopal teaching as if the authority of the bishop were the ultimate criterion, when what counts is the authority of Christ, the One Teacher, whom the bishop represents.

In the theology of the manuals, the ground of the distinction between divine faith and religious submission is that there are two distinct authorities in question. The motive for an act of divine faith is the unfailing authority of God, whereas the motive for religious submission to a bishop is the authority of the bisho[24] The problem with this is the separation of the bishop from Christ, for the bishop has no independent authority whatever. All his authority to teach in the Church comes to him from Christ, and he exercises it all the time under the influence of the Holy Spirit, so that he can act 'in the person of Christ'. When he teaches the truth, when he exercises his office 'authentically,' he is teaching 'in the person of Christ,' and his teaching is to be accepted as from Christ, with divine faith. If he teaches anything else, such teaching must be recognised as counterfeit. This approach to the matter resolves a further difficulty with the manualist theology. The manuals teach that one is obliged to give internal religious assent to all episcopal teaching, and the standard position is that such assent should

---

[24] On this see the summary of the theology of the manuals in Charles C. Curran, Robert E. Hunt, <u>Dissent In and For the Church: Theologians and *Humanae vitae*</u> (New York: Sheed & Ward, 1969), 42-48.

be conditional, because the possibility of error cannot be excluded. The difficulty with this is that we have it on the excellent authority of Cardinal Newman that such a thing is impossible. There is no such thing as conditional assent. Assent of its very nature is unconditional. According to Cardinal Newman,

> assent is in its nature absolute and unconditional.[25] ... We might as well talk of degrees of truth as of degrees of assent.[26] ... I do not know then when it is that we ever deliberately profess assent to a proposition without meaning to convey to others the impression that we accept it unreservedly, and that because it is true.[27] ... If human nature is to be its own witness, there is no medium between assenting and not assenting.[28]

My grasp of the epistemology of this is not such as I can uphold this position with full certainty, but, in this matter, I am more inclined to believe Newman than the manualist theologians, and I take it as a corroboration of the approach being developed here that it removes a position which he considers to be absurd.

In order to clarify the points being made here, it is useful to make the comparison with a position put forward by Ladislas Orsy, who writes: 'The faithful have a right to be informed correctly, as far as possible, concerning what point of doctrine belongs to the core of our Christian beliefs and what does not. In the first case, their response ought to be a surrender to the Word of God, alive in the church. In the second case, it must be a religious *obsequium*, an attitude essentially different from an act of faith. This distinction is vital.'[29] This is the polar opposite of

---

[25] John Henry Cardinal Newman, A Grammar of Assent, (Notre Dame/London: University of Notre Dame Press, 1979), 135. Same idea is repeated on pages 47, 50, and 145.
[26] Ibid, 146.
[27] Ibid, 147-48.
[28] Ibid, 148.
[29] Orsy, 'Reflections on the Text of a Canon,' 234.

the position being developed here. On this understanding, there is no relevenat distinction between what is core and what is peripheral in the faith; there is the one Word of God proclaimed in its totality. And there is no such thing as a religious submission distinct from the assent of faith; there is only faith in the one Word of God. And this resolves a difficulty of Orsy with the Profession of Faith of 1989. He protests that 'under the heading of Profession of Faith candidates for offices have to declare their acceptance of doctrines which are not of faith,'[30] and argues that this 'can lead to a misguided perception: definitive and non-definitive propositions can be seen as being as important as the articles of faith.'[31] On the position being developed here, Orsy is wrong in this, and the Congregation for the Doctrine of the Faith is also wrong to separate these other propositions into separate categories. The Profession of Faith of 1989 is properly so-called because these extra paragraphs are basically an illusion, and they both properly coalesce into the first paragraph, so that our assent is only demanded to what is of faith.

Compare the position being developed here with a good representative of the manualist tradition. Francis Sullivan sums up his position in this way: 'As I understand it, then, to give the required *obsequium religiosum* to the teaching of the ordinary magisterium means to make an honest and sustained effort to overcome any contrary opinions I might have, and to achieve a sincere assent of my mind to this teaching.'[32] On the standard principles, this does not seem such a bad approach. A bishop has learned the faith carefully and he was chosen as a bishop on the basis of a general judgment that he knew the faith of the Church and could teach it accurately. One is entitled to assume that, if he is certain that what he is teaching is the faith of the Church, then it is so, and the onus is on the Christian to make every effort to accept it. However, this position fails to advert to the point which makes all the difference,

---

[30] Ladislas Örsy, S.J., The Profession of Faith and the Oath of Fidelity: A Theological and Canonical Analysis (Dublin: Dominican Publications, 1990), 19.
[31] Ibid, 32.
[32] Sullivan, <u>Magisterium</u>, 164. Same in Francis A. Sullivan, S.J., <u>Creative Fidelity: Weighing and Interpreting Documents of the Magisterium</u> (Dublin: Gill & Macmillan Ltd, 1996), 24.

whether the teaching in question is true or false. On that everything depends. If the teaching is true, and is the genuine teaching of the Church, then my difficulties are my own and need to be overcome. If, on the other hand, the teaching is false, and my difficulties arise from a better grasp of the teaching of the Church than is behind the teaching being presented, then a completely different situation arises. If, in fact, the bishop is mistaken and his teaching is erroneous, a crisis arises which must be resolved. He must be brought to change his teaching or be disciplined. The 'honest and sustained effort' is not required of me in this case, but of the bishop who is teaching error in place of Christian truth, and all my energies should be devoted to helping him to correct his error.

I owe complete religious submission of will and intellect to God alone, to Christ the One Teacher who teaches in his humanity from his place at the right hand of the Father in heaven. He sends his Holy Spirit into my heart as the Interior Teacher who illuminates my mind and makes the word of Christ clear to me. With this foundation, I owe religious submission of intellect and will to the bishops of the Church, indeed, but only insofar as they truly speak for God. I accept that the College of Bishops, acting in Council or through the Pope alone, is the supreme authority in the Church and has the right and the duty to make the final judgment in matters of faith and their definitive judgments I accept completely as the very word of Christ himself who ensures the truth of what they decide. Apart from those definitive judgments, I cannot accept the word of any bishop, even the Pope, as final, and must follow my conscience, illuminated by the Holy Spirit, even if it leads me into dissent from a particular teaching of the bishops or the Pope, subject always to the final judgment of the Church speaking definitively through the College of Bishops. I can, and do, normally take it for granted that what is officially taught in the Catholic Church is really the teaching of the Holy Church, and I adhere to it with religious submission of will and intellect. However, the case can arise when something seems wrong to me, and I can no longer submit in good conscience.

Submission to *Authentic* Teaching

The difference between the position being advocated here and the current position hangs on the meaning of the word 'authentic'. *Lumen gentium* § 25 teaches that 'this religious submission of will and intellect is to be given, in a special way, to the authentic Magisterium of the Roman Pontiff, even when he does not speak *ex cathedra* …'[33] In the manuals, the word 'authentic' was taken to mean simply 'authoritative', referring to teaching given seriously and in the proper form. It would seem that this is how the word was understood at the Second Vatican Council. In a note attached to *Dei verbum* § 10, the Theological Commission says of decisions of the Magisterium, that they are all 'authentic' and therefore possess authority, where it is clear that this is effectively a definition of the word.[34] Betti reports that some of the Council Fathers asked that 'authentice' be changed to 'auctoritative' to avoid the ambiguity in the word 'authentic', and that the Doctrinal Commission refused the suggestion because in theological terminology 'authentice' means 'authoritatively'.'[35] It is commonly understood that authentic judgments are simply judgments made by the proper authorities in due form, and that the word 'authentic' does not carry the connotation of true and correct which the word normally bears in English. And so it was not unusual in the manuals of theology to speak of teaching which was 'merely authentic', referring to the ordinary teaching of the Pope especially, where a definitive judgment was not involved.[36] I suggest that this usage needs to be challenged. If it is argued that the authentic judgments of magisterial authorities are to be accepted, then the word should carry the connotation of true and correct, for truth

---

[33] Decrees of the Ecumenical Councils, Volume Two: Trent to Vatican II, Ed. Norman Tanner, S.J. (London/Washington: Sheed & Ward/Georgetown University Press, 1990), 869.11-15.

[34] Gil Hellín, Dei Verbum, 76, III (A).

[35] Betti, 'L'Ossequio,' 451, footnote 100. Reference is made to Umberto Betti, La dottrina del concilio Vaticano II sulla trasmissione della Rivelazione (Spicilegium Pontificii Athenaei Antoniani, 26, Rome 1985), 160, 181, 278.)

[36] See for instance J. Salaverri, 'De Ecclesia Christi,' in Sacrae Theologiae Summa, I (Madrid: BAC, 1962), 704.

and correctness do not follow automatically from the propriety of the form. Consider the example of Patriarch Nestorius preaching against the motherhood of Our Lady in the Santa Sophia in Constantinople. This was authoritative teaching by a very high authority in the Church, and yet it was erroneous. It is being argued here that the word 'authentic' must be given its full meaning, if the doctrine is to be sound. In that case, the role of the One Teacher is implicitly recognised, and the only authentic teaching is the teaching of Christ through the ministry of the bishops, and that teaching must be true.

The position developed here brings a resolution to the complaints made against the exercise of doctrinal authority by the proactive papacy ever since the eleventh century. As was noted earlier, according to Congar: 'The Reforms of the 16th century ... were ... a refusal of an *unconditional* authority of the Church, and particularly of the Pope.'[37] It is to be noted that the complaint against the authority of the Pope as being absolute, unconditional, and discretionary, was also made without distinction against the Church itself. In the Reformed understanding of Catholic theology, echoing no doubt one strand of Catholic theology at the time, the authority of the Church and the authority of the Pope are effectively the same thing. It is being suggested here that the fundamental flaw here is the identification of the Church with the Pope, or the College of Bishops, the human authorities in the Church, and treating the Church-mystery as of no account. There is a legitimate complaint to be made against an unconditional claim on behalf of the Pope, who is a fallible human being, but not against an unconditional claim on behalf of the theandric Church, the Bride and the Body of Christ, the Incorporation of the Holy Spirit. There can be no grounds for and no legitimate demand for any control over the teaching of this Church. It is the teaching of Christ and the Holy Spirit and it must be accorded total implicit faith.

It is wrong to insist that Christians accept unconditionally episcopal or papal teaching which may be mistaken, even if only in exceptional cases. Enjoying a presumption of truth does not suffice to ground

---

[37] Congar, Vraie et fausse réforme dans l'Église 374. (Emphasis in the original.)

the response of Christian faith. The response of Christian faith is to Christ teaching, and it is unconditional. The appropriate response to mistaken teaching, from whomever it may come, can only be to reject it. The proper response to ordinary episcopal teaching must, therefore, be conditional. In this light it is necessary to interpret carefully an exhortation of the Congregation for the Doctrine of the Faith: 'In any case there should never be a diminishment of that fundamental openness loyally to accept the teaching of the Magisterium as it is fitting for every believer by reason of the obedience of faith.'[38] The ambiguity in the meaning of the word 'magisterium' underlies the difficulty of this exhortation. If the Magisterium of the Holy Church is meant, then the exhortation is completely valid, and is to be accepted without any reservation. If, however, the teaching of the bishops is meant, the willingness to accept episcopal teaching can only be conditional.

Obedience Except where there is Sin

An appropriate analogy for the response to a bishop teaching is provided by the traditional doctrine regarding the response of a religious to his superior commanding.

There are differences, of course, the most obvious being that between teaching and commanding, but there are also clear similarities. It has not been much used in the tradition, but two canonists, Wernz and Vidal, who were standard commentators in the early twentieth century, have written that the interior approval of the faithful to an episcopal teaching 'has something of the provisional to it and is founded on the presumption that the authentic teacher of doctrine does not err unless there is a strong suspicion to the contrary. Therefore we owe obedience of the intellect to the teacher much as we owe obedience of the will to a superior issuing a legitimate command - unless there is a strong suspicion that he is commanding something morally wrong.'[39] The structure of the proper submission to episcopal teaching is the same

---

[38] Donum veritatis, § 29.
[39] Wernz/Vidal, Ius Canonicum IV/2 (Romae, 1935), n. 617.

as the structure of religious obedience, and the theological foundation is basically the same. One author has explained this foundation in the following manner:

> [Christ] lives in the midst of us in his Body the Church. Obedience to Christ thus becomes obedience to his Church as the propagator of God's word, as the living power of Christ alive in her.[40] ... Such comprehensive obedience can and dare only be offered to a man whose own will is, down to the smallest and most insignificant details, wholly identified with the will of God. But this is true only of Christ; to him alone, the Holy One, is total obedience due. But Christ is alive and present for every Christian in the Church. And such obedience is only permitted within the Church and as religious obedience.[41]

Brunner is speaking here of obeying the superior in practical matters, but the response to a bishop teaching the faith is fundamentally the same. St Ignatius of Loyola, a great master of obedience, summed up the matter when he wrote that 'in all things into which obedience can with charity be extended, we should be ready to receive the command just as if it were coming from Christ our Saviour ... persuading ourselves that everything is just and renouncing with blind obedience any contrary opinion and judgment of our own in all things which the superior commands and in which no species of sin can be judged to be present.'[42] He says that we must obey the superior in all things possible, as long as there is no sin involved. And in this St Ignatius was following the traditional understanding of religious obedience throughout the tradition, beginning with St Basil the Great in the East

---

[40] August Brunner, <u>A New Creation: Towards a Theology of the Christian Life</u> (London: Burns & Oates, 1955), 115.

[41] Ibid, 118.

[42] <u>The Constitutions of the Society of Jesus and Their Complementary Norms</u> (The Institute of Jesuit Sources: St Louis, 1996), [547].

and St Augustine in the West.[43] St Ignatius did not formulate any norms for a conflict situation, but his practice and the experience of the Society of Jesus over the last four centuries led to their formulation by a recent General Congregation, and they are summarized in the Complementary Norms.[44] The same approach should apply to the Christian response to episcopal teaching. The religious sees Christ in the superior and obeys the command of the superior fully, as long as no species of sin is found in it [refer to the Constitutions]. Similarly, the Christian sees Christ in the Bishop and accepts the Bishop's teaching fully, as long as no species of error is found in it. The qualification is required in both instances, because the mediator in each case is a fallible human being, and the possibility of sin in one case and error in the other, simply cannot be excluded. Every effort is made to accept the teaching proposed, as the teaching of Christ, but it is not permissible, much less meritorious, to assent to what is perceived as error. And this possibility of error in magisterial teaching must be allowed for. It is a flaw in the standard theology of the matter that this possibility is vaguely noted, but not systematically treated. The Congregation for the Doctrine of the Faith, in the Instruction, *Donum veritatis* § 17, wrote: 'It is also to be borne in mind that all acts of the Magisterium derive from the same source, that is, from Christ who desires that His People walk in the entire truth.' This formula is ambiguous, with the ambiguity noted already. If by 'Magisterium' is meant the Magisterium of the Holy Church teaching the whole truth always and everywhere, it is true to say that every act of this Magisterium is from Christ and therefore infallible. However, if by 'Magisterium' the episcopal Magisterium is meant, it simply cannot be asserted that every episcopal teaching is from Christ and, therefore, infallible. An erroneous teaching is not from Christ and cannot claim his divine authority.

---

[43] On this see Fr. Manuel María Espinosa Pólit, S.J., Perfect Obedience: A Commentary on the Letter of Obedience of St. Ignatius of Loyola (Westminster, Maryland: The Newman Bookshop, 1947), 182-84.

[44] Complementary Norm, § 154. The Constitutions of the Society of Jesus and Their Complementary Norms (The Institute of Jesuit Sources: St Louis, 1996), 223-24.

It has been quite a long road to reach this resolution of the issue of the appropriate submission that must be offered to papal, as to any episcopal, teaching. At the end of it all, it is interesting to note how close the fundamental principle is to that formulated by William of Ockham (1300-59) when he wrote: "The rule of our faith is the Sacred Scripture and the doctrine of the universal Church, which cannot err. To it one must always have recourse in all questions concerning faith. To it and not to the Supreme Pontiff if he opposes it, one must give the most firm faith."[45] If Ockham's *ecclesia universalis* is understood as the whole Church, clergy and laity spread throughout the world, the principle is a formula for anarchy and the tension we have been experiencing for centuries. If, on the other hand, it is understood as the Holy Church, which subsists in the Catholic Church, it represents precisely the doctrine we have been developing in these pages. As we can imagine, this principle does not remove all tension, but it does allow us to formulate procedures which can guide us when tensions arise.

---

[45] Tractatus contra Ioannem XXII, in Richard Scholz, Unbekannte Kirchenpolitische Streitshriften, 1914, vol. 2, 398.

Chapter 15

Legitimate Dissent from Official Teaching

The groundwork has now been done and it is time to deal explicitly with the problem of dissent. Before presenting an alternative view, the current understanding can be briefly recalled again. The right to dissent from official teaching is a standard part of the manualist tradition of theology.[1] It is understood that the ordinary magisterium of the Pope is fallible, and that dissent is, therefore, possible. This approach was granted a certain level of official approval at the Second Vatican Council. In the final stage of the drafting of *Lumen gentium* § 25, 'three Fathers raised the case of a theologian who could not assent *internally*, on reasonable grounds, to a doctrine which had not been infallibly proposed.' The reply of the Theological Commission was: 'On this case the approved theological expositions should be consulted.'[2] The Congregation for the Doctrine of the Faith, in one of the documents sent to Charles Curran, gave a good exposition of the current standard doctrine.

> The assistance of the Holy Spirit, in which the Church believes, moves the faithful to accept every authentic teaching, in the absence of valid and certain

---

[1] On this see Curran, Hunt, <u>Dissent In and For the Church</u>, 41-44; Komonchak, 'Ordinary Papal Magisterium and Religious Assent,' 71-72.
[2] Gil Hellín, <u>Lumen Gentium</u>, 255.

arguments to the contrary. (For) ... the noninfallible magisterium ... enjoys the presumption of truth grounded in the above-mentioned assistance of the Holy Spirit. Insofar as the individual theologian does not have reasons which appear to be clearly valid to him and which derive from his competence in the matter in question to suspend or refuse assent to the teaching of this authentic magisterium, he must heed its teaching, even while recognizing that it might in an exceptional case be mistaken, since it does not enjoy the guarantee of infallibility.[3]

In these expositions the conditions necessary to justify dissent were not clearly worked out, and were mostly quite general and vague. One, Palmieri, could write that 'religious assent is owed when there is nothing which could prudently persuade one to suspend his assent.'[4] Some suggest that only a theologian could find himself in such a situation[5], but the normal position is that any Catholic is entitled to make this judgment. This is the tradition to which Curran and the large group of theologians in the United States were appealing to justify their dissent from *Humanae vitae*. They summed it up, accurately, in saying: 'It is common teaching in the Church that Catholics may dissent from authoritative, noninfallible teachings of the magisterium when sufficient reasons for so doing exist.'[6] It seems to me that this is most unsatisfactory and quite unworkable approach to the matter of

---

[3] Observations of the Sacred Congregation for the Doctrine of the Faith on some writings of Father Charles Curran (July 1979) in Curran, Faithful Dissent, 118.

[4] D. Palmieri, De Romano Pontifice cum prolegomeno De Ecclesia (2nd edition, Prato: Giacchetti, 1891, 719.

[5] For example H. Dieckmann, De Ecclesia, t. II (Freiburg: Herder, 1925), 116 and J. Salaverri, De Ecclesia Christi in Sacrae Theologiae Summa, t. I (Madrid: B.A.C., 1955), 720.

[6] Joseph A. Komonchak, 'Ordinary Papal Magisterium and Religious Assent,' in Readings in Moral Theology No. 3: The Magisterium and Morality, edd. Charles E. Curran and Richard McCormick, S.J. (New York / Ramsey: Paulist Press, 1982), 67-90 at 77.

the Christian response to teaching in the Church. The position quoted from Palmieri almost reads like a *reductio ad absurdum*! We are exhorted to offer our assent when nothing prudently persuades us otherwise! Consider that as a theory of religious obedience! A religious is to obey his superior unless something prudently persuades him otherwise! Is this not a formula for chaos?

The problem with this approach is that it considers the role of the human minister in ecclesial teaching as primary. In the quotation given from the Congregation for the Doctrine of the Faith, the teacher is the 'authentic' 'non-infallible' magisterium. It has to be taken that this designation refers to the bishops teaching in the Church. In this perspective the role of the Holy Spirit is the secondary one of providing 'assistance' to this episcopal teaching. When the focus is kept on the bishops and the body of episcopal teaching is considered as a unitary whole, a confusion arises. Charles Curran always made clear that the right to dissent applied only to 'some' undefined teachings. However, without some way of discerning precisely which teachings are involved, the qualification is ineffective. The presence of Christ and the Holy Spirit guarantees that, in a general way, the body of official teaching in the Catholic Church is the infallible teaching of the Holy Church. The presence of sin in the concrete Church, at every level, means that 'some' official teachings may be, and inevitably will be, erroneous. Any particular proposition within this ordinary teaching of the bishops is likely to be the teaching of the Church. But it may be an error, or merely a human opinion, masquerading as Christian truth, and therefore a misuse of the apostolic authority. The reality of the situation is such that there is no way of knowing in advance which is the case.

The solution to the problem is to begin from the beginning. Our response of faith is given to God, speaking through Christ in the power of the Holy Spirit. This divine economy of revelation is the Holy Church which proclaims the Word of God always and everywhere and is to be obeyed fully in everything she teaches. This is the ordinary teaching of the Church to which all are completely bound, from the bishops to the least of the lay faithful. Dissent from this teaching of the Church is heresy and its implication automatic excommunication, for communion in the Church is founded on the truth. Every Christian has direct access to this teaching of Christ the One Teacher, teaching from his place at the Father's right hand, illuminated as each Christian is from within by the Interior Teacher, the Holy Spirit of truth. That is the fundamental situation of teaching in the Church, from which all the rest must be judged. This sets the primary context for any possible legitimate dissent from episcopal teaching in the Church. All of us, from the bishops to the least of the lay faithful, are bound by this teaching of the Holy Church, subsisting in the Catholic Church. The International Theological Commission has made the same point in different terms: 'In this common service of the truth, the Magisterium and theologians are both bound by certain obligations: They are bound by the word of God. ... They are both bound by the 'sensus fidei' (supernatural appreciation of the faith) of the Church of this and previous times.'[7]

This allows a first principle to be established that, even in the event of a perceived obligation to dissent from official teaching in the Church, one's fundamental commitment to the Catholic Church remains intact. We believe that the promise of Christ guarantees the Catholic Church against any fundamental flaw, so there can never be any question of abandoning the Church, no matter how bad things might look to a given individual.[8] As Rahner has formulated the point at greater length:

> For the Catholic the Church is absolute in the sense that he knows that the Church is the enduring and imperishable home of his salvation, the ground of truth, the inexhaustible well-spring of grace, the representative of the visible presence of Christ's grace until the end. And all this refers to the hierarchical

---

[7] International Theological Commission (1975), 'The Ecclesiastical Magisterium and Theology,' in <u>Readings in Moral Theology No. 3: The Magisterium and Morality</u>, edd. Charles E. Curran and Richard McCormick, S.J. (New York / Ramsey: Paulist Press, 1982),151-160 at 153.

[8] Karl Rahner, <u>The Dynamic Element in the Church</u> (Freiburg / London: Herder / Burns & Oates, 1964), 44.

> Church. Consequently, for anyone who has once accepted by faith this Church as the measure of his life, there is no point of vantage outside this Church from which he might oppose her, no court of appeal to which he might take a claim against her. If he struggles and argues with her, it is a struggle and a debate within the Church herself. He is speaking to the human members and ministers of this Church and appealing to guiding principles and a spirit which they recognize as their own and to which they concede they are themselves subject and willingly subject. For a Catholic every 'clash' with the Church is always an occurrence recognized by the Church herself as an expression of her own life and only to the extent that it is such a thing. In that sense, therefore, the Church is an 'absolute' for the Catholic. Simply because she is one with Christ, who for him is the Absolute made man, and because she declares herself to be one with Christ.[9]

Congar has also made clear this fundamental difference between a genuine Catholic reformer and a heretic who is willing to abandon the Church.

> Rather than taking Christianity as *given* in the Church, as an *existing reality* to which one must accommodate oneself, the heretic considers it to be an *object* of thought to be constructed by the mind. For the heretic the critical and constructive operation of the spirit has priority; for the faithful Catholic, submission to the deposit and living *in* the Christian reality in the bosom of the Church has priority and reasoning only comes after. Reason operates with a great freedom, indeed, but *in the Church* and according to her spirit.

---

[9] Ibid, 48-49.

For the heretic, the Church is, or can be, still to be found, to be reconstructed; for the faithful Catholic, she exists concretely, and one must serve her, be nourished by her, work in her.[10] ... And so it follows that the reformer who wishes to remain in communion, the Church must always be accepted as <u>given</u>, and not only on the intellectual level, but on the level of reality. One must never for a moment place oneself outside of her in order to judge her, but one must remain committed within her concrete reality, even, and indeed especially, if she requires, in some respect, to be reformed.[11]

It is within this context then that a given episcopal teaching must be received. A Christian must judge the teaching within the faith of the Church, as he sees it. Seckler has written: 'A theologian is bound to serve the truth of the Christian faith, *as he sees it*. Otherwise he is only a functionary. It belongs to his vocation, to make his contribution, knowing that ultimately *only God* knows who understands his Word and that he has the *last* judgment on the truth and worth of a theological position.'[12] Walter Kasper has put the point strongly, when he writes: 'The authority of the Church's ministry reaches only as far as the gospel ... We follow Church leaders only to the extent that they themselves follow Christ. ... Some situations oblige one to obey God and one's conscience rather than the leaders of the Church. Indeed, one may even be obliged to accept excommunication rather than act against one's conscience.'[13] And Joseph Ratzinger has made the same point in relation to papal teaching in particular: 'Criticism of papal pronouncements will be possible and even necessary, to the degree that they lack support in Scripture and the Creed, that is, in the faith of

---

[10] Congar, <u>Vraie et fausse réforme dans l'Église</u>, 228.
[11] Ibid, 229.
[12] Seckler, 'Die Kirchlichkeit,' Ch. 7, § 4, 161-83, at 167, footnote 75.
[13] Walter Kasper, <u>Leadership in the Church: How Traditional Roles Can Serve the Christian Community Today</u> (New York: Crossroad, 2003), 110-111.

the whole Church.'[14] It does not mean that there is an absolute license to dissent from any magisterial teaching which is not definitive. The teaching from which I am dissenting may be in fact the teaching of the Church, though it has not yet been judged as such definitively. On the other hand, the teaching may not be the teaching of the Church and my dissent will, therefore, contribute to the purification of the teaching of the College of Bishops by ridding it of what does properly belong to it. I may be a heretic, like Arius, who denied the divinity of Christ before the Council of Nicaea, or I may be a genuine reformer, like Congar, de Lubac, Rahner, Courtney Murray *et al.* who helped to purify the teaching of the College of Bishops at the Second Vatican Council.

Charles Curran claimed the right to dissent from 'some' 'non-infallible' magisterial teaching, because such teaching in fallible. On the position being developed here, that justification is not correct. The proper distinction to apply does not regard the infallibility of teaching, but its definition. All are agreed that defined doctrine is binding and that the possibility of dissent only arises in regard to teaching which is not defined. There is no difficulty identifying teaching that is not defined, whereas the distinction between what is taught infallibly or not is complicated by the duality between the Holy Church and the Catholic Church. Hence the importance of the 'some'! Before a judgment can be made as to the legitimacy of dissent, it has to be known whether or not the teaching in question is or is not the teaching of the Holy Church. If it is, then no one is entitled to dissent, and such dissent is material heresy. The ultimate difficulty here is that only a dogmatic definition can remove all doubt as to the status of a doctrine as the teaching of the Church. Short of such a definition there is a grey area where dissent can be justified subjectively even though it not legitimate in fact.

It is in this context that we must seek the answer to a question which arose in the reaction to the disciplinary action taken against Charles Curran. The statement made by more than 750 theologians from around the United States noted that the Congregation for the Doctrine of the Faith did not make any claim that any of the teachings

---

[14] Ratzinger, <u>Das Neue Volk Gottes</u>, 144.

for which Curran was being disciplined fulfilled the conditions necessary for an infallible pronouncement. On this basis it concluded that the 'underlying assumption of the letter, therefore, is that dissent from noninfallible teachings effectively places one outside the body of Catholic theologians,' and wondered 'Which noninfallible teachings are serious enough to provoke such a result, and how are those teachings determined?'[15] This question goes to the heart of the matter, but it lacks its proper context. The underlying assumption of the Congregation for the Doctrine of the Faith is not 'that dissent from noninfallible teachings effectively places one outside the body of Catholic theologians'. The Congregation made clear that it accepts the standard manualist view that dissent from what should properly be called undefined teachings is possible within Catholic theology. I suggest that the underlying, but unarticulated, assumption of the Congregation is the one presented here, that dissent from any teaching of the infallible Holy Church places one outside the body of Catholic theologians. Hence the validity of the Statement's question as to which teachings these are and how they are determined. The Congregation is certain that the teachings for which Curran was disciplined belong to the teaching of the Holy Church and disciplined Curran on that basis.

This makes sense on the position being proposed here. The full teaching of the Church, the Holy Church, is binding on all and it is a primary responsibility of the College of Bishops to insist that this teaching be accepted. The vigilance of the bishops cannot be restricted to the defined teaching of the Church, but must extend to the whole teaching of the Church in its full extent. When, therefore, a teaching of the Church comes into dispute, the bishops are still bound to ensure that it be clearly taught and fully accepted by all. It is here that the difficulty arises of discerning which official teachings which are not defined do actually belong to the teaching of the Holy Church. In the case in point, the Congregation for the Doctrine of the Faith offered no

---

[15] Statement signed by some past presidents of the Catholic Theological Society of America and the College Theology Society (eventually signed by 750 Catholic theologians in US) in Faithful Dissent, 283.

criteria for their judgment in the matter, but simply assumed that their faith judgment was correct and acted accordingly. The validity of the procedure will need to be discussed in due course, but it seems clear to me that this is what in fact occurred.

Good Faith Presumed

On the basis of this approach to dissent certain standard approaches need to be reviewed. On the standard theory of dissent much is made to turn on an assessment of the subjective judgment of the dissenter. In the Instruction, *Donum veritatis*, the Congregation for the Doctrine of the Faith offers some criteria to be used in judging whether or not a theologian's difficulties with a doctrine are well-founded. It makes one contention which covers a lot of ground, in saying that 'the judgement of the subjective conscience of the theologian' would not justify dissent, 'because conscience does not constitute an autonomous and exclusive authority for deciding the truth of a doctrine.'[16] Certainly, the personal judgment of the theologian does not justify dissent objectively, but what else is the theologian to use in forming his own judgment about the matter besides his conscience? Because my own conscience is not the final judge of doctrine does not mean that I must not use it in making my judgements. There is no alternative; my own conscience is ultimately all that I have to judge with. Even in accepting the teaching of Church infallibly proposed there is my own subjective judgment to accept it. If the definitiveness of the judgement is not clear to me I must follow my conscience in doubting it, or in rejecting it if I have what appears to me to be sufficient reason for so doing. There is no alternative. Cardinal Newman was greatly exercised about the doctrine of papal infallibility during the run up to the First Vatican Council, and he spoke about his own efforts to sort out the doctrine in his own mind. He said: 'One can but go by one's best light. Whoever is infallible I am not; but I think I am bound to argue out the matter and to act, as if I were - till the Council decides - and then if God's infallibility is against me, to

---

[16] Donum Veritatis § 28.

submit at once, still not repenting of having taken the part which I felt to be right ... We can but do our best.'[17] And Cardinal Ratzinger says much the same thing. 'I couldn't deny a present conviction that I had reached to the best of my abilities. That isn't possible, you see.'[18] So, one point that should be taken for granted is the good faith of the dissenter. We can and must presume that everyone is following the light of truth with sincerity. A classic example is Nestorius, who preached his doctrine against the theotokos from his pulpit as Patriarch of Constantinople and felt it his duty to discipline the members of his flock who believed that Our Lady is the Mother of God He even wrote informing the Pope, Celestine I, of his campaign, and the trouble it caused him.[19] It is clear that Nestorius had a solid faith conviction that the doctrine he was preaching was true, and the same can be presumed of every dissenter. Maintaining the discipline of the faith requires no animosity against anyone, just a clear-headed love for the truth. One must, therefore, take issue with the position proposed by Cardinal Bertone, when he was secretary of the Congregation for the Doctrine of the Faith. He said: 'The basic data cannot be ignored: at the root of dissent is the *crisis of faith*.[20] ... As one of its first manifestations, the spiritual crisis of faith brings with it *a crisis of obedience to the Magisterium's authority*, which is a crisis in the authority of the Church founded on the divine will.'[21] It is wrong to attribute lack of faith to everyone who dissents from an undefined doctrine. Even in a case where such dissent must eventually be seen to be illegitimate, it can still be justified subjectively on the basis

---

[17] To Whitty, April 12, 1870 in Wilfrid Ward, The Life of John Henry Cardinal Newman, Volume II (New York: Longmans, Green, and Co., 1913), 295.

[18] Joseph Cardinal Ratzinger, Salt of the Earth: Christianity and the Catholic Church at the End of the Millenium, An Interview with Peter Seewald, (San Francisco: Ignatius Press, 1997), 15.

[19] On this see Philip Hughes, The Church in Crisis: A History of the General Councils, 325-1870 (New York: Image Books, 1964), 55-56.

[20] Archbishop Tarcision Bertone, S.D.B., "The Magisterium of the Church and the *Professio Fidei*," in Proclaiming the Truth of Jesus Christ: Papers from the Vallombrosa Meeting (Washington, D.C.: United States Catholic Conference, 2000), 31-48 at 40.

[21] Ibid, 41.

of an honest mistake made in good faith. The ultimate test of one's good faith comes when a doctrine is defined and the teaching of the Holy Church is made clear beyond any doubt, but not before then.

In order to justify dissent from the teaching of the Pope or the College of Bishops, it is necessary to appeal to the Holy Church, the mystery which lies within and beneath the institution as we experience it. Our experience of the Church is clouded by sin. Every single member of the Church Militant is a sinner, from the Pope to the least of the lay faithful, and that fact has its implications at every level. It means that there is inevitably going to be error mixed in with the teaching, even of the Pope. The 'hidden' dimension of the Church, to which Luther and the other Reformers appealed, is ultimately the joint presence of Christ and his Holy Spirit, the two divine Persons sent on mission by the Father for our salvation. The only court of appeal higher than the College of Bishops is God, but since God speaks in and through the Church, the College of Bishops still retains its essential role in formulating a definitive answer to any question of faith. It follows, therefore, that the 'dissenter' must still leave the final judgment of the matter with the College of Bishops, which must either accept or reject the criticism. If the College judges that the position with which the dissenter disagrees is in fact the teaching of the Church, then he is wrong, and the doctrine under discussion will move into the category of doctrines judged definitively, and any suffering he may have undergone will have borne fruit for the whole People of God. Newman had a formula to express this, which he put at the end of his *Essay on Development*, and which has been much imitated since: 'It is scarcely necessary to add that he now submits every part of the book to the judgment of the Church, with whose doctrine, on the subjects of which he treats, he wishes all his thoughts to be coincident.'[22] A more recent theologian, who had problems with the authorities of the Church, said the same: 'I once more submit my efforts and endeavors

---

[22] An Essay on the Development of Christian Doctrine, John Henry Cardinal Newman (New York: Image Books, 1960) with a foreword by Gustave Weigel, S.J., 28.

to the consideration of my theological peers and to the judgment of the church's doctrinal authority.'[23] Heretics do not choose the position they do in order to be wrong; they choose it in good faith, believing it to be true. They become heretics formally only when the definitive judgement of the Church goes against them and they refuse to accept it.

On the basis of what has been said, it is necessary to criticise a set of guidelines on dissent drawn up by the Conference of Bishops of the United States just after the publication of *Humanae vitae*, which run as follows:

> When there is question of theological dissent from non-infallible doctrine, we must recall that there is a presumption in favor of the Magisterium. Even non-infallible authentic doctrine, though it may admit of development or call for clarification or revision, remains binding and carries with it a moral certitude, especially when it is addressed to the universal Church, without ambiguity, in response to urgent questions bound up with faith and crucial to morals. The expression of theological dissent from the Magisterium is in order only if the reasons are serious and well-founded, if the manner of the dissent does not question or impugn the teaching authority of the Church and is such as not to give scandal. ... Even responsible dissent does not excuse one from faithful presentation of the authentic doctrine of the Church when one is performing a pastoral ministry in Her name.[24]

---

[23] Jacques Dupuis, S. J., Christian and the Religions: From Confrontation to Dialogue (London / New York: Orbis Books / Darton, Longman & Todd, 2002), 263.
[24] Norms of Licit Theological Dissent; National Conference of Catholic Bishops, (Excerpted from Human Life in our Day, 1968), in Readings in Moral Theology No. 6: Dissent in the Church, edd. Charles E. Curran and Richard McCormick, S.J. (New York / Mahwah: Paulist Press, 1988),127ff. at 127-28.

The Bishops are making the mistake of considering the ordinary teaching of the Bishops as a whole and characterizing it as 'non-infallible'. What they are referring to is doctrine which has not been declared definitively, and which should not be simply categorized as 'fallible'. For, within this ordinary teaching of the Pope or the Bishops there is the fundamental distinction that has been developed here. The bulk of it is the teaching of the Church <u>simpliciter</u>, and is, therefore, taught infallibly, albeit not definitively, with the infallibility of the Church, and what is not the teaching of the Church can only be human traditions mistaken as the teaching of the Church. There is no such thing as 'non-infallible authentic doctrine' which 'remains binding and carries with it a moral certitude, especially when it is addressed to the universal Church, without ambiguity, in response to urgent questions bound up with faith and crucial to morals.' The only binding doctrine is the teaching of the Church and it is taught infallibly, with the infallibility of the Church, and from it no dissent is legitimate, private or public. The only legitimate dissent is from teaching which purports to be the teaching of the Church, but which in fact is not. This is the one and only criterion for dissent, and it is objective. Subjective considerations are fundamentally irrelevant. These speak to the good faith of dissenters and this can be presumed in every case, since it can be taken for granted that no one will dissent from the teaching of the Pope or the Bishops without reasons which appear to him 'serious and well-founded.' The matter of the manner of the dissent is one that calls for prudential judgements in particular situations and is not of fundamental importance either. What is of greater importance is the manner of the magisterial intervention to resolve the situation, for the bishops bear the greater responsibility from the burden of the office which they are called to carry.

The United States bishops insist that the manner of the dissent must 'not question or impugn the teaching authority of the Church.' Legitimate dissent must be based on the teaching authority of the Church. It appeals to the Magisterium of the Church against the bishops who are abusing it, as the dissenter sees it. They also insist that the manner of the dissent must not give scandal. Certainly, scandal must be avoided as much as possible, but on the hypothesis being advocated here, it is difficult to see how it can be avoided completely. If the dissent is legitimate, the situation is scandalous already, insofar as the bishops of the Church are misusing their office and teaching error in the place of Christ's truth. It is wrong, therefore, to say that 'even responsible dissent does not excuse one from faithful presentation of the authentic doctrine of the Church when one is performing a pastoral ministry in Her name.' For if the dissent is responsible the doctrine from which one dissents is not authentic doctrine but error, and one must not present it as authentic doctrine but resist it as a misuse of apostolic authority.

The *Obligation* to 'Dissent'

The 'right to dissent' then becomes, on this understanding, an obligation to proclaim the faith of the Church. St Augustine formulated the duty to tell the truth in his usual trenchant manner:

> One must therefore tell the truth, especially when a difficulty makes it all the more urgent that the truth be told. Let those grasp it who can. Far be it that, in keeping silence out of consideration for those who might not be able to understand, not only truth be frustrated, but those be left in error who could have grasped the truth and thus escaped their error. … How fearful we are that the truth may harm those who will not be able to understand! Why are we not afraid that if we remain silent, those who could have understood will be deceived.[25]

One famous dissident theologian, Ignaz von Döllinger, who could not accept the teaching of the First Vatican Council on the authority of the Pope to make a definitive doctrinal judgment on his own, based

---

[25] De Bono Perseverantiae, cha 16, as quoted in John R. Quinn, The Reform of the Papacy: The Costly Call to Christian Unity (New York: The Crossroad Publishing Company, 1999), 68-69.

his resistance on these principles. He wrote that 'we believe our piety owes its first duties to the divine institution of the Church and to the truth, and it is precisely this piety which constrains us to oppose, frankly and decisively, every disfigurement or disturbance of the one or the other.'[26] He quotes St. Bernard, who wrote, 'It is better that scandal arise than that truth be abandoned.'[27] One can have no quarrel with the principles enunciated here. Döllinger turned out to be wrong, and he was wrong to refuse to accept the judgment of the First Vatican Council. He was, however, fully entitled to follow his conscience prior to the definitive judgment, and the principles he was following are fully legitimate. More recently, the point was well made by Joseph Komonchak who wrote: 'Again, given the real possibility of error, is there not a responsibility imposed upon each qualified member of the Church, who believes he has detected an error, to seek to correct it? Does he not have this responsibility to truth itself? ... to the Church? ... toward the members? ... what I have called the possibility of public dissent can well be described as the right, or indeed the obligation, to dissent publicly.'[28]

Ratzinger has no doubt that true love of the Church and a genuine obedience can lead to the obligation to speak out against abuses which can and do arise in the Church. He writes: 'It stands to reason, then, that in this way obedience *as* obedience takes on a new aspect: the obligation of 'bearing witness,' the duty to strive for the integrity of the Church, to battle against the 'Babylon' within her that raises its head not only among the laity, not only among individual Christians, but even higher up within the very core of the Church's structure.'[29] And this 'bearing witness' need not be easy. As Ratzinger says, 'it is

---

[26] Ignaz von Döllinger (writing as Janus), The Pope and the Council (London, Oxford, and Cambridge: Rivingtons, 1869), x-xi.

[27] Melius est scandalum oriatur quam veritas relinquatur, in Ignaz von Döllinger (writing as Janus), The Pope and the Council (London, Oxford, and Cambridge: Rivingtons, 1869), xi.

[28] Komonchak, 'Ordinary Papal Magisterium,' 83.

[29] Joseph Ratzinger, 'Free Expression and Obedience in the Church,' in The Church readings in theology (New York: J. Kenedy & Sons, 1963), 194-217 at 211-12.

evident that even within the Church such bearing of witness will now as ever prove painful, open as it is to misunderstanding, suspicion, even condemnation.' And he is not sparing in his disparagement of those who would remain silent out of fear of the suffering involved. 'Meanwhile, the servility of the sycophants (branded by the genuine prophets of the Old Testament as 'false prophets'), of those who shy from and shun every collision, who prize above all their calm complacency, is not true obedience. The true obedience is that which remains obedient even while bearing witness in suffering; it is that obedience which is forthright truthfulness and which is animated by the persistent power of love. ... What the Church needs today, as always, are not adulators to extol the status quo, but men whose humility and obedience are no less than their passion for truth; men who brave every misunderstanding and attack as they bear witness; men who, in a word, love the Church more than ease and the unruffled course of their personal destiny.'[30] In offering criteria for discernment of the validity of witness, he first lays down: 'Obviously, when one confronts the deposit of faith as such, criticism must cease.'[31] With that fundamental principle accepted, the norm is 'truth'. 'Truth, as well as love, possesses a right of its own and over sheer utility it takes precedence – truth from which stems that strict necessity for prophetic charisma, and which can demand of one the duty of bearing public witness. For were it necessary to wait for the day when the truth would no longer be misinterpreted and taken advantage of, we might well find that it had lost all effect.'[32] He lays down a number of restrictions that might apply in certain situations, while still recognizing that no set of rules can cover every situation. 'But again in these matters, all things taken into consideration, there is no absolute norm except for the necessity of an obedient decision made in the light of the faith.'[33]

---

[30] Ibid, 212. See also the remarks on page 209.
[31] Ibid, 213.
[32] Ibid.
[33] Ibid, 214.

Public Dissent

The issue of public dissent needs now to be addressed. The Congregation for the Doctrine of the Faith accepts the standard doctrine allowing for the possibility of 'private' dissent, but deny that this constitutes a right to public dissent. In the correspondence with Curran, they wrote that 'this suspension of assent does not provide grounds for a so-called right to public dissent, for such public dissent would in effect constitute an alternative magisterium contrary to the magisterium of Christ given to the apostles and constantly exercised through the hierarchical magisterium in the Church.'[34] As was noted at the beginning, this point was considered by the Congregation and by Curran to be the key point at issue between them, and it was at the top of the list of errors for which Curran was finally disciplined. The Congregation provided a further development of its thinking on this issue in Donum veritatis, where the situation of a theologian having difficulty with a magisterial teaching was considered, and suggestions were made as to what he might do in such a situation. The Congregation wrote:

> If, despite a loyal effort on the theologian's part, the difficulties persist, the theologian has the duty to make known to the Magisterial authorities the problems raised by the teaching in itself, in the arguments proposed to justify it, or even in the manner in which it is presented. He should do this in an evangelical spirit and with a profound desire to resolve the difficulties. His objections could then contribute to real progress and provide a stimulus to the Magisterium to propose the teaching of the Church in greater depth and with a clearer presentation of the arguments. In cases like these, the theologian should avoid turning to the 'mass media', but

---

[34] Observations of the Sacred Congregation for the Doctrine of the Faith on some writings of Father Charles Curran (July 1979) in Faithful Dissent, 118.

> have recourse to the responsible authority, for it is not by seeking to exert the pressure of public opinion that one contributes to the clarification of doctrinal issues and renders service to the truth.[35]

The major flaw in this approach is that it does not consider the one case which makes all the difference, the case, that is, when an episcopal teaching is simply wrong. This is the case which the medieval thinkers had in mind in dealing with the traditional doctrine that a Pope can only be judged when he falls into heresy. And as Congar, pointed out, this case is one which must be dealt with seriously, for this is ultimately the only justification for legitimate dissent. Joseph Ratzinger understood the possibility of error following inevitably from the sin which is in the Church. For the reality of sin in the Church is a permanent reality, and it has concrete implications, affecting all the members, even those in positions of authority. 'Grace, being absolute, implies of itself human inadequacy, and such human inadequacy justifies criticism of those in the Church. To repeat then, these men <u>are</u> the Church and that Church cannot be considered as pure abstraction, independent of and divorced from these her human members.'[36] And there can be no doubt that Ratzinger had the bishops of the Church in mind, exercising their function of teaching in the Church. In his commentary on <u>Dei Verbum</u>, he made this quite clear. He wrote that 'we must say that fear of the terrifying possibilities of the teaching office can equally be dispelled only through confidence in the Spirit that guides his Church. This is, however, in no way intended to devalue or remove the place of vigilance.'[37] He spoke sympathetically of Luther's effort to challenge the authorities of his day on the basis of scripture, and wrote that 'there exists something like a certain independence of scripture as a separate, and in many respects perfectly unambiguous, criterion in face

---

[35] <u>Donum veritatis</u>, § 30.
[36] Ratzinger, 'Free Expression and Obedience in the Church,' 203.
[37] Joseph Ratzinger, 'Dogmatic Constitution on Divine Revelation: Origin and Background', in <u>Commentary on the Documents of Vatican II, Volume III</u>, (London / New York: Burns & Oates / Herder and Herder, 1969), 155-166, at 194.

of the Church's magisterium. That was undoubtedly a correct insight on Luther's part, and in the Catholic Church not enough place has been accorded to it on account of the claims of the magisterium, the intrinsic limits of which have not always been sufficiently clearly perceived.'[38]

If we are speaking of legitimate dissent, the difficulties must be with the teaching in itself, for dissent is only legitimate when the teaching is erroneous. This means that legitimate dissent is not really dissent at all, but only appears to be such because of an erroneous official teaching. In this case, the so-called 'dissent' is in fact the genuine teaching of the Church, and it is the official teaching which is the truly dissident position. The Congregation does not take this possibility into account. The only progress mentioned is proposing the teaching of the Church in greater depth, so the possibility of an error is not envisaged, for, in that case, it would be required to propose the teaching of the Church correctly, rather than incorrectly. When the assumption is made, and Catholic theology has a great difficulty making it since the Reformation, everything changes. Now there is not only a right to dissent, but an obligation to dissent and a corresponding obligation to remedy the situation. In this situation it may indeed be appropriate to speak of an 'alternative Magisterium'. On the assumption that the official Magisterium has fallen into error, an alternative is required and the truth is, on this hypothesis, with the dissident and not the bisho

The Congregation recognises the duty of the theologian to make the problem known, but only to the magisterial authorities. On the assumption that there is error in the current teaching, surely more is required. Everyone in the Church has the right to know if a given official teaching is erroneous, as Curran and his colleagues pointed out at their press conference in 1968. The teaching of the Church is everyone's business, and error in teaching is a serious matter. It is a scandalous situation which requires to be remedied urgently. Remember the situation prior to the Second Vatican Council when the official

---

[38] Joseph Ratzinger, 'Revelation and Tradition,' in Karl Rahner and Joseph Ratzinger, Revelation and Tradition, Quaestiones Disputatae 17 (New York: Herder and Herder, 1965), 26-49 at 48.

position was still the refusal to recognise the value of ecumenism or religious freedom and so on. In these cases it was the official position which was causing the scandal, and making it known to the Roman authorities of the time would have made no difference at all. The matter had to be made more widely known so that the world-wide episcopate could make its influence felt. And public debate was required for the issues to be clarified. It is unrealistic to suggest that having recourse to the responsible authority is sufficient in these matters. The evidence of history makes it clear that doctrinal development does not come so easily. The responsible authorities are fallible and sinful men like all the rest of us, and they require a certain amount of human pressure to be brought to a right frame of mind, if a change is required. The fear of the 'mass media' is not appropriate in the Church. The mass media represent an important channel of communication within the Church, and every member of the Church has a legitimate interest in the discernment of the teaching of the Church. It is not a matter for select committees working behind closed doors. A comment made by St Robert Bellarmine in a letter to Pope Clement VIII in the context of the controversy *De auxiliis* is relevant here. He wrote to the Pope: 'You say that the question appertains to the faith, but if that be so it is everybody's concern, according to the dictum of Pope Nicholas. Therefore it should be discussed in the full light of day, and not secretly, with a mere handful of advisers.'[39] The Church has nothing to fear from publicity. The truth is going to triumph, and the more people who know about it the better. The point has been made strongly by one theologian in connection with the *Humanae vitae* crisis. He pointed out that the fact that the discussion is 'a matter of immediate and urgent practical consequence for millions of persons, both Catholic and not, has already moved the matter from the remote and private rooms of theologians out into the forum of public concern.'[40] And he continued:

---

[39] James Brodrick, S.J., The Life and Work of Blessed Robert Francis Cardinal Bellarmine, S.J., Volume II (Burns Oates and Washbourne: London, 1928), 59.
[40] Komonchak, 'Ordinary Papal Magisterium and Religious Assent,' 82.

Further, if there is a real possibility of error, may it not be argued that the Church has nothing to fear from public discussion? If the teaching is correct, the Spirit will show (as has not yet been shown) why it is correct. If the teaching is incorrect, it can only be corrected if there is given to bishop and to theologian the freedom to explore the matter. Since collaboration is a necessary part of the theological endeavor, it is difficult to see how such exploration can remain private. No theological journal is so abstruse and no language so arcane that its publication cannot overnight become known to the world. It is not certain that one can even speak of private discussion or dissent any longer.[41]

Submissive Silence?

With these principles in place it is possible to review the position of the Congregation for the Doctrine of Faith which permits private dissent but forbids its publication. If private dissent is legitimate and public dissent is not, what then is the dissident theologian to do? In this connection Curran poses a question to the CDF: 'Is silentium obsequiosum the only legitimate response for a theologian who is convinced that there are serious reasons which overturn the presumption in favor of the teaching of the authoritative noninfallible hierarchical magisterium?'[42] By his use of the phrase silentium obsequiosum in this question, Curran is making reference to a dispute on the issue which arose during the Jansenist controversy. The Jansenists could not accept a papal decree against them and offered to observe a 'respectful silence' in regard to it. One Pope, Clement IX, was willing to make do with this position and accepted it officially in a papal brief of Jan. 14, 1669, thus ushering in a period of calm in the controversy known as the Clementine Peace. However, a later Pope, Clement XI, at the request

---

[41] Ibid, 83.
[42] Curran, Faithful Dissent, 154.

of Louis XV, condemned this attitude of respectful silence. In the bull <u>Vineam Domini Sabaoth</u> (16 July 1705), he declared 'that all sons of the Church should learn to listen to the Church, not only by keeping silence, but obeying interiorly, which is the true obedience of the orthodox man' and that "respectful silence' does not suffice.' (DS 2390) The Congregation for the Doctrine of the Faith is implicitly advocating this 'respectful silence' as the proper response to a magisterial teaching which one cannot accept, and the policy is no more acceptable now that it was in that earlier day. Pope Clement XI is quite right that assent, of its very nature interior, to the teaching of the Church is the only genuine response. It has been argued here that dissent is only legitimate if it is correct and the official teaching dissented from is mistaken, and in that case the dissent must be made public because it is, in this case, the genuine teaching of the Church. There can be no legitimate distinction between interior and exterior assent; the two must go together in any human being. In disciplinary matters the situation is different, for truth and error do not enter in. If I disagree with a decision in such matters and, having made all due representations to have the decision reversed, the decision is upheld, I can still accept it while continuing to disagree with it. In this case a 'respectful silence' is legitimate. When the truth is at stake, however, the situation is different. I cannot allow error to masquerade as truth in the official teaching of the Church without protest. It is my Christian duty to everything within my power to correct the situation. It follows, therefore, that on the principles being advocated here, the Congregation for the Doctrine of the Faith is simply wrong in denying the right to public dissent.

The further question arises as to possible limitations on the appropriate from of the public dissent. In this regard Pope John Paul II wrote, on one occasion:

> <u>Dissent</u>, in the form of carefully orchestrated protests and polemics carried on in the media, <u>is opposed to ecclesial communion and to a correct understanding of the hierarchical constitution of the People of God</u>. Opposition to the teaching of the Church's Pastors

cannot be seen as a legitimate expression either of Christian freedom or of the diversity of the Spirit's gifts. When this happens, the Church's Pastors have the duty to act in conformity with their apostolic mission, insisting that *the right of the faithful* to receive Catholic doctrine in its purity and integrity must always be respected.[43]

And Cardinal Ratzinger, commenting on *Donum veritatis*, had similar things to say:

> The instruction distinguishes between healthy theological tension and true dissent, in which theology is organized according to the principle of majority rule, and the faithful are given alternative norms by a 'counter-magisterium.' Dissent thus becomes a political factor, passing from the realm of thought to that of a 'power-game.' This is where a theologian's use of mass media can be dangerous.[44]

In the same commentary Cardinal Ratzinger allowed that some publicity is appropriate for a dissident view. He said of the dissident theologian that 'we have not excluded all kinds of publication, nor have we closed him up in suffering ...'[45] These strictures are only reasonable on the assumption that the official teaching in question is fundamentally correct and needs only minor adjustment. If, however, the teaching is simply erroneous, the Pope and the Congregation for the Doctrine of the Faith are in no position to be laying down rules about the publicity due to the genuine teaching of the Church. On the hypothesis being proposed here, it is the official teaching which is wrong. It is causing the scandal in the Church and urgently needs to be corrected, and all means necessary for that purpose are in order. Every Christian has the

---

[43] Veritatis Splendor § 113.
[44] Origins 20 (1990-91), 119.
[45] Ibid.

right to know if an official teaching is erroneous, and the mass media are a fully legitimate means of communicating this information.

Of interest in this context also is the case of von Döllinger who made use of the mass media, and defended his use in strong terms. For von Döllinger deliberately set out to use public opinion as a means to exert influence on the debate around the First Vatican Council. And in his famous speech to the Munich congress in 1863 he said: 'It is theology which confers being and force to a proper and healthy public opinion in religious and ecclesiastical matters, and to this opinion all must yield, even the leaders of the Church and the bearers of authority. Like prophecy in the Old Testament times, which stood beside the ordained priesthood, so also in the Church there is an extraordinary authority which stands beside the ordinary authorities, and this is public opinion. Through it theological science exercises its compelling power, which in the long run nothing can withstand.'[46] Seckler is critical of this position, but for the wrong reason, in my view, when he writes: 'Here we are no longer speaking of theology, which *opportune importune* exercises its *scientific* service of witness in the face of all powers. ... Theology no longer works only as a science with scientific methods, but as an *Agitator*, which uses public opinion in support of goals, which it believes it cannot otherwise achieve.'[47] Seckler is critical of the appeal to public opinion because it is not a proper academic procedure, which is true. The appeal to public opinion in the Church is not an academic matter. It is an appeal to the supernatural sense of the faith of the whole Church, and that is a fully legitimate procedure. Von Döllinger is wrong in his opinion of the role of theology in forming public opinion in the Church, for that is the function primarily of the Holy Spirit in person. The primary human formers of public opinion in the pilgrim Church are the bishops, and theologians and everyone else has their own appropriate role in the process too. In the situation we are considering, any Christian who is convinced that a given official teaching is erroneous is fully entitled to do all in his power to correct the

---

[46] Seckler, 'Kirchliches Lehramt,' 48.
[47] Ibid, 48-49.

situation, including the appeal to the whole Church through the mass media. History provides examples of this legitimate effort. According to Newman's account of the Arian crisis, the ordinary faithful had an important part to play in maintaining the purity of the Church's faith. One recalls also the uproar that was caused by Pope Pius IX's *Syllabus of Errors*. Many of the ordinary faithful were shocked and scandalised by Pope Pius's extreme opinions in the matter of Church/State relations, and these opinions had to be moderated by judicious explanation at the time and by eventual abandonment at the Second Vatican Council.

This repudiation of the mass media from theological discussion is of a piece with the attitude of the Congregation for the Doctrine of the Faith towards the faithful in general. One of Charles Curran's questions to the Congregation was on this issue. He asked: 'Can the ordinary faithful prudently make a decision to act against the teaching of the ordinary authentic noninfallible hierarchical magisterium?'[48] The 'Observations' on page 1 says no: 'The ordinary member of the faithful, lacking expertise in a particular question, could not prudently trust himself to human wisdom or theological opinion in making a decision, in the face of the authentic teaching of those who 'by divine institution ... have succeeded to the place of the apostles as shepherds of the Church...' LG 20[49] Enough has been said already in dealing with the ambiguity of speaking of an 'authentic' teaching in this connection. If the teaching is truly authentic, then no one at all is free to dissent from it, bishop or theologian or any other. If, on the case under consideration, the teaching is authoritative but wrong, then it becomes possible to see that the Congregation is mistaken in the attitude it is adopting. The discernment of the teaching of the Church is not a matter of 'expertise in a particular question.' It is a matter of the supernatural sense of the faith to which all in the Church have equal access. Every Christian can and must discern the faith of the Church. Expertise has its role to play in laying out the issues involved, but every educated Catholic is entitled

---

[48] Curran, Faithful Dissent, 156.
[49] Observations of the Sacred Congregation for the Doctrine of the Faith regarding the Reverend Charles E. Curran (July 1979) in Faithful Dissent, 118.

to judge matters of the faith. If a reasonable doubt exists in a given case, and there can be no question at all of legitimate dissent without some grounds for reasonable doubt, then everyone is entitled to the benefit of that doubt.

Archbishop (now Cardinal) Levada saw the reality of public dissent in its true colours. He saw that it was not contributing towards the growth in understanding of Church teaching, but implied a direct criticism of the magisterial teaching and the claim that one's own position was correct, which it does, and must, of necessity. He concluded: 'Hence the person who dissents publicly, that is, who presents conclusions as a decision at which they have arrived in contradiction to the teaching of the church, must also understand that this decision implies a certain separation from the tradition of the church which is handed on in the magisterium under the guidance of the Holy Spirit for the belief of the Christian faithful.'[50] What Cardinal Levada said here is true, if the teaching in dispute is in fact the genuine teaching of the Church, which he is implicitly taking for granted. In that case the dissent is illegitimate and is in fact heresy, and should be condemned as such. If, on the other hand, the dissenter is correct, it is the magisterial authorities who are the material heretics and they must be brought to change their position as a matter of urgency. The problem is insoluble if one continues to speak of dissent as if the truth of the matter did not enter into consideration. There is no doubt that Cardinal Levada's presumption will apply for the most part. It is unthinkable that in the Church of the God the bishops could be mostly wrong in what they teach. However, in matters of divine faith, 'for the most part' is no use. As Christians, we believe in God absolutely, and we are entitled to receive his word absolutely, with no confusion at all. When confusion arises and public dissent proliferates, the bishops have an urgent responsibility to clarify the situation. Condemning public dissent in general is not helpful at all; it simply does not help to clarify the situation. There comes a time when a

---

[50] Archbishop William Levada; 'Dissent and the Catholic Religion Teacher', in Readings in Moral Theology No. 6: Dissent in the Church, edd. Charles E. Curran and Richard McCormick, S.J. (New York / Mahwah: Paulist Press, 1988),133ff. at 147.

definitive judgment must be made. If there is the smallest possibility of error in episcopal teaching, that possibility must be taken into account. When an issue has become the focus of widespread public interest and concern, special measures are called for in order to bring about a resolution. The ordinary teaching procedures no longer suffice. The time has come for a definitive judgment.

The Obligations of the Bishops

The fundamental obligation of the bishop is to proclaim the full truth of Christ. In doing this, he has to follow his conscience also and insist on the faith of the Church, as he understands it, being preached and accepted in the Church. That hardly needs to be said, but it still remains the fundamental truth of the matter, and it means, in practice, that the first reaction of the bishops in the face of dissent from official teaching will normally be suspicious and negative. And, no doubt, rightly so. But, in the context of all that has been said, the possibility needs also to be faced that the bishop could be wrong. The darkness of intellect caused by original and actual sin affects the bishops as it affects every Christian, and bishops need to be aware of the problem. The fact of the matter is, as Rahner has pointed out on more than one occasion, that the official representatives of the Church can be, have been and are sinners. 'And since they can in fact commit sin, since they can be culpably narrow, culpably egoistic, self-satisfied, obstinate, sensual or indolent, this sinful attitude of theirs will naturally affect also those actions which they initiate precisely as ecclesiastics and in the name of the Church as acts of the concrete Church.'[51] And Rahner has elaborated the implications of this for the proper attitude of bishops in re.

> The representatives of the Magisterium must, in
> the name of this Magisterium, state explicitly and

---

[51] 'The Church of Sinners,' Theological Investigations 6 (Baltimore/London: Helicon Press/Darton, Longman & Todd, 1969), 253-269 at 261.

> also practice: We also are men when we make our judgments, men who should not be rash and full of prejudice, but who unavoidably are such. Apart from the case of definitive judgments of the Pope or a Council which are guaranteed free from error by the Spirit of the Church, we can – and even the Pope – err in our judgments and have done so even into our own day. That is something which goes without saying, which the rights and requirements of the function of Magisterium does not remove. It is our duty to operate under this risk …[52]

Ratzinger has also expressed his mind on the issue of the attitude the authorities should adopt in this matter.

> Now we can say something concerning the role of the institution and of office as such. The Church needs the spirit of freedom and of sincere forthrightness because she is bound by the command, 'Do not stifle the Spirit' (1 Thess. 5:19), which is valid for all time. Upon hearing such words, who can help but recall Paul's account of his collision with Peter in Gal 2:11-14. … if it was weakness in Peter to have compromised the freedom of the gospel for fear of James' supporters, it was his greatness which enabled him to accept the liberty of Paul, who 'rebuked him to his face.'[53]

In this light, he suggests that the Church today might be lacking in that greatness of spirit of St Peter, when he asks: 'might she not be taken to task for holding the reins a bit too tightly, for the creation of too many norms, so that not a few of these helped abandon the century to disbelief rather than save it? In other words, might she not be rebuked

---

[52] Karl Rahner, 'Theologie und Lehramt,' in <u>Stimmen der Zeit</u> 198/6 (June 1980) 363-375 at 364.
[53] Ratzinger, 'Free Expression and Obedience in the Church,' 214.

for trusting too little that power of truth which lives and triumphs in the faith, for entrenching herself behind exterior safeguards instead of relying on the truth, which is inherent in liberty and shuns such defenses?'[54]

One commentator recommended to bishops St Paul's remark in 2 Cor 4:7 that 'we have this treasure in earthen vessels,' and remarked: 'To speak frankly, this word of modesty seems to me to represent the alpha and the omega of the virtues of an episcopal magisterium which is credible and acceptable from the ethical point of view.'[55] And Pope John Paul II made recommendations in this regard which are helpful. He was reflecting on the erroneous judgment made in the Galileo Affair when he wrote: 'The pastoral judgment that the Copernican theory required was difficult to make, insofar as geocentrism seemed to be a part of scriptural teaching itself. It would have been necessary all at once to overcome habits of thought and to devise a way of teaching capable of enlightening the people of God. Let us say, in a general way, that the pastor ought to show a genuine boldness, avoiding the double trap of a hesitant attitude and of hasty judgment, both of which can cause considerable harm.'[56] Pope Paul VI has expressed the need for humility in the face of criticism. 'We have to accept criticism with humility and reflection and admit what is justly pointed out. Rome has no need to be defensive, turning a deaf ear to observations which come from respected sources, still less, when those sources are friends and brothers.'[57]

The Curran Case Revisited

In the light of the principles developed here, it is possible to resolve a number of issues raised by the manner in which the Congregation for the Doctrine of the Faith dealt with the Curran case. The Congregation

---

[54] Ibid, 215.
[55] André Naud, Pour une éthique de la parole épiscopale (Éditions Fides, 2002), 19.
[56] Pope John Paul II's Address to the Pontifical Academy of Sciences on October 31, 1992 in Origins 22 (1992-93), 370-74 at 372.
[57] 'Address to the Roman Curia, September 21, 1963,' AAS 55 (1963), 797.

initially presented the issue of public dissent as the central point in their case against Curran. While affirming that private dissent can be legitimate in certain circumstances, it denied the legitimacy of public dissent in all circumstances. Curran was given reasonable grounds for his conclusion that this was the important issue at stake. He accepted without hesitation the judgment that his positions on the moral issues were in dissent from official teaching, but believed that these points were 'primarily illustrative of the more fundamental issues involved.'[58] And yet, in the end, the issue of public dissent played no part in the final judgment against Curran; the whole focus was on the moral norms from which Curran was dissenting.

The fundamental question is whether or not these norms are part of the teaching of the Holy Church. As was pointed out by the theologians who supported Curran, the Congregation did not make any claim that any of the specific moral teachings for which Curran was disciplined fulfil the conditions necessary for an definitve pronouncement, and they asked the question 'Which noninfallible teachings are serious enough to provoke such a result, and how are those teachings determined?'[59] This question is badly posed. There are no noninfallible teachings of the Church. The teachings in question are not definitive. If they belong to the teaching of the Holy Church, they are taught infallibly with the infallibility of the Church. If they do not belong to the teaching of the Holy Church, they are not taught at all, but are human opinions in need of correction. The Congregation offered no justification for its position that dissent from these particular doctrines is out of order, but I suggest the reason must have been that the Congregation judged that these moral norms belong to the faith of the Church and that no one has the right to dissent from them, even though they have not yet been defined. In its letter of September 17, 1985, the Congregation told Curran 'that the authorities of the Church cannot allow the present

---

[58] Curran; 'Public Dissent in the Church,' 390.

[59] Statement signed by some past presidents of the Catholic Theological Society of America and the College Theology Society (eventually signed by 750 Catholic theologians in US) in Charles E. Curran, Faithful Dissent (London: Sheed & Ward, 1987), 282-284 at 283.

situation to continue in which the inherent contradiction is prolonged that one who is to teach in the name of the Church in fact denies her teaching.'[60] That is the Congregation's judgment, which it is entitled to make, and it must act on it. The fact that the Congregation did not continue to insist on the prohibition of public dissent implies that they did not understand this position as being part of the teaching of the Church in the same way.

This would also explain another aspect of the Congregation's action to which Curran took particular exception. In one letter to Curran the Congregation gave him references to magisterial documents supporting each of the doctrines in dispute. Curran was familiar with them all, and in spite of them he was still convinced of his dissident position. Then, in 1983, the Congregation presented Curran with the set of moral teachings from which he was dissenting and called on him to revise his positions. The Congregation wrote: 'We would now like to invite you to indicate in writing to this Congregation whether or not you would like to revise those positions in clear public dissent from the Magisterium.'[61] In the 1985 letter, the Congregation offered Curran the following advice: 'In your letter you indicated that you had not taken the positions you have, without 'a great deal of prayer, study, consultation and discernment.' This fact inspires us to hope that by further application of these means, you will come to that due adherence to the Church's doctrine which should characterize all the faithful.'[62] In response to this Curran has commented that he found this attitude to be insulting. 'I have dedicated my life as a Catholic theologian to the pursuit of truth. If I change my position on important issues, I believe there is a strong moral obligation to state that as clearly as I can in the same way and manner that I stated the contrary positions.'[63]

---

[60] Curran, Faithful Dissent, 250.
[61] Letter of Congregation to Curran, May 10, 1983 in Charles E. Curran, Faithful Dissent (London: Sheed & Ward, 1987), 198.
[62] Curran, Faithful Dissent, 250.
[63] Curran's Response on August 24, 1984 in Charles E. Curran, Faithful Dissent (London: Sheed & Ward, 1987), 234.

If the situation is properly understood, there is no reason for Curran to be insulted by the Congregation's action and attitude. The Congregation is informing Curran of its judgment that these norms belong to the faith of the Church, and, on that premise, no one has the right to dissent. The Congregation has a public responsibility to insist that the faith of the Church be accepted and taught throughout the Church and dealt with Curran accordingly. Curran disagrees with the Congregation's judgment, but he should recognise its right to make it and to act on it. He has no reason to consider himself insulted if the Congregation for the Doctrine of Faith deems him to be a material heretic when he denies the faith of the Church, as it sees it. Given the premise that it judges these moral norms to be part of the faith of the Church, it has no alternative.

There was also confusion caused by the precise disciplinary action taken against Curran. As was noted earlier the academics who supported Curran asked the question: 'If one is declared no longer a Catholic theologian, does that modify in any way the theologian's relation to the Catholic Church itself? If so, how? If not, what does such a declaration mean?'[64] I suggest that what the disciplinary action means is that Curran is adjudged to be dissenting from doctrines which belong to the faith of the Church but which have not been defined as such. If Curran were in dissent from defined doctrine, the penalty would be excommunication. Given that these moral norms are not defined, and yet the responsible authority judges them to belong to the faith of the Church, this lesser disciplinary action is taken, where Curran can remain a priest in good standing in his diocese but cannot teach theology in any Catholic faculty.

---

[64] Statement signed by some past presidents of the Catholic Theological Society of America and the College Theology Society (eventually signed by 750 Catholic theologians in US) in Charles E. Curran, Faithful Dissent (London: Sheed & Ward, 1987), 282-284 at 283.

Institutionalizing Dissent?

Richard McCormick has made the suggestion that dissent is to be accepted as a normal part of the life of the Church. He has written that 'the magisterial function in the Church is much more a matter of a teaching-learning *process*, in which dissent should play a positive, nonthreatening role. It is part of the ordinary way of progress in human growth in understanding. I must insist on this: *we must learn to institutionalize dissent and profit from it.*'[65] In support of this view he quotes Pope John Paul II, writing at an early stage as Karol Wojtyla: 'The structure of a human community is correct only if it admits not just the presence of a justified opposition, but also the effectiveness of opposition which is required by the common good and the right of participation.'[66] According to McCormick this dialectic of the democratic process is true of the Church in the same way as of any other human community.[67] On this basis he wonders what the bishops are called upon to do in the face of dissent. Can they simply ignore it, or are they invited to a new reflection on the matter? If they ignore it, 'then the key theological issue embedded in dissent has not been faced.'[68] For McCormick, '[w]hen a question is the object of a genuine dispute in the Church, the very worst thing to do is to close the conversation, decree a solution and select as consultants only those who will support it,' and he considers this 'a quite modest and unthreatening conclusion.'[69]

Responding to this suggestion provides an opportunity to rehearse some of the fundamental principles developed in this book. McCormick

---

[65] Richard A. McCormick, S.J., 'Dissent in the Church: Loyalty or Liability?,' in *The Critical Calling: Reflections on Moral Dilemmas Since Vatican II* (Washington, D.C.: Georgetown University Press, 1989), 25-46 at 42.
[66] Karol Wojtyla, *The Acting Person* (Boston: D. Reidel, 1979), 343.
[67] McCormick, 'Dissent in the Church: Loyalty or Liability?,' 42.
[68] Richard A. McCormick, S.J., 'Dissent in the Church: Loyalty or Liability?,' in *The Critical Calling: Reflections on Moral Dilemmas Since Vatican II* (Washington, D.C.: Georgetown University Press, 1989), 25-46 at 44.
[69] Richard A. McCormick, S.J., 'The Chill Factor in Contemporary Moral Theology,' in *The Critical Calling: Reflections on Moral Dilemmas Since Vatican II* (Washington, D.C.: Georgetown University Press, 1989), 71-94 at 72.

himself was quoted earlier to the effect that ecclesiology determines one's understanding of dissent, and I would contend that the flaw in McCormick's view springs from a flawed ecclesiology. For the Church is not like any other human institution; it is a theandric institution and that makes all the difference. Christ is the one teacher in the Church, teaching the whole Word of God in and through the Church by the incorporation of the Holy Spirit. The epistemology of faith is, therefore, quite unlike the epistemology of other forms of human knowledge. The 'ordinary way of progress in human growth in understanding' does not apply. Our knowledge in faith comes from above by a divine light and does not come by human inquiry in the normal manner, where differences of opinion are inevitable and disagreements are an essential part of the dialectical development. The faith of the Church is known in its global totality to all in the Church. It can happen that particular points are unclear for different reasons and it can take a long time for a point to crystallize into doctrine. The long maturation of the Marian doctrines are the prime examples of this. When, however, a doctrine has become established as official teaching in the Church, a particular stage in the development of doctrine has already been reached. Given that the holy Church of Christ subsists in the Catholic Church, the providence of God must ensure that the official teaching of the Catholic Church will be identical with the genuine teaching of the holy Church, and that must be our first assumption if the question arises. It cannot, therefore, be taken for granted that dissent from official teaching, however widespread it may be, implies a problem with the teaching. McCormick has offered his opinion: 'Concretely, if large segments of the community do not see the analyses and conclusions of an authoritative teacher, it is a sign that (a) either the matter is not sufficiently clear, sufficiently mature for closure, or (b) that it is badly formulated or (c) that it is wrong.'[70] McCormick does not even consider the possibility that the teaching is quite clearly formulated and is correct, and that it is the dissenters who are wrong. For him, 'we shall always be in trouble when members of the hierarchy, or the CDF, or even the Holy Father reassert

---

[70] McCormick, 'Dissent in the Church: Loyalty or Liability?' 37.

conclusions as *certain and binding* when such conclusions do not have theological support. But let us be accurate on the source of that trouble and confusion. It is not primarily public criticism by theologians. It is first of all and at root a problem of the use of authority.'[71]

If a given teaching is, in fact, the teaching of the holy Church of Christ, the responsible authorities in the Church must insist upon it, regardless of how widespread dissent from it may be. If the sense of faith of the bishops discerns the teaching to be the *'certain and binding'* faith of the Church, it is the duty of their office to proclaim it against any opposition whatever. And they are entitled, and indeed obliged, to take the measures which McCormick deems so reprehensible. In this case, the dissent cannot be granted equal status with obedient acceptance, for such dissent is heresy and is dividing the Church, and dissenters must always be aware of the possibility, even the probability, that such is the case in their particular case. If, on the other hand, the dissenters are correct and their dissent is legitimate, an even worse scenario emerges. In this case, it is the bishops who are wrong. They are teaching error, or at best mere human opinion, as the teaching of the holy Church of Christ and are thereby misusing their apostolic office, and also dividing the Church.

Dissent, therefore, is either heresy or prophecy; there is no middle ground of a general vagueness where no one is clear what is going on. It is possible for theologians to disagree on points of theology and to agree to differ. When a responsible authority in the Church makes a formal judgment that a given doctrine belongs to the faith of the Church and begins to insist on it as official teaching, a new situation arises. The authority of Christ has been invoked and the agreement to differ is no longer an option. This is the situation Pope Pius XII referred to in *Humani generis* when he laid down that after a formal judgment of the Pope a point of doctrine could no longer be considered a mater for free theological debate. It does not mean that the papal judgment is inerrant. It does mean that the position is now official teaching and possesses a new level of seriousness. If it is correct, the doctrine is the teaching of the

---

[71] McCormick, 'The Chill Factor in Contemporary Moral Theology,' 74.

Holy Church and must be accepted by all. If it is incorrect, the doctrine represents a misuse of apostolic authority and must be corrected as soon as possible. McCormick is wrong, therefore, to claim that his claim for the legitimacy of his dissent is 'nonthreatening'. It is threatening to the unity of the Church. All dissent from official teaching divides the Church and the situation calls for urgent resolution. It cannot be 'institutionalized'. We may profit from it, indeed, but only when it has been overcome and the situation finally resolved, one way of the other.

Chapter 16

The Resolution of the *Humanae vitae* Crisis

Having established general principles regarding magisterium and dissent, we are now in a position to consider the specific case from which we began, the ongoing crisis in the Church over *Humanae vitae*, applying the principles which have been presented. We can begin with a brief presentation of the historical background to the situation in which we find ourselves.

The condemnation of contraception was universal in the Christian community until the twentieth century. Noonan has given us a wonderful short summary of the tradition in the matter.

> "The propositions constituting a condemnation of contraception are ... recurrent. Since the first clear mention of contraception by a Christian theologian, when a harsh third-century moralist accused a pope of encouraging it, the articulated judgment has been the same. In the world of the late Empire known to St. Jerome and St. Augustine, in the Ostrogothic Arles of Bishop Caesarius and the Suevian Braga of Bishop Martin, in the Paris of St. Albert and St. Thomas, in the Renaissance Rome of Sixtus V and the Renaissance Milan of St. Charles Borromeo, in the Naples of St. Alphonsus Liguori and the Liège of Charles Billuart, in

the Philadelphia of Bishop Kenrick, and in the Bombay of Cardinal Gracias, the teachers of the Church have taught without hesitation or variation that certain acts preventing procreation are gravely sinful. No Catholic theologian has ever taught, "Contraception is a good act." The teaching on contraception is clear and apparently fixed forever."[1]

In the wider Christian community the new ideas in regard to contraception began to appear early in the twentieth century. At the Lambeth Conferences of the Anglican Communion in 1908 and 1920 attempts were made to change the teaching, but the condemnation continued to be upheld.[2] Then, at the Lambeth Conference of 1930 a decree was passed sanctioning the use of contraceptive means for the good of marriage. This first breach in the long-standing and universal Christian consensus was formally repudiated by Pope Pius XI in *Casti connubii* that same year, and his teaching was peacefully accepted among Catholics. During the years that followed, other Christian denominations followed the Anglican lead one after another and the morality of contraception was eventually accepted by the World Council of Churches in 1959.[3] It wasn't until the 1960's that division began to appear in the Catholic Church. Indeed, the public manifestation of the division can be dated rather precisely. In 1963, two well-qualified observers, John C. Ford, S.J. and Gerald Kelly, S.J. wrote that, although certain matters concerning the recently developed contraceptive pills were still theologically obscure, at least one thing was clear and certain, and this was that, according to the authoritative teaching of the Church

---

[1] John T. Noonan, *Contraception: A History of Its Treatment by the Catholic Theologians and Canonists* (Cambridge, Mass.: Harvard Univ., 1965), 6.

[2] John T. Noonan, *Contraception: A History of Its Treatment by the Catholic Theologians and Canonists* (Cambridge, Mass.: Harvard Univ., 1965), 409.

[3] Ibid, 490.

and the unanimous opinion of the theologians, to use the pills as contraceptives is gravely sinful.[4] They elaborated:

> The teachings of the Catholic Church on the question of contraceptive birth control are well known and universally applicable. Every method of contraception which interferes with the progress of marital activity towards its natural goal of conception is intrinsically wrong and in violation of natural law. The use of pills for the immediate purpose of impeding fertility, whether in the male or the female, represents likewise an unnatural interference with the natural tendency of the reproductive activity. These principles are accepted by all theologians of the Catholic Church, and they must be the starting point of any discussion of secondary questions on the subject of population control about which there may be difference of opinion and possibility of deeper insight.[5]

Before the end of that same year, 1963, three articles appeared which argued for the moral acceptability of the use of anovulant pills[6], and the universal consensus in the Catholic Church on the matter was shattered and has yet to be restored.

---

[4] J. C. Ford, S.J. and G. Kelly, S.J., *Contemporary Moral Theology: II. Marriage Questions* (Cork: The Mercier Press, 1963), 375.

[5] Ibid, 376.

[6] Louis Janssens, 'Morale conjugale et progestogènes', *Ephemerides Theologicae Lovanienses* 39 (1963), 787-826 ; Willem van der Marck, O., 'Vruchtbaarheidsregeling. Poging tot antwoord op een nog open vraag', *Tijdschrift voor Theologie* 3 (1963), 379-413; Josef Maria Reuss, 'Eheliche Hingabe und Zeugung: Ein Diskussionsbeitrag zu einem differenzierten Problem', *Tübinger Theologische Quartalshrift* 143 (1963), 454-76.

It was in that same year also that Pope John XXIII decided to form a commission to settle the question discreetly.[7] On 27 April 1963 the Secretary of State, in the name of Pope John XXIII, asked the Swiss Dominican H. De Riedmatten to form 'a small group of experts to examine the demographic problem under its many aspects (medical, moral, social, economic and statistical) and to propose effective proposals to maintain the moral order which is under attack.'[8] Before dealing with the working of the Commission, the brief but significant appearances of the issue at the Second Vatican Council must be mentioned. On 23 October 1964 Archibishop Pericle Felici, Secretary of the Council, announced that the question of artificial birth-control would be removed from the competence of the Council since there already existed a special commission to deal with it.[9] Despite this announcement, in the General Congregation on October 29, the matter was raised by Cardinals Léger, Suenens, and Alfrink, together with the Melkite Patriarch Maximos IV Saigh of Antioch. Bernard Häring reported on what happened that day:

> There was a great upset and the moderators were told not to allow any more talks in this direction, especially since these men had received the applause of the majority of the council. It was on one of these days I was asked by the press panel whether Ottaviani did not also receive a strong applause and I said, yes he did, only with the difference that he received a strong applause from very few hands. But [for the others] there was applause and a manifestation from many hands.[10]

---

[7] Chiron, L'infaillibilité, 330. For his report on the functioning of the papal commission Chiron based himself primarily on de Locht, Les Couples et l'Église. Chroniques d'un témoin (Paris, 1979). 122-250.
[8] Ibid, 331.
[9] Peter Hebblethwaite, Paul VI: The First Modern Pope (Paulist Press: New York / Mahwah, 1993), 394.
[10] Philip S. Kaufman, O.S.B., Why You Can Disagree ... and Remain a Faithful Catholic (New York: Crossroad, 1991), 4.

Although the Council could not discuss the issue, it still had to be mentioned in the section of *Gaudium et spes* dealing with marriage and the family. The text of this document, which had been approved by the Council by 2052 to 91 votes, did not meet with Pope Paul VI's approval and led to the 'papal bombshell' of 24 November 1965. On that day, the Mixed Commission supervising the redaction of the document received a letter from the Secretary of State in which he said: 'I announce to you that the August Pontiff desires that ... there are certain points which must of necessity be corrected ... concerning the section which treats of 'promoting the dignity of marriage and the family".[11] It then demanded explicit mention of *Casti Connubii* and Pius XII's address to midwives, and went on: 'Secondly, it is absolutely necessary that the methods and instruments used to make conception ineffectual - that is to say, the contraceptive methods which are dealt with in the encyclical *Casti Connubii* - be openly rejected; for in this matter admitting doubts, keeping silent or insinuating that such opinions may perhaps be admitted, can bring about the gravest dangers in public opinion.'[12] In the final version of *Gaudium et spes*, *Casti Connubii* is cited, but in a footnote and flanked by Pope Paul's address to the Cardinals describing the origin of the Pontifical Commission and its purpose, highlighting the fact that the matter was under review at the time.[13]

At the first plenary meeting of the full Papal Commission of 51 members, which took place in Rome from 25-29 March 1965, the question of the irreformability of the pronouncements of the Magisterium was posed, and 'many' of the members of the commission 'while recognising that it is not infallible, considered that [*Casti Connubii*] could not be put in question.'[14] However, the debates brought about a change in the minds of some members. The closing vote revealed that seven members of the theological section of the commission held for the irreformability and twelve for the reformability of the condemnation of

---

[11] Hebblethwaite, Paul VI, 443.
[12] Ibid, 563.
[13] Ibid, 445.
[14] Chiron, 332 quoting de Locht, 150.

contraception.¹⁵ In the last session, 13 April - 25 June 1966, a group of sixteen Cardinals and bishops was chosen to supervise the work and make the final decision on the documents produced. After two weeks of debate on the irreformability of the teaching of *Casti Connubii*, the members were asked to respond to two questions: '1. Is the doctrine of the encyclical irreformable? 2. Is contraception intrinsically evil in itself?' Of the nineteen theologians, only four considered the teaching of *Casti Connubii* irreformable and contraception to be intrinsically evil. 'The principal, and quasi-unique argument of these four was that the Church could not err on this point. ... In the face of this difficulty which, for them, was insurmountable, any argument about the content of the doctrine carried little weight.'¹⁶ From 19-26 June, fifteen of the sixteen Cardinals and bishops met to supervise the work of the Commission, since Bishop Karol Wojtyla was detained in Cracow. On 23 June a text written by six theologians of the 'majority' favouring the reformability of the doctrine was discussed. On 24 June, three questions were put to the vote, two of which are of interest: Is the intrinsic illiceity of every contraceptive intervention certain? 2. Can the liceity of contraceptive intervention, in the terms employed by the majority of the theological experts of the Commission, be affirmed in continuity with the Tradition and the declarations of the supreme Magisterium? To the first question, nine voted against the certainty of the intrinsic evil of contraception. For two the illiceity was certain, for one other with certain reservations, and there were three abstentions. To the second question, nine voted Yes, five No, with one abstention.¹⁷ All this simply confirms what has long been well known, that the uncertainty about this doctrine reached into the highest levels of the College of Bishops. And the experience of the Papal Commission tends to give the impression that open debate on the matter would favour a change in the doctrine, since it seems that a good number of bishops had their minds changed by the discussions.

---

[15] De Locht, 151.
[16] Ibid, 182-83.
[17] Chiron, 233.

Following the submission of the report of the Papal Commission there was a period of three years while Pope Paul VI studied the question and suffered under its weight. During this period Pope Paul insisted that the Church was not in a state of doubt on the issue. In an address to the Cardinals on 29 October 1966, Pope Paul said that the existing norm in the matter of contraception must still be followed and that it should not be considered as not binding 'as if the teaching authority of the Church were now in a state of doubt, whereas it is in a period of study and reflection.'[18] Elsewhere he said: 'One should not say the Church is in a state of doubt or is not sure of itself. The Church is well-informed on all the latest data about contraception. Maybe something has changed? In that case, let's see what science has discovered that our ancestors did not know. Let's see if something should be changed in the law.' Summarising the position, the papal press secretary, Monsignor Fausto Vallainc, said that if the Church changed its position on birth control, this would not imply doubt at any moment; it would be a change from one state of certitude to another.[19] Many people had difficulty with this, and Pope Paul's denial that doubt existed was the reason given by Charles Davis for his decision to leave the Catholic Church. According to Davis: 'The papal statement was dishonest - it was a diplomatic lie, covering over an awkward but plain fact.'[20] For Davis it was 'evident even to the world at large that the teaching authority of the Catholic Church, namely, the Pope and bishops, is ... in a state of bewildered and anxious doubt concerning the previously strongly affirmed stand against contraception. The failure to issue a clear statement after widespread questioning and years of study is sufficient proof of that.'[21] He considered the 'attempt to allow for future change without, however, admitting doubt' to be impossible, and to be 'illustrated with beautiful absurdity by the Vatican Press Officer in the statement already quoted that the Church was not

---

[18] Charles Davis, A Question of Conscience (New York: Harper & Row, 1967), 97-98.
[19] Ibid, 65-66.
[20] Ibid, 93.
[21] Ibid, 98.

in a state of doubt, but that when the Pope issued his decision it would pass from one state of certainty to another.'[22]

I suggest that the apparent absurdity of Pope Paul's position is resolved by the distinction that has been made between the Magisterium of the Church and the Magisterium of the bishops. Davis only attended to the latter, and had lost all sense of the Magisterium of the Holy Church. Pope Paul VI was solid in his conviction that the teaching of the Church could not change, and the infallibility of the Church demands no less. The One Teacher, Christ, teaching in the power of the Holy Spirit, teaches the one Truth always and everywhere. The Pope and the bishops were certainly unsure, as Davis and everyone else could see, but the Holy Church can never be unsure. Pope Paul VI was clearly envisaging the possibility of a change in the doctrine which would still be in basic continuity with what went before, and that has to be true of any legitimate change. There is a good precedent for the kind of thing involved, in Pope Pius XII's recognition that the use of the safe period would be legitimate as a means of birth control. That was a change in basic continuity with the past, a passing from one state of certainty to another. And whatever the outcome of all the discussion on this issue, that fundamental principle has to be upheld. The majority of the Papal Commission believed that the continuity of Church teaching could survive the lifting of the absolute prohibition. And they had to do so, for the infallibility of the Church is the most basic doctrine of all and must be upheld at all costs.

Then in July 1968 *Humanae vitae* was issued upholding the traditional condemnation of contraception and its reception was mixed at every level in the Church. The spokesman who presented the document to the press on behalf of the Holy See, Archbishop Fernando Lambruschini, made a statement on the occasion in which he pointed out that 'attentive reading of the encyclical *Humanae vitae* does not suggest the theological note of infallibility. ... It is not infallible.'[23] This point was also made

---

[22] Ibid, 99.
[23] 'Statement Accompanying Encyclical *Humanae vitae*,' Catholic Mind, vol. 66, no. 1225 (September 1968), 54-55.

by a number of episcopal conferences in response to the encyclical. The Austrian bishops said that *Humanae vitae* 'does not contain an infallible dogma,'[24] and the Canadian bishops that it does not contain 'any point of divine and Catholic faith.'[25] This was basically the point that was broadcast by Charles Curran and his colleagues at their press conference where they stated that 'a loyal Catholic could dissent from such noninfallible teaching.'[26] It is clear enough what these comments are referring to, but the analysis presented in this book suggests that the point made is not accurate, due to the common confusion between infallibility and definition. What is really meant, and which is true, is that Pope Paul VI did not define the doctrine in *Humanae vitae*. The issue of the infallibility of the teaching is different. Whatever the Church teaches in this matter, she teaches infallibly, for she can teach no other way. If Pope Paul VI is correct that the condemnation of contraception is the teaching of the Church, then that doctrine is taught infallibly, with the infallibility of the Church. And in that case the document would contain a point of divine and Catholic faith and an infallible dogma, contrary to what the Austrian and Canadian bishops had to say. The only way that *Humanae vitae* can fail to contain a point of divine and Catholic faith and an infallible dogma is if Pope Paul VI was wrong in his judgment as to the teaching of the Church. And, in that case, he would be guilty of a very serious misuse of his apostolic office in teaching error in the name of Christ, and the genuine teaching of the Church would then need to be uncovered and proclaimed as a matter of urgency.

One must be careful of one's language here. Consider the following comments made by two theologians. Bruno Schüller has written: 'That the Church could be faced with the necessity of revising its current

---

[24] Curran, Hunt, Dissent In and For the Church, 199.
[25] Horgan, 79.
[26] Curran, Faithful Dissent, 17.

position on contraception is difficult for many to accept.'[27] And another theologian, Joseph Komonchak wrote that

> it may be objected that if the papal position on artificial birth control is wrong, we are faced with an extremely serious doctrinal error. For many centuries the Church would have been giving incorrect moral guidance, and there are theologians who believe it impossible for the Spirit ever to permit the Church to fall that seriously into error. In reply, it can be pointed out that it is a very risky business to try to predict how much of evil (whether the evil of sin or the evil of error) God might permit to creep into the Church. There are enough cases in which the Church has been wrong in the past, and there are no *a priori* grounds on which it can be demonstrated that it could not be wrong again.[28]

The ambiguity in the meaning of the word 'Church' needs to be noted here. It is clear that Schüller and Komonchak are thinking of the empirical Catholic Church, and the mystery of the holy Church is nowhere on their minds. 'The Church,' the Body and the Bride of Christ, the Incorporation of the Holy Spirit cannot revise its position on anything. If the teaching on contraception is erroneous, then it never was and never can have been 'the teaching of the Church'. It is manifest that it has been 'the official teaching of the Catholic Church' for centuries past and continues to be so today. If that teaching is erroneous the many Popes and bishops who have been teaching it have all been systematically misusing their office and the need for correction would then be obvious.

---

[27] Bruno Schüller, S.J., 'Remarks on the Authentic Teaching of the Magisterium of the Church,' in <u>Readings in Moral Theology No. 3: The Magisterium and Morality</u>, edd. Charles E. Curran and Richard McCormick, S.J. (New York / Ramsey: Paulist Press, 1982), 14-33 at 14.
[28] Komonchak, 'Ordinary Papal Magisterium and Religious Assent,' 80-81.

It is important that this unavoidable implication of dissent be squarely faced, and the dissenter from the doctrine has to recognise what he is doing. He is effectively accusing Pope Paul VI, and Pope Pius XI and Pope Pius XII and all the Popes and bishops who have taught this doctrine, of material heresy, in teaching error in the place of Christian truth. This was a point made strongly by the theologians who wrote the Minority Report of the Papal Commission on Birth Control. They wrote:

> If contraception were declared not instrinsically evil, in honesty it would have to be acknowledged that the Holy Spirit in 1930 (*Casti Connubii*), in 1951 (address of Pius XII to mid-wives) and 1958 (address to the Society of Haematologists in the year of Pius XII's death), assisted the Protestant Churches, and that for half a century did not protect Pius XI, Pius XII and a large part of the Catholic hierarchy against a very grave error, one most pernicious to souls; for it would have suggested that they condemned most imprudently, under the pain of eternal punishment, thousands upon thousands of human acts which were now approved.[29]

The dissenter must appeal from the Pope to the Holy Church, to the Pope and the College of Bishops better informed, and, given the widespread nature of the dissent and its steady perdurance despite all the best efforts to deal with it, the only possible resolution of the situation is for a definitive judgment to be made one way or the other. The recognition of the implications of their actions in this matter is especially important for the episcopal conferences who issued statements in this sense. The episcopal conferences of Austria, Belgium, Canada, and Scandinavia, which drew attention to the option of dissent from Pope Paul's teaching, cannot simply leave the matter there. They have raised the possibility that this teaching may be erroneous and they have

---

[29] Peter Harris, et. al., On Human Life, 195.

a responsibility to ensure that the true teaching is made clear for us all. It is not acceptable to cast doubt on Pope Paul's teaching without making any effort to correct the situation, if he is wrong.

A Dogmatic Definition

If it is accepted that a definitive judgment is necessary, it is good to be clear that such a definitive statement has not yet been made, contrary to what has been suggested at the highest level. In 1997 the Pontifical Council for the Family issued a *Vademecum for Confessors Concerning some Aspects of the Morality of Conjugal Life*, in which it was stated at § 2.4: 'The Church has always taught the intrinsic evil of contraception, that is, of every marital act intentionally rendered unfruitful. This teaching is to be held as definitive and irreformable.' The Council is stating its conviction that this teaching is the genuine teaching of the Church, and that it is therefore irreformable. However, when it says that the teaching is to be held 'as definitive', it must be speaking loosely, for it is clear to all that the teaching has not been defined, in the relevant technical sense. The Holy See has been working to support the doctrine in the Church all these years. Pope John Paul II has reiterated the doctrine on many occasions. Charles Curran was disciplined for his dissent from this teaching, among others. It is well known that acceptance of the doctrine of the Holy See in this matter, indeed on all matters of consequence, is one of the criteria demanded of candidates for episcopal office.[30] All this makes clear the strong conviction of the Holy See in the matter, but it does not constitute a dogmatic definition. From the nature of the case, a dogmatic definition will be obvious to all. It is a clear statement by an ecumenical council or a Pope speaking with his own authority which settles an issue definitively, once and for all. And that has not yet been done.

There are two main arguments currently in use against the possibility of such a dogmatic definition. There are those who argue that the failure

---

[30] On this see Thomas J. Reese, S. J., <u>Archbishop: Inside the Power Structure of the American Catholic Church</u> (San Francisco: Harper & Row, 1989), 32-35.

to make a dogmatic definition of an absolute moral norm, implies the recognition by the Church that such a thing is impossible. One moral theologian, Bernhard Fraling interprets this as a deliberate renunciation on the part of the Church, and contends that if the Church were convinced that such matters belonged to the core of the deposit of faith, she could not have behaved in this way.[31] It has already been argued in this book that the moral doctrine of the Church belongs fully to the deposit of faith. There is only One Teacher in the Church, Christ our Lord, and he teaches the whole Gospel as a unitary whole, and the moral teaching of the Church belongs with full right to the essential core. One can also ask if it is reasonable to interpret the lack of definition of moral matters as a deliberate choice, for there is an alternative, and to me more plausible explanation. Until 1968 there has never been an occasion when a definitive judgment was needed. When Pope Pius XI rather solemnly recalled the Church's prohibition of contraception in *Casti Connubii*, it was received without any notable difficulty by the Church at large. The large-scale rejection of Pope Paul's encyclical represents a completely new situation in the Church. One can go along with Fraling to the extent certainly that the Church now faces the obvious option of making a definitive judgment in moral matters, and it now seems urgently necessary in a way that it has never done before. If the failure to make a definitive judgment continues indefinitely, one might begin to see the force of Fraling's argument, but for the moment it seems to me that Fraling is being precipitate in arguing from the *non esse* to the *non posse*, and that only a definitive judgment can clear the air.

A new obstacle to a possible definition has recently been brought forward by the Congregation for the Doctrine of the Faith. In the *Commentary on the Profession of Faith of 1989* the Congregation suggests

---

[31] Bernhard Fraling, 'Hypertrophie lehramtlicher Autorität in Dingen der Moral? Zur Frage der Zuständigkeit des Lehramtes aus moral-theologischer Sicht', in Lehramt und Sexualmoral (Düsseldorf: Patmos, 1990), 95-129 at 127.

that the Magisterium of the Church can teach a doctrine 'to be held *definitively* with an act which is ... *non-defining*.'[32] It explains:

> *Such a doctrine can be confirmed or reaffirmed by the Roman Pontiff, even without recourse to a solemn definition*, by declaring explicitly that it belongs to the teaching of the ordinary and universal Magisterium ... Consequently, when there has not been a solemn form of a definition, but this doctrine ... is taught by the ordinary and universal Magisterium, ... such a doctrine is to be understood as having been set forth infallibly. The declaration of *confirmation* or *reaffirmation* by the Roman Pontiff in this case is not a new dogmatic definition, but a formal attestation of a truth already possessed and infallibly transmitted by the Church.[33]

The then Secretary of the Congregation, Archbishop (now Cardinal) Bertone, explained why this new procedure was adopted. He gave the encyclicals *Veritatis splendor* and *Evangelium vitae* and the apostolic letter *Ordinatio sacerdotalis* as examples of this new non-defining definition, and offered the reason: 'If we were to hold that the Pope must necessarily make an *ex cathedra* definition whenever he intends to declare a doctrine as definitive because it belongs to the deposit of faith, it would imply an underestimation of the ordinary, universal Magisterium, and infallibility would be limited to the solemn definitions of the Pope or a Council, in a way that differs from the teaching of Vatican I and Vatican II, which attribute an infallible character to the teachings of the ordinary, universal Magisterium.' The Pope simply

---

[32] Congregation for the Doctrine of the Faith, 'Commentary on the Concluding Formula of the 'Professio fidei'', AAS 90 (1998) 547; L'Osservatore Romano (Eng. Ed.), 15 July 1998, 4. (Emmphasis in the original.)

[33] Ibid, 547-48. This new doctrine had appeared earlier in Cardinal Ratzinger's Introduction to Dall''Inter Insigniores' all''Ordinatio sacerdotalis': Documenti e commenti by the Congregation for the Doctrine of the Faith, Libreria Editrice Vaticana, 1996, 19.

'formally declares that this doctrine already belongs to the faith of the Church and is infallibly taught by the ordinary universal Magisterium as divinely revealed or to be held in a definitive way.' Cardinal Bertone concludes: 'In the light of these considerations, it seems a pseudo-problem to wonder whether this papal act of *confirming* a teaching of the ordinary, universal Magisterium is infallible or not. In fact, although it is not *per se* a *dogmatic definition* (like the Trinitarian dogma of Nicaea, the Christological dogma of Chalcedon or the Marian dogmas), a papal pronouncement of *confirmation* enjoys the same infallibility as the teaching of the ordinary, universal Magisterium, which includes the Pope not as a mere Bishop but as the Head of the Episcopal College.'[34]

One has to suggest here that the problem posed by the interpretation of these papal interventions is not 'pseudo' but real. The most obvious difficulty is that a non-defining definition is a contradiction in terms. The act is either a definition or it is not. Confirming and reaffirming the teaching of the ordinary Magisterium is what the Pope does all the time, in any teaching document. There is nothing else the Pope can do, for the teaching of the ordinary Magisterium covers the whole range of Christian truth. What differentiates the extraordinary from the ordinary Magisterium is precisely definition, and, if the Pope does not define the doctrine, his act is another act of the ordinary Magisterium and, effectively, nothing is changed by it. Cardinal Bertone argues that making a definition would underestimate the ordinary Magisterium, so that infallibility would be limited to definitions. This is not so. The definitions of all the Councils in no way underestimated the infallibility of the ordinary Magisterium, as this argument would seem to suggest that they did. There is the widespread confusion at work here between definition and infallibility. What a definition adds is simply definition, not infallibility. The ordinary Magisterium of the Church is infallible in all that it teaches, but, from the nature of the case, it is incapable of definition. Definition is only possible by an act of an ecumenical

---

[34] Archbishop Tarcisio Bertone, 'A proposito della recezione dei Documenti del Magistero e del dissenso pubblico,' L'Oss. Rom. (December 20, 1996) 1, col. 5-6; 5, col. 4-6; 'Theological Observations by Archbishop Bertone,' L'Oss. Rom [English ed.] (January 29, 1997) 6-7 at 6, col. 3.

Council or the Pope, acting on behalf of the College of Bishops as a whole. Whatever procedure is used, it has to be declared to be, and easily seen to be, a definition.

The confusion here has been occasioned by a formula introduced quite late into the text of *Lumen gentium* § 25, when it taught that the worldwide episcopate enjoys the charism of infallibility when it teaches a doctrine 'to be held definitively'. Cardinal Ratzinger refers to the matter in his *Introduction*: 'According to the definition of Vat. I and the teaching of Vat. II in LG 25, the Magisterium of the Pope enjoys the charism of infallibility when it proclaims *with a definitive act* a doctrine regarding faith and morals. The entire episcopal body enjoys the same infallibility, when, conserving the bond of communion within itself and with the Successor of Peter, it teaches a judgement to be held definitively. This means that the Magisterium can teach a doctrine regarding faith and morals as *definitive*, either with a *definitive act (solemn judgement)* or with an *act which does not have the form of a definition*.'[35] Cardinal Ratzinger takes it that the situations are identical, when a Pope or a council defines a doctrine or the when the worldwide episcopate teaches a doctrine 'to be held definitively'. It is not so, however. Teaching a doctrine 'to be held definitively' is not at all the same thing as defining a doctrine. The worldwide episcopate in its ordinary teaching teaches the faith of the Church which is to be held definitively in all its parts. The worldwide episcopate, however, cannot *teach* anything definitively apart from an ecumenical council. Holding a doctrine definitively means holding it firmly and with unshakeable certainty, and we all do this with the whole teaching of the Church. Teaching a doctrine definitively means crafting a definite and clear formulation and making a final judgment about it. These are two quite different things, and this choice of the word '*definitive*' in this sentence of *Lumen gentium* § 25 embodies the confusion between infallibility and definition and is not helpful at all. The confusion appears in another statement of the Congregation for

---

[35] Introduction to Dall''Inter Insigniores' all''Ordinatio sacerdotalis': Documenti e commenti by the Congregation for the Doctrine of the Faith, Libreria Editrice Vaticana, 1996, 19.

the Doctrine of the Faith: 'The essential point is that *the Magisterium can teach a doctrine infallibly without necessarily having recourse to the form of a (solemn) definition*.'[36] This is true. The Magisterium of the Holy Church teaches everything that it teaches infallibly; it can do no other. But it cannot teach *definitively* without a definition.

And the implications of this confusion entered into by the Congregation for the Doctrine of the Faith are serious indeed. The logic of this position is that the College of Bishops is never again to define doctrine for fear of undermining the infallibility of the Church. This is Hirscher's mistake in reverse with consequences even more serious than Hirscher first envisaged. For now the College of Bishops is being encouraged to avoid the most important single act they are empowered to perform in the exercise of their Magisterium. The Bishops must remember that they are not infallible, individually or collectively. The bishops of the Church are one and all sinful and fallible men. The infallibility of the Church belongs exclusively to God, to the one Teacher Christ and his Holy Spirit. The bishops of the Church participate in that infallibility when they teach the truth of Christ authentically, that is accurately and truly. The one thing the bishops are empowered to do is to define doctrine, so that it is made clear to all without any possibility of ambiguity what the teaching of the Church in a given matter really is. When that happens the subjective certainty of faith which we all have all the time, is transformed into the objective ecclesial certainty which is only available when doctrines are defined. And one has to protest against this new policy which would deprive us all of that objective certainty to which we are entitled in certain critical circumstances, when the normal consensus is not available in the Church as a whole. This does not undermine the force of the universal magisterium but supports and confirms it. It is never the function of a definition to propose a new formulation but always to confirm an existing certainty. The formulation emerges through the process of development of the

---

[36] "Some Brief Responses to Questions Regarding the *Professio Fidei*," in Proclaiming the Truth of Jesus Christ: Papers from the Vallombrosa Meeting (Washington, D.C.: United States Catholic Conference, 2000), 31-48 at 62.

deposit of faith, often in response to the denial of a certainty already existing implicitly, and the function of the extraordinary magisterium is to make a definitive judgment of the truth of the formulation already in place.

And this new 'non-defining definition' simply does not work in practice. Pope Pius XI, in *Casti Connubii*, 'confirmed and reaffirmed' the teaching of the ordinary and universal Magisterium in the matter of contraception and it did not constitute a definition. Pope Paul VI, in *Humanae vitae* 'confirmed and reaffirmed' the ordinary and universal Magisterium again, and it still did not constitute a definition. When a definition is required, no amount of ordinary confirmation and reaffirmation will produce one; only a definition can do it. This is the truth in Hirscher's original insight, that there is an inevitable margin for error and discussion in the formulation of the teaching of the ordinary and universal Magisterium. The teaching is infallible in all its parts, with the infallibility of the One Teacher, but our assimilation of it is subject to the fallibility our darkened intellects. It is being argued here that the situation in the Church has reached a critical stage in regard to the teaching of *Humanae vitae* and the moral doctrine of the Church in general. There is much confusion, division and uncertainty in these matters, and this is not how it should be in the Church of God. The College of Bishops has a serious responsibility to take the matter in hand and resolve this situation. Clear and definitive statements of the Church's moral doctrine are called for so that we can all know one way or the other what the teaching of the Church in this area truly is.

Part 2

Defining the Truth about Contraception

There is another aspect of definition which is most relevant here. Definition occurs on two levels, on the level of understanding and on the level of judgment. In order to be defined a doctrine must be stated clearly and authoritatively. It must be clear that the doctrine is being stated definitively, with no possibility of appeal. This is definition on the level of judgment, and is a matter of a decision made by the responsible authority in question, whether it be an ecumenical council or a Pope. Definition on the level of understanding is different. This means that the doctrine is understood clearly and distinctly so that no one can have any doubt as to what is meant. This is not simply a matter of a decision by the responsible authority but is the work of theology, and it can require many years and even centuries for its achievement. The suggestion to be made here is that the effort has already twice been made to define the truth about contraception at the level of judgment, but that these efforts have failed because the matter is not yet clearly defined at the level of understanding.

At the time of its issuance there was a considerable body of opinion which held that the statement of Pope Pius XI in *Casti connubii* represented an infallible definition of the immorality of contraception.[1] The Pope did speak in most solemn terms to the effect that 'the Catholic Church, to whom God has entrusted the defence of the integrity and purity of morals, standing erect in the midst of the moral ruin which surrounds her, in order that she may preserve the chastity of the nuptial union from being defiled by this foul stain, raises her voice in token of her divine ambassadorship and through Our mouth proclaims anew ...'[2] One could reasonably interpret this as introducing a statement *ex cathedra* on a matter of faith and morals to be held by all the faithful. Despite this solemnity of the declaration, however, it will be argued that the document fails in the other essential condition of an infallible definition, that it clearly define the doctrine being proclaimed along the lines of the genuine Christian tradition.

And again there is a certain body of opinion which would see Pope Paul VI's statement in *Humanae vitae* as such an infallible definition.[3] And there is a certain plausibility to this interpretation, for Pope Paul made his statement with considerable solemnity and he was speaking to the whole world, and the whole world was listening to a degree greater than for any papal statement ever made before. Again it will be argued that, despite its apparent Gallic clarity, *Humanae vitae* did not clearly define the doctrine at the level of understanding, so that it was unambiguously clear what the teaching of the Church in the matter truly is and why it is so.

There are four questions to which clear answers must be given before definition is achieved. What is contraception? Is it wrong? If it is wrong, Why is it wrong? and How do we know that it is wrong? Two of these questions, Is it wrong?, and How do we know it is wrong?, refer to the level of judgment. And two of these questions, What is contraception?, and Why is it wrong?, refer to the level of understanding. It will be

---

[1] The opinions are recorded in J. C. Ford, S.J. and G. Kelly, S.J., *Contemporary Moral Theology: II. Marriage Questions* (Cork: The Mercier Press, 1963), 263-70.
[2] DS 3717.
[3] See, for instance, Ermengildo Lio, o. f. m., *Humanae vitae e infallibilità: Paulo VI, il Concilio, e Giovanni Paulo II* (Città del Vaticano: Libreria Editrice Vaticana, 1986).

suggested here that there is confusion about what contraception is, about why it is wrong, and about how we know that it is wrong, and these confusions must be cleared up before a definition is possible that can clear the air in the Church.

Chapter 17

The Procreative Principle

An essential part of the process of defining the moral status of contraception is the definition of just what the act of contraception consists in. Is contraception a sexual act or an act against life? Most of those discussing the issue currently understand contraception to be a sexual act. The Minority Working Paper of the Papal Commission on Birth Control gave the following definition: '*Contraception* is understood by the Church as any use of the marriage right in the exercise of which the act is deprived of its natural power for the procreation of life through human intervention.'[1] According to Elizabeth Anscombe the traditional teaching is that 'you turn copulation into a wrong and shameful act if before or during or after the act you do something that you suppose destroys the possibility of conception and do this in order to destroy that possibility.'[2] William E. May gives a definition along the same lines: 'Contraception ...entails (a) the choice to have intercourse and (b) the choice to get rid if whatever procreativity results in this act of intercourse.

---

[1] "The Minority Working Paper, 23 May 1966," in Peter Harris, et. al., On Human Life, 170.

[2] G. E. M. Anscombe, "You Can have Sex without Children: Christianity and the New Offer," *Ethics, Religion and Politics* (Minneapolis: University of Minnesota Press, 1981), 82-96 at 84.

One can thus rightfully speak of contraceptive intercourse ...'[3] Martin Rhonheimer writes: '*Contraception* is, objectively and essentially, an integral part of one's sexual behaviour...'[4] And Janet E. Smith has the same view: 'As is well known, the Church has always taught that contraception belongs in the same class as masturbation, and so on, since all these acts are considered to be perverted sexual acts.'[5] It could even be argued that this position constitutes the official teaching of the Church based on *Evangelium vitae* § 13, which teaches that 'contraception ... contradicts the full truth of the sexual act as the proper expression of conjugal love [and] is opposed to the virtue of chastity in marriage...'

Cognate with this understanding of what contraception is, the reason given for the judgment of the immorality of the action is its failure properly to respect the procreative purpose of sexual intercourse, and this reason is given in the papal teaching on the matter. The section on contraception in *Casti connubii* is remarkably short and very little background or explanation is given. The central affirmations can be quickly reviewed. Pope Pius prefaces his solemn condemnation of contraception with a one-sentence rationale: 'Since, therefore, the conjugal act is destined by nature for the begetting of children, those who in exercising it deliberately frustrate its natural power and purpose sin against nature and commit a deed which is shameful and intrinsically vicious.'[6] He then proceeds immediately to his solemn declaration that 'any use whatsoever of matrimony exercised in such a way that the act is deliberately (*de industria hominum*) frustrated in its natural power to generate life is an offence against the law of God and of nature, and those who indulge in such are branded with the guilt of a grave sin.'[7]

---

[3] William E. May, *Sex, Marriage and Chastity: Reflections of a Catholic Layman, Spouse and Parent* (Chicago, Illinois: Franciscan Herald Press, 1981), 114.

[4] Martin Rhonheimer, *Etica de la procreación* (Madrid: Ediciones Rialp, S. A., 2004), 141.

[5] Smith, *Humanae Vitae*, 360.

[6] DS 3716.

[7] DS 3717.

The ground for the condemnation of contraception is the procreative purpose of sexual intercourse.

In *Humanae vitae*, Pope Paul VI formulates one of the central principles of his argument as follows: 'The Church, nevertheless, in urging men to the observance of the precepts of the natural law, which it interprets by its constant doctrine, teaches that each and every marital act must of necessity retain its intrinsic relationship (*per se destinatus permaneat*) to the procreation of human life.' (*Humanae vitae*, § 11) And what is arguably his central principle is his teaching about the inseparable connection between the two meanings of sexual intercourse. Pope Paul VI stated that the teaching of the Church in this matter 'is based on the inseparable connection, established by God, which man on his own initiative may not break, between the unitive significance and the procreative significance which are both inherent to the marriage act.' (*Humanae vitae*, § 12) Much more will need to be said about this inseparability principle in due course, but for the moment I simply state that I agree with Richard McCormick's view that it is basically a development of the traditional procreative principle.[8] If this is correct, it would appear that Pope Paul VI, like Pope Pius XI earlier, is basing his condemnation of contraception on the basis of its failure to properly respect the procreative purpose of sexual intercourse.

The Establishment of the Procreative Principle

The argument to be made here is that the procreative principle is ultimately unsuccessful in grounding the moral judgment on contraception. In order to do that it is necessary first to review the development of the principle and to establish that this principle did not in fact ground the original judgment of the Church in this matter and that, therefore, its ultimate failure should come as no real surprise. The analysis of the establishment of the procreative principle in its role as justifying the condemnation of contraception can be focussed on

---

[8] Richard McCormick, S. J., *The Critical Calling: Reflections on Moral Dilemmas since Vatican II* (Washington, D. C.: Georgetown University Press, 1989), 214.

three determinative stages; the initial establishment of the traditional teaching on contraception and the role of the procreative principle, if any, at that stage, the highly influential contribution of St. Augustine, and the synthesis made by St. Thomas.

The First Three Centuries

Early on, Noonan provides a valuable summary of what he calls the 'Scriptural structure' of the doctrine on contraception. He asserts that the New Testament doctrine on sexuality, 'in which the rule on contraception is born,' can be reduced to eight themes: 'the superiority of virginity; the institutional goodness of marriage; the sacral character of sexual intercourse; the value of procreation; the significance of desire as well as act; the evil of extramarital intercourse and the unnaturalness of homosexuality; the connection of Adam's sin and the rebelliousness of the body; the evil of "medicine."'[9] He reviews the relevant texts and concludes: 'These particular texts of the New Testament on virginity, marriage, intercourse, sin, "medicine," provide the basis from which the doctrine on contraception is developed.'[10] He correctly notes that contraception is not mentioned anywhere in the New Testament, and that none of the topics directly relevant to the subject, 'the intention with which intercourse in marriage may be sought; the lawfulness of marriage by the sterile; the role of pleasure in marriage,'[11] were mentioned either. And yet he remains confident that the doctrine on contraception emerged from this matrix. He is quite clear that it was influenced by the religious, philosophical and social context of the time, and he writes: 'Within the intellectual and social context of the Roman Empire, the vital acts of selection, discrimination, emphasis, and application of the biblical texts were performed. In this collaboration between the Christian community and the written word, under the

---

[9] John T. Noonan, *Contraception: A History of Its Treatment by the Catholic Theologians and Canonists* (Cambridge, Mass.: Harvard University Press, 1965), 37.
[10] Ibid, 45.
[11] Ibid.

pressures generated by Roman life, the teaching on contraception took shape."[12]

He places a particular emphasis on the role of the Stoics, "whose influence, if more transitory, was as real as that of Scripture."[13] The Stoic approach to sexuality had a particular appeal for the early Christian moralists. The Stoic watchwords were nature, virtue, decorum, freedom from excess, and the early Fathers were happy to make use of them in their turn. The Stoics were suspicious of the role of passion in marriage and sought a more solid basis for its primordial role in human life. 'Plainly that basis was its necessary part in the propagation of the race. By this standard of rational purposefulness, self-evident and supplied by nature, excess in marital intercourse might be measured. This view of marriage was to seem right and good to many Christians.'[14] Thus did the norm of the essential procreative end of sex and marriage first enter Christian moral thinking. The Stoic philosophers taught that marital intercourse is morally right only if its purpose is procreative and that, therefore, intercourse for pleasure, even within marriage, is reprehensible.[15] Noonan concludes his analysis as follows: 'If one asks, then, where the Christian Fathers derived their notions on marital intercourse — notions which have no express biblical basis — the answer must be, chiefly from the Stoics. ... It is not a matter of men expressing simple truths which common sense might suggest to anyone with open eyes. It is a matter of a doctrine consciously appropriated. The descent is literary, the dependence substantial.'[16] And not alone was the general doctrine on sexual morality strongly influenced by the Stoic theories, but 'the doctrine on contraception, as it was fashioned, largely depended on them.'[17] It is a view that Noonan repeats regularly throughout his book, that the doctrine on contraception emerged as a response to the conditions of the time, and mainly under the influence

---

[12] Ibid, 45-46.
[13] Ibid, 46.
[14] Ibid.
[15] Ibid, 47.
[16] Ibid, 48.
[17] Ibid, 49.

of Stoic doctrine. He notes correctly that the Stoic marital ethic was generally accepted, in the West at least, and goes on: 'If intercourse when nature itself prevented impregnation was wicked, it would seem, a fortiori, that intercourse would have been regarded as seriously sinful when a human agency made fruitful insemination impossible. Contraception stood condemned by the express conditions required for any lawful intercourse.'[18] [I have stuff about the logic somewhere else.] He concludes his summary of the early development as follows: 'The position of the first three centuries on contraception is, then, enmeshed with the Alexandrian commitment to the Stoic rule on procreative purpose and the Stoic view of nature.'[19]

There is a problem with this interpretation which was adverted to by John Finnis, who wrote:

> A constant theme of Noonan's book is that the condemnation of contraception somehow followed from the condemnation of intercourse engaged in without procreative purpose. He never stops to consider how wholly implausible it is to assert that the grave sinfulness of contraception, universally taught, somehow followed from the venial sinfulness of lack of procreative intent in intercourse, taught by some but only some of the Church's teachers. Nor does he show us any theologian at any time making the connection that he treats as virtually the key to the whole matter.[20]

There is no doubt, as Noonan points out, that the Stoic doctrine of the necessity of procreative intent for lawful intercourse immediately implies, *a fortiori*, the wrongfulness of contraception. But it is also true, as Finnis observes and on the basis of the evidence in Noonan's own book, that not a single Church Father of any period made that

---

[18] Ibid, 77.
[19] Ibid, 104. See also 56.
[20] John Finnis, '*Humanae Vitae*: Its Background and Aftermath' *International Review of Natural Family Planning* (1981), 141-53 at 151.

connection. The issue at stake here is not hard to discern. If it were true that the condemnation of contraception were to any degree dependent on the Stoic condemnation of the lack of procreative intent in intercourse, it would follow that, when the error of the Stoic position is discerned the condemnation of contraception loses, to that degree, its solid foundation. For it is now evident and generally accepted that a procreative intent is not necessary for the justification of sexual intercourse. However, the fact of the matter remains that the Stoic formulation of the evident reality that marriage and sexuality have a procreative purpose had no impact whatever on the formation of the moral norm about contraception. The genuine foundation of the moral norm lies in the other stream of tradition dealing with the protection of human life in its origins, and that point will be established in the second part of the book. In the meantime, the mistaken establishment of the procreative principle as foundational to the doctrine needs to be explained, and the key figure in that process was St. Augustine.

St Augustine on the Procreative Purpose[21]

St. Augustine first developed his ideas on sex and marriage at the very beginning of his writing career, in his polemic against the Manichees who believed that procreation is evil. Rebutting this error, St. Augustine formulated his position that not alone is procreation a fundamental human good, but that it is the very reason for marriage, even the only reason for marriage. In one text he reminds the Manichees of their avoidance of intercourse after menstruation because that is taken to be the time when the woman is fertile, and so procreation can be avoided. From this it follows, he argues, that, for them, marriage is not for the procreation of children but to satisfy sexual desire. He affirms his doctrine that marriage is for the procreation of children,

---

[21] As well as Noonan, helpful on St. Augustine is Louis Janssens, 'Morale conjugale et progestogènes,' *Ephemerides Theologicae Lovanienses* 39 (1963), 787-826 at 794-803 and 'Chasteté conjugale selon l'encyclique *Casti connubii* et suivant la Constitution Pastorale *Gaudium et spes*', *Ephemerides Theologicae Lovaniensis* 42 (1966), 513-54 at 517-29.

and concludes with one of his pithy aphorisms: 'If there is a wife there is matrimony. But there is no matrimony where motherhood is avoided; for then there is no wife.'[22] He brings forward different arguments. He finds a first reason in the etymology of the word *matrimonium*: 'Marriage (*matrimonium*) is so called because a woman marries for no other reason than to become a mother (*mater*)'[23] He invokes the universal conviction that 'the value of marriage for all peoples and all men is generation.'[24] But he stresses particularly the Roman tradition, from which the Christians took the marriage contract (*tabulae nuptiales*) which declared that procreation is the *raison d'être* of marriage and which was recited at the wedding ceremony and signed by the bisho[25] It is to be noted immediately that St. Augustine is drawing all his substantive arguments in this matter from natural considerations based on reason alone, no doubt influenced by the Stoic doctrine with which he was familiar, although he never explicitly adverts to it. He does add some putative arguments from Scripture, but they cannot really be taken seriously. He refers to 1 Tim 5:14: 'So I would have younger widows marry, bear children, rule their households, and give the enemy no occasion to revile us,' and suggests that this text represents support from St. Paul for the thesis that generation is the reason for marriage.[26] In his interpretation of Gen 2:18: 'Then the LORD God said, "It is not good that the man should be alone; I will make him a helper fit for him."', St. Augustine eliminates all other possible interpretations in order to conclude that procreation is the sole motive for God's granting a helpmate to man.[27] St. Augustine's position on this matter is manifestly

---

[22] 'Si enim uxor est, matrimonium est. Non autem matrimonium est ubi datur opera ne sit mater: non igitur uxor.' *De moribus ecclesiae catholicae*, lib. 2, c. 18, 65, CSEL 90, ??; PL 32, 1373.

[23] 'Matrimonium quippe ex hoc appelatum est, quod non ob aliud debeat femina nubere, quam ut mater fiat.' *Contra Faustum*, XIX, c. 26 (PL 42, 365).

[24] 'Bonum igitur nuptiarum per omnes gentes atque omnes homines in causa generandi est.' *De bono coniugali*, c. 24, n. 32 (PL 40, 395).

[25] *Sermo* 332, n. 4 (PL 38, 1463) ; *De moribus Ecclesiae et Manichaeorum*, c. 18, n. 65 (PL 32, 1372).

[26] *De bono coniugali*, c. 24, n. 32 (PL 40, 394.)

[27] *De genesi ad litteram* IX, c. 5, n. 9 (PL 34, 396.)

clear, that 'the propagation of children is the first and natural and legitimate reason for marriage,'[28] and he makes the point repeatedly.[29] It is equally clear that this proposition is based on reason alone, and has no solid scriptural foundation whatever.

In fact the only truly relevant Scriptural witness seems to contradict the Augustinian doctrine, for is the attribution of this exclusively procreative significance to sexual intercourse not opposed to the order of St. Paul that a husband should give her due to his wife and the wife to her husband (1 Cor 7:3) with no reference to procreation at all? St. Paul says: 'Do not deprive one another, except perhaps for a limited time, that you may devote yourselves to prayer; but then come together again, so that Satan may not tempt you because of your lack of self-control. Now, as a concession, not as a command, I say this.' (1 Cor 7:5-6). Despite St. Paul's advice which bears no reference whatever to procreative intent, St. Augustine still holds that to seek intercourse beyond the need of procreation is a venial sin. He finds a justification in the last clause quoted, which he knew as '*Dico secundum indulgentiam* or *veniam*' (1 Cor 7:6) Following the interpretation of St. Jerome, he translated *venia* as pardon and concludes that where there is pardon there is sin: '*Neque enim conceditur secundum veniam, nisi peccatum*'[30] And St. Augustine finds this sin in intercourse sought beyond the limits or procreation.[31] Is St. Augustine's insistence that first natural and legitimate cause of marriage is procreation not against St. Paul's teaching that marriage is a remedy for incontinence in 1 Cor 7:1-6? St. Augustine sees no contradiction and continues to insist that absolute primacy of procreation.[32]

Some ten years later, in his argument with Faustus, a Manichean bishop, he repeats the point:

---

[28] 'Propagatio itaque filiorum ipsa est prima et naturalis et legitima causa nuptiarum' (*De coniugiis adulterinis*, II, 12, 12 (PL 40, 479).
[29] Janssens, 'Chasteté conjugale,' 519-20.
[30] *Contra Faustum*, XXX, c. 5 (PL 42, 494).
[31] *De bono coniugali*, c. 10, n. 11 (PL 40, 381).
[32] Janssens, 'Chasteté conjugale.' 522-23.

> For what you most of all detest in marriage is that children be procreated, and so you make your Auditors adulterers of their wives when they take care lest the women with whom they copulate conceive. They take wives according to the laws of matrimony by tablets announcing that the marriage is contracted to procreate children; and then, fearing because of your law, lest they infect a particle of God with the foulness of their flesh, they copulate in a shameful union only to satisfy lust for their wives. They are unwilling to have children, on whose account alone marriages are made.[33]

At another point in the same book, he makes the point again with one small addition. He affirms his fundamental premise that marriage is only for procreation, and continues: 'But the perverse law of the Manichees commands that progeny above all be avoided by those having intercourse, lest their God, whom they complain is bound in every seed, should be bound more tightly in what a woman conceives. Therefore their God by a shameful slip is poured out rather than bound by a cruel connection.'[34] The 'shameful slip' is obviously a reference to *coitus interruptus*, but it is clear that the method of avoiding procreation is not relevant to St. Augustine's argument; it applies equally to periodic abstinence as to any other method of controlling procreation. Twenty years later again, in a book on divorce and remarriage, *De nuptiis et concupiscentia*, St. Augustine repeats this doctrine: 'It is lawless and shameful to lie with one's wife where conception of offspring is avoided. This is what Onan, the son of Judah, did, and God killed him for it. You may marry to give an outlet for your incontinence, but you ought not to temper your evil so that you exterminate the good of

---

[33] *Contra Faustum* 15.7, CSEL 25¹: 429-30. Translation from John T. Noonan, *Contraception: A History of Its Treatment by the Catholic Theologians and Canonists* (Cambridge, Mass.: Harvard University Press, 1965), 122.

[34] *Contra Faustum* 22.30; CSEL 25¹:624. Translation from John T. Noonan, *Contraception: A History of Its Treatment by the Catholic Theologians and Canonists* (Cambridge, Mass.: Harvard University Press, 1965), 121.

marriage, that is, the propagation of children'[35] Noonan tells us that this 'is the first use of the fate of Onan by a prominent theologian as an argument against contraception in marriage.' And he adds that 'Augustine's main objection rests on his teaching on the procreative purpose of marriage.'[36] Noonan's latter point is obviously true, but his first point is not quite accurate. St. Augustine does not use the Onan story as an argument against contraception precisely. He uses it as an argument against the avoidance of procreation by any means, including the periodic abstinence he was familiar with from his Manichean days.

It is worth pausing here to reflect on the implications of this. It has already been noted that the very first application of the procreative principle of sexual morality by the Stoic philosophers was a mistake. The notion that a procreative intention was required to justify intercourse, though it was accepted by most of the early Fathers and continued to be relied upon for 1,500 years was eventually uncovered as erroneous. Now, St. Augustine applies the principle in his turn, and immediately comes up with an erroneous result. We now know that St. Augustine was wrong to conclude from the fact that marriage and sexual intercourse have procreation as an end, that the avoidance of procreation is morally wrong and that it destroys marriage. We now know that the avoidance of procreation can be a perfectly legitimate goal within marriage when the circumstances call for it. On this Noonan comments: 'In the history of the thought of theologians on contraception, it is, no doubt, piquant that the first pronouncement on contraception by the most influential theologian teaching on such matters should be such a vigorous attack on the one method of avoiding procreation accepted by the twentieth-century Catholic theologians as morally lawful.'[37] More than piquant; it is a very serious matter. That St. Augustine's first application of the procreative principle in the matter of contraception should be mistaken is surely a sign that something is fundamentally wrong here. And what sense can now be made of Augustine's principle that 'there is no

---

[35] De adulterinis coniugiis, 2. 12.12, CSEL 41, 396.
[36] Noonan, Contraception, 138.
[37] Ibid, 120.

matrimony where motherhood is avoided'? This can only be understood as rhetoric, and very dangerous rhetoric at that. St. Augustine was well aware in other places that marriage is formed by the consent of man and woman and that it is indissoluble. To suggest that any choices of the spouses can break that union is to demean marriage, and is a serious mistake. The conclusion cannot be avoided that St. Augustine was doubly wrong here. He was wrong to exaggerate the importance of procreation in marriage, and he was wrong to underestimate the solidity of marriage. We can say that nothing good has come from the procreative principle so far, and much that is wrong and has caused trouble in the Church, and is still wreaking havoc among us.

At around the same time, 419-20, as he wrote *De adulterinis coniugiis*, St. Augustine wrote another book on marriage, *De nuptiis et consupiscentiae*. In this book also, the topic of contraception comes up in passing, and as Noonan tells us: 'It is the only passage in Augustine dealing with artificial contraceptives.'[38] It is also by far the most famous, for it entered the traditional collections under the incipit *Aliquando*. St. Augustine is making this larger point we have met already that avoiding procreation in sexual relations voids marriage. He writes:

> I am supposing that then, although you are not lying for the sake of procreating offspring, you are not for the sake of lust obstructing their procreation by an evil prayer or an evil deed. Those who do this, although they are called husband and wife, are not; nor do they retain any reality of marriage, but with a respectable name cover a shame. ... Assuredly if both husband and wife are like this, they are not married, and if they were like this from the beginning they come together not joined in matrimony but in seduction. If both are not like this, I dare to say that either the wife is in a fashion

---

[38] Ibid, 136.

the harlot of her husband or he is an adulterer with his own wife.[39]

In the middle of this passage, at the '...', St. Augustine digresses and speaks of couples whose determination to avoid offspring leads to the practice of contraception, abortion or infanticide.

> They give themselves away, indeed, when they go so far as to expose the children who are born to them against their will; for they hate to nourish or to have those whom they feared to bear. Therefore a dark iniquity rages against those whom they unwillingly have borne, and with open iniquity this comes to light; a hidden shame is demonstrated by manifest cruelty. Sometimes [*Aliquando*] this lustful cruelty, or cruel lust, comes to this, that they even procure poisons of sterility, and, if these do not work, extinguish and destroy the fetus in some way in the womb, preferring that their offspring die before it lives, or if it was already alive in the womb to kill it before it was born.[40]

Noonan's comment on this passage needs to be reviewed. He writes:

> This vehement passage ... is a fundamental text. It is the only passage in Augustine dealing with artificial contraceptives. ... It provided later canon law with its term for contraceptives, "poisons of sterility." Under the heading *Aliquando*, it was to become the medieval locus classicus on contraception. Formally, unequivocally, passionately, Augustine here condemned contraception practiced by the married.[41] ... The "homicide" argument favored by Jerome and Chrysostom is not

---

[39] *De nuptiis et concupiscentia* 1.15.17, CSEL 42:229-30.
[40] Ibid.
[41] Noonan, Contraception, 136.

> relied on. There is a close association in Augustine's mind, and in contemporary practice, of infanticide, abortion, and contraception. The association gives a sting to his critique.[42]

The importance of this text in the development of the notion that contraception is a sexual sin is obvious, and we will follow the gradual increase of its influence in due course. Noonan's central affirmation here, however, cannot be accepted. It is simply not true to say that, in this text, St. Augustine 'formally, unequivocally and passionately condemned contraception practiced by the married.' Noonan's only interest is in contraception, so it appears to him that St. Augustine's mention of abortion and infanticide is merely giving 'a sting to his critique' of contraception. St. Augustine was not dealing formally with any of these matters. The book was written as part of his argument with the Pelagians, and deals with fundamental matters in the theology of grace and original sin, and their relationship to marriage and concupiscence, as the title indicates. The question of contraception and birth control only entered in incidentally. It is also clear from the text that St. Augustine does not treat of the use of 'poisons of sterility' in any way differently from his treatment of abortion or infanticide. He primarily condemns the avoidance of procreation, as he has done consistently from the beginning, and he mentions these more serious matters in a rhetorical flourish, not in a formal statement at all.

One must also take issue with Noonan's remark that 'the "homicide" argument favored by Jerome and Chrysostom is not relied on'. This gives the impression that some other argument is relied on, where the plain fact of the matter is that St. Augustine is not arguing about this matter at all. He simple mentions all these forms of behaviour, contraception, abortion and infanticide, in the same breath and all considered as a single set of related ways in which the basic refusal to accept children can be made effective. St. Augustine simply takes it for granted that these actions are reprehensible, he doesn't argue the matter in any way

---

[42] Ibid.

whatever. These points are important because they point to the fact that St. Augustine was not teaching about contraception, and helps to explain how his contributions in this matter made no impact on the development of doctrine in this area for centuries to come. Noonan tells us that Augustine's doctrine on marriage 'centering on the procreative requirement, was to be preserved for a thousand years in the Christian West.'[43] There is no doubt about this, but it is important to be clear also that he had no formal doctrine on the matter of contraception specifically, as distinct from the avoidance of procreation by whatever means including periodic abstinence.

As well as his mistaken application of the procreative principle in the matter of fertility control, St. Augustine also maintained the mistaken doctrine of the Stoics that intercourse without procreative intent is a sin. For him, sexual intercourse is only fully legitimate when it is engaged in for the sake of procreation. He recognises that the fault in not having a procreative purpose is not a serious one; it is not adultery or fornication.[44] However, to demand intercourse for any other reason is a venial sin.[45] St. Augustine was well aware that this conclusion ran totally counter to the experience of married Christians. As he observes himself: 'Never in friendly conversations have I heard anyone who is or who has been married say that he never had intercourse with his wife except when hoping for conception.'[46] This fact, however, did not deflect him from following the course of his logic to its conclusion. Nor was he deterred by the fact that his conclusion also ran counter to the advice of St. Paul in 1 Cor 7:5 when he says to spouses that they should not abstain from sexual intercourse lightly 'so that Satan may not tempt you because of your lack of self-control.' St. Paul clearly is counselling spouses to have sexual intercourse for a reason which has nothing whatever to do with the procreative purpose of the act. St. Augustine

---

[43] Ibid, 138.
[44] *De bono coniugali* 6.6, CSEL 41: 195-95.
[45] 'Exigere autem (concubitum) ultra generandi necessitatem (est) culpae venialis'. *De bono coniugali*, c. 7, n. 6.
[46] *De bono coniugali* 13.15, CSEL 41, 208. Translation and reference in Noonan, *Contraception*, 130.

overcomes the apparent contradiction by means of an interpretation of what St. Paul says immediately afterwards. For he then adds: 'Now as a concession, not a command, I say this.' (1 Cor 7:6) The phrase here translated 'as a concession' kata. suggnw, mhn was translated by St. Jerome as *secundum indulgentiam,* and St. Augustine followed St. Jerome in interpreting it as implying pardon for a sin. According to Janssens, it is universally accepted now that St. Paul is simply affirming the liceity of having sexual intercourse, and Jassens remarks: 'This biblical text, now properly understood, was obviously a hard blow to the traditional position which invoked the authority of St. Paul in support of the thesis that every act of intercourse unnecessary for procreation was at least a venial sin.'[47]

Just to complete this section I would like to comment on a remark of Noonan which summarizes his, and the general, understanding of St. Augustine's role in this matter. Noonan says of St. Augustine that he, 'comprehensively and passionately, synthesized his own experience, the Stoic rule on procreation, the teaching on original sin, the need to protect life, into a rule on contraception.'[48] There can be no doubt that St. Augustine formed a synthesis of the matters Noonan mentions, but I dispute the fact that he synthesised them into a rule on contraception. St. Augustine never at any stage dealt with contraception as an issue on its own. He mentioned it in passing as part of his arguments in more general aspects of the reality of marriage, and it is clear that he was dealing with a doctrine already established which he used for other purposes. The synthesising of his doctrine into a rule on contraception came later, and it is to that development that we must now turn.

The Medieval Developments

A most important development occurred at a very early stage in the revival of theology in the Middle Ages, when the influence of St. Augustine began to wax extremely strong in the West. The direction of subsequent tradition was set by the two great medieval collectors of

---

[47] Janssens, 'Chasteté conjugale,' 538.
[48] Noonan, *Contraception,* 106.

texts, Gratian and Peter Lombard, both of whom chose *Aliquando* as the leading text on the issue of contraception. Noonan explains well what happened.

> If Augustine is the most important single authority on contraception, and if a single statement of his is to be taken as the epitome of his doctrine, then the use of *Aliquando* by Gratian and Lombard is the most important teaching on contraception in the Middle Ages. The text is presented in both under almost identical headings. Gratian's heading is "They are Fornicators, Not Spouses Who Procure Poisons of Sterility" (*Decretum* 2.32.2.7). Lombard's lead sentence is "Those who indeed procure poisons of sterility are not spouses but fornicators" (*Sentences* 4.31.3). Each embeds the text in a discussion of the Augustinian goods of marriage, and each follows it with a chapter on abortion. The effect is to distinguish carefully the specific fault of contraception from the specific fault of abortion, and to place centrally within the teaching on marriage Augustine's passionate rejection of contraception as destructive of the marital relation.[49]

The influence of the ideas at work in the summaries of Gratian and Lombard is still strong in the discussion of contraception, as we shall see, and it is important to recall that Gratian and Lombard and Noonan, who follows them, all misrepresent St. Augustine's thought in a fundamental point. St. Augustine did not reject contraception as destructive of the marital relation; he did not explicitly reject contraception at all. He only mentioned it in passing on two occasions. What he passionately rejected was the avoidance of procreation whether by periodic abstinence or contraception or abortion or infanticide. And, as has been pointed out already, his passionate conviction was mistaken.

---

[49] Ibid, 174.

The avoidance of procreation does not vitiate the marital relation in any way, and the question which is still a real one is whether or not contraception has that effect.

What is true, as Janssens points out, is that the substance of the sexual morality of St. Augustine, according to which procreation is the only natural *raison d'être* of marriage and the natural order consists in conforming to the procreative function of the sexual act, was taken up by the great scholastics and made precise in their elaboration of the natural law.[50] He focuses on the teaching of St. Thomas, since his influence remains preponderant in the theological tradition. For St. Thomas the end of sexual intercourse is procreation, without any qualification, and this is the principle he applies. He never deals explicitly with the issue of contraception or the avoidance of procreation within marriage as an explicit question. Unlike St. Augustine who had to deal with the issue in his polemic against the Manichees in favour of procreation, St. Thomas was building a system and this issue found no place in it. The 'poisons of sterility', the traditional rubric under which the question would have arisen, find no mention at all in the works of his maturity. He only deals with *coitus interruptus* in the context of a general treatment of sexual morality, and so the tradition began which considers contraception to be a sexual sin.

He lays down a basic principle, which is best formulated in *De Malo*, q. 15, a. 1 c.: 'Sometimes the disorder of desire is also accompanied by a disorder in the very external act as such, as happens in every use of the genital organs outside the conjugal act. And every such act is evidently disordered of its very self, since we call every act that is not properly related to its requisite end a disordered act. For example, eating is disordered if it be not properly related to bodily health, for which end eating is ordained. And the end of using genital organs is to beget and educate offspring, and so every use of the aforementioned organs that is not related to begetting and properly educating offspring is as such disordered. And every act of the aforementioned organs outside the sexual union of a man and a woman is obviously unsuitable for

---

[50] Janssens, 'Chasteté conjugale,' 529.

begetting offspring.'[51] How this principle applies to sexual morality is synthesised in II-II, q. 154. Fornication, adultery, rape and incest are wrong because certain essential conditions appropriate to sexual intercourse are not met. More serious than these are what St. Thomas calls 'sins against nature', no doubt following St. Paul's reference in Romans 1:26 to sexual relations which are 'against nature' (para. fu, sin). He lays down his principle in the first article that 'insofar as the generation of offspring is impeded there is the sin against nature, which is to be found in every sexual act from which generation cannot follow.'[52] He develops this argument in article eleven where he points out that masturbation, bestiality and homosexuality fall under this category, and also any sexual intercourse 'where the natural manner of lying together is not used, either in regard to an inappropriate instrument or to other monstrous and bestial manners of lying.'[53] What is noteworthy in this is that St. Thomas is not speaking of contraception at all. He doesn't even mention *coitus interruptus*. Under the use of an inappropriate instrument he, presumably, has in mind oral and anal intercourse which can be chosen for reasons other than the avoidance of procreation. And what the 'other monstrous and bestial manners of lying' might be can be left to the fertile imagination of those who wish to follow the thought. The tradition which built on these foundations found *coitus interruptus* and subsequently the use of a condom to fall within this category of 'sins against nature', but St. Thomas does not speak of such matters here or anywhere else. As Noonan remarks, the criticism of *coitus interruptus* was normally made in terms of its unnaturalness, and the explicit criticism of contraception under the rubric of the 'poisons of

---

[51] English translation in *On Evil*, trans. Richard Regan (Oxford: Oxford University Press, 2003), 421.
[52] II-II, q. 154 a.1c: '*Uno modo, quia habet repugnantiam ad finem venerei actus. Et sic, inquantum impeditur generatio prolis, est vitium contra naturam, quod est in omni actu venereo ex quo generatio sequi non potest.*'
[53] Q. 154, a. 11c : '*si non servetur naturalis modus concumbendi, aut quantum ad instrumentum non debitum; aut quantum ad alios monstruosos et bestiales concumbendi modos.*'

sterility' was usually made applying the 'homicide' argument.[54] What is noteworthy is that St. Thomas fails to treat the 'poisons of sterility' and the explicit question of contraception anywhere in his mature works. Why that may be is not clear, but it certainly has the effect of side-lining the treatment of contraception as a life issue, and further solidifying the perception that contraception is a sexual matter and not a life issue at all. It is worth noting for future reference that St. Thomas is not 'proving' that these actions are morally wrong; he gets that from Scripture and Tradition. The procreative principle he got from St. Augustine and he put these elements together in an elegant system which makes eminent sense and lasted uncontested for a long time.

The principle being applied, that every sexual act from which generation cannot follow, would also condemn sterile intercourse, but St. Thomas never has the occasion to draw that conclusion. He does have occasion to come close in the *Summa contra Gentiles*, chapter 122. There he repeats his principle that every emission of seed from which generation canot follow is against the good of man, and if this is done deliberately it is a sin. He emphasises that he has in mind a situation where generation cannot follow from the nature of the act chosen, *secundum se*. If it only happens *per accidens* there is no sin, as in the case where the woman happens to be sterile. What St. Thomas might have said about intercourse chosen deliberately for its sterility we will never know, and it is not easy to speculate. What is of interest to us is the fact that St. Thomas never deals explicitly with the issue of contraception at all.

St. Thomas also maintains the position first elaborated by the Stoics and upheld by St. Augustine that intercourse without procreative intent is sinful. The act of intercourse is only free of all fault when both spouses choose it with a view to procreation, 'for in intercourse which goes beyond the limit of what is necessary for procreation the one who asks (*petitio debiti*) commits a sin and only the one who responds (*redditio*

---

[54] Noonan, *Contraception*, 246.

debiti) is irreproachable.'[55] Noonan also reports that St. Thomas held this view, but he suggests that his adherence to it may have been less than full, when he observes that St. Thomas took this stand in his work on the *Sentences* (4.31.2.2, ad 2), and that it was an historical accident which enhanced the significance of this relatively youthful work, for St. Thomas did not live to complete the portion of the *Summa theologica* which would have dealt with the purposes of marriage. Accordingly, according to Noonan, 'the youthful commentary on the *Sentences* had to serve as his final statement on the subjective elements in marital intercourse and … was commonly reproduced as part of the "Supplement to the *Summa theologica*."'[56] This suggestion of Noonan doesn't stand up to examination, for the point is made in the commentary on *First Corinthians* written in 1273, just a year before St. Thomas died.

John Finnis seeks to rebut the standard view that St. Thomas held the doctrine at all, but his effort does not stand u[57] St Thomas makes the point explicitly in the two texts mentioned by Janssens, *In 1 Cor. 7, lect. 1* and *In 1 Thess. 4, lect. 1*, and in that mentioned by Noonan, *IV Sent.* d. 31 q. 2 a. 2 ad 2. In a short note appended to his chapter on 180, Finnis adverts only to the last of these three texts and considers it insignificant because it 'says merely that choosing intercourse only to avoid one's own temptations to fornication [extra-marital sex] is [lightly] wrong; it says nothing whatever about procreative purpose.' He goes on to suggest that 'the main reply to this very article … clearly contradicts Noonan by stating that *either* procreation or *fides* suffices as a reasonable motive for marital intercourse …' He opines that 'Noonan's entire influential account is flawed from top to bottom by his failure to observe … that *seeking* the 'giving of what is due' (the 'rendering the debt', as he lamely translates *reddere debitum*) is never condemned by Aquinas even in contexts where procreation is out of the question…' The problem here is that Finnis has missed the point completely. Noonan's translation as

---

[55] Janssens, 'Chasteté conjugale,' 534-35. He quotes *In 1 Cor.*, 7, lect. 1 and the course notes *In I Thess.*, 4, lect. 1.
[56] Noonan, *Contraception*, 248.
[57] *Aquinas : Moral, Political, and Legal Theory* (Oxford University Press, 1998), 143-54.

'rendering the debt' is accurate, literal and traditional and makes it easy to formulate the distinction between *petitio debiti* ('seeking the debt') and *renditio debiti* ('rendering the debt') which St. Augustine's flawed interpretation of 1 Cor 7:3 requires. According to Augustine, followed quite clearly by St. Thomas, 'seeking the debt' without procreative intent is a venial sin, while 'rendering the debt' to the spouse 'seeking' it is without moral fault. For Finnis to speak of 'seeking the giving of what is due' indicates that this distinction is completely lost on him, since it is the distinction between the 'seeking' and the 'giving' which is crucial. Although the text 'says nothing whatever about procreative purpose', Finnis himself understands, apparently without realizing the fact, that it does not need to be mentioned, for he deduces correctly that the action being analysed is seeking intercourse 'only to avoid one's own temptations to fornication,' which is precisely what 'without procreative intent' means. Finnis then tells us that the text 'merely' says that such choosing intercourse without procreative intent 'is [lightly] wrong.' Finnis is right, of course, that that is all it says. But that is all that Noonan, along with everyone else, says that it says, and that is the whole point. Being '[lightly] wrong' is what a venial sin is, and it would appear that earlier Christians took this 'light' wrongness more seriously than does Finnis. For this is precisely what weighed upon the Church for all those centuries and it took from Martin LeMaistre in the fourteenth to Gury in the nineteenth century to work it out of our system. Finnis should have stopped to think how odd it would have been for such expenditure of energy to be required to clarify a point that Aquinas had clarified already, and nobody had noticed all this time.

The Disintegration of the Procreative Synthesis

The centuries from the fifteenth on have witnessed the slow but steady disintegration of the synthesis completed by St. Thomas, and the process continues today with no obvious end point in view. Janssens and Noonan both begin their accounts with Martin Lemaistre (1432-81), one of the first and most influential promoters of the new understanding of sexual intercourse.[58] Lemaistre took issue with the doctrine which originated with the Stoics and was accepted by the early Fathers of the Church and maintained by St. Augustine and St. Thomas and the general tradition after them, that a procreative intention is required for the legitimacy of sexual intercourse. He begins by establishing that common to St. Augustine and St. Thomas was the thesis that procreation is the only valid reason for sexual intercourse. He counters this with his own thesis that not every act of intercourse chosen for a different motive is opposed to the virtue of chastity.[59] The controversy continued over the following four or five centuries. Noonan considers the new position to be established by the middle of the eighteenth century but, for Janssens, it was not finally resolved until the nineteenth century, when, in the *Compendium theologiae moralis* of J. Gury, it became standard doctrine that fostering the mutual love of the spouses was a sufficient motive to justify sexual intercourse beyond what is necessary for procreation.[60] The change meant that while 'the tradition required that the spouses should only have sexual relations which *positively seeking* procreation, the new understanding simply required that *they do not positively exclude* procreation ...'[61] Thus was the longest-standing proposition based on the procreative purpose of intercourse finally abandoned as mistaken.

Another step was taken when the positive exclusion of procreation by the deliberate choice of sterile intercourse was seen to be legitimate. In 1853 the question was raised about the legitimacy of sexual relations restricted to the infertile period, and the official reply by the Sacred Penitentiary was that the practice was acceptable, as long as nothing was done to impede conception. 'In other words, the Sacred Penitentiary simply condemned once again the vitiation of the conjugal act.'[62] After the publications by Ogino (1929) and Knaus (1930), which provided a scientific basis, the practice of periodic abstinence became more common as a means of birth control and was fully sanctioned by Pope

---

[58] Noonan, *Contraception*, 303-40; Janssens, 'Chasteté conjugale,' 537-43.
[59] Janssens, 'Chasteté conjugale,' 537-38.
[60] Ibid, 539.
[61] Ibid, 540.
[62] Ibid.

Pius XII in 1951.⁶³ This meant that it was seen to be a legitimate option for a married couple to have sexual intercourse while positively excluding the possibility of procreation, the very choice which St. Augustine had condemned so vehemently when practised by the Manichees. Thus was St. Augustine's fundamental position, that the avoidance of procreation was immoral, developed on the basis of his understanding of the procreative purpose of intercourse finally set aside. Noonan's summary of the implications here is worth recording for the discussions to come. He wrote: 'Use of the sterile period ... was now fully sanctioned. The substantial split between sexual intercourse and procreation, already achieved by the rejection of Augustinian theory, was confirmed in practice.'⁶⁴ This has to be recognized as a somewhat controversial conclusion, especially in the light of the 'inseparability principle' espoused by Pope Paul VI as the cornerstone of his teaching in *Humanae vitae*. That matter will be dealt with in due course.

In the light of these developments it was now found necessary to re-formulate the procreative principle. Where St. Augustine, followed by St. Thomas and the tradition generally, had understood procreation to be the (one and only) purpose of intercourse, it was now accepted that other purposes had to be recognised. In the light of this, the position was now adopted that procreation was the primary purpose of intercourse, and the unitive purpose was to deemed secondary to it. This was the position adopted by the encyclical *Casti connubii*. It recognised that, even beyond the necessity of procreation, sexual relations can be praiseworthy. It justified such intercourse on the basis of what it called the secondary ends of marriage and sexual intercourse, the unitive purpose,⁶⁵ as long as the intrinsic nature of the act is safeguarded and its due ordination to the primary end.⁶⁶

---

63   'Address to the Italian Catholic Society of Midwives, October 29, 1951', AAS 43 (1951), 845-46.
64   Noonan, Contraception, 447.
65   Janssens, 'Chasteté conjugale,' 541.
66   '*Dummodo salva semper sit intrinseca illius actus natura ideoque eius ad primarium finem debita ordinatio.*' 59. DS 3718 ; AAS 22 (1930), 561.

The next stage in the process was the challenge to this new formulation, initiated by Herbert Doms in a book published in 1935.[67] Doms argued that human sexuality differs from that of the other animals, so that the biological end can no longer be considered the primary end. Intercourse is always an expression of interpersonal love. Only a *few* acts of intercourse lead to conception but, on the human level, *every* act of intercourse, in virtue of its very nature, must express the mutual love of the spouses. On April 1, 1944 the Holy Office issued a decree rejecting Doms's theory in favour of the traditional view. It repudiated the opinion of those who denied that the primary end of marriage is the procreation and education of children, or who held that the secondary ends are not essential subordinate to the primary end, but are equally principal and independent.[68] Despite this authoritative intervention, the new view grew in strength more and more as new ideas gained ground in the Church. And eventually, the Second Vatican Council, in the pastoral constitution *Gaudium et spes*, confirmed the personalist vision. It does not speak of primary and secondary ends, but specifically states, in § 50, that marriage is not instituted solely for procreation and that while marriage is instituted for this purpose, that other ends of marriage are not to be considered secondary (*non posthabitis ceteris matrimonii finibus*), thus effectively contradicting the decree of the Holy Office on the matter.

The Council also proposed a doctrine on the role of sexual intercourse in marriage which finally returns to the Pauline teaching in *1 Corinthians* and marks a definitive overcoming of the Augustinian view which had held sway for so long. In *Gaudium et spes*, the Council recognizes the difficulty that a prolonged period of continence can present a marriage couple, and observes that 'where the intimacy of married life is broken off, it is not rare for the faithfulness to be imperilled and its good of offspring (*bonum prolis*) ruined. For then the upbringing of the children and the courage to accept new ones are both endangered.' (GS 51) Janssens comments that this must be the first

---

[67] *Vom Sinn und Zweck der Ehe. Eine systematische Studie* (Breslau, 1935).
[68] DS 3838.

time a magisterial document affirms that continence in marriage can be dangerous and in this way opposes the genuine meaning of 1 Cor 7:5 to the erroneous interpretation which weighed on the theological tradition for such a long time.[69] It was noted before that St. Augustine developed his theory of the procreative purpose on rational grounds and without scriptural warrant, but Janssens goes even further in his criticism of the Augustinian contribution here. He wrote:

> The great merit of the reaction against the traditional conception consists in having regained contact with the Christian doctrine, as enunciated by St. Paul in 1 Cor 7:1-6. It is evident that, in this passage, St. Paul justifies marriage and sexual intercourse for other motives than procreation. Of this latter he says not a word. Today many exegetes think that in this text St. Paul was reacting expressly against rigorist tendencies which, directly or indirectly, were inspired by the traditional conception. To the extent that this hypothesis is confirmed, one would even have to say that the new theory has freed us from a non-Christian conception, attacked by the Apostle and yet placed under his patronage by a centuries-long theological tradition based on the erroneous interpretation St. Jerome and St. Augustine gave to the controverted phrase: *dico secundum indulgentiam* (1 Cor 7:6).[70]

Whatever the final judgment on this issue may be, it can hardly be disputed that these developments raise serious questions about the use of the procreative principle as a guide to sexual morality. Each conclusion reached on the basis of the principle has eventually, sooner or later, been found to be erroneous. The Stoics first concluded to the need of procreative intent in intercourse and were followed in this by St. Augustine and the whole Western tradition until the conclusion

---

[69] Janssens, 'Chasteté conjugale,' 549.
[70] Ibid, 543.

was found to be a mistake and had to be abandoned. St. Augustine concluded that the deliberate avoidance of procreation in marriage was morally wrong and this conclusion had to be abandoned eventually as mistaken. It has finally been recognised that procreation is not the only purpose of sexual intercourse, and it may not even be the primary purpose. If, therefore, contraception is judged to be immoral on the basis of the procreative principle, can we be sure of the solidity of this judgment. As Janssens asks: 'In this new situation, does the argument retain its peremptory force? Once it is admitted that sexual intercourse can be licit apart from procreation, that it can be justified by other motives, and that one can exclude procreation from one's *intention* to the degree that one can *intentionally* limit intercourse to the infertile times, does the old argument still work?'[71] And that final question is the one to which we must now move.

---

[71] Ibid, 542-43.

Chapter 18

The Failure of the Procreative Principle

Although the procreative principle was slowly but surely losing its power to convince since the fifteenth century, it still remained in place as an official argument against contraception. According to a careful interpreter, Gerald Kelly, Pope Pius XI and Pope Pius XII, 'in explaining their teaching that contraceptive practices and direct sterilization are against the natural law, stressed *one* reason: namely, that these things are contrary to the natural purpose of the generative act and the generative faculty.[1] ... In the last analysis, the argument from finality is *the* argument against artificial birth prevention.'[2] Not long after Kelly was becoming aware that there were difficulties with the argument. He summarized what had become known as the 'perverted faculty' argument, the one developed by St. Thomas, as we saw: 'To use a natural faculty in such a way as to frustrate an essential purpose of its use is intrinsically immoral. But contraception involves the use of the reproductive faculty in such a way as to frustrate an essential purpose of its use. Therefore, contraception is intrinsically immoral.'[3] In his

---

[1] Gerald Kelly, S. J., *Medico-Moral Problems* (Dublin / London: Clonmore & Reynolds Ltd / Burns Oates Ltd, 1960), 157.
[2] Ibid, 158.
[3] Gerald Kelly, "Contraception and Natural Law," in *Proceedings of the Eighteenth Annual Convention, The Catholic Theological Society of America, 1963* (New York, 1964), 25-45 at 36.

address to the Catholic Theological Society of America, he adverted to one sign of weakness. The same argument had been used to justify the condemnation of lying as intrinsically evil, and when that judgment came to be revised and the decision not to tell the truth in certain circumstances was seen to be justifiable, it was seen that the 'perverted faculty' argument was not watertight. He recalled that this difficulty had been pointed out some years earlier. E. J. Mahoney had seen the difficulty this involved for the argument over contraception and asked: 'What is to prevent our opponent from expressing the hope that Catholic theologians will similarly find themselves able to depart from it in circumstances where there is a just and reasonable cause for preventing the birth of children?'[4]

Despite its difficulties, the essential role of the procreative principle continued to be upheld. The *Minority Working Paper*, produced by the four moral theologians who supported the traditional teaching, was strong on its importance, when they wrote: 'Once one has set aside this principle, one would also be setting aside a *fundamental* criterion, up until the present time unshaken in its application to many acts which have always been considered by the Church to be serious sins against chastity.'[5] Another influential moral theologian of that same time could write that 'if the use of sex can be divorced from all reference to procreation there is no such thing as sexual morality.'[6] And John Noonan considered that the whole edifice of sexual morality depended on this principle. He wrote:

> As long as there was no argument against fornication
> based on the demands of love, as long as the main
> rational argument against fornication rested on the

---

[4] *American Ecclesiastical Review*, 79 (1928), 237. Quoted by Gerald Kelly, "Contraception and Natural Law," in *Proceedings of the Eighteenth Annual Convention, The Catholic Theological Society of America, 1963* (New York, 1964), 25-45 at 37, footnote 22.

[5] "The Minority Working Paper, 23 May 1966," in Peter Harris, *et. al.*, *On Human Life*, 198.

[6] Kelly, "Contraception and Natural Law," 45.

treatment of the fornicating act as normally generative, to allow the lawfulness of contraception would have been to favor fornication. Similarly, the argument establishing all the sins against nature – masturbation, bestiality, sodomy – rested on the assumption that any prevention of insemination was unnatural. The argument was seriously disturbed if coitus interruptus was in any case admitted. Again, as long as there was no ethic based on the requirements of love between persons, it seemed dangerous to disturb the rational foundation of a whole range of sexual morality.[7]

There was even the suggestion that the principle was revealed. The Minority Report reviewed the Scripture evidence and in conclusion asked the rhetorical question as to whether, 'by the law set forth in Sacred Scripture, is not a general prohibition for acting sexually against the good of procreation included?'[8] And as late as 1980 John Finnis: 'For my part, I think that the teaching on contraception is implicit in the New Testament revelation; for what makes sense of the multiple prohibitions of various forms of sexual conduct is the unstated principle that sexual actions opposed to or insufficiently related in form to the good of procreation and the procreative type of act are wrongful for that very reason.'[9] And Pope Paul VI, in *Humanae vitae*, seems to present the principle as Church teaching: 'The Church, nevertheless, in urging men to the observance of the precepts of the natural law, which it interprets by its constant doctrine, teaches that each and every marital act must of necessity retain its intrinsic relationship to the procreation of human life.' (*Humanae vitae*, § 11.)

Then, in the early 1960s, despite all its traditional and official support, the argument began to lose its power to convince. As one commentator remarked at the time: 'Few arguments in the domain

---

[7] Noonan, Contraception, 356-57.
[8] "The Minority Working Paper, 200.
[9] John Finnis, *'Humanae Vitae*: Its Background and Aftermath' *International Review of Natural Family Planning* 4(1980), 141-53 at 152.

of morality seem as unpersuasive to the great majority of Americans as the customary natural-law arguments against contraception as a "frustration of the generative act".[10] As recalled earlier, the first explicit rejection became public in Catholic moral theology in the three articles of 1963. These three based their case on the unitive dimension of sexual intercourse. Intercourse is not only a potentially procreative act, but is actually and in itself a unitive act. While it is true that contraception frustrates the procreative aspect of the act, it fully respects the unitive aspect and, in fact, facilitates it by removing tensions or fears capable of impairing the expression of love in married intercourse, and so can be justified when there are valid reasons for avoiding procreation.

An added complication to the arguments against contraception was introduced by the development of the anovulant pill. For Janssens, writing in 1963, the important value of chemical contraceptives is that their use respects the conjugal act in its natural structure and so preserves its full unitive significance.[11] Unlike coitus interruptus or mechanical barrier methods of contraception, the use of the Pill does not vitiate the performance of the act of intercourse, and in this it is similar to the practice of restricting intercourse to the infertile part of the menstrual cycle. This view of the matter also formed an important part of the argument in the other two articles which broke the Catholic consensus that year. Willem van der Marck argued that the integrity of the sexual act must be preserved because of its anthropological and sacramental significance.[12] And in a critical review of these articles, Gerald Kelly summarizes Bishop Reuss's article as follows: 'According to the bishop's analysis, the couple may never resort to birth-control methods which interfere with the natural structure of the marriage-act. This act must always keep its natural symbolism of total self-giving. This is an absolute. But, since sterilization does not interfere with the

---

[10] Paul M. Quay, S.J., "Contraception and Conjugal Love," in Smith, ed., <u>Why Humane Vitae was Right: A Reader</u>, 19. This is a reprint of an article published in *Theological Studies* 22 (1961), 8-40.

[11] Louis Janssens, 'Morale conjugale et progestogènes,' *Ephemerides theologicae Lovanienses* 39 (1963), 787-826 at 820-21.

[12] Valsecchi, *Controversy*, 43.

natural structure of the act, and since sterile days may be deliberately chosen when periodic continence is practiced, the bishop argues that sterilization is not absolutely ruled out as a solution ...'[13] For the bishop, 'it is a natural law absolute that the natural structure of the conjugal act must be preserved. ... The act itself must express total love, without reservation.'[14] The irony of this situation will be revealed in due course, but the fact remains that on the basis of the procreative principle the use of the anovulant pills appeared an attractive alternative to *coitus interruptus* because it did not directly interfere with the act of sexual intercourse so that the newly discovered unitive purpose could appear to justify sterilized intercourse on its own.

Karol Wojtyla's Argument

Given the subsequent election of its author as Pope John Paul II, the argument in Karol Wojtyla's book *Love and Responsibility* needs to be examined, for it contains the application of the procreative principle in a pure form. According to Wojtyla intercourse 'must be accompanied by awareness and willing acceptance' of the procreative dimension of the act.[15] The point is foundational in Wojtyla's theology of this matter. He makes the point repeatedly. 'Sexual (marital) relations have the character of a true union of persons as long as a general disposition towards parenthood is not excluded from them.'[16] And 'the personalistic value of the sexual relationship cannot be assured without willingness for parenthood. ... Willing acceptance of parenthood serves to break down the reciprocal egoism ... behind which lurks the will to exploit the person.'[17] And again: 'In marital intercourse both shame and the normal process of its absorption by love are connected with the

---

[13] Gerald Kelly, S.J., 'Confusion: contraception and "the pill",' *Theology Digest* 12 (1964), 123-30 at 127.
[14] Ibid, 129.
[15] Karol Wojtyla (Pope John Paul II), *Love and Responsibility* (London: Collins, 1981), 227.
[16] Ibid, 229.
[17] Ibid, 230.

conscious acceptance of the possibility of parenthood. ... If there is a positive decision to preclude this eventuality sexual intercourse becomes shameless.'[18] And yet again: 'When we write about morality in sexual relations and in marriage we always stress that it depends on conscious and willing acceptance by the man and the woman of the possibility of parenthood.'[19] From all this he concludes: 'This acceptance is so important, so decisive that without it marital intercourse cannot be said to be a realization of the personal order. Instead of a truly personal union all that is left is a sexual association without the full value of a personal relationshi'[20] Wojtyla concedes that a positive intention to procreate is not required to justify sexual intercourse.[21] But there must be a positive relationship to procreation of some kind, for the deliberate exclusion of the possibility is immoral. 'By definitively precluding the possibility of procreation in the marital act a man and a woman inevitably shift the whole focus of the experience in the direction of sexual pleasure as such. The whole content of the experience is then "enjoyment", whereas it should be an expression of love with pleasure as an incidental accompaniment of the sexual act.'[22] As formulated, this condition is not precise enough, for it would also render periodic abstinence immoral, for there is also the 'deliberate exclusion' of procreation in that case. Wojtyla was aware of this, of course, and subsequently adds: 'We need only remind ourselves that what we call here "deliberate exclusion" means quite simply prevention by artificial means.'[23] Wojtyla may say that, but it simply is not true. 'Deliberate exclusion' does not mean quite simply prevention by artificial means. It means quite simply deliberate exclusion, which can be achieved by periodic abstinence. The fact of the matter is that Wojtyla's major premise is unsound. Sexual intercourse between spouses does not require a willing acceptance of procreation; it does not require any particular reference to procreation at all. For

---

[18] Ibid, 231.
[19] Ibid, 232.
[20] Ibid, 228.
[21] Ibid, 233.
[22] Ibid, 234-35.
[23] Ibid, 235.

centuries Christian thinkers had no doubt that a procreative intention was necessary to justify sexual intercourse. The manner of speaking is significant. There was a suspicion about sexual intercourse, so that the act needed justification. Now Wojtyla says that it requires an acceptance of procreation in order to be justified. He says that this acceptance is such that it can survive the deliberate exclusion of procreation by limiting intercourse to the sterile period of the woman's cycle. It is only the deliberate exclusion by artificial means which removes the required 'acceptance'. It would seem rather that sexual intercourse between married people does not require any justification at all. It is a normal part of married life and it happens without any ulterior motives of any kind. It is not performed for unity or for procreation. These purposes are built into the act, but need not form part of the conscious intention of the couple. The desire to have intercourse arises and is satisfied without any special reflection. Looking for the significance on the level of intention does not seem to be appropriate at all.

Elizabeth Anscombe's Arguments

Another early effort at producing a rebuttal of the new justification of contraception was that of Elizabeth Anscombe.[24] One prong of her approach was a presentation of the classical argument using the synthesis of St. Thomas built on the principle of the procreative purpose of intercourse. She wrote that

> the ground of objection to fornication and adultery was that sexual intercourse is only right in the <u>sort</u> of set-up that typically provides children with a father and mother to care for them. If you can turn intercourse

---

[24] G. E. M. Anscombe, "You Can have Sex without Children: Christianity and the New Offer," *Ethics, Religion and Politics* (Minneapolis: University of Minnesota Press, 1981), 82-96. This is a reprint of an article written in the early 1960s and the argument was published in pamphlet form as G. E. M. Anscombe, *Contraception and Chastity* (London: Catholic Truth Society, 1975).

into something other than the reproductive type of act ... then why, if you can change it, should it be restricted to the married? Restricted, that is, to partners bound in a formal, legal, union whose fundamental purpose is the bringing up of children? For if that is not its fundamental purpose there is no reason why for example "marriage" should have to be between people of opposite sexes. ... But if sexual union can be deliberately and totally divorced from fertility, then we may wonder why sexual union has got to be married union. If the expression of love between the partners is the point, then it shouldn't be so narrowly confined.[25]

On this basis she affirms that 'contraceptive intercourse is faulted ... because ... [T]he action is not left by you as the kind of act by which life is transmitted, but is purposely rendered infertile, and so changed to another sort of act altogether."[26] And she then sets up her *reduction ad absurdum*: 'If contraceptive intercourse is permissible, then what objection could there be after all to mutual masturbation, or copulation in vase indebito, sodomy, buggery, ...? It can't be the mere pattern of bodily behaviour in which the stimulation is procured that makes all the difference! But if such things are all right, it becomes perfectly impossible to see anything wrong with homosexual intercourse, for example.'[27]

The earlier logic, from the Stoics on, was that a procreative intention was necessary for legitimate intercourse, and that demand had to cede to reality. Now the claim is that the intrinsic procreative purpose of intercourse is essential to its validity. The difficulty, however, remains as to how this new formulation fits with the accepted validity of deliberately chosen sterile intercourse. Sterile intercourse is clearly

---

[25] G. E. M. Anscombe, "Contraception and Chastity," in Janet E. Smith, ed., Why Humane Vitae was Right: A Reader (San Francisco: Ignatius Press, 1993), 121-46 at 123.
[26] Ibid, 135.
[27] Ibid, 136.

unapt for procreation. One can even say that it is <u>intrinsically</u> unapt for the purpose. It is, indeed, the <u>sort</u> of act which can, normally, be procreative. But it is chosen now for its sterility, for its very unaptness for procreation. Anscombe's argument is that if intercourse can be legitimately separated from procreation, then the whole edifice of sexual morality collapses. But intercourse can be legitimately separated from procreation by the systematic use of the sterile period. It would then follow, if her major premise holds, that the whole edifice of sexual morality has collapsed in the Catholic Church since Pope Pius XII formally recognised the validity of sterile intercourse. A number of points can be made in this situation. The first is that the whole edifice of Christian sexual morality does not depend on any logical foundation which we have to be able to work out. Christian morality is a teaching from above. It does not depend on our philosophical justification for its validity. It can hardly be doubted that the structure of sexual morality is related to the procreative purpose of sex and marriage. It was clear to the Stoic philosophers in Ancient Rome and it can hardly be seriously doubted by any fair-minded thinker. But it is one thing to concede the general point, and quite another to use it as a major premise in order to establish difficult moral demands.

Anscombe had another part of her argument which focussed on the intention involved in contraception, which was designed specifically to meet the arguments in defence of the new anovulant pills. She again takes as her major premise the same principle enunciated by St. Thomas that sexual acts intrinsically unapt for generation are morally wrong, and her effort is to fit the new contraceptive techniques to this pattern. She accepts the point that some female contraceptive methods do not interfere directly with the act of intercourse, since 'the acts remain intrinsically apt for generation, physically speaking, and are made not to be apt for it only by incidental circumstances.'[28] She goes on to argue that, if the acts are not altered physically, then any change which will vitiate the act must be on the level of the intention with which they are performed. She wrote that 'if acts *not* of an inherently non-procreative

---

[28] Anscombe, "You Can have Sex without Children," 85.

kind are non-procreative in virtue of further circumstances, then surely *only* the anti-conceptional intent could be objectionable.'[29] She spells out the effect of the contraceptive intention as follows:

> *considered as intentional actions*, artificially contraceptive acts of intercourse *are* intrinsically unapt for generation. It is true that *just considered physically* they may be acts of an intrinsically generative type; but since the physical circumstances that make the acts in the concrete case non-generative, are produced on purpose by the agent so that they may be non-generative, they cannot be considered intrinsically generative *as intentional actions*.[30]

The crucial challenge which Anscombe has to meet is to be able to formulate clearly, on her intentionality principle, the distinction between the use of contraceptives and the use of periodic abstinence, and she does so as follows:

> In contraceptive intercourse you intend to perform a sexual act which, if it has a chance of being fertile, you render infertile. Qua your intentional action, then, what you do is something intrinsically unapt for generation and, that is why it does fall under that same condemnation. There's all the world of difference between this and the use of the 'rhythm' method. For you use the rhythm method not just by having intercourse now, but by not having it next week, say; and not having it next week isn't something that does

---

[29] Ibid. She is followed in this logic by Brian J. Shanley, O. in 'The Moral Difference between Natural Family Planning and Contraception,' *Linacre Quarterly* 54 (1987), 48-60 at 50-52 and Martin Rhonheimer in"Contraception, Sexual Behavior, and Natural Law: Philosophical Foundations of the Norm of 'Humanae Vitae'" *Linacre Quarterly*, May, 1989, 20-57 at 22.

[30] Ibid, 86. (Emphasis in the original.)

something to today's intercourse to turn it into an infertile act; today's intercourse is an ordinary act of intercourse, an ordinary marriage act.[31]

But does this work? Is the distinction clear at the level of intention where Anscombe places all the moral significance? In a sympathetic critique of Anscombe's contribution Jenny Teichmann formulates the difficulty well. She summarizes Anscombe's argument as being that sexual intercourse accompanied by the use of contraceptives is wrong because it 'embodies an intention to avoid conception.'[32] She then poses the fundamental problem.

> Even if it is wrong to say that individual acts of safe period sex embody the intention to avoid conception might one not correctly describe the whole programme of choosing only safe period acts as embodying that intention? The intention here occurs, not indeed as a cause of the infertility of this or that act, but rather as the cause of the infertility of a particular couple, of a particular couple's sexual life.'[33] … It seems then that we are left with the following question: if an *action* is condemnable because it embodies a certain intention, will a *programme of behaviour* which embodies that same intention also be condemnable, and if not why not? At present I do not see any way of finding an answer to this question.[34]

With these questions in mind, let us look again at Anscombe's intentionality principle and give the full quotation from her text. She

---

[31] Anscombe, Contraception and Chastity, 19.
[32] Jenny Teichman, "Intention and Sex" in *Intention and intentionality : essays in honour of G.E.M. Anscombe*, edd. Cora Diamond and Jenny Teichman (Brighton: Harvester Press, 1979), 147-61 at 152.
[33] Ibid, 155-56.
[34] Ibid, 156.

wrote that 'if acts *not* of an inherently non-procreative kind are non-procreative in virtue of further circumstances, then surely *only* the anti-conceptional intent could be objectionable; and this in itself is *not* regarded as vitiating acts of intercourse, if use of the 'safe period' is permitted.'[35] Am I missing something, or is Anscombe not contradicting herself in this sentence. *Only* the contraceptive intent can be objectionable, and yet it is *not* regarded as vitiating acts of intercourse since periodic abstinence is permitted! But can this argument from intention alone be considered to be convincing at all? Can anything be changed in its intrinsic nature simply by taking thought? Can an act of intercourse be changed from procreative to non-procreative simply by one's intention in performing it? It seems clear to me that this issue simply cannot be resolved at the level of intention, for an intention is wrong only if the act intended is wrong, and that is the point to be proved.

The Inseparable Connection of the Unitive and Procreative Dimensions

In *Humanae vitae*, Pope Paul VI stated that the teaching of the Church in this matter 'is based on the inseparable connection, established by God, which man on his own initiative may not break, between the unitive significance and the procreative significance which are both inherent to the marriage act.' (*Humanae vitae*, § 12) This is a strong and clear statement, and Richard McCormick, in his reaction to the encyclical takes it at its face value, and with reason, when he says: 'It seems that the whole weight of the Encyclical's teaching that a contraceptive act is "intrinsece inhonestum" (n. 14) derives from this analysis. In fact, Pope Paul says just that.'[36] In that same paragraph of the encyclical Pope Paul affirmed that he believed that 'our contemporaries are particularly capable of seeing that this teaching is in harmony with human reason.' This expectation was not borne out in practice. A

---

[35] Anscombe, "You Can have Sex without Children." 85.
[36] *Theological Studies* 29 (1968), 727.

typical reaction was that expressed in the editorial of the United States Catholic newspaper the *National Catholic Reporter*. The editorial noted that the entire weight of the encyclical rests on the single assertion of an inseparable connection between the unitive and procreative dimensions of sexual intercourse. It recognises that there is obviously a connection, and then asks: 'But is the connection *inseparable*? How do we *know* that it is inseparable? On what basis is it asserted that separating the two functions of the marriage act, by means of contraception, is *evil*?'[37] These are legitimate questions and they raise questions in regard to the inseparability principle which need to be addressed.

A first point to note is that Pope Paul is asserting a moral, not a factual, inseparability, for the possibility of separating the two aspects in practice is obvious and creates the moral problem. The encyclical admits as much in the previous paragraph when it points out that sexual intercourse chosen during the infertile period is legitimate since 'its natural adaptation to the expression and strengthening of the union of husband and wife is not thereby suppressed.' Richard McCormick considers this recognition of a *de facto* separation of the unitive and procreative dimensions in periodic continence as a contradiction in the encyclical[38], but that doesn't really make sense. It would be foolish to deny the obvious possibility of separating the two dimensions of intercourse, and, in any case, it is clear that Pope Paul has a moral inseparability in mind when he speaks of an 'inseparable connection, established by God, which man on his own initiative may not break'. The question remains, however, as to the solidity of the foundation for this moral inseparability.

According to McCormick, the one who was more than anyone else associated with systematizing the notion of inseparability was Joseph Fuchs.[39] Speaking of the two ends of intercourse, Fuchs laid down his premise that 'the Creator *united* this double aspect. The sexual faculty

---

[37] Editorial from the *National Catholic Reporter*, August 7, 1968 in *The Catholic Case for Contraception*, ed. Daniel Callahan (London: Arlington Books, 1969), 136-46 at 140-41.
[38] *Theological Studies* 29 (1968), 728.
[39] Ibid, 727.

has but *one* natural actuation in which the generative and oblative aspects specify each other.'[40] From this it follows that 'an act which is not apt for procreation is by this very fact shown to be one which is *of itself* not apt for the expression of conjugal love; for the sexual act is one.'[41] McCormick reports further:

> Many of us accepted this approach for a number of years and argued that contraceptive inteference could not be viewed as a merely biological intervention. Rather, we argued, it was one which affected the very foundation of the act as procreative and hence as unitive of persons; for by excluding the child as the permanent sign of the love to be expressed in coitus, one introduced a reservation into coitus and therefore robbed it of that which makes it objectively unitive.[42]

Whereas previously it was enough to say that contraception was wrong simply because it attacked the procreative aspect of intercourse. Now that periodic abstinence was recognised as a method of avoiding procreation, the procreative principle alone was no longer considered sufficient to establish the immorality of contraception. In that situation the effort now was to argue that an attack on procreation was also an attack on the unitive dimension, that the two are inseparable. The new principle was needed and the one Fuchs and McCormick used was the quality of self-gift inherent in sexual intercourse. As McCormick put it: 'Acts that do not preserve a completeness of donation (e.g., condomistic intercourse and *coitus interruptus* or withdrawal) fail to express the relationship of total oblation. By more or less detracting from the total self-gift, such acts do not create unity in one flesh, and to that extent

---

[40] Joseph Fuchs, S. J., *De castitate et ordine sexuali* (3rd ed.), (Rome: Gregorian University Press, 1963), 80.
[41] Ibid, 45.
[42] *Theological Studies* 29 (1968), 727-28.

they are separative.'[43] The inseparability of the unitive and procreative dimensions implies 'that we may use the procreative aspect of the act as a practical criterion of complete self-giving. Because the act is one, we cannot negate the act in one aspect and not in the other'[44] McCormick asked the question as to why the procreative aspect could be used as a criterion for the proper performance of the sexual act, and therefore for completeness of self-giving, and gave this answer:

> First of all, the procreative demands are clear and definite and resist the abuse to which the term "self-giving" is liable. Secondly, the union of spouses, when complete and total, strives for permanence and stability. The child is not simply a biological result of the act; he is a person – a living and permanent symbol of the union of persons. But as symbol he contains the thing symbolized. Hence it is quite natural that the procreative capability of the human effort should be highlighted as the criterion for the completeness of donation in sexual union.[45]

These reasons seem to be somewhat weak as well as overly general. To be clear and definite and resistant of abuse is a secondary consideration and would need some more fundamental point to carry conviction. The notion of the child as an expression of parental self-donation is odd, and, in any case, it would tell against the avoidance of procreation by periodic abstinence. These considerations seem to be simply the old procreative principle under another guise. It is no wonder that McCormick was himself doubtful of the force of his arguments. At the conclusion of his efforts he wrote:

---

[43] Richard A. McCormick, S. J., 'Conjugal Love and Conjugal Morality: A re-evaluation of the Catholic position in terms of total marital commitment,' *America* January 11, 1964, 38-42 at 39.
[44] Ibid, 40.
[45] Ibid.

> When there is withdrawal or appliance contraception, the rejection of total self-giving would seem relatively clear ... Sterilization procedures empty the donation of its fullness, the more especially where permanent sterilization renounces any future decision for parenthood. This latter point may be more difficult for the limited human intelligence to see, even though sterilization is a more radical attack on total self-giving. I doubt that we shall ever be able to demonstrate such a conclusion with the satisfying click of the adding machine. ... Without the sure guidance /41 of the Church's authentic teaching, we might not conclude that sterilization impairs self-giving – at least with regard to temporary sterilization (e.g., by hormonal pills such as Enovid), where there are cogent reasons for the avoidance of pregnancy.[46]

This line of argument did not impress many people at the time, even as staunch an upholder of the traditional position as Germain Grisez. He observes that the 'gist of the phenomenological argument is that sexual intercourse ... represents objectively the mutual, total self-giving of man and woman.'[47] From this it follows that no reservations and obstacles must be allowed to interfere with the definitive and exclusive surrender of man and wife to one another, and, since contraception introduces such an obstacle, the practice is an offense against the meaning of the conjugal act. He then concludes: 'One way to understand this argument is to assume at the beginning that the withholding of one's effective generative power, whether or not one's partner approves, is a withholding of part of what *ought* to be given in the mutual self-giving. If the argument is understood in this way, however, it will not prove

---

[46] Ibid, 40-41.
[47] Germain Grisez, *Contraception and the Natural Law* (Milwaukee: The Bruce Publishing Company, 1964), 33.

that contraception is immoral, for it proceeds on the supposition that it is."[48]

Subsequent events have shown that these arguments did not suffice to maintain their conviction of the immorality of contraception for Fuchs and McCormick. Fuchs was the most famous of the moralists on the Papal Commission who changed his mind in the course of the discussions, and McCormick's agonising journey is well documented in his *Notes on Moral Theology* in *Theological Studies* over the relevant years. Even so, this is precisely the argument used much later by Monsignor Cormac Burke in his effort to ground the inseparability principle appealed to by Pope Paul VI in *Humanae vitae*.[49] Monsignor Burke summarizes the argument in favour of contraception on the basis that it respects the quality of sexual intercourse as unitive and points out that this implies that the two aspects are separable. To this he replies:

> This thesis is of course explicitly rejected by the Church. The main reason why contraception is unacceptable to a Christian conscience is, as Paul VI puts it in "Humanae Vitae", the "inseparable connection, established by God ... between the unitive significance and the procreative significance which are both inherent to the marriage act" (HV 12).[50] ... this connection ... is the very ground of the moral evaluation of the act.[51]

Monsignor Burke has made a strong claim here. The thesis of separability has been explicitly rejected by Pope Paul VI in *Humanae vitae*, but one cannot conclude from that without further ado that it has been explicitly rejected *by the Church*. One can reasonably claim that contraception has been explicitly rejected *by the Church*, though even

---

[48] Ibid, 33-34.
[49] Cormac Burke, "Marriage and Contraception," in Smith, ed., Why Humane Vitae was Right: A Reader, 153-69. The article first appeared in the *Linacre Quarterly* 55 (Feb. 1988), 44-55.
[50] Ibid, 155.
[51] Ibid, 156.

that is disputed by many, but a single statement in one encyclical does not establish the principle of inseparability as the teaching *of the Church*.

In his article Monsignor Burke sets out 'to show why one cannot annul the procreative aspect or the procreative reference of the marital act without necessarily destroying its unitive function and significance.'[52] The principle he uses is the one used earlier by Fuchs and McCormick, the donative quality of sexual intercourse, and this argument is also subsequently used by Pope John Paul II in *Familiaris consortio*, § 32:

> When couples, by means of recourse to contraception, separate these two meanings that God the Creator has inscribed in the being of man and woman and in the dynamism of their sexual communion, they act as "arbiters" of the divine plan and they "manipulate" and degrade human sexuality-and with it themselves and their married partner-by altering its value of "total" self-giving. Thus the innate language that expresses the total reciprocal self-giving of husband and wife is overlaid, through contraception, by an objectively contradictory language, namely, that of not giving oneself totally to the other. This leads not only to a positive refusal to be open to life but also to a falsification of the inner truth of conjugal love, which is called upon to give itself in personal totality.

And Pope John Paul II elaborates the point further in one of his catechetical homilies on the theology of the body, going so far as to state that in this is to be found the essential evil of contraception.

> The conjugal act 'signifies' not only love, but also potential fecundity, and therefore it cannot be deprived of its full and adequate significance by artificial means. In the conjugal act it is not licit to separate the unitive aspect from the procreative aspect, because both the

---

[52] Ibid, 154.

one and the other pertain to the intimate truth of the conjugal act: the one is activated together with the other and in a certain sense the one by means of the other. This is what the encyclical teaches. Therefore, in such a case the conjugal act deprived of its interior truth, because artificially deprived of its procreative capacity, ceases also to be an act of love. It can be said that in the case of an artificial separation of these two aspects, there is carried out in the conjugal act a real bodily union, but it does not correspond to the interior truth and to the dignity of personal communion: communion of persons. This communion demands in fact that the "language of the body" be expressed reciprocally in the integral truth of its meaning. If this truth be lacking, one cannot speak either of the truth of self-mastery, or of the truth of the reciprocal gift and of the reciprocal acceptance of self on the part of the person. Such a violation of the interior order of conjugal union which is rooted in the very order of the person, constitutes the essential evil of the contraceptive act.[53]

The inseparability principle is presumed here. We saw earlier the efforts of Fuchs and McCormick to provide a coherent basis for it and their lack of success. In his article Monsignor Burke takes a different approach, attempting to use the principle of self-donation to ground the inseparability of the unitive and procreative aspects of sexual intercourse in the very physiology of the act. He wrote:

> The greatest expression of a person's desire to give *himself* is to give the *seed* of himself. ... In human terms, this is the closest one can get to giving one's self conjugally and to accepting the conjugal self-gift of another, and so achieving spousal union. Therefore,

---

[53] John Paul II, Reflections on Humanae Vitae (Boston: St. Paul Editions, 1984), 33-34.

what makes marital intercourse express a <u>unique</u> relationship and union is ... the sharing of a *power* – an extraordinary life-related, creative, physical, sexual power.[54]

On this basis his argument runs:

> Now, if one deliberately nullifies the life-orientation of the conjugal act, *one destroys its essential power to signify union*. ... In contraceptive sex, no unique power is being shared, except a power to produce pleasure. But then the uniqueness of the marital act is reduced to pleasure. Its significance is gone.[55] ... Instead of accepting each other totally, contraceptive spouses reject part of each other, because fertility is part of each one of them. They reject part of their mutual love – its power to be fruitful. A couple may say, 'We do not want our love to be fruitful.' But if that is so, there is an inherent contradiction in their trying to express their love by means of an act which, of its nature, implies fruitful love: and there is even more of a contradiction if, when they engage in the act, they deliberately destroy the fertility-orientation from which precisely it derives its capacity to express the uniqueness of their love.[56]

There are a number of difficulties with this. The first relates to the very use of the concept of self-giving in this context. What does it mean to give oneself to another person. The paradigmatic text underlying the notion is 1 Timothy 2:6 which tells us that Jesus 'gave himself as a ransom for all.' Our Lord gave his life (yuch,) (Matt 20:28; Mark 10:45), and we understand that what is being referred to is his acceptance of death for us. Giving of oneself means giving one's possessions, one's

---

[54] Burke, "Marriage and Contraception," 157.
[55] Ibid, 158.
[56] Ibid, 159.

time, one's property, etc., and it is understood that the gift is more or less difficult and costly. How does any of this apply to the case of sexual intercourse? The urge to have sexual intercourse is a natural and strong drive, sometimes difficult to control, and it is not immediately obvious how the notion of self-gift on any possible analogy with the self-gift of Jesus to us can be applied to it. There is an enormous amount of self-giving in married and family life, but sexual intercourse is simply not part of it. The gift of themselves involved in rearing children, the feeding at night, the continual demands through the day. This is the kind of area where genuine self-giving occurs. The gift of time and energy to listen to one's spouse. It can happen that an act of intercourse can be a selfless act, when one is not well or the mood is wrong. But to speak of self-giving in the case of the normal ecstatic experience of sexual intercourse is to use language in an obscure and confusing manner. In marriage as a whole there is a total and mutual giving of self, faithful and exclusive until death, but how can that be said to be true for an individual act of intercourse?

A further problem with the argument is it applies equally to the systematic use of the sterile period for intercourse. By restricting intercourse to the sterile period, the spouses are withholding the procreative power from their intercourse. They are robbing their intercourse of its ability for two to become one flesh through the new life they could create. Pope John Paul does not say that the act of sexual intercourse that is not open to procreation is not truly unitive. He is always careful to say that the act of sexual intercourse *artificially deprived* of its procreative capacity is not truly unitive. He has to say that, otherwise he is back in the old problem which dogged the understanding of sexual intercourse since the Stoics first got their theory off the ground. The difficulty here is that it is not easy to see how the artificiality of the sterilization affects the unitive capacity of the intercourse. The acts are physically identical, the overall intention is the same in both cases. What difference does it make to the act of intercourse itself that the woman has taken the pill ahead of time? Orgasm is a biological function of a very high intensity. If it can be properly understood as self-giving at all, it seems to me that it is self-giving of quite a low level.

Genuine self-giving cannot surely be so attractive that one has to work hard to resist the temptation to indulge in it in quite inappropriate circumstances. Pointing to the ejaculation of semen as the man 'giving' of his very body to his beloved is an odd kind of romanticizing of a very fundamental biological function. And the same can be said of considering this function as a statement on the level of sharing truth with another, and the tampering with the semen as a 'lie'

A completely different argument is proposed to ground the inseparability principle by Martin Rhonheimer, and the fact that he takes a different approach entirely might reasonably be taken as a further sign of the failure of the self-donation principle. For him the malice of contraception lies in a failure of what he calls procreative responsibility, manifested in the unwillingness to accept the disruption demanded by periodic abstinence. Rhonheimer opens his argument with the assertion that it is '[o]nly on the background of an already deeply implanted contraceptive mentality,' that 'periodic continence may appear unreasonable.'[57] This does not seem right to me, to begin with. It is not necessary to have 'a deeply implanted contraceptive mentality' in order that periodic continence should seem unreasonable. All that is necessary is that one does not agree with the official teaching of the Catholic Church that contraception is intrinsically evil. For periodic abstinence is unreasonable, unnecessary and even absurd, apart from a solid conviction that contraception is morally wrong. One abstains from intercourse during the fertile times for the simple reason that one believes contraception is a sin. Otherwise the thought would not cross one's mind. If one considered contraception morally acceptable and wished to have sexual intercourse during a fertile period, then one would simply use contraception. Obviously, then, as Rhonheimer points out, '[c]ontraception signifies that to avoid conception, sexual behavior need not be modified.'[58] Of course, it need not be modified, if contraception is an acceptable option, and that is the point of contraception. And Rhonheimer finds all the moral problem with

---

[57] Rhonheimer, "Contraception, Sexual Behavior, and Natural Law," 42.
[58] Ibid, 43.

contraception in this unwillingness to modify one's sexual behavior in order to avoid conception. He writes: 'Contraception is problematic precisely because of the fact that it renders needless a specific sexual behavior informed by procreative responsibility; it also involves a choice against virtuous self-control by continence.'[59] This argument seems to me to be perfectly circular. The only conceivable reason for periodic abstinence is the conviction that contraception is wrong. It cannot therefore be the ground of the immorality of contraception that one is unwilling to abstain periodically, when periodic abstinence only makes sense on the prior conviction that contraception is wrong.

These efforts to ground the inseparability of the unitive and the procreative dimensions of intercourse in a new principles of total self-giving or procreative responsibility do not seem to achieve their goal. And if they did succeed, it would mean that inseparability is not the real principle involved. For the efforts to establish the inseparability principle begin from yet another principle, the quality of self-donation deemed to be inherent in the act of sexual intercourse, or procreative responsibility as the case may be. On that showing it would mean that the real principle being applied is the principle of self-donation or procreative responsibility and the inseparable connection is a conclusion derived from the deeper principle. One is therefore led to sympathise with the view of Richard McCormick that the inseparability principle is simply the traditional procreative principle re-elaborated in a different form: 'Many have seen this notion of inseparability and its implication as a linear descendent – indeed, a prolongation – of the analysis of intercourse as an *actus naturae* with a single procreative purpose.'[60]

One thing is abundantly clear and that is that the inseparability principle to which Pope Paul appealed so confidently has not succeeded in convincing many people. And so it would appear that Pope Paul's belief that our contemporaries are particularly capable of seeing that the teaching is in harmony with reason was not well founded. The experience of the succeeding forty years belies the notion utterly.

---

[59] Ibid.
[60] McCormick, *The Critical Calling)*, 214.

And why should it be so easy to see? The procreative significance of intercourse is obvious, and always has been. The recognition of the unitive significance is a comparative novelty in the Church. How can it be said to be evident that the two are inseparably connected in some way? St. Augustine based his doctrine on the procreative significance alone and took it too far. He had no sense of the unitive significance and believed that intercourse was for procreation alone. He concluded that any attempt to avoid procreation was therefore illegitimate and that judgment of his has had to be revised all these centuries later. Can it not be legitimately deduced from this that there are circumstances when the unitive significance can be legitimately separated from the procreative and sought for its own sake while taking deliberate steps to ensure that procreation does not occur? It seems to me to be a reasonable interpretation of the use of periodic abstinence that one is separating the unitive and procreative significances of intercourse in so doing. Nature separates the two significances all the time. The existence of the female rhythm of fertility and infertility can reasonably be taken to mean that God himself has built into the structure of sexual relations that the two significances are separated so that the couple can enjoy a freedom in their sexual relations which does not excessively result in procreation. Why choose as the basis of the doctrine a principle which seems to be so obviously counter to what nature itself allows.

Grisez's New Version of the Procreative Argument

The strongest rejection of the classical argument based on the procreative purpose of intercourse is to be found in an early work of one of the staunch defenders of the traditional position on contraception, Germain Grisez. In his book presenting a new argument of his own, he sets about comprehensively demolishing the traditional synthesis which had held sway from St. Augustine and St. Thomas. He first of all outlines and then rebuts the general principle that acting against the natural function of human systems is against the natural law. He begins: 'Arguments proceeding within the framework of conventional natural-law theory always include the following incomplete syllogism: *Contraception is intrinsically immoral because by it one engaging in intercourse prevents his act from attaining its natural end.*[61] This is the major premises of the "perverted-faculty argument," and Grisez rejects it as follows: 'This major has never seemed obvious to many although some have claimed it to be self-evident. Whether it were evident in itself or not, it would need to be explained in some way that would reveal why the natural teleology of human functions requires absolute moral respect. Simply to assume this principle against someone who is defending the liceity of contraception is to beg the question.'[62] He considers this more general principle as it applies in the particular case of sexual ethics: 'Any sexual activity apart from the conditions necessary for it to be suited of itself to the procreation and proper education of children is intrinsically immoral.'[63] And again he rejects it, saying that 'the most telling reason against using this general principle of sexual ethics to support the specific proposition about contraception is that the general principle itself is neither evident nor easily proved. Moreover, the argument that contraception may not be intrinsically immoral implies precisely that this general principle admits of exceptions. Consequently, simply to assert the general principle is to beg the question.'[64] Grisez's rejection of this whole tradition based on the procreative principle is sweeping and total: 'It is only unfortunate that those who wished to show the intrinsic immorality of contraception assumed the first logically adequate major premise which came to hand – one indefensible because it is more general than is required – instead of examining the specific nature of the contraceptive act. The many attempts over the years to show the intrinsic immorality of contraception using this faulty premise have exposed Catholic moral thought to endless ridicule and surely have caused harm in other ways.'[65]

---

[61] Grisez, *Contraception and the Natural Law*, 20.
[62] Ibid, 27-28.
[63] Ibid, 26.
[64] Ibid.
[65] Ibid, 31.

Grisez himself proposed a new argument against contraception. As an alternative to the traditional synthesis he has set aside, Grisez develops a new theory of the natural law based on the idea that there are basic principles formulating the goods which every human being must seek and which bind everyone always and everywhere. He identifies procreation as one of these goods and uses the corresponding principle as the ground for the condemnation of contraception. He writes:

> According to the theory of the moral law which I outlined ..., there is a fundamental affirmative precept of moral law corresponding to each of man's basic natural inclinations. ... To show that contraception is intrinsically immoral, therefore, we need only show it to be a direct violation of one of the basic principles. ... The principle violated by contraception is that procreation is a human good worthy of man's pursuit, and that human acts suited to achieve this good should be done. This is a basic moral principle. It is one of the primary sources of all human practical reasoning. It obligates all men and holds true at all times."[66]

The structure of Grisez's argument is remarkably similar to the traditional argument he rejected, and one can react to it in just the same way as he reacted to the traditional argument. One can simply say, as Grisez did, that this new principle 'is neither evident nor easily proved. Moreover, the argument that contraception may not be intrinsically immoral implies precisely that this general principle admits of exceptions. Consequently, simply to assert the general principle is to beg the question.'[67] Furthermore, Grisez's argument fares no better than the others that have been examined in making clear the distinction between artificial contraception and periodic abstinence. The practice of periodic abstinence is a means of avoiding procreation and is, therefore, a form of behaviour which goes against this fundamental human good

---

[66] Ibid, 76.
[67] See above at footnote X.

of procreation, and stands condemned by Grisez's new principle. By its condemnation of an acceptable form of behaviour, therefore, Grisez's new principle also fails.

The realization of the weakness of the arguments behind the condemnation of contraception has been around for quite some time. In the concluding stages of the work of the Papal Commission on birth control, the group of moral theologians representing the majority of the Commission drew up a document presenting an 'Argument for Reform' of the teaching on contraception. They pointed to the fact that 'today many of the best theologians who defend the illicitness of every contraceptive intervention because of the past teaching of the Church, concede that they do not have a convincing argument based on reason or natural law.'[68] In its editorial reaction to the publication of *Humanae vitae*, the *National Catholic Reporter* complains against the encyclical that 'by failing to present a respectable rationale for the stand it takes, it imposes an impossible burden on Catholic teachers and confessors ...'[69] More recently, after a thorough examination of two contemporary arguments in favour of the traditional condemnation of contraception, Gareth Moore concludes: 'So I think the attempts ... find a solid detailed basis in reason for the traditional Christian and modern Catholic ban on contraception fail. I have not seen another one that is at all convincing, and I do not know how to generate one myself.'[70] It seems to me that Moore's reaction would be very widely shared, and it seems sound to me.

---

[68] "The "Argument for Reform" 27 May 1966," in Peter Harris, et. al., On Human Life: An Examination of Humanae Vitae (London: Burns & Oates, 1968), 203-15 at 205.

[69] Editorial from the *National Catholic Reporter*, August 7, 1968, *The Catholic Case for Contraception*, ed. Daniel Callahan (London: Arlington Books, 1969), 136-46 at 140.

[70] Gareth Moore, O., *The Body in Context: Sex and Catholicism* (London: SCM Press, 1992), 178.

Chapter 19

The Failure of the Arguments Interpreted

On the basis of what has been presented so far, it is possible to offer some points of interpretation which help to explain the situation in which we find ourselves. Given that the procreative principle has been the leading argument underpinning the condemnation of contraception for so long, it becomes quite understandable that the ultimate collapse of the arguments based on this principle would lead to a widespread loss of conviction about the value of the moral judgment involved. This is certainly the line of thought underlying the dissenting position. The *eminence grise* of the dissent, Louis Janssens, in his two important articles[1], considers no other basis for the traditional position, and I have found no dissenting theologian taking any different line. With a single exception, which will be dealt with at a later stage, the same is true of all those defending the traditional doctrine. It has to be recognised, therefore, that the dissent on this issue has a *fundamentum in re*.

In this light, a plausible explanation is required as to how this argument first emerged and how it has survived for so long. Everyone admits that the condemnation of contraception has been an element of the Christian tradition from the earliest times. The dissenting view holds that this long-standing tradition is based on the procreative principle, and is not a genuine Christian tradition bearing the word of God, but a

---

[1] Janssens, 'Morale conjugale,' 513-54.

human tradition deriving from some other source. Corroborative of this position is the fact which has been pointed out earlier that the principle of the procreative purpose of intercourse was not of Christian origin. The early Fathers inherited it from the Stoic philosophers and we saw St. Augustine basing it on natural reasoning, while giving incidental and not very apposite Scriptural references. Karl Rahner has offered a hermeneutical key which can point a way forward here. In one of his articles, he discussed the issue of moral argument and offered a suggestion as to how invalid moral arguments can carry force.

> There are also *false* (historically time-conditioned, global, instinctively operating) convictions which then seek objective expression in explicit conceptual 'proofs', so that to anyone who shares these convictions the proofs are obvious and they are put forward and defended with the absoluteness with which people cling to such a prescientific global conviction, even though the latter is false or at least questionable. ... The actual development and history of moral theology in the Church has to do largely, not only with the destruction of incorrect or uncertain theological arguments as such, but with the demolition of such prescientific instinctive convictions which are false or unproved, but hitherto made the explicit arguments seem 'obvious'.[2]

I suggest, therefore, that there is a 'prescientific global conviction' which can explain the emergence of the procreative principle and its survival for so long, and it is the natural instinct of self-preservation of the species. That sexual intercourse has a procreative purpose is self-evident, and the only question is as to its precise moral implications. The high value placed on fecundity and a large family is a feature of all traditional cultures, and it finds its perfect expression in the biblical injunction: 'Be fruitful and multiply and fill the earth and subdue

---

[2] Karl Rahner, S.J., 'On Bad Arguments in Moral Theology,' *Theological Investigations 18* (London: Darton, Longman & Todd, 1984), 74-85, at 78.

it …' (Gen 1:28). This positive injunction has deep roots in traditional cultures and leads to an instinctive abhorrence of any form of birth control. There is even one explicit condemnation of contraception, which is based on this logic, to found in the writings of the Stoic philosopher Musonius Rufus. He appeals to traditional laws prohibiting birth control, and goes on: 'How then could it be that we are not acting unjustly and unlawfully, when we do things contrary to the wish of these lawmakers, godly and god-favored men, whom it is considered good and useful to follow? And we act against their wish when we prevent our women from having many children. How could we not be sinning against our ancestral gods and against Zeus, protector of the family, when we do such things?'[3]

This instinct has found expression also in the Judaeo-Christian tradition. Among the Jews it takes the form of the duty to propagate the race which is imposed on every Jewish man. The duty to procreate the race did not survive in the Christian tradition because of the new ideal of virginity. In fact one of the first evidences of Christian influence on Roman law is a decree of the Emperor Constantine in 320 terminating a part of the traditional legislation encouraging procreation, and, in later decrees, the special privileges of large families and the penalizing of childless couples were both ended in the year 410. However, despite the fact that the traditional positive injunction had to be moderated in Christianity, I suggest that the instinct remained operative and transferred its focus on to the purposes of sexual intercourse and the strong resistance to the notion of birth control in marriage. Understood in this way, the procreative principle condemns birth control without distinction of means. It is not surprising, therefore, that the first time the principle was applied, St. Augustine condemned the Manichean practice of periodic abstinence. And it makes sense also of the fact that no argument based on the principle has ever been able to distinguish between the practice of artificial contraception and periodic abstinence.

---

[3] Musonius Rufus, 'Should All Children Born be Brought Up?' as quoted in Stobaeus, *Florilegium* 75.15, in Musonius, *Reliquiae*, ed. Hense. Text, reference and translation in Noonan, *Contraception*, 48-49.

The procreative purpose of intercourse certainly has moral implications. It can reasonably ground the restriction of intercourse to the married, without demanding that the procreative purpose of every act of intercourse. It can also reasonably ground the positive injunction to have children, unless there are compelling reasons to avoid having them. What it cannot do is to ground the moral judgment of the means used to avoid procreation, and that has only become clear over long centuries of careful reflection.

This understanding can also help to make sense of an unresolved difference of opinion between the Papal Commission on Birth Control and *Humanae vitae*. The Majority Report of the Papal Commission suggested that the self-evident procreative purpose of marriage and sexuality should be understood as being a quality of marriage and the family rather than of the individual act of sexual intercourse. It said: '"The responsible procreative community" is always ordered towards procreation; this is the objective and authentic meaning of sexuality and of those things which refer to sexuality (affectivity, unity, the ability to educate). So we can speak of the "procreative end" as the essential end of sexuality and of conjugal life.'[4] In this perspective it could be considered morally acceptable to render some acts of intercourse infertile when the overall procreative good of the family unit called for it, for 'the morality of sexual acts between married people takes its meaning first of all and specifically from the ordering of their actions in a fruitful married life, that is one which is practised with responsible, generous and prudent parenthood. It does not then depend upon the direct fecundity of each and every particular act.'[5] In *Humanae vitae* referred to this argument as an application of 'the so called principle of totality', and considered the question: 'Could it not be admitted, in other words, that procreative finality applies to the totality of married life rather than to each single act?' (*Humanae vitae* § 3) Later in the encyclical, Pope Paul rejected the argument with a paraphrase of Romans 3:8, 'it is never

---

[4] "The "Argument for Reform" 27 May 1966," in Peter Harris, et. al., On Human Life, 213.

[5] "The Theological Report of the Commission, 26 June 1966," in Peter Harris, et. al., On Human Life, 232.

lawful, even for the gravest reasons, to do evil that good may come of it, and concluded: 'Consequently, it is a serious error to think that a whole married life of otherwise normal relations can justify sexual intercourse which is deliberately contraceptive and so intrinsically wrong.' Pope Paul was criticised for his treatment of this matter.[6] It was point out, correctly, that he did not really respond to the argument at all. He simply assumed the point to be proved, that artificial contraception is intrinsically evil, and on that premise, the argument obviously fails.

It seems to me that there is a good logic in the position of the Report of the Papal Commission. The result of the analysis that has been made is that the procreative principle does not properly apply to each and every act of intercourse, but can reasonably be applied to married life as a whole, in the manner outlined by the Majority Report. Pope Paul did not attempt an answer to this argument, and this can be taken as a corroboration of the position being proposed here, that there is no answer based on the procreative principle. The procreative principle cannot be used effectively to condemn artificial contraception. On the other hand, it cannot be used effectively to condone it. The argument of the Majority Report simply points to the failure of the procreative principle. It leaves the issue of artificial contraception unresolved. It means that the argument against artificial contraception, if there is one, must lie elsewhere. And this point needs to be pressed. It has already been pointed out that the procreative purpose of intercourse was not the basis on which the condemnation of contraception was established. It was not used by St. Augustine to condemn contraception. His mention of contraception and his spirited condemnation of it had other sources, and it was only mentioned incidentally as part of a different argument. It was not used by St. Thomas to condemn contraception. He used it to condemn *coitus interruptus*, not as form of contraception but as a form of unnatural sexual intercourse. It came to be taken as the basis for the condemnation of contraception in later centuries when nothing else

---

[6] See for instance Richard A. McCormick, S. J., in his *Notes on Moral Theology* in *Theological Studies*, 29 (1968), 730-31.

seemed to be available. And as soon as other methods of contraception were discovered its weakness was revealed.

Faith or Reason?

The failure of all the arguments based on the procreative principle to establish the moral norm in regard to contraception raises a more fundamental question still. What is the role of rational argument in establishing the moral norms taught by the Church? The universal consensus seems to hold that successful rational arguments are essential in the process of establishing these moral norms. In an earlier chapter we have seen that Pope Paul VI, in *Humanae vitae*, gives some reason to believe that he himself is of that mind. He claimed that the Magisterium has a special role as 'interpreter' of the natural law, and presented moral arguments in favour of the doctrine. He presented no Scriptural witness in support of the teaching and the earliest reference to the tradition is to the Catechism of the Council of Trent. Louis Janssens observes that the encyclical refers to no argument from scripture, but appeals to natural law and rational principles, and concludes: 'Thus the document places itself on a plane where the final word is given not to authority, but to the overriding validity of the reasons proposed.'[7] If, as we have been forced to concede, the arguments do not prove the point, then a serious situation arises. As the editorial comment on the encyclical in the *National Catholic Reporter* pointed out, '[t]he reason all this is critically important is that the encyclical makes no pretense of finding authority in God's revelation for stating that contraception is against God's will. The teaching is founded on natural law, the encyclical says. To discover the natural law requires the use of reason, to explain and defend it requires the presentation of arguments drawn from reason.'[8] This expectation of rational arguments to establish the norm was widespread

---

[7] Janssens, 'Considerations on "Humanae Vitae",' 244.
[8] Editorial from the *National Catholic Reporter*, August 7, 1968, *The Catholic Case for Contraception*, ed. Daniel Callahan (London: Arlington Books, 1969), 136-46 at 142.

when the encyclical was published. Richard McCormick noted that many theologians had come to the conclusion that the traditional norms in this matter were genuinely doubtful and that the Majority Report of the Papal Commission represented the more probable opinion, and then went on: 'Hence, when *Humanae vitae* appeared, we read it eagerly looking for the new evidence or the more adequate analyses which led Paul VI to his reaffirmation of traditional norms.'[9]

This expectation of the encyclical is not universal. Martin Rhonheimer says: 'In my opinion, "Humanae Vitae" ... did not intend to provide a philosophical (ethical) reason why contraception violates natural law; it only wanted to affirm that it does. Nor does "Humanae Vitae" explicitly refer to any definite natural law concept. It applies, in the light of revelation (Holy Scripture and Tradition), its perennial, prophetical teaching on the matter to new developments in the field of contraceptive devices without putting forward a properly philosophical argument.'[10] Rhonheimer may very well be right here, but it has to be conceded that Pope Paul did not make clear what precisely he was doing in this regard and what he wrote is patient of the other interpretation. Whatever about the correct interpretation of *Humanae vitae*, the trust in the power of rational argument to ground the teaching of specific moral norms still waxes strong in Catholic moral theology. Martin Rhonheimer himself introduces the basic statement of his position on contraception with the statement that his aim is 'to show by rational arguments where the ethical problem of contraception is situated.'[11] He believes that 'the analysis of the demands based on the natural law is, in the first place, a task of philosophical ethics. The *fundamental* argument which demonstrates that contraception is, in principle and for all, an illicit action, must be, therefore, of an ethical-philosophical

---

[9] *Theological Studies* 29 (1968), 733.
[10] Martin Rhonheimer, "Contraception, Sexual Behavior, and Natural Law: Philosophical Foundations of the Norm of 'Humanae Vitae'" *Linacre Quarterly*, May, 1989, 20-57 at 23.
[11] Martin Rhonheimer, *Etica de la procreación* (Madrid: Ediciones Rialp, S. A., 2004), 28.

nature.'[12] He points out that *Humanae vitae* teaches that contraception violates natural law 'and that's why it is first of all a *philosophical* issue. ... the basic argument will therefore be an argument on the philosophical level.'[13] It is not only Rhonheimer, but all the defences of the traditional position approach the matter in this way, and therein, in my opinion, lies a fundamental cause of the whole malaise we face.

For the fact of the matter is that a moral norm taught by the Church cannot be based on rational argument. The Holy Church of Christ can only teach on the basis of revelation; it possesses no other resource. A moral norm taught by the Church must be based on Scripture and Tradition, not on rational argument. There can, therefore, be no 'new' argument against contraception. Germain Grisez, in his early work, rejected the traditional arguments and proposed a new one of his own. I contend that any such new argument stands condemned *ipso facto*, for, from the Christian point of view, it is simply impossible that the foundation of the condemnation of contraception can be based on an argument which is completely new. The Church's teaching on any matter, including its teaching on moral matters, must of its very nature be based on Scripture and Tradition. The foundation of the teaching must have its roots in the past and, therefore, a totally new argument cannot possibly be its ultimate basis. The fundamental flaw is in the assumption that the condemnation of contraception is based on any such argument, whether the earlier ones or Grisez's own.

And this same point can be made about Pope Paul's appeal, in *Humanae vitae*, to the principle of the inseparability of the procreative and unitive dimensions of sexual intercourse. As has been noted already, many consider this to be the old procreative principle presented in a new form. Others, Rhonheimer goes in here? If, in fact, the principle really is new, I suggest that it fails the fundamental test of a proper foundation of Church doctrine, precisely on the grounds that it is new. Producing a new foundation for a Church doctrine defeats its own purpose. It implies that the foundations previously relied upon have

---

[12] Ibid, 30.
[13] Rhonheimer, "Contraception, Sexual Behavior, and Natural Law," 20.

been found to be inadequate, and when it fails itself in turn, a very strong impression is created that there is no solid foundation at all. But what is absolutely certain is that it is not the traditional basis of the doctrine on contraception.

On the basis of his examination of the tradition Germain Grisez concludes that '[i]t is a sign of the basic flaw in scholastic natural-law theory that it provided only question-begging arguments for specific norms of Christian morality.'[14] I suggest that Grisez misunderstands what it was that the scholastic theologians were doing. They weren't developing the specific norms of Christian morality on the basis of their natural-law theory. That is impossible. The norms of Christian morality are given by revelation and accepted by faith. The moral theories developed to try to explain the norms were efforts to understand norms already given, not efforts to establish them from scratch. It should cause no surprise, therefore, that the arguments would often be question-begging, since the conclusions were in fact given in advance. It seems to me that John Noonan has things exactly right when he says: 'It is, I suggest, evident that the appeal to a given "nature" was a way of teaching. The invocation of "nature" reinforced positions already taken.'[15] Noonan is speaking here about the reflections of the early Christian writers, but his comment applies equally to the whole of the Church's moral tradition. And, of course, it simply does not work as a justification for a Christian teaching, to find philosophical principles however exalted which purport to 'prove' the point. Christian teaching, of its nature, must be traditional. Its presentation cannot be that the teaching is this and the reason is that. It has to be presented, plausibly, in the form; the teaching is this, and it has always been this, for it has been taught by so-and-so and so-and-so always. Philosophical underpinnings of a Christian teaching are all very well, but they can only be presented as helps. If they are presented as the very reason for the teaching, something is radically wrong.

---

[14] Germain Grisez, *The Way of the Lord Jesus*, vol. 1, *Christian Moral Principles* (Quincy, IL: Franciscan Press, 1983), 105.

[15] Noonan, <u>Contraception</u>, 75.

The Role of Authority

The ultimate authority in matters of moral doctrine as in matters of dogma generally rests with the Magisterium of the Holy Church. Towards the end of *Humanae vitae* Pope Paul VI appealed to priests, especially teachers of moral theology, to give an example of sincere obedience to the magisterium of the Church. "For, as you know, the pastors of the Church enjoy a special light of the Holy Spirit in teaching the truth. And this, rather than the arguments they put forward, is why you are bound to such obedience."[16] This does not make sense if Pope Paul is being understood to be presenting rational arguments as the basis of his teaching. If, however, he is speaking as a Christian pastor in the person of Christ, then his position does make sense. He is not speaking as an independent 'interpreter' of the natural law, but as an authoritative interpreter of the Christian tradition, which is his role as Pope. In this case, his judgment can be respected even though he has not presented the grounds of his judgment clearly.

Richard McCormick seems to be challenging the whole notion of magisterial authority to teach the moral doctrine of the Church, when he writes:

> Where teaching authority is claimed within a religious community and where this authority is associated by divine design with officeholders (the hierarchy), there is the tendency that such authoritative teaching will become self-validating, that is, it will be regarded as correct simply because it is proposed by authorities. ... Such perspectives have a devaluating effect on the importance of moral argument and analysis, and the processes which nourish them. Moral positions will be regarded as correct regardless of the arguments or analysis used to support them. When moral analysis is devalued and replaced by authoritative

---

[16] Humanae vitae, § 28.

assertions in the public consciousness, there is the grave danger that it will become careless and undisciplined. The nonfunctional easily becomes the neglected. That this can happen is evident in the types of moral argument sometimes made by manualist theologians to uphold ecclesiastical positions.[17]

Later in the same chapter McCormick adds that 'when "loyalty to the Holy See" becomes the test of the legitimacy of a moral argument, then things are upside down. Truth becomes subordinate to institutional purposes and the instruments of its search. ... if we are never to be allowed to question the pronouncements of those who administer a moral code, then we are no longer dealing with morality but with authority.'[18]

It can be granted to McCormick that there are evident dangers involved in having human authorities acting in the person of Christ in the supervision of his deposit of faith and morals. The critical situation in which we now find ourselves is sufficient proof that much has gone badly wrong in traditional moral theology and teaching. However, *abusus non tollit usum*. The whole of the first part of this book was to establish the principle that there can be a legitimate criticism of the bishops of the Church, but that the genuine teaching of the Holy Church must be accepted by all without demurral. 'Loyalty to the Holy See' cannot be the ultimate test of a Christian position, but 'loyalty to the Holy Church' can and must be. There is no avoiding the fact that, in the Christian community, in matters of faith, which includes morals, authority has an ultimate role to play.

So what are we to make of an authoritative intervention where the arguments given do not convince? Rahner has given us a useful hermeneutical key for this situation as well. He points out that a true and genuine tradition of the Church can be hidden beneath a veneer of

---

[17] Richard A. McCormick, S.J., 'Moral Argument in Christian Ethics' in *The Critical Calling: Reflections on Moral Dilemmas Since Vatican II* (Washington, D.C.: Georgetown University Press, 1989), 47-69 at 52-53.
[18] Ibid, 62.

poor argumentation. He speaks of the situation where, 'for example, a correct global understanding of Christian *revelation* can be presumed behind an argument questionable in itself,'[19] and of 'the "right" that can exist behind a bad argument in moral theology, presented perhaps in a certain way without meeting any opposition and often sustained by a long history of moral theological teaching in the Church, since the conviction of the correctness of what was to be proved prevailed long before the appearance of the proof itself…'[20] If the traditional condemnation of artificial contraception is to be upheld the basis must lie elsewhere, and so we must now examine another line of tradition which has a much better claim to be the genuine Christian tradition in this matter.

---

[19] Rahner, 'On Bad Arguments in Moral Theology,' 77.
[20] Ibid, 78.

Chapter 20

The Genuine Tradition on Contraception

In his thorough presentation of the whole tradition on contraception, John Noonan makes clear that there are, in fact, two streams of tradition in the matter. He deals with both streams of tradition and their interrelationship, and it is his opinion that both aspects made a contribution to the formation of the teaching on contraception: 'The rule on contraception will be seen to have this double aspect: in part the outgrowth of a theory of sexual control, in part justified as a protection of life.'[1] He presents both aspects fairly and well, but his judgment is coloured by the widespread assumption, which he shares, that contraception is ultimately a matter of sexual morality. The argument here is that this judgment is mistaken, and that the condemnation of contraception is not as a matter of sexual morality at all. The establishment of the procreative principle has been analysed with a view to showing that its role in the matter is ultimately chimerical and not real at all. It was found to be without foundation either in Scripture or the early tradition, and to have arisen during the second millennium by using references of St. Augustine to contraception in a manner he had never envisaged. The plan now is to present an account of the real foundation of the doctrine which is located in the protection of human life in its origins.

---

[1] Noonan, *Contraception* 85. See also 91.

The genuine Christian tradition on contraception lies along the other line which sees contraception as a life matter, and is based on the sacredness of the human generative process. The scriptural foundation of this tradition is familiar enough, but it is not very well understood; the story of Onan's sin in Genesis 38. The key verses of the text run as follows:

> Then Judah said to Onan, "Go in to your brother's wife and perform your duty as brother-in-law to her and raise up seed (spe, rma) for your brother. But Onan knew that the seed (spe, rma) would not be his; so when he went in to his brother's wife he spilled (the seed) on the ground, lest he should give seed (sper, ma) to his brother. And what he did was evil in the sight of the Lord, and he killed him also. (Genesis 38:8-10)

What did Onan do that merited death? 'Was Onan punished for his disobedience, for his lack of family feeling, for his egotism, for his evasion of an obligation assumed, for his contraceptive acts, or for a combination of these faults?'[2] The exegetes differ on the answer to this question. The most commonly accepted interpretation is that Onan was killed for his breach of the Levirate law. Janssens, in his famous article of 1963, simply states this as something taken for granted; 'But the exegetes tell us that the reason for the divine punishment was the violation of the Levirate law, laid down in Deuteronomy (Deut. 25:5-10).'[3] This interpretation, however, cannot be sustained. The punishment for breaking this law, outlined in Deuteronomy 25:5-10, is to be publicly shamed not to be put to death. The capital offence must be sought elsewhere. Now, what Onan actually did was to 'waste' (Hebrew) or to 'spill' (Greek), the discreet Biblical manner of describing Onan's act of *coitus interruptus*. Neither Hebrew nor Greek has an object for these verbs but, beginning with St. Jerome's Latin translation[4], it has

---

[2] Noonan, *Contraception*, 35.
[3] Janssens, 'Morale conjugale et progestogènes,' 816.
[4] Noonan, *Contraception*, 102.

been common practice to insert the object 'seed', which appears three times in verses 8 and 9. Neither Hebrew nor Greek could use this word as the object for these verbs because, in those languages, the human 'seed' refers to offspring, as it does throughout both Testaments. The Bible does not have our ease with straightforward and crude references to physiological functions, but it would appear that already in the time of St. Jerome the Latin word for 'seed', *semen*, was already being applied to the male ejaculate. This concrete manner of thinking which bears within it the close connection between the male seed and the child to be born is foundational for the line of tradition to be reviewed here, and I see no reason why the obvious interpretation, that Onan was killed for what he concretely did in 'wasting the seed', should be set aside.

I suggest, therefore, that the true scriptural foundation of the tradition which condemns contraception is to be found in the biblical understanding of the unity of the whole human generative process which is implicit in the use of the word 'seed' to mean offspring through the whole Bible.[5] As the use of the word in Gen 38:8-9 indicates, the mind swings between the initiation of the process in sexual intercourse and its completion in the adult human being. The understanding is implicit here that the sacredness of human life is a continuous reality from its beginning, not in conception as a more developed understanding of biology would suggest but in sexual intercourse which initiates the human generative process. Whether or not this can be taken as the full interpretation of the Onan story, it represents an understanding of the sacredness of the functions of human generation which is a

---

[5] Gen 4:25; 13:16; 15:3, 5, 13; 16:10; 17:9; 19:32, 34; 21:12, 13, 23; 22:17; 24:60; 26:4, 24; 28:14; 32:13; 38:8, 9; 46:6;, 7; 48:11, 19; Exod 32:13; Lev 21:15; 22:13; Num 5:28; 14:24; 21:30; 23:10; 24:20; Deut 3:3; 4:37; 10:15; 25:5; 30:19; Joshua 24:3; 1 Sam 1:11; 2:20, 31; 24:22; 2 Sam 7:12; 2 Kings 11:1; 14:27; 1 Chron 16:13; 17:11; 2 Chron 22:10; Ezra 2:59; 9:2; Neh 7:61; Tobit 4:12; 8:6; 2 Macc 7:17; Ps 21:10; 22:23, 30; 25:13; 37:25, 26, 28; 69:36; 89:4, 29, 36; 102:28; 105:6; 106:27; 112:2; Job 5:25; Wisdom 3:16; 10:15; 12:11; 14:6; Sirach 10:19; 44:12, 13, 21; 46:9; 47:20, 22; Mal 2:15; Isaiah 1:4, 9; 14:20, 22, 30; 15:9; 41:8; 43:5; 44:3; 45:25; 48:14, 19; 53:10; 54:3; 57:3, 4; 61:9; 65:9, 23; 66:22; Jer 7:15; 23:8; 26:27; 38:27; Ezek 31:17; Dan 3:36; 13:56; Matt 22:24, 25; Mk 12:19, 20, 21, 22; Lk 20:28; Jn 8:33, 37; Acts 7:6; Romans 4:18; 9:7, 8, 29; 1 Cor 11:22; Gal 3:19, 29; Heb 11:18.

constant in the Christian tradition. It finds a first, programmatic, formulation in a short text of Clement of Alexandria, one of the first of the Christian Fathers to condemn contraception. He wrote: 'Because of its divine institution for the propagation of man, the seed is not to be vainly ejaculated, nor is it to be damaged, nor is it to be wasted.'[6] In the same text, he alludes to the fact that Moses forbade husbands to approach their wives at the time of menstruation 'for it is not right to contaminate with corrupt matter of the body the fertile part of the seed soon to become a human being.'[7] In these texts, the 'seed' has already now been clearly applied to the male ejaculate, and there is the explicit reference to its sacral character as the source of new life. Clement makes no reference to the Onan story, but his short text could stand as a comment upon it.

The role of contraception in the attack on life did not loom that large in the minds of the early Fathers, for there were bigger fish to fry at the time. As Noonan reports: 'The conventional Roman attitude to fetal and infant life was strikingly callous.'[8] Even infanticide was considered to be within the remit of the father of the family. Obviously enough, the condemnation of infanticide and abortion had to come first. There has always been the recognition of different levels of gravity in abortion depending on the state of the foetus in the womb, but the clear statement of St. Basil the Great is the one which has stood the test of time. He wrote: 'A woman who deliberately destroys a fetus is answerable for the taking of life. And any hairsplitting distinction as to its being formed or unformed is inadmissible with us.'[9] This respect for life in the womb was pushed back to cover the whole generative process in its full extent. Noonan sums up the development: 'Combating the prevailing indifference, the Christians taught that all life must be inviolate, and

---

[6] Paedogogus 2.10.91.2, GCS 12:212. Reference and translation in John T. Noonan, *Contraception: A History of Its Treatment by the Catholic Theologians and Canonists* (Cambridge, Mass.: Harvard University Press, 1965), 93.

[7] *Paedogogus* 2.10.92.1. *Sources Chretiennes* 108, 176-78.

[8] Noonan, *Contraception*, 85.

[9] Letters 188, PG 32:672. Reference and translation in Noonan, *Contraception*, 88, footnote 40.

using the terms the law reserved for the killing of adults, they charged that not only the destruction of existing life but the interruption of the life-giving process was homicide and parricide. They were led to attach sanctity not only to life but to the life-giving process.'[10]

It is within this context that the patristic tradition on contraception is to be properly understood. According to Noonan, 'the first fairly clear reference to contraception by a Christian writer is in the *Elenchos* or *Refutation of all the Heresies* written between 220 and 230.'[11] This document is a vehement attack on Pope Callixtus who had permitted marriages involving those whom the civil law did not recognise. Noonan summarizes the relevant section in this way:

> The consequence of this innovation, according to the *Elenchos*, is that 'as, on account of their prominent ancestry and great property, the so-called faithful want no children from slaves or lowborn commoners, they use drugs of sterility (*atokiois pharmakois*, "anti-bearing drugs") or bind themselves tightly in order to expel a fetus which has already been engendered' (*Elenchos* 9.12.25, GCS 26:250). This conduct, the critic of Callixtus concludes, is 'adultery' and 'murder.' Adultery stigmatizes the relationship; 'murder,' the acts of contraception and abortion.[12]

This first record of Christians using contraceptives employs the technical term for contraceptives in use at the time, and although such drugs could also be abortifacients, it appears that they were primarily meant as contraceptives. The categorization of 'murder' was not a novelty, for, among the Jews, the Talmud and Philo had said the same of the destruction of semen.[13] In view of discussions to come as the tradition progresses, it is worth dwelling on a number of aspects of

---

[10] Noonan, *Contraception*, 88.
[11] Ibid, 93.
[12] Ibid, 94.
[13] Ibid.

this first reference to contraception in the Christian tradition. The contraceptive method is chemical contraception, 'anti-bearing drugs', which in the strange twists of history would emerge again in the middle of the twentieth century as an apparent novelty. There is no argument, no discussion, no effort to 'prove' the immorality of contraception by natural law arguments or any other. The moral judgment is simply affirmed as something taken for granted. And there is no hesitation in seeing contraception and abortion as two closely related activities, both interfering in the human generative process which is seen as sacrosanct, in line with the biblical tradition from which the condemnation springs.

The next patristic mention of contraception is more than a century later by St. Ambrose in a commentary on the book of Genesis, and again we will let John Noonan tell the story.

> Commenting on the variety of birds whose creation is described by Genesis, he exclaimed, 'Let men learn to love their children from the pious custom of crows.' Crows sedulously cared for their tender young. But 'the women of our race' are different. The poor abandon their offspring. The rich 'lest their patrimony be divided among several, deny their own fetus in their uterus and by a parricidal potion extinguish the pledges of their womb in their genital belly, and life is taken away before it is transmitted' (*Hexameron* 5.18.58, CSEL 32¹:184).[14]

This is not a very exact statement of a condemnation of contraception. But neither is abortion clearly meant, since 'life is taken away before it is transmitted.' And this is a common theme of all these interventions, that life can be attacked in its sources, before it actually comes to be. Despite the fact that the life is not yet formed, the potions are deemed to be 'parricidal,' which means the killing of a relative, in this case, one's child. Again we note the same points as before. St. Ambrose is speaking of chemical contraception, *parricidalibus sucis*, and the same

---

[14] Ibid, 99.

confusion almost to the point of identity of contraception and abortion. His condemnation is an *obiter dictum* in a Scripture commentary of a moral judgment taken for granted and requiring no argument.

All these same points apply to a pithy sentence of St. Jerome which would be quoted down the centuries: 'Others, indeed, will drink sterility and murder a man not yet born.'[15] St. Jerome's remark occurs in a general description of the moral depravity of the times in a letter encouraging a disciple to virginity. So again we have an *obiter dictum* of a moral condemnation, taken for granted, of chemical contraception, *sterilitatem praebibunt*, which is practically equated with abortion, with no discussion and no argument.

The strongest statement of all is that of St John Chrysostom:

> Why do you sow where the field is eager to destroy the fruit? Where there are medicines of sterility? Where there is murder before birth? You do not even let a harlot remain only a harlot, but you make her a murderess as well. Do you see that from drunkenness comes fornication, from fornication adultery, from adultery murder? Indeed, it is something worse than murder and I do not know what to call it; for she does not kill what is formed but prevents its formation. What then? Do you contemn the gift of God, and fight with his laws? What is a curse, do you seek as though it were a blessing? Do you make the anteroom of birth the anteroom of slaughter?[16]

It is bad enough, we are inclined to think, to call contraception murder. But St. John calls it 'something worse than murder.' His thought can only be that sterilization prevents numerous new lives,

---

[15] 'aliae vero sterilitatem praebibunt et necdum sati hominis homicidium faciunt.' *Letter 22, To Eustochium* 13, CSEL 54:160.9-11. Translation in Noonan, *Contraception*, 100.

[16] Homily 24 on the Epistle to the Romans, PG 60: 626-27. Reference and translation in Noonan, *Contraception*, 98.

and so, from that perspective, can be considered worse than a single murder. Chrysostom made the same point in other homilies, when he declared that those who desire to avoid children as a burden 'mutilate nature, not only killing the newborn, but even acting to prevent their beginning to live,'[17] and that 'those who castrate themselves ... do the work of "murderers".'[18] And all the same points apply yet again to his condemnation of contraception. These are homilies where argument is not used, but rather the condemnations assumed to be commonly known; all that is used is rhetoric. The contraception is chemical, atokia, and is not only practically equated with abortion, but seen as even worse.

Finally, the most influential statement of the point, given its dominance in the Western theological tradition, is that of St. Augustine. Before examining it, one point is worth stressing in the witness we have been following so far. In none of the texts we have met is there any mention of the procreative purpose of sexual intercourse. In fact there is no mention of sexual intercourse at all. The focus in every instance is on the generative process, and contraception is condemned as an interference in that process comparable to abortion. It is only in St. Augustine that sexual intercourse becomes an issue, and that for the obvious reason that he is discussing marriage. His mention of contraception is an *obiter dictum* like all the rest, but it is in a discussion of sexual intercourse and so it was that a link was forged which is to weigh on this debate ever after. He wrote:

> I am supposing that then, although you are not lying for the sake of procreating offspring, you are not for the sake of lust obstructing their procreation by an evil prayer or an evil deed. Those who do this, although they are called husband and wife, are not; nor do they retain any reality of marriage, but with a respectable

---

[17] *Homily 28 on Matthew* 5, PG 57:357. Reference and translation in Noonan, *Contraception*, 99.

[18] *Homily 62 on Matthew* 19, PG 58:599. Reference and translation in Noonan, *Contraception*, 95.

name cover a shame. They give themselves away, indeed, when they go so far as to expose the children who are born to them against their will; for they hate to nourish or to have those whom they feared to bear. Therefore a dark iniquity rages against those whom they unwillingly have borne, and with open iniquity this comes to light; a hidden shame is demonstrated by manifest cruelty. Sometimes [Aliquando] this lustful cruelty, or cruel lust, comes to this, that they even procure poisons of sterility [sterilitatis venena], and, if these do not work, extinguish and destroy the fetus in some way in the womb, preferring that their offspring die before it lives, or if it was already alive in the womb to kill it before it was born.[19]

Noonan's commentary on this is worth hearing.

This vehement passage ... is a fundamental text. It is the only passage in Augustine dealing with artificial contraceptives. ... It provided later canon law with its term for contraceptives, 'poisons of sterility.' Under the heading *Aliquando*, it was to become the medieval locus classicus on contraception. Formally, unequivocally, passionately, Augustine here condemned contraception practiced by the married. ... The 'homicide' argument favored by Jerome and Chrysostom is not relied on. There is a close association in Augustine's mind, and in contemporary practice, of infanticide, abortion, and contraception. The association gives a sting to his critique. But the acts are distinguished. The fetus in the womb, not yet alive, is the fetus in the forty days before ensoulment. The 'poisons of sterility' are intended to achieve their deadly effect before conception; the

---

[19] Marriage and Concupiscnence 1.15.17, CSEL 42.229-30. Reference and translation in Noonan, *Contraception*, 136.

other means are used if they fail, and a fetus has been conceived.[20]

The points made in regard to every text we have met all apply here again. The contraception is chemical, the condemnation taken for granted, and the emphasis is on the generative process and the close parallel with abortion. One of Noonan's comments needs to be nuanced a little. He points out that St. Augustine did not appeal explicitly to the 'homicide' argument used by the other Fathers. It is true that St. Augustine did not call contraception murder as all those before him had done, but it is wrong to speak of the 'homicide' *argument*. None of these Fathers, including St. Augustine himself, is arguing the matter at all; the condemnation they are recalling is something they are taking for granted and assuming as accepted by their readers. And, although he does not call contraception murder, he links it closely with abortion as all the others do.

The presuppositions of this condemnation of contraception as an attack on life need to be clarified and Noonan gives an excellent commentary on the matter. He introduces a section entitled *The Christian Meaning of "Homicide"* in this way:

> If this desire to protect life is understood, the significance of the terms in which the Christian writers criticize contraception is illuminated. It will be found that the words applied to contraception are 'parricide,' 'worse than murder,' 'killing a man-to-be.' ... The Christian writers are using this language rhetorically and morally, just as, rhetorically and morally, they attacked abortion as homicide and parricide.[21]

He considers the obvious hypothesis that this manner of condemning contraception was due to a misunderstanding of the biological process involved, understanding the male seed as somehow already a little

---

[20] Noonan, *Contraception*, 136.
[21] J Ibid, 88.

human being. He examines the state on biological understanding at the time and reports: 'Three theories of procreation existed, all of them assigning a major role in procreation to the male seed. ... But under no theory was the male seed itself equal to a "man," for under no theory was it maintained that the seed already had a soul.'[22] He explains:

> It is abundantly clear from these discussion that the most anyone contends is that ensoulment occurs at conception; the dominant view is that the fetus becomes a man only when 'formed.' ... In the light of such views of the fetus, no one could have confused the seed with a man or meant to say that destruction of the seed was literal homicide.[23]

And he concludes:

> When the second- and third-century Christians apply the term 'parricide,' then, they do so in a conscious effort to enlarge the legal meaning to condemn what they believe is morally wrong. ... The protection of life leads to the prohibition of interference with life at the fetal stage. It is only one step to extend this protection to the lifegiving process.[24]

This then, it is being argued, is the genuine Christian tradition behind the condemnation of contraception, and it may be useful to make the point yet again. In his summary comments on the emergence of the condemnation of contraception during the first three centuries, Noonan keeps insisting that there were two strands of tradition at work, the Stoic emphasis on the procreative dimension of sexual intercourse as well as the strong sense of the 'poisons of sterility' being an attack on

---

[22] Ibid, 89.
[23] Ibid, 90.
[24] Ibid, 91.

human life in its beginnings. He makes the point on pages 85 and 91 and then concludes the chapter as follows:

> The position of the first three centuries on contraception is, then, enmeshed with the Alexandrian commitment to the Stoic rule on procreative purpose and the Stoic view of nature. Remove those parts of the testimony, and what is left is the contention that contraception attacks life – a contention with much claim to be heard when embryonic life needed protection, but not intended literally. Beyond this protection of existing life lies the assumption that the life-giving process is itself sacred, a cooperation with God immune from interference; St. John Chrysostom alone expresses this position distinctly. This was the state of the doctrine on contraception when the Church experienced a trauma as profound as that of Gnosticism – the competition of the Manichees – and when a writer appeared who, comprehensively and passionately, synthesized his own experience, the Stoic rule on procreation, the teaching on original sin, the need to protect life, into a rule on contraception: St. Augustine.[25]

Hopefully, enough has been said ot make clear the important flaw in this analysis. Noonan reports no instance of any early Christian writer linking the condemnation of contraception with the Stoic rule on procreative purpose in sexual intercourse, for the simple and good reason that there was none. There were no such 'parts of the testimony' and there is no need for any removal, and therefore 'what is left is the contention that contraception attacks life.' The texts we have presented and analysed make it evident that the condemnation was based on the perception that human life is sacred in its beginnings, and on that

---

[25] Ibid, 105-06.

perception alone. The Stoic rule had no influence whatever on the emergence of the condemnation of contraception.

This interpretation is borne out by what happened subsequently, as the condemnation of contraception hardened into an official position in the course of the second half of the first millennium. Summarizing the development of the doctrine from 500-1100, Noonan remarks: 'The Augustinian analysis of contraception as a destruction of the goods of marriage was not used. It was Jerome's analysis of the contraceptive act as homicide which was employed.'[26] The first Bishop to make the condemnation of contraception the official doctrine in his diocese was Caesarius of Arles (470-542), and his condemnation was forthright indeed.[27] He wrote:

> Who is he who cannot warn that no woman may take a potion so that she is unable to conceive or condemns in herself the nature which God willed to be fecund. As often as she could have conceived or given birth, of that many homicides she will be held guilty, and, unless she undergoes suitable penance, she will be damned by eternal death in hell. If a woman does not wish to have children, let her enter into a religious agreement with her husband; for chastity is the sole sterility of a Christian woman.[28]

The condemnation of contraception as a sin against life crystallized during this second half of the first millennium, mainly in the penitentials. The focus was on the use of potions to avoid conception and the sin was understood as a form of homicide. Noonan notes that *coitus interruptus* is rarely mentioned in these documents and that the absence of a more widespread allusion to the Onan text seems to indicate that this method

---

[26] Ibid, 144.
[27] J Ibid, 145.
[28] *Letter*, printed as *Sermo* 1.12, *Corpus Christianorum (Series Latina)* 103, 9. Reference and translation in Noonan, *Contraceptio*, 146.

of contraception was not much used at the time.[29] This tradition came to formulation in a text which appears first in a collection by Regino of Prüm (840-915), and which would continue in use until the revision of the canon law in 1917 under the incipit *Si aliquis*: 'If someone to satisfy his lust or in deliberate hatred does something to a man or woman so that no children be born of him or her, or gives them to drink, so that he cannot generate or she conceive, let it be held as homicide.'[30]

We have reached the end of the first millennium, and so far only one writer in that whole period has linked the condemnation of contraception with the Stoic insight into the role of procreation in sexual intercourse, St. Augustine. Now, however, the situation begins to change as St. Augustine's influence makes itself more and more felt in Western theology. About 1094, Ivo of Chartres (1040-1115) set out to make a bigger and more contemporary collection of legal texts. He dropped *Si aliquis* and instead used five texts from St. Augustine, the most important of which was the quotation from *De nuptiis et concupiscentia* we have seen earlier, beginning with the word *Aliquando*. On this Noonan remarks that 'Ivo thereby put into the stream of theological speculation a classic and neglected denunciation of artificial contraception; at the same time, he implicitly advanced the view that contraception was a sin against marriage, not a form of homicide.'[31] In the middle of the twelfth century, when the most influential collections of texts were made, the two great editor-compilers, Gratian and Lombard, both chose to include *Aliquando* and omitted *Si aliquis*. This choice will be most significant. According to Noonan: 'If Augustine is the most important single authority on contraception, and if a single statement of his is to be taken as the epitome of his doctrine, then the use of *Aliquando* by Gratian and Lombard is the most important teaching on contraception in the Middle Ages.'[32]

---

[29] Noonan, *Contraception*, 161.
[30] *Churchly Discipline and the Christian Religion* 2.89, PL 132:301. Reference and translation in Noonan, *Contraception*, 168.
[31] Noonan, *Contraception*, 172.
[32] Ibid, 174.

From this point on, there are two rationales of the condemnation of contraception developing side by side, one seeing it as a sexual matter and the other as a life matter. The former has been presented already, so we will concentrate here on the further progress of the latter. Despite the choice made by Gratian and Lombard, as Noonan reports: 'In the first half of the twelfth century the old view of contraception as homicide was also current. As the reform movement gathered strength in Italy with German support, the *Decretum* of Burchard was widely used. Here *Si aliquis* was the principal text against contraception.'[33] A century later, in 1230, the Dominican Raymond of Pennaforte (1175-1275) began, at the direction of Pope Gregory IX, to make a collection of authoritative decrees. In the new *Decretals* he adopted *Si aliquis* with a slight variation in word order and inserted it as chapter 5 of book V, title 12, 'Voluntary and Chance Homicide.' It reads as follows: '*He who does magic or gives poisons of sterility is a homicide*. If anyone to satisfy his lust or in meditated hatred does something to a man or woman or gives something to drink so that he cannot generate, or she conceive, or offspring be born, let him be held a homicide.'[34] In Noonan's view: 'With the inclusion of *Si aliquis* in this papally sponsored law for the universal Church, the official opposition to contraception reached its apogee.'[35]

It would seem that the two approaches to contraception divided between the theologians and the canonists, the theologians following St. Augustine, as interpreted by Peter Lombard, while the canonists held to the earlier tradition. According to Noonan the turning away from the rhetoric of 'homicide' began with St Albert in his commentary on the Sentences.[36] In his treatment of the 'poisons of sterility', in *IV Sent.* 31.18, 'Albert did not mention *Si aliquis* by name, but he drew from the theory underlying it three arguments against his own doctrine.' He took the rhetorical statements literally and rebutted them with ease.[37]

---

[33] Ibid, 173.
[34] Gregory IX, Decretals 5.12.5, Corpus Iuris Canonici, vol. 2, ed. Friedberg
[35] Noonan, *Contraception*, 178.
[36] Ibid, 233.
[37] Ibid, 234.

In his commentary on the Sentences, St Thomas followed his master in his reserved approach to the homicide rhetoric and fails to mention the 'poisons of sterility' at all in his later works.[38] St. Alphonus Liguori (1696-1787) dropped this line of analysis totally. Nowhere in his *Moral Theology* is contraception linked to homicide or related to the provisions of *Si aliquis*.[39] Noonan sums up: 'With St. Alphonsus the homicide approach ended its theological life.'[40]

Seeing contraception as a life matter may have been dropped by the theologians, but it continued to be used by the canonists and the catechists. Again according to Noonan, the common position, initiated by Hostiensis (1200-1271) in the *Golden Summa* 5, "Homicide," 1, and followed by the *Gloss*, was that contraception was "interpretively" homicide.'[41] And so it continued for subsequent centuries. 'If none of the great theologians of this theological age was eager to treat contraception as homicide, the more common later analysis followed Hostiensis. Contraception was "interpretively" homicide'[42] The rhetoric was not only applied to the use of 'poisons of sterility', but to *coitus interruptus* as well, the most illustrious proponent of this position being St. Bernardine of Siena (1380-1444). In a sermon on 'The Frightful Sin Against Nature,' he quoted a statement, attributed at the time to St. Augustine, that 'those labouring under this vice are killers of men, if not by the sword, yet in fact.'[43] The Catechism of the Council of Trent emphatically restated the teaching, saying that 'it is a most grave crime for those joined in matrimony to use medicines to impede the conceptus or to abort birth: this impious conspiracy in murders must be extirpated' (2.7.13).[44] And the text of *Si aliquis* remained part of the canon law until the revision of the Code in 1917. To quote Noonan yet

---

[38] Ibid.
[39] Ibid, 364.
[40] Ibid, 365.
[41] Ibid, 233.
[42] Ibid, 235.
[43] *The Eternal Gospel* 15.2.1. Reference and translation in Noonan, *Contraception*, 237.
[44] Noonan, *Contraception*, 361.

again: 'To the extent that the canonical and catechistical classification was followed, the designation as "homicide" remained an objection to contraception by potion and poison.'[45]

That the use of the 'homicide' rhetoric would be abandoned is readily understandable, but the fundamental principle of the inviolability of the generative process did not disappear completely. It found an authoritative presentation in the teaching of Pope Pius XII on contraception. In an address to obstetricians the Pope spoke of the marvellous collaboration of the parents, and of nature and of God in the process of the generation of a new human life. 'Nature puts at man's disposal the whole chain of causes which will result in the appearance of a new human life. It is for man to release this vital force and it is for nature to develop its course and bring it to completion. When once man has done his part and set in motion the marvellous process which will produce a new life, it is his bounden duty to let it take its course. He must not arrest the work of nature or impede its natural development.'[46] In his most formal statement of the doctrine, he taught that 'any attempt by the spouses in the completion of the conjugal act or *in the development of its natural consequences*, having the aim of depriving the act of the force inherent in it or *of impeding the procreation of a new life*, is immoral.'[47] Both the relevant principles are invoked here, the procreative purpose of sexual intercourse and, by the clauses highlighted, the inviolability of the generative process.

One commentator on the papal teaching on contraception suggested that the basic principle being invoked was not the procreative purpose of intercourse but the inviolability of the generative process. Gerald Kelly wrote that 'Pius XI (and later Pius XII) was primarily interested in the divinely established order for the beginning of human life. His basic analytical principle, therefore, is not the immorality of misusing a

---

[45] Ibid, 365.
[46] Allocution to the Convention of Italian Catholic Obstetricians, 29 October 1951, AAS 43 (1951), 835-36 at 836.
[47] 'Address to the Italian Catholic Society of Midwives' AAS 43 (1951), 843. [Italics mine.]

natural faculty, but rather the substantial inviolability of the divine plan for human life, in its beginning and in its continuation.[48]

Kelly went on to develop and ground the principle at work.

> Whether we speak of the *opus hominum* and *opus naturae* or of the essence and integrity of the marital act, it is clear from the teaching of both popes that each of these phases of generative function is part of a divine plan that man is not free to change. But why this inviolability? Because these things constitute the natural prelude to the *opus Dei*, which is the creation of the spiritual and immortal soul. Hence, according to the divine plan, these functions are life-giving – and the life they help to give is human life. This is the ultimate specific reason for their inviolability. Just as innocent human life itself is inviolable, so those things which immediately pertain to the beginning of human life are also inviolable.[49]

So, for Kelly, it is not the procreative purpose of sexual intercourse which provides the basic principle, but 'the inviolable divine plan for the *beginning of human life*.'[50] And this is to be recognised as 'our basic natural-law argument for the inviolability of both the marriage act and the generative faculty.'[51] And Kelly was not unique in this approach. In their text book, Ford and Kelly, mention 'authors (Merkelbach, for instance) who ... put the malice of contraception in the positive interference with the physiological processes of reproduction.'[52] And, in the very first article mentioned in Valsecchi's survey by F. J. Connell,

---

[48] Gerald Kelly, "Contraception and Natural Law," in *Proceedings of the Eighteenth Annual Convention, The Catholic Theological Society of America, 1963* (New York, 1964), 25-45 at 36-37.

[49] Ibid, 30.

[50] Ibid, 31. (Emphasis in the original.)

[51] Gerald Kelly, S.J., 'Confusion: contraception and "the pill",' *Theology Digest* 12 (1964), 123-30 at ???

[52] JFord and Kelly, *Contemporary Moral Theology 2*, 366.

C.SS.R., the principle is laid down that the use of the pill is illicit because 'any direct and positive interference in the processes of human generation, whether before, during or after copulation, is a transgression of the law of God.'[53]

Strangely, given its almost total eclipse today, in what is known as the 'Minority Working Paper', the group of moral theologians who argued in favour of maintaining the traditional official teaching on contraception presented this argument from the sacredness and inviolability of the generative process as the first of their arguments. They pointed out that 'the Fathers, theologians, and the Church itself have always taught that certain acts and the generative processes are in some way specially inviolable precisely because they are generative,'[54] and then went on to explain: 'This inviolability was explained for many centuries by the Fathers, the theologians and in Canon Law as analogous to the inviolability of human life itself. This analogy is not merely rhetorical or metaphorical, but it expressed a fundamental moral truth. Human life already existing (*in facto esse*) is inviolable. Likewise, it is also in some sense inviolable in its proximate causes (*vita in fieri*). ... This quasi-sacredness of natural human life ... is extended in the teaching of the Church to the acts and the generative processes in as much as they are such.'[55] And the majority group in the Commission, in their 'Argument for Reform' also observed that the 'principal argument is founded on the inviolability of the sources of life; like human life itself, it is said, they do not fall under the dominion of man but pertain to the dominion of God.'[56]

This line of tradition finds its place also in *Humanae vitae*. Pope Paul VI's encyclical is a complex document, and there is no doubt that the inviolability of the generative process is not invoked explicitly as a ground underlying the judgment on contraception. There are, however, aspects of the doctrine in the document which point in its direction.

---

[53] F. J. Connell, C.SS.R., 'The contraceptive pill', *The American Ecclesiastical Review* 137 (1957), 50-51.
[54] 'The Minority Working Paper, 23 May 1966,' 178-79.
[55] Ibid, 179.
[56] "The "Argument for Reform" 27 May 1966," 208.

Pope Paul appealed a number of times to the respect due to nature and natural processes. In § 10, he writes: 'If we consider first the biological processes, responsible parenthood means an awareness of, and respect for, their proper functions. In the procreative faculty human reason discerns biological laws that pertain to the human person.' In § 13, the encyclical says that

> to experience the gift of married love while respecting the laws of conception is to acknowledge that one is not the master of the sources of life but rather the minister of the design established by the Creator. Just as man does not have unlimited dominion over his body in general, so also, and with more particular reason, he has no such dominion over his specifically sexual faculties, for these are concerned by their very nature with the generation of life, of which God is the source. 'Human life is sacred—all men must recognize that fact,' Our predecessor Pope John XXIII recalled. 'From its very inception it reveals the creating hand of God.'

In § 14, which is the centre of the encyclical, the basic teaching is summarized as follows:

> Therefore We base Our words on the first principles of a human and Christian doctrine of marriage when We are obliged once more to declare that the direct interruption of the generative process already begun and, above all, all direct abortion, even for therapeutic reasons, are to be absolutely excluded as lawful means of regulating the number of children. Equally to be condemned, as the magisterium of the Church has affirmed on many occasions, is direct sterilization, whether of the man or of the woman, whether permanent or temporary. Similarly excluded is any action which either before, at the moment of, or after

sexual intercourse, is specifically intended to prevent procreation—whether as an end or as a means.

Stated thus in its bare essentials, the teaching bears directly, in all its various parts, on the full scope of the generative process. And the same point appears once more in § 16, where the first reason given distinguishing periodic continence from contraception is formulated as follows: 'In the former the married couple rightly use a faculty provided them by nature. In the latter they obstruct the natural development of the generative process.' Pope Paul VI does not say so, but his teaching is fully and directly in the line of tradition being presented here, which sees contraception as a life issue. The first sentence of § 14 is a perfect summary of this tradition, teaching that the 'direct interruption of the generative process' is immoral.

This completes the basic account of the tradition treating contraception as a life matter, and the contention here is that this represents the genuine Christian tradition on the issue. Treating contraception as a matter of sexual morality is a false trail based on a misunderstanding of certain incidental references to it in St. Augustine's various writings on marriage matters. In one place, Noonan wonders what might have happened if St. John Chrysostom had been the dominant guide in the matter of contraception, rather than St. Augustine. St. John Chrysostom completely ignored the Stoic notion of marriage, and in this he certainly was not followed, in the West at least. Noonan does recognise a fundamental point, when he writes: 'If the other teachings of Chrysostom had ... been adopted, that the marital act is sacral and that the interruption of the procreative process is worse than murder, no concrete difference for the rule of contraception would have followed.'[57] It is being contended here that Noonan's conditional formulation of this matter is inappropriate, for, despite all appearances to the contrary, this is exactly what in fact has happened.

---

[57] Noonan, *Contraception*, 139.

Chapter 21

The Inviolability of the Generative Process

Drawing together the fruits of this survey of the tradition judging contraception as a life issue, one can assert that the principle underlying the judgment is the inviolability of the generative process. It is necessary, therefore, to be clear as to what one has in mind when one speaks of the generative process, for the duality in the tradition on the matter means that the emphasis can be different depending on one's point of view. Charles Curran, for instance, saw clearly that this is the heart of the matter. He admitted that his 'disagreement with the accepted teaching goes to the most basic and fundamental level - the stewardship which man has over his sexuality and generative functions,'[1] and insisted that this is the point upon which the discussion should be focussed.[2] It would seem, however, that Curran's notion of the generative process is significantly different from the one being developed here. At one stage in his book, commenting on a controversy between Cardinal Cajetan and Martin Le Maistre in the 16th century, Noonan isolated a number of issues essential to the discussion. One question he raised, which seems to me of fundamental importance, is: 'In the sexual, generative, and educative process, what part of the process is taken as a unit for moral

---

[1] Charles E. Curran, *New Perspectives in Moral Theology* (Notre Dame / London: University of Notre Dame Press, 1976), 203.
[2] Ibid, 207.

judgment?'[3] He judges that 'Cajetan takes as the unity for moral judgment the entire process of intercourse, insemination, conception, birth, and education,'[4] and that is certainly one possible option. The normal option in the contemporary literature is to focus on the act of sexual intercourse and begin one's reflections there, as Curran does. The contention here is that, in order to judge the moral status of contraception in line with the genuine tradition of the Church, the proper option is to focus on the generative process from sexual intercourse to the birth of the child as the appropriate unit for moral judgment. Whatever the means used, contraception denotes the termination of the generative process prior to conception, in order to ensure that conception does not take place. The male can be sterilized prior to intercourse in order to ensure that the ejaculate contains no sperm. Or coitus interruptus can be practised to ensure that no sperm are deposited in the woman's sexual tract. Or one of the various barrier methods can be use to ensure that any sperm is blocked from reaching its goal. Or the woman can be sterilized, temporarily by chemical means or permanently by surgical, so that no egg is released for fertilization. Regardless of the means, the action intended is the same; to terminate the generative process prior to conception so that conception does not take place. And that is the action which the Christian tradition condemns as immoral on the basis of the inviolability of the whole generative process which shares in the sacredness of human life.

What difference does it make whether the focus is on sexual intercourse or on the whole generative process? There are a number of differences which seem crucial to me. The principal difference is that the sacredness of the generative process is the principle we receive from Scripture and Tradition. The procreative purpose of sexual intercourse is a human insight. The procreative purpose is self-evidently true, but it does not succeed in grounding the moral judgments in the matter of fertility control. For some centuries now the focus has been firmly

---

[3] Noonan, <u>Contraception: A History of Its Treatment by the Catholic Theologians and Canonists</u> (Cambridge, Mass.: Harvard University Press, 1965), 355.
[4] Ibid, 356.

on the act of sexual intercourse as the morally relevant part of the generative process. *Coitus interruptus* and the condom were the actions analysed in the moral theology textbooks, and they were judged as unnatural sexual acts, for, as it seems, chemical contraceptives were no longer much in use. The older tradition which focussed on the whole generative process from intercourse to birth was completely forgotten, and the inviolability principle underlying the traditional condemnation of the 'poisons of sterility' was no longer used. This, however, is the revealed principle underlying the moral judgment of the Church in this matter and it must be restored to its proper place if the situation is to be resolved.

It has to be admitted that the sacredness and inviolability of the generative process in its initial phase is not obvious, in the way that the procreative purpose of intercourse is. In a contribution made shortly after *Humanae vitae* was issued, Michael Novak argues forcefully against the sacredness of the elements of the generative process, the male seed and the female egg. He asks: 'Is the ovum more sacred that the brain, the heart, the blood, the kidneys?'[5] And he tells us: 'I have never understood why there is anything especially sacred about male sperm. It is plentiful and a bodily juice like many others.'[6] These are fundamental questions, indeed. Why are the male sperm and the ovum sacred? St. Thomas teaches, following Aristotle, that there is something divine in the human seed. He is discussing the sins against life in the *De malo*, and he points out that actual homicide is not the only serious sin against life. He points out that taking away a person's means of subsistence is also a serious sin against life and continues: 'Even more closely ordained to human life than any external things is human seed, in which there is found a human being *in potential*, so that Aristotle could say in his *Politics* that there is something divine in human seed.'[7] The only argument available on the philosophical level is that these elements of our biology are sacred by association with the new life to

---

[5] Michael Novak, "Frequent, Even Daily, Communion", *The Catholic Case for Contraception*, ed. Daniel Callahan (London: Arlington Books, 1969), 92-102 at 95.
[6] Ibid, 98.
[7] De malo, q. 15 a. 2 c.

which they lead. If that is not convincing, one must appeal to faith and point out that the sacredness of these generative elements has been recognised in the Judaeo-Christian tradition since its very beginning and is now established as part of our faith. Novak's argument against the sacredness cannot be said to carry much force. The fact that male sperm is plentiful does not tell against its sacredness. Human beings are plentiful also, and yet each is sacred. Human beings are animals like many others, and yet they are sacred in a special way. The sperm and the ovum are sacred because they are the living organisms which unite in the formation of the new human being. Ultimately the recognition of this sacredness is a matter of Christian faith.

A more sophisticated challenge to the sacredness and inviolability of the generative process was formulated by Mgr J. M. Reuss, the Auxiliary Bishop of Mainz, in one of the three ground-breaking articles of 1963.[8] He recalled the use of the principle of totality as it is applied in the case of therapeutic surgical interventions. In such cases it is legitimate to sacrifice a part of the human body or to suppress an organic function when this is necessary for the good of the whole person. He suggests that this same principle can also include the sacrifice of generative function when it is judged to be necessary for the total well-being of the spouses. He concludes that 'no absolute and valid unalterability is possessed in all circumstances by biological and physical factors and processes in themselves: on the contrary, intervention in these processes, when motivated by a proportionately good result, is always permissible'[9] This line of thought was also taken up in the Majority Report of the Papal Commission on Birth Control. In its rebuttal of the traditional arguments against contraception, the Report had this to say: 'The principal argument is founded on the inviolability of the sources of life; like human life itself, it is said, they do not fall under

---

[8] J. M. Reuss, 'Eheliche Hingabe und Zeugung: Ein Diskussionsbeitrag zu einem differenzierten Problem', *Tübinger Theologische Quartalschrift* 143 (1963), 454-76.

[9] Ambrogio Valsecchi, *Controversy: The birth control debate 1958-1968* (Washington-Cleveland: Corpus Books, 1968), 45. On this see also Gerald Kelly, S.J., 'Confusion: contraception and "the pill",' *Theology Digest* 12 (1964), 123-30 at 127.

the dominion of man but pertain to the dominion of God.'[10] The rebuttal of this argument proceeded in two stages. In the first stage, the respect due to nature in general was relativized. The Report asserted that 'an unconditional respect for nature as it is in itself ... pertains to a vision of man which sees something mysterious and sacred in nature, and because of this fears that any human intervention tends to destroy rather than perfect this very nature.'[11] In the second stage, the respect due to human life in particular was also relativized.

> The sources of life, just as existent life itself, are not more of God than is the totality of created nature, of which he is the creator. The very dignity of man created to the image of God consists in this: that God wished man to share in his dominion. ... To take his own or another's life is a sin not because life is under the exclusive dominion of God but because it is contrary to right reason unless there is question of a good of a higher order. It is licit to sacrifice a life for the good of the community. It is licit to take a life in capital punishment for the sake of the community, and therefore from a motive of charity for others. Suicide is a sin because it is contrary to right reason and opposed to man's destiny.[12]

Having laid down these principles the Report went on to observe that 'there is a certain change in the mind of contemporary man. He feels that he is acting more in conformity with his rational nature, created by God with liberty and responsibility, when he uses his skill to intervene in the biological processes of nature so that he can achieve the ends of the institution of matrimony in the conditions of actual life, than if he abandons himself to chance.'[13] The argument is summed up

---

[10] 'The "Argument for Reform" 27 May 1966,' 208.
[11] Ibid.
[12] Ibid.
[13] Ibid, 209.

in the programmatic statement: 'Man is the administrator of life and consequently of his own fecundity.'[14] In its concluding paragraphs the Report gave many reasons why a change was called for in the teaching of contraception, new knowledge in different areas and social changes, but 'most of all, a better grasp of the duty of man to humanize and to bring to greater perfection for the life of man what is given in nature.'[15]

The Report is basing its position on the human vocation to 'fill the earth and subdue it' (Genesis 1:28). Human beings have the right to apply their ingenuity and technology in order bring nature under human control. The question, however, regards the limits of human dominion over natural phenomena. In his response to *Humanae vitae*, Bernard Häring comments on what the encyclical has to say on this issue of human dominion over the generative process. Pope Paul wrote that 'Just as man does not have unlimited dominion over his body in general, so also, and with more particular reason, he has no such dominion over his specifically sexual faculties, for these are concerned by their very nature with the generation of life, of which God is the source.' (HV, § 13) Häring fills out the major premise of Pope Paul's argument, when he writes: 'Modern medicine is based on a *reasonable, limited* dominion over the organism. Good medical art rejects any *arbitrary* interference with the biological functions, but it does intervene whenever it is to benefit not only the biological organism but *the whole person*.' The logic of this should have led to the conclusion that, just as man has a real but limited dominion over his body, he should have a similar real but limited dominion over the generative process. *Humanae vitae*, on the contrary, concluded that man has 'no such dominion' over the generative process. According to Häring, 'this total difference between "limited dominion" and "no such dominion" demands a special proof.'[16] Häring also comments on Pope Paul's use of a quotation

---

[14] Ibid, 213.
[15] 'The Theological Report of the Commission 26 June 1966,' in Peter Harris, et. al., On Human Life, 234.
[16] Bernard Häring, 'The Inseparability of the Unitive-Procreative Functions of the Marital Act,' in Charles Curran (ed.), *Contraception: Authority and Dissent* (London : Burns & Oates, 1969), 176-92 at 181.

from Pope John XXIII's encyclical *Pacem in terris*, to the effect that human life is sacred: 'Here again we encounter unequal members in the comparison: the absolute sacredness of the *biological laws and rhythms* is compared and equated with the sacredness of *human life*. ... Biological functions, including the human sperm and ovule, are not human life nor the inception of human life.'[17] And there is the rub. Häring demands a 'proof' that the generative process shares in the sacredness of human life in general. If he is looking for a 'proof' on the level of reason, I certainly cannot provide it. A 'proof', however, is available on the level of faith. I contend that the Christian Tradition tells us that the generative process also shares in this sacredness of human life, and that its inviolability must be respected accordingly, setting limits on our human dominion over it. The principle of totality applies properly within the limits of an individual organism, so that any part of the organism can be sacrificed for the good of the whole. If the traditional position is accepted, it seems that the totality principle stops short at the generative dimension of human biology, presumably on the basis that it transcends the limits of the individual organism in its orientation to the new life to be formed. Justifying this position on the basis of reason is not easy, but it is being taken here that the inviolability of the generative process is a given of Christian revelation which cannot be set aside.

Taking it, then, that the inviolability of the generative process from intercourse to birth is the basic principle to be applied in this matter, it is possible now to tackle the fundamental question, What is contraception? or more accurately, What is the action which the Church condemns? For the word 'contraception' does not specify the action precisely. The concept 'contraception' means any action which is undertaken in order to avoid or prevent conception; it focuses on the end rather than the means. One can legitimately speak of periodic abstinence as a means of contraception, so that in order to be clear that one has the physical interventions in mind, one has to specify one's meaning and speak of 'artificial' contraception. It is being contended here that the action condemned by the Church is, using the formula of Pope Paul VI in

---

[17] Ibid, 182.

Humanae vitae, the 'direct interruption of the generative process' prior to conception, by whatever means. The intervention can be prior to sexual intercourse in sterilization, whether surgical or chemical, or by the placing of a barrier of some kind. It can take place during intercourse, whether by *coitus interruptus* or the use of a condom. Or it can take place after intercourse by the use of a douche or one of the new post-coital drugs. Whatever the means, the aim is to terminate the generative process before conception occurs. The matter is not commonly understood in this way, and so there is no single word which sums up what is common to all these interventions, but the argument here is that the act which the tradition condemns is the termination of the generative process prior to conception, or the contraceptive interruption of the generative process.

One commentator who understands the matter along these lines is Dietrich von Hildebrand who made it the foundation of the moral judgment of contraception. He wrote: "The sinfulness of artificial birth control is rooted in the arrogation of the right to separate the actualized love union in marriage from a possible conception, to sever the wonderful, deeply mysterious connection instituted by God."[18] It is on this basis that von Hildebrand distinguishes contraception from the practice of periodic abstinence when he affirms: 'The sin consists in this alone: the sundering by man of what God has joined together – the *artificial, active* severing of the mystery of bodily union from the creative act to which it is bound at the time.'[19] A disciple of von Hildebrand, Josef Seifert even interprets Pope Paul VI's inseparability principle in this way. Commenting on the doctrine of 'inseparability' in *Humanae vitae*, he writes: 'What can the concept "inseparability" mean? What is primarily intended is that it is never morally permissible actively to separate the marital act from procreation. ... It is never permitted deliberately and directly to break the link between sexual intercourse and procreation, or that between the beginning of the process of impregnation which

---

[18] Dietrich von Hildebrand, "The Encyclical *Humanae Vitae*: A Sign of Contradiction," in Janet E. Smith, ed., <u>Why Humane Vitae was Right: A Reader</u> (San Francisco: Ignatius Press, 1993), 47-82 at 71.

[19] Ibid, 81.

leads to conception and conception itself.'[20] It seems to me that Seifert is correct in his basic contention, but wrong in interpreting Pope Paul VI's inseparability principle in this sense. The inseparability involved here is rather that invoked by Pope Pius XII at an earlier stage when dealing with artificial procedures in favour of fertility. He taught that 'the Church has likewise rejected the ... attitude which would attempt to separate, in generation, the biological activity from the personal relation of the married couple. ... Never is it permitted to separate these various aspects to the point of excluding positively either the procreative scope or the conjugal embrace.'[21] The link between sexual intercourse and conception is the generative process, and the inseparability of the two is grounded in the inviolability of that process. Von Hildebrand and Seifert speak of separating intercourse from conception, but I suggest that what they are referring to is more clearly formulated as the contraceptive termination of the generative process already begun.

If we take it, then, that the action which the Church finds to be morally objectionable is the contraceptive termination of the generative process, a number of points can be clarified. We can deal first with the contention that the act is not a sexual act as it is commonly taken to be. It is useful to refer here to the argument made in this connection by Germain Grisez and three of his colleagues.[22] It is obvious that in the normal course of things a person practises contraception in view of acts of sexual intercourse that are planned. Despite this, Grisez *et. al.* contend that 'the definition of contraception neither includes nor entails that one who does it engages in sexual intercourse.'[23] In support of this contention they consider the case of a dictator controlling the

---

[20] Josef Seifert, "Der sittliche Unterschied zwischen natürlicher Empfängnisregelung und künstlicher Empfängnisverhütung," in Ernst Wenisch (ed.), *Elternschaft und Menschenwürde: Zur Problematik der Empfängnisregelung* (Vallendar-Schönstatt: Patris Verlag, 1984), 191-242 at 203.

[21] Address to the Second World Congress on Fertility and Sterility, May 19, 1956. AAS 48 (1956), 470.

[22] Germain Grisez, Joseph Boyle, John Finnis, William E. May, "'Every Marital Act Ought to be Open to New Life,': Toward a Clearer Understanding,' *The Thomist* 52 (1988), 365-426.

[23] Ibid, 370.

population of his territory by adding a contraceptive chemical to the public water supply. He is interfering in the generative process of other couples, and his act of contraception bears no relation to his own acts of sexual intercourse. And so, such an act of contraception is clearly not a sexual act. This might seem a far-fetched example, but the notion of hostile contraception against other people is part of the tradition in this matter, and is known to the Penitentials. One of the groups encountered in the texts 'are those resorting to magic to cause sterility out of hostility. The texts ... imply that herbs causing sterility might ... be foisted on an unwary neighbor. Regino speaks of prevention of generation or conception out of "meditated hatred" (*Churchly Disciplines* 89, PL 132:301).'[24] And this type of act continued to be envisaged in the law as codified in *Si aliquis*. Another point revealing the separation of contraception and sexual intercourse is the fact that contraception can be chosen and practised after intercourse. After rape, efforts might reasonably be made to prevent conception, but the same choice could be made after a normal act of intercourse. A new emergency contraceptive pill, Plan B, can be taken up to three days after intercourse and still claims a 90% success rate in preventing conception.

The efforts to rebut these arguments focus on the fact that an act of contraception only arises in the wake of an act of sexual intercourse. Martin Rhonheimer simply argues from the fact that 'babies come into being as a consequence of a human (sexual) act,' so that you cannot perform the act of contraception] unless you simultaneously choose to engage in sexual intercourse ...'[25] The latter part of Rhonheimer's argument falls in the face of the two examples given. A person involved in hostile contraception or post-coital contraception is not simultaneously choosing to engage in sexual intercourse. And the fact that babies come from sexual intercourse does not establish the connection, for the same could be said of abortion and infanticide and, indeed, any form of homicide. All these acts are related to sexual

---

[24] Noonan, Contraception, 159.
[25] Rhonheimer, "Contraception, Sexual Behavior, and Natural Law," 29. See also Smith, *Humanae Vitae*, 361.

intercourse, albeit at a greater and greater distance, but this relationship does not at all constitute them as sexual acts. And the same holds exactly for contraception. Grisez states the case baldly, but accurately: 'Considered as a technological intervention in a biological process, contraceptive behavior need only prevent the fertilization of an ovum by a sperm.'[26] When the act is clearly understood as the contraceptive termination of the generative process, the distance from intercourse is brought more clearly to mind, and the case against considering it to be a sexual act is made easier. The Fathers who first dealt with the chemical contraceptives were thinking of the generative process and condemned any interference in it, and we must do the same. By focusing clearly on the generative process, of which sexual intercourse is but the necessary initiation, the true nature of the 'artificial' contraceptive interventions is made clear.

We can next treat of the crucial test case for the moral priniciple underlying this issue and consider how it fares in making the distinction between periodic abstinence and the various physical contraceptive interventions. A famous argument of Louis Janssens is one which is based on the moral equivalence of artificial contraception and periodic abstinence as means of birth control. He sets up his major premises as follows: 'It is also said that *coitus interruptus* and the use of contraceptive means are immoral since the conjugal act must never *positively* exclude procreation. But this positive exclusion seems to be also present in the practice of periodic continence. To exclude something in our action implies that one excludes it not only by *intention* but also by the choice of a *means* which is the external act.'[27] He then points out, correctly, that the choice of periodic abstinence springs from a positive intention to exclude procreation and involves the choice of a programme which constitutes a means to that end. He then speaks about the role of time in human action and suggests that periodic abstinence 'creates an obstacle of the *temporal* order by the exclusive choice of sexual relations only

---

[26] Germain Grisez, *The Way of the Lord Jesus, Volume Two: Living a Christian Life* (Quincy, Illinois: Franciscan Press, 1992), 509.
[27] Janssens, 'Morale conjugale et progestogènes,' 817.

during the infertile periods, just as the use of mechanical contraceptive means constitutes an obstacle of the *spatial* order in raising a material partition between the organs of the spouses.'[28] He then concludes, again quite correctly, that though the two methods of birth control may be different 'the reason for the difference cannot be that that the use of contraceptive means positively excludes procreation, for the practice of periodic continence also excludes it positively, by intention and by the choice of means.'[29] It has to be recognised that the notion of a 'temporal barrier' constitutes a clever tactic in the effort to establish the moral equivalence of periodic abstinence and the various barrier methods of contraception, and it has prove difficult to pinpoint precisely the fallacy underlying the concept. If it is recognised, however, that the contraceptive termination of the generative process once begun is the action which the Church deems to be morally objectionable, then the matter can be resolved without great difficulty. Even if one concedes Janssens' novel concept of a 'temporal barrier,' it becomes apparent that the 'temporal barrier' is being set up precisely to avoid this forbidden act, the contraceptive termination of the generative process once begun. For one abstains from sexual intercourse so that one will not initiate a generative process foreseen to be fertile, precisely in order that one will not subsequently need to terminate it, knowing that this is forbidden. The weakness in Janssens argument is that he focuses on the end of contraception and does not attend sufficiently carefully to the difference of the means used. His failure to advert to the significance of the generative process and its inviolability makes it impossible for him to see what that difference is.

In another place, Janssens attempts to establish the equivalence of periodic abstinence and artificial contraception by widening the notion of sterilization to include the former. He wrote:

> One moralist for example defines direct sterilization: 'every human intervention which has as its primary

---

[28] Ibid.
[29] Ibid, 818.

purpose (*finis operis*), deliberately intended (*finis operantis*), to suppress (porter atteinte a) the generative power, whether it is a matter of the sterilization of the person, or of particular sexual acts.' If this definition is exact, periodic continence would also be a direct sterilization. In positively excluding fecundity – by the choice of the act and by intention – it is a human intervention which has as its primary purpose, deliberately intended, to suppress (porter atteinte a) the generative power of sexual acts in particular. However it is generally admitted that periodic continence is not an intrinsically evil practice and that it has, therefore, a positive moral value if the intention governing it is good.[30]

In response to this, one must again concede Janssens basic point that periodic abstinence involves the positive, deliberate exclusion of procreation and the use of a means to achieve that purpose. On that level, the level of intention, there is no difference between the different means of contraception. But to categorize periodic abstinence as sterilization does not work. One abstains from intercourse precisely to avoid the need to sterilize it. Sterilization is a physical intervention designed to terminate the generative process as soon as it begins, and that is what is condemned.

Another effort to formulate the difference between periodic abstinence and artificial contraception seeks to see one as 'natural' and the other as 'unnatural', as in Natural Family Planning. Many fail to be convinced. Michael Novak has written:

> I do not understand why it is "unnatural" to block the spatial flow of the sperm so that it does not fertilize the ovum – to block it by diaphragm, or condom, say (however disagreeable such devices are) – and yet not

---

[30] Ibid, 821.

"unnatural" to time placement of the sperm so that it does not fertilize an ovum. In either case, human intelligence is directing the process so that the ovum will not be fertilized. ... I do not understand why spatial objects are blameworthy, while temporal gaps are not. Both are equally "natural" (or "unnatural").[31]

Novak is correct in his assertion that in all the various means of contraception, periodic abstince included, 'human intelligence is directing the process so that the ovum will not be fertilized'. All can be considered to be 'artificial' methods of controlling nature, and 'unnatural,' in that somewhat extended sense. The difference, however, lies in the fact that all the 'disagreeable' devices terminate the generative process, whereas abstinence is undertaken precisely to avoid this forbidden procedure. The 'disagreeable' devices are 'unnatural' in the precise and fundamental sense that they are against the natural law, which is just another way of saying that they are immoral.

It seems appropriate to deal here with another rather important intervention in the debate about contraception, that of one of the great philosopher/theologians of the twentieth century, Bernard Lonergan. In a letter written in September 1968, to a priest asking for advice in preparation for the meeting of the Canadian Bishops to deal with the crisis arising after the issuance of *Humanae vitae*, Bernard Lonergan gave his opinion as to why the teaching of the Church in this matter was no longer valid. According to Lonergan, 'traditional Catholic doctrine on the sexual act followed rigorously from the position adopted by Aristotle in his *De generatione animalium*.' On the Aristotelian position, again according to Lonergan, 'it was clear that every act of insemination was of itself procreative and that any positive interference was an act of obstructing the seed in its exercise of its efficient causality.'[32] This position is now known to be erroneous.

---

[31] Novak, "Frequent, Even Daily, Communion," 84.
[32] *Letter of Bernard Lonergan on contraception and the natural law*, edd. Frederick E. Crowe, Robert M. Doran in *Lonergan Studies Newsletter*, 11 March, 1990, 7-8 (here 7).

> Insemination and conception are known now to be quite distinct. The act of inseminating is not an act of procreating in the sense that of itself, per se, it leads to conception. The relation of insemination to conception is just statistical and, far more frequently than not, insemination does not lead to conception.[33]

It is Lonergan's view that this change in biological understanding is a major factor behind the change in Catholic thinking on this issue.

Is Lonergan correct in this? Did the Catholic position arise from Aristotelian biology and is it now based in any way on any theory of the biology of procreation? The traditional teaching on contraception, as it has been presented here, shows no signs whatever of the influence of Aristotle's biology. Whatever about Clement of Alexandria and the later Fathers involved, there is no doubt that the writer of the book of Genesis had no familiarity with Aristotle. And yet the concrete sense of a relationship between the male seed and the human offspring is all that is required to ground a condemnation of any interference in the process. Anyone who performs an act of coitus interruptus has all the grasp necessary of the link between intercourse and conception to ground a moral judgment. The fact that sexual intercourse initiates a process which leads to the birth of a new human being is all the basis needed to make a judgment in the matter. Whether the relationship is direct or statistical is irrelevant. In either case, a person who succeeds in disrupting the process, so that a birth which might have occurred does not in fact occur, has interfered directly in the generative process, and that is what is wrong.

Lonergan offers a new formulation of his own of the principle governing moral discernment in these matters.

> So there arises the question whether this statistical relationship of insemination to conception is sacrosanct and inviolable. Is it such that no matter what the

---

[33] Ibid.

circumstances, the motives, the needs, any deliberate modification of the statistical relationship must always be prohibited? If one answers affirmatively, he is condemning the rhythm method. If negatively, he permits contraceptives in some cases. Like the diaphragm and the pill, the menstrual chart and the thermometer directly intend to modify the statistical relationship nature places between insemination and conception.[34]

Lonergan has here formulated the prohibition of contraception in a new form. He formulates the essence of the human generative process as 'the statistical relationship of insemination to conception.' He argues that, on this basis artificial contraception and periodic abstinence are morally equivalent. Even granting his odd formulation, it still seems odd to suggest that there is no difference between abstinence and contraception in their effect on the statistical relationshi There is surely no moral fault in controlling this statistical relationship by abstaining from sexual intercourse. All of us do it some of the time, and some of us try to do it all the time. The moral issue only properly arises when one attempts to control the statistical relationship within an instance of the generative process already begun. Until a generative process is initiated by sexual intercourse the moral question does not arise. And when the generative process has begun, the statistical relationship is irrelevant. The statistical relationship implies that there is a certain probability of success for any given instance of intercourse. Whatever the probability of that given instance, the contraceptive intervention attempts to bring the probability down to zero, and that intervention is what is adjudged to be an attack on human life in its beginnings, and therefore considered to fall under the condemnation of the fifth commandment.

---

[34] Ibid, 7-8.

Chapter 22

Some Objections Answered

Having presented the life-tradition in the matter of contraception and argued that the underlying principle is the inviolability of the generative process and that the action condemned by the Church is the contraceptive termination of that process, it is necessary now to deal with some of the objections and difficulties to which this analysis might be subject.

The long-standing reaction to this approach has been to ignore it or to treat it as of no great significance, for the lack of appreciation of the significance of the traditional condemnation of contraception as a sin against life is currently almost complete. In the collection of essays defending *Human Vitae*, published in 1993 on the 25th anniversary of the encyclical, only one article mentions the tradition at all, and that only in order to explain it away. In the editorial introduction to Elizabeth Anscombe's article, Janet Smith commends it as offering 'a helpful explanation of many of the peculiarities of the historical condemnation of contraception, for instance, its being categorized with the sin of homicide.'[1] Anscombe relates that 'contraception by medical methods ... had previously been characterized as homicide throughout the dark ages. And this seems a monstrously unreasonable stretching of the idea of homicide.' She goes on to explain that 'the reason why it

---

[1] Smith, ed., <u>Why Humane Vitae was Right: A Reader</u>, 119.

seemed to be so in the dark ages ... was that it was taken for granted that medical methods were all abortifacient in type.' According to Anscombe, the fault lay in the inadequacy of the ancient knowledge of the biological realities, so that ignorance of the existence of the ovum led to an over-estimation of the role of the 'seed' in the generative process. She concludes: 'So that is the explanation of the curiosity that historically medical contraception was equated with homicide – it was equated with homicide because they thought it was that sort of thing, the sort of thing that destroying the fertilized ovum is.'[2]

It is clear enough from the presentation of the tradition already provided that Anscombe's interpretation of the 'homicide' argument is unsatisfactory. None of the witnesses brought forward ever thought that contraception was actually homicide; their knowledge of the biological realities involved was in every case sufficient to avoid that mistake. Of course, it has to be recognised that they were unable to be certain that the use of 'poisons of sterility' was not homicide, for that doubt remains to this day about certain chemical interventions. The argument throughout was that contraception is 'interpretively' homicide, as Noonan felicitously formulated the matter. The situation now is that even this 'interpretive' approach, which sees contraception as a life issue at all, is widely rejected, and the rejection finds its clear formulation in the emphasis placed on the difference between contraception and abortion. It was noted in the life tradition that these two were seen as closely related, in that they are both forms of interference in the generative process whose inviolability was the fundamental principle being invoked. Now it is the distinction which is emphasised. The distinction between contraception and abortion is also strongly made even by most of the moral theologians who condemn both. According to Martin Rhonheimer: 'To mention contraception in the same context as abortion is to risk the reproach levelled now and again at the magisterial practice of the Catholic Church: to link illicitly contraception and abortion is to trivialize the evil of abortion as much as

---

[2] Anscombe, "Contraception and Chastity," 128.

to injure those couples who use contraceptives for serious reasons.'[3] He reports that the mention of the life argument at the Congress of Moral Theologians in Rome in 1988 provoked an outcry of indignation in German-speaking countries. In response to this, at the press conference which followed the congress, Rhonheimer, together with other co-organizers and speakers, declared themselves against this 'irritating' argument.[4] Even Pope John Paul II has clearly affirmed the moral distinction between contraception and abortion. In *Evangelium vitae* §13, he declares: 'Certainly, from the moral point of view contraception and abortion are *specifically different* evils: the former contradicts the full truth of the sexual act as the proper expression of conjugal love, while the latter destroys the life of a human being; the former is opposed to the virtue of chastity in marriage, the latter is opposed to the virtue of justice and directly violates the divine commandment "You shall not kill".'

The principle which grounds the similarity between contraception and abortion, and which was used throughout the life-tradition, is the inviolability of the generative process. All the contraceptive interventions, like abortion, are means of interfering in the generative process. Contraception, as the name implies, prevents conception, so that there is no question of homicide, but both prevent the birth of the child who would have been the fruit of a particular generative process already begun. An early preventative form of contraception, such as the permanent sterilization of either partner, allows one to maintain a conceptual distance between contraception and abortion. However, there are forms of contraception for which the boundary between the two is so close that it is not always possible to be clear whether a particular chemical method is acting as a contraceptive or an abortifacient.[5] It was this close proximity of the two procedures which led the early Fathers to adopt the 'homicide' rhetoric and to speak of contraception as 'interpretively' homicide. On this basis they

---

[3] Rhonheimer, *Etica de la procreación*, 15.
[4] Ibid, 29.
[5] On this see John Guillebaud, *The Pill and Other Hormonal Contraceptives: The Facts* (Sixth edition) (Oxford University Press, 2005), 207-210.

saw the particular fault in effective contraception and sterilization that they prevent multiple human lives, where abortion can affect only one. Speaking of 'homicide' in the context of contraception is clearly rhetoric, for human life is not yet formed. Beneath the rhetoric, however, is the reality of the inviolability of the generative process and the fact that contraceptive termination of the generative process is a procedure closely related to abortion, so that both are to be seen as attacking human life in its sources. This way of viewing the matter, it seems to me, is not optional. Its basis in Scripture and Tradition establishes it as part of the teaching of the Church to which all are bound. The relevant question is this: were the biblical writer and these early Fathers correct in seeing the disruption of the generative process as an attack on human life which is to be assessed as being on a continuum which leads from contraception through abortion to infanticide? These are three different human acts, certainly. But do they form a continuum within the generative process leading to an adult human person so that they are to be judged as part of one coherent reality, the process leading form sexual intercourse to adult humanity? I contend that the biblical usage of 'seed' to mean 'offspring' encapsulates in a concrete manner the insight involved, that the whole process from intercourse to adult humanity is one continuum to be assessed as a unit. I contend that the great Fathers of the Church made that insight their own and this is the foundation of the development of doctrine leading from the commandment, 'Thou shalt not kill', to the prohibition of contraception. I repeat that this, in my opinion, is the central question in this whole matter. If it is to be upheld that contraception is indeed a different species of act from abortion, that it is not fundamentally an attack on the human generative process, then there is no solid traditional argument against it.

There is no doubt that contraception, the contraceptive termination of the generative process, is different from abortion or infanticide, in that the new human life is not yet formed, and that difference grounds the exception to the rule which arises in the case of self-defence against rape. The issue arose in a famous case in the early 1960's when it was deemed morally acceptable for nuns to take anovulant pills to guard themselves against the possibility of being made pregnant if they were raped during the the civil disturbances taking place in the Congo at the time. According to Valsecchi, in his account, this case and its solution marked a point of transition in the discussion of contraception, in that it brought out into the open some latent doctrinal trends which were important during the course of the subsequent controversy.[6] The moralist from the Lateran University in Rome, Fernando Lambruschini, who later became famous for remarks he made at the Vatican press conference introducing *Humanae vitae*, had a clear view of the matter. He had not doubt that the use of the anovulant pills is a deliberate act of sterilization which aims precisely at the prevention of conception.[7] Lambruschini justified this intervention on the principle that 'when a physical and physiological process is in opposition to a pre-existent moral and spiritual right, precedence must be given to the latter'.[8] Valsecchi highlights the novelty of the situation, where a case of deliberate contraceptive sterilization is defended. Previously such contraceptive sterilization had been considered to be intrinsically evil, and this admission of an exception was new and surprising. Valsecchi then goes on: 'Following the irresistible course of logic, from the nun who fears to suffer violent assault to the wife who cannot resist her husband's unjust will, we find ourselves drawn still further forward ... until we reach a point where it appears possible to wonder whether, in marriage, the woman who deprives herself of her fertility capacity for the whole of that period when she has neither the right nor the duty to exercise it, may perhaps not be acting against the natural moral order, even if she is interfering with a physiological process.'[9] It is clear that this intervention has to be seen as a deliberate interference in the generative process already begun, but the difference which admits the exception is that one is entitled to defend oneself against unlawful aggression. Until conception occurs, the preliminary part of the process is still part of the unjust attack and the right to self-defence applies. As Germain Grisez remarks: 'The measures taken in this case are a defense

---

[6] Valsecchi, *Controversy*, 26.
[7] Ibid, 28.
[8] Ibid, 29.
[9] Ibid, 35-36.

of the woman's ovum (insofar as it is a part of her person) against the rapist's sperms (insofar as they are part of his person).'[10] The situation mirrors exactly that of self-defence against an unjustified attack on one's person more generally. One is entitled to defend oneself even to the point of taking the life of the aggressor, and this is not seen as breaching the principle of the inviolability of human life. Similarly, one is entitled to defend oneself against rape even to the point of terminating the invasive generative process prior to conception, and this is not to be seen as breaching the principle of the inviolability of the generative process.

Is it Physicalism?

The tradition which discerns the moral unacceptability of contraception in its interference with the human generative process needs to respond to a serious objection that such respect for a biological process is mere physicalism. The rejection of 'physicalism' is general in the discussion and it is important to be clear what precisely is being rejected and why. It is useful in this regard to consider the contribution of Richard McCormick which spans the years before and after *Humanae vitae*. In an article published in 1964 as part of the new debate on the anovulant pill, McCormick has this to say: 'The apparent naturalness of temporary direct sterilization by steroid hormones has failed to shake the conviction of theologians that this application is incompatible with man's limited rights over his physical integrity. This is the *basic* principle according to which direct sterilization is rejected.'[11] McCormick reports as the basic principle at that time our limited rights over our 'physical integrity'. It has been argued here that the genuine tradition of the Church teaches respect for the integrity of the human generative process, so it is necessary to discern just what McCormick had in mind.

---

[10] Germain Grisez, *The Way of the Lord Jesus, Volume Two: Living a Christian Life* (Quincy, Illinois: Franciscan Press, 1992), 512.
[11] Richard A. McCormick, S. J., 'Family Size, Rhythm, and the Pill,' in *The Problem of Population* (Notre Dame: University of Notre Dame Press, 1964), 58-84 at 79.

At the time, McCormick expressed his dissatisfaction with the basic principle of respect for physical integrity. On sterilization he wrote:

> Sterilization is a word like contraception; that is, verbally it focuses on a physiological phenomenon. It is quite natural therefore, that the principles basic to the rejection of direct sterilization should begin at this level. It is my opinion, however, that to be fully adequate to the human situation, the rejection of sterilization must eventually reach the level of interpersonal relations.[12]

He made the same point in regard to contraception, when he wrote

> that these acts are physically or biologically contraceptive. Such acts are even named *contraceptive* acts because of this effect. Hence their morality has often been argued against merely in terms of the fact that they cannot allow conception to occur (and conversely, the morality of so-called 'natural' acts has been upheld in terms of the fact that they *can* allow conception to occur).[13]

McCormick is thinking here of contraception as an act of sexual intercourse performed with its procreative potential removed and is not convinced by the rationale of its condemnation. He wrote that 'it has always been an uphill battle to convince the popular mind that rhythm differs from contraception. Traditionally, it has been said that though the physical results are the same (avoidance of pregnancy), the means used are morally different. Contraception mutilates the integrity of the reproductive act; rhythm leaves this integrity untouched. Assuredly this is correct, though one can regret a formulation that seems to derive basic morality from reproductive integrity alone and not from personal

---

[12] Ibid, 79-80.
[13] Ibid, 39.

relationships.'[14] In his view 'the deliberate removal of the power to procreate does not necessarily identify the ultimate reason for the immorality. ... Sterilization is unfortunately a word like contraception. Describing as it does a physiological phenomenon, it forces attention on the physical frustration of procreative potential. Perhaps we theologians have been less than fully accurate in condemning sterilization exclusively for this reason.'[15]

McCormick's unease with this argument led eventual to its abandonment as incapable of grounding the judgment of the moral unacceptability of contraception and sterilization. He came to reject arguments which 'absolutize a biological aspect of the human person by equating the unequatable: human life and the sources of human life. Depriving a person of life is one thing; depriving oneself of the power to procreate is a remarkably different thing and ought not to be treated in an identical way ethically.'[16] He considers this to be at the basis of the argument in *Humanae vitae*. 'In any number of places in the Encyclical the biological structure and the processes of nature are accepted as the determinants of meaning. (nos. 10, 11, 13, 16, 17) They are said to represent God's plan and therefore to be morally normative.'[17] Bernard Häring makes a similar point and also sees respect for biology as the key to *Humanae vitae*.

> *Humanae Vitae* confines the procreative meaning of the marital act to the faithful observance of biological laws and rhythms. It implies therein that God's wise and divine plan is revealed to the spouses through these absolutely sacred physiological laws. This is undoubtedly the philosophy underpinning the argumentation of the

---

[14] Ibid, 41.
[15] Ibid.
[16] McCormick, *The Critical Calling*, 277.
[17] *Theological Studies* 29 (1968), 729.

whole encyclical. It goes so far as to declare biological laws as absolutely binding on the conscience of men.[18]

And Janssens follows the same line. In his critical response to *Humanae vitae*, Janssens finds the heart of the encyclical's teaching in its call for the respect to shown to biological processes. He writes: 'The distinction between artificial means and periodic continence is that the latter respects "the development of natural processes" (HV 16). Thus the entire problem is reduced to a consideration of respect for natural processes, based on the principle, often repeated in *Humanae Vitae* (HV 10, 12, 13, 16, 17), that God's creative intention is expressed immediately in biological functions.'[19] He sees this as the fundamental dividing line in the whole matter: 'All in all, it is foreseeable that after the publication of the encyclical – just as before it – there will remain two tendencies…; with respect to the concrete norms of the means of regulating birth, some couples will take as their standard respect for biological functions and processes, others will form their consciences according to the personalist criteria of responsible parenthood and mutual self-giving in the context of true love.'[20] Not surprisingly, therefore, Richard McCormick offers as his opinion that 'a rather well-educated guess would say that the vast majority of theologians will conclude that the analyses of *Humanae vitae* build upon an unacceptable identification of natural law with natural processes.'[21]

To what extent these criticisms bear directly on the teaching of *Humanae vitae* is not easy to discern, for the encyclical is a complex document with many strands whose interpretation is not always a simple matter. Martin Rhonheimer rejects the interpretation of the critics of the encyclical: 'According to these critics, "Humanae Vitae" teaches that the biological patterns inherent in the human generative faculty must

---

[18] Bernard Häring, 'The Inseparability of the Unitive-Procreative Functions of the Marital Act,' in Charles Curran (ed.), *Contraception: Authority and Dissent* (London : Burns & Oates, 1969), 176-92 at 180.
[19] Janssens, 'Considerations on "Humanae Vitae",' 248.
[20] Ibid, 252.
[21] *Theological Studies* 29 (1968), 733.

never be acted against, but respected.'[22] In his opinion: 'Interpreting "Humanae Vitae" in this way, its critics had an easy job of rejecting its doctrine.'[23] And for John Finnis the encyclical 'carefully avoids the old arguments about "natural processes..."'[24] Whatever about *Humanae vitae*, what is clear is that the criticisms do bear directly on the interpretation of the Christian tradition being advocated in this book. If it is correct to say that what the Church condemns is the contraceptive termination of the generative process and that this condemnation is based on respect for the inviolability of the generative process, then respect for biological processes is at the heart of the matter.

And it is not only the dissenting theologians who oppose making respect for biological processes the foundation of the moral norm. The same is also true of the theologians who support the traditional position. Martin Rhonheimer, for instance, repudiates such an idea. He writes: 'For discovering what is wrong with contraception, one must not concentrate on questions like: "What's wrong with obstructing the procreative process in having its natural course?"'[25] Rhonheimer considers the biological reality to be basically irrelevant. He says: 'Notice that the description of contraception which I adopt is absolutely independent of what is happening on the physical level...,'[26] and tells us that '[b]y adopting this description, we will be able to point out that the reason why contraception is wrong is not because it violates naturally given structures of the generative faculty or other "natural" laws, for not every act of preventing conception implies such violations or interferences with natural processes...'[27] He is confident that the moral norm cannot be based on such respect for biological processes, at least he says that 'to my knowledge ... nobody ... has ... provided a compelling argument in favor of the *moral* relevance of *never* deliberately impeding

---

[22] Rhonheimer, "Contraception, Sexual Behavior, and Natural Law," 21. The critics he refers to are Bernard Häring and Charles Curran.
[23] Ibid.
[24] Finnis, '*Humanae Vitae*: Its Background and Aftermath,' 151.
[25] Rhonheimer, "Contraception, Sexual Behavior, and Natural Law," 46.
[26] Ibid, 30.
[27] Ibid, 31.

insemination during the marital act.'[28] Brian Shanley similarly affirms that 'the issue is in no way determined by mere biological or physical factors.'[29] And Kevin Flannery is of the view that '[t]he immorality of contraception has little to do with how spermatozoa get to ova.'[30] John Finnis seems to see the move away from any concern with the biological level an important mark of progress, when he says that 'the whole confused debate of 1959 to 1968 and its resolution in *Humanae Vitae*, a document that carefully avoids the old arguments about "natural processes," has as an episode rather cleared the air about the bases of ethics – of natural law and of Catholic moral teaching.'[31] The undervaluing of the biological reality of the generative process appears even in the Minority Report which was arguing precisely in favour of its inviolability. There we read: 'This inviolability is always attributed to the act and to the process, which are biological; not inasmuch as they are biological, but inasmuch as they are human, namely inasmuch as they are the object of *human acts* and are destined by their nature to the good of the human species.'[32] These theologians distinguish between what is 'biological' and what is 'human'. They seem to suggest that the human generative act and process only become human 'inasmuch as they are the object of human acts', and not already human simply by the fact that they 'are destined by their nature to the good of the human species.' This may be quibbling, but the point seems so important to me, and it seems to be that the biological reality of the generative process is not properly respected by any of the contributors to this discussion at all.

Even the group of thinkers who have appealed explicitly to the life-tradition have fallen into the trap of disrespecting the biological

---

[28] Martin Rhonheimer, 'The Contraceptive Choice, Condom Use, and Moral Arguments Based on Nature: A Reply to Christopher Olsen,' *National Catholic Bioethics Quarterly* 7 (2007), 273-91 at 280.

[29] Brian J. Shanley, O., 'The Moral Difference between Natural Family Planning and Contraception,' *Linacre Quarterly* 54 (1987), 48-60 at 52.

[30] Kevin Flannery, S. J., 'Philosophical Arguments against and for Humanae Vitae,' *Anthropotes* 10 (1994), 189-204 at 193.

[31] Finnis, '*Humanae Vitae*: Its Background and Aftermath,' 151.

[32] 'The Minority Working Paper, 23 May 1966,' 179.

reality.[33] They begin their argument by making a distinction between 'contraception' and the 'contraceptive act'. They write: '"Contraception" signifies only the prevention of *conception*, but the contraceptive act seeks to impede *the beginning of the life of a possible person*. The distinction is only conceptual, but we think it important, for the explicit reference to new life calls attention to the fact that contraception is a contralife act.'[34] In order to locate how contraception is an attack on life, Grisez *et al.* find it necessary to move away from the physical level and on to the level of the intention. They say that contraception means *only* the prevention of conception, implying that the prevention of conception is not morally significant. For them the attack on life is in the further intention of preventing the 'beginning of the life of a possible person'. This move to the level of the further intention does not work, however, because preventing the beginning of the life of a possible person can be a legitimate goal, and there is the obvious and legitimate means of achieving that goal which is to abstain from sexual intercourse. The logic applied by Grisez *et al.* is unable to distinguish between artificial contraception and periodic abstinence. In his textbook produced subsequently, Grisez recognises that couples using artificial means of contraception can be doing so for the acceptable motive of proper family planning, and then go on to locate the malice of that use as follows:

> But in choosing contraception as a means to this further good, they necessarily imagine a new person coming to be if he or she is not prevented, they want that imagined person not to be, and they efficaciously will that he or she never be. That will is a contralife will. Therefore, considered as a moral act, each and every contraceptive act necessarily is contralife."[35]

---

[33] Germain Grisez, Joseph Boyle, John Finnis, William E. May, "'Every Marital Act Ought to be Open to New Life,': Toward a Clearer Understanding," The Thomist 52 (1988), 365-426.
[34] Ibid, 366.
[35] Grisez, The Way of the Lord Jesus: Volume Two, 509.

The weakness of this analysis is revealed by the fact that it applies equally to those who choose to plan their families by periodic abstinence. Paralleling exactly Grisez's formulation, one could write:

> In choosing periodic abstinence as a means to this further good, they necessarily imagine a person coming to be if he or she is not avoided, they want that imagined person not to be, and they efficaciously will that he or she never be. That will is a contralife will. Therefore, considered as a moral act, each and every period of abstinence from sexual intercourse necessarily is contralife.

The fact of the matter is that on the level of the acceptable goal of proper family planning, the intentions can be exactly identical, as was explicitly recognised by Pope Paul VI in *Humanae vitae* (§ 16). The choice to plan one's family inevitably involves a choice not to have a child who might otherwise be born. It is not helpful to characterize this choice not to have a child as a choice against life. The choice is made on the basis that bringing another child into the world in the particular circumstances would be inappropriate, and that is a legitimate choice *for* life, for the fullness of life of those already born and against an impoverished life for the prospective child. So it is quite wrong to characterise such a choice as a choice against life without a proper consideration of all the circumstances involved. It sheds no light on the moral situation, for the immorality of artificial contraception simply is not to be located on this level of the couple's overall intention where there is no difference between contraception and periodic abstinence.[36]

A further weakness of this approach is that it distracts people and prevents their focussing on the point which renders contraception morally unacceptable. In her rebuttal of this approach to the matter, Janet Smith wrote that '[t]he likening of a contraceptive will to a homicidal

---

[36] This point is made in the criticism of this approach offered by Gareth Moore, O., *The Body in Context: Sex and Catholicism* (London: SCM Press, 1992), 165-78, and by Rhonheimer in "Contraception, Sexual Behavior, and Natural Law," 29.

will, no matter how qualified, still seems far-fetched.'[37] There is no doubt that contraception does not involve a homicidal intention. It is precisely a choice to prevent conception so that a human life does not begin and there cannot therefore be any question of homicide. Contraception can be chosen precisely in order to avoid the possibility of being placed in the situation where one would be tempted to commit homicide by abortion or infanticide. Grisez *et al.* do not help matters at all by formulating the sense of contraception as an attack on life in this manner. It is so obviously wrong and so easy to ridicule that it brings the whole argument into disrepute. It is precisely what happened before and led to the loss of the sense of the condemnation of contraception along this line which has brought us to the impasse we now face.

The fundamental point being argued here is that the moral analysis must focus specifically on the physical act of contraceptive intervention itself. The distinction Grisez *et al.* make between 'contraception' and the 'contraceptive act' is the obverse of the one being made here. For them 'contraception' is the physical interference in the generative process and it 'only' prevents conception, whereas the 'contraceptive act' is the avoiding of a new life. Here 'contraception' is understood as referring to the overall intention to avoid conception and it can reasonably apply to periodic abstinence, and the 'contraceptive act' is the physical act, of whatever kind, which disrupts the generative process to prevent conception. And it is this act of physical interference which is morally objectionable according to the Christian tradition. For there is no difference between conception and the beginning of the life of a human being. Conception is the beginning of the life of a human being and the malice of artificial contraception is to be located precisely in the positive interference in the process of human generation in order to prevent conception.

If this survey presents an accurate picture of the situation, it would seem that there is unanimity right across the board against the interpretation of the life tradition being advocated here. If the inviolability of the generative process is the basic principle operating

---

[37] Smith, *Humanae Vitae: A Generation Later*, 363.

in the Christian condemnation of contraceptive termination, then the issue is fundamentally 'determined by mere biological or physical factors,' and has everything 'to do with how spermatozoa get to ova'. Contraceptive termination is wrong precisely 'because it violates naturally given structures of the generative faculty or other "natural" laws ... [and] implies such violations or interferences with natural processes.' It is to be hoped that Rhonheimer will no longer feel able to say that 'nobody has provided a compelling argument in favor of the *moral* relevance of *never* deliberately impeding insemination during the marital act.' For the whole thrust of this book is to propose that Scripture and Tradition provide precisely such an argument. But is it 'physicalism' to base the condemnation of contraceptive termination on respect for the inviolability of the generative process? For that is what Scripture and the Fathers have done. 'Physicalism' can only refer to an *undue* respect for physical reality. Presumably, all would agree that respect for human life represents an appropriate respect for physical reality, and such respect may be deemed to be 'physical', but should not be condemned as 'physicalist'. The question at issue in the matter of contraception is as to how far that respect reaches back into the sources of life in the generative process. The tradition has understood the whole generative process from intercourse to birth as a unified totality, under God's direct authority and beyond human dominion. From the moment of conception, the generative process is a nascent human being. For the short period prior to conception, is it to be considered simply as a biological process to be dealt with at will, according to the principle of totality, where the part can legitimately be sacrifice in favour of the whole? It seems to me that the tradition is clear that the respect for human life stretches back to the very beginning of the generative process, that such respect is not 'physicalism,' and that it forms the basis of the Church's moral norm in this matter.

Chapter 23

A Dogmatic Definition

It is time now to bring this long journey to its conclusion. The aim has been to bring a final resolution to the crisis affecting the Catholic Church in the matter of contraception, and to make the case that this can only be achieved by a formal definition of the the truth of the matter by an Ecumenical Council. It has been argued already that definition is required on two levels, the level of understanding and the level of judgment, and understanding must come first. We begin, then, by resuming what has been said in answer to the questions, What is contraception? and Is it wrong?

Is contraception instrinsically evil? The answer to this question can only be that it depends on what you mean by contraception. If contraception means deliberately avoiding or preventing conception while engaging in sexual intercourse, then it need not be wrong at all, for these goals can be achieved by periodic abstinence. What the Church condemns as intrinsically evil is the contraceptive termination of the generative process. This involves interfering on the physiological level by any of the various means available so that a given act of intercourse cannot achieve conception. Obviously abstinence does not involve such interference; it is chosen precisely in order to avoid it. In the essential central paragraph 14 of *Humanae vitae*, Pope Paul VI formulated the teaching of the Church in this matter.

> Therefore We base Our words on the first principles of a human and Christian doctrine of marriage when We are obliged once more to declare that the direct interruption of the generative process already begun and, above all, all direct abortion, even for therapeutic reasons, are to be absolutely excluded as lawful means of regulating the number of children. Equally to be condemned, as the magisterium of the Church has affirmed on many occasions, is direct sterilization, whether of the man or of the woman, whether permanent or temporary. Similarly excluded is any action which either before, at the moment of, or after sexual intercourse, is specifically intended to prevent procreation—whether as an end or as a means.

The summary principle which includes everything taught here is that the 'direct interruption of the generative process already begun' is intrinsically evil. Before conception it is contraceptive; after conception it is abortifacient, and both are intrinsically evil. This is the clear statement of the teaching of the Church in this matter, and this first clarification is an essential first step on the road to a dogmatic definition.

The next question to be dealt with is, Why is this wrong? It is not wrong on the basis of the procreative finality of sexual intercourse, as has been argued for centuries now. *Coitus interruptus* and coitus with a barrier in place can be judged using the procreative principle, and are seen to be unnatural sex acts which can be numbered with intercourse *in vase indebito*, homosexual intercourse and bestiality. But, in so far as they are contraceptive in intent, they must be seen as means of terminating the generative process just as it begins, and can then be numbered with sterilization, whether surgical or chemical, and post-coital contraception. These latter are not affected by the procreative principle, and therein lies its weakness and ultimate failure to deal with the moral issue involved here. The principle underlying the Church's condemnation is the inviolability of the generative process, so that a termination, whether before or after conception, is immoral.

Herein lies a fundamental weakness in the two major magisterial interventions in the matter, *Casti connubii* and *Humanae vitae*. Pope Pius XI's pronouncement in *Casti connubii* was remarkably brief.

> Since, therefore, the conjugal act is destined by nature for the begetting of children, those who in exercising it deliberately frustrate its natural power and purpose sin against nature and commit a deed which is shameful and intrinsically vicious.[1] ... And he solemnly declares that 'any use whatsoever of matrimony exercised in such a way that the act is deliberately frustrated in its natural power to generate life is an offense against the law of God and of nature, and those who indulge in such are branded with the guilt of a grave sin.'[2]

The Pope's teaching is presented here as being based solely on the procreative principle. And the same is true of *Humanae vitae*, which states that the teaching is based primarily on the procreative principle.

> The Church, nevertheless, in urging men to the observance of the precepts of the natural law, which it interprets by its constant doctrine, teaches that each and every marital act must of necessity retain its intrinsic relationship to the procreation of human life. This particular doctrine, often expounded by the magisterium of the Church, is based on the inseparable connection, established by God, which man on his own initiative may not break, between the unitive significance and the procreative significance which are both inherent to the marriage act.[3]

---

[1] DS 3716.
[2] DS 3717.
[3] *Humanae vitae*, the last sentence of § 11 and the first sentence of § 12.

This procreative principle is not the traditional basis of the Church's teaching and ultimately fails to ground that teaching, and these facts go a long way to explaining why both these pronouncements failed to convince the Church at large. An ultimate definition of the genuine teaching of the Church in this matter must base itself on the traditional principle involved, the inviolability of the generative process.

The fourth and final question must now be addressed, How do we know it is wrong? This epistemological question is the most fundamental of all, and it explains why this book has been so long. There are a number of misconceptions clouding the issue here, and they had to be removed before the matter could be dealt with fully and definitively. Firstly, it is a matter of faith not reason. The moral prohibition belongs to the natural law, but the truth has been revealed to us by Scripture and Tradition. And here lies another weakness in the teaching of the two encyclicals. Pope Pius XI's appeal to tradition was as brief as the teaching.

> Small wonder, therefore, if Holy Writ bears witness that the Divine Majesty regards with greatest detestation this horrible crime and at times has punished it with death. As St. Augustine notes, 'Intercourse even with one's legitimate wife is unlawful and wicked where the conception of the offspring is prevented. Onan, the son of Juda, did this and the Lord killed him for it.'(*De coniug. adult.*, lib. II, n. 12.)

This is quite unsatisfactory as an appeal to Scripture and Tradition. The Scripture reference is apposite, indeed, but the sole reference to St. Augustine places it in the flawed context of the procreative tradition which ultimately fails to ground the teaching. And *Humanae vitae* is even weaker in this regard. There is no appeal to Scripture at all, and the earliest traditional text mentioned is the Catechism of the Council of Trent.[4] As has been noted already, Pope Paul VI, in his introduction to the encyclical, claimed that he was speaking on the basis of his role

---

[4] *Humanae vitae*, § 14, footnote 16.

as an 'interpreter' of the natural law, and this seems to imply that he has a superior moral insight and that this is the basis on which his teaching is to be accepted. It is small wonder, therefore, that so many readers of these encyclicals expected to be convinced by the reasons given, and when that did not happen they could not accept the teaching. In his summing up of the grounds for his dissent from the encyclical, Richard McCormick had this to say:

> In the light of these reflections it is the opinion of the compositor of these Notes that the intrinsic immorality of every contraceptive act remains a teaching subject to solid and positive doubt. This is not to say that this teaching of *Humanae vitae* is certainly erroneous. It is only to say that there are very strong objections that can be urged against it and very little evidence that will sustain it. One draws this conclusion reluctantly and with no small measure of personal anguish. With proper allowance made for one's own shortcomings, pride, and resistance, what more can a theologian say?[5]

I take it that that 'strong objections that can be urged against' the encyclical are those which have been accepted here, that the arguments given simply do not work. However, I must take issue with McCormick's view that there is 'very little evidence that will sustain it'. Of course, all the evidence is traditional and of faith, not reason. For the dissident position to stand, it must explain the long-standing teaching on this matter in the Church as flawed to its core. It has been argued here that the procreative tradition is indeed flawed, but that there is another, life tradition, which grounds the teaching fully. An ultimate definition of the matter must, therefore, make clear that the teaching is a matter of faith, and present fully the Scriptural and Traditional basis on which it rests.

---

[5] *Theological Studies* 29 (1968), 727.

There are other points of confusion which need to be clearly resolved. It must be clearly stated that the teaching is a revealed doctrine to be received with divine and Catholic faith. There remains a solid and widespread doubt that the absolute moral norms can be divinely revealed and that they can be the object of a dogmatic definition. The only way that doubt can be finally removed is by the very act of making such a definition.

It must be made clear that the absolute moral norms, including this one, are in no way secondary matters belonging to a so-called secondary object of infallibility. The Congregation for the Doctrine of the Faith has expressed such an opinion, and it is important that any such notion be finally and fully laid to rest. It needs to be made clear that this is the unanimous teaching of all the bishops of the Church. At the time of *Humanae vitae*, a number of episcopal conferences expressed doubts about the status of the teaching, and, to my knowledge, have never retracted their comments. It must now be made clear that such episcopal reservations have been completely withdrawn. It is being argued here that all these goals can only be achieved by a dogmatic definition of an ecumenical council.

Made in the USA
Middletown, DE
25 February 2024